MARXISM IN SOUTHEAST ASIA

MARXISM IN
SOUTHEAST ASIA

A Study of Four Countries

Edited, with an Introduction and Conclusion,

by

FRANK N. TRAGER

Consultant,
The RAND Corporation

With Contributions by

JEANNE S. MINTZ • I. MILTON SACKS
JOHN SEABURY THOMSON • DAVID A. WILSON

STANFORD UNIVERSITY PRESS
STANFORD, CALIFORNIA   1959

Stanford University Press
Stanford, California
London: Oxford University Press

© 1959 by The RAND Corporation

INTRODUCTORY NOTE

The editor and the authors are grateful to The RAND Corporation for a research grant which enabled them from May 1956 to July 1957 to prepare this study of Marxism in Southeast Asia. Each of the authors has had the benefit of field experience and continuous professional specialization in the area. The editor had the additional advantage, provided by The RAND Corporation, of revisiting Southeast Asia during the late spring and summer of 1956. Now that we have finished our investigations and the writing of the study, we are collectively aware that were we enabled to start again, the result would probably diminish our errors of omission and commission. For we have learned much in the doing of the job. However, the exigencies of time do not permit such luxury. If our study helps others to proceed in depth and clarity, we shall be satisfied despite our shortcomings.

To exhibit, in part, our indebtedness to other students in the field, we have provided detailed footnotes. We deemed this the more necessary because, despite the existence of several noteworthy country studies, data about our subject are sparse and elusive. To acknowledge the official and unofficial aid we have received in each of the four countries and in the capitals of the former metropolitan powers would require a list of several hundred names. To all these our profound thanks for encouragement and support. To Mrs. Marina S. Finkelstein I am specially indebted for a valiant editorial effort beyond my capabilities and patience.

FRANK N. TRAGER

New York City
September 30, 1959

CONTENTS

1

THE STUDY DEFINED

FRANK N. TRAGER

This study has a threefold purpose: to identify the nature of Marxism in selected countries of Southeast Asia; to determine its relationship, avowed and hidden, to indigenous and similar ideologies; and to relate these findings to current political processes and activities, domestic and international, in the selected countries. Four Southeast Asian countries have been the focus of this study: Burma, Thailand, Viet Nam, and Indonesia.

In the twentieth century the peoples of these countries—with the exception of Thailand—successfully conducted revolts against alien political, economic, and sociocultural domination. Marxism was an important element in rationalizing their revolt. It is still today an ingredient in the social philosophies of the ruling elites. It serves as a banner under which revolutionary Communist forces seek to undermine and to overthrow the existing non-Communist governments.

Both the history of Marxism and the present scope of its influence on national policy show considerable variation from one to another of the four countries under study. Burma, nurturing a Marxist tradition since the mid-1930's, witnessed the effective organization of the Thakin nationalist movement and for the decade following independence had a government which, through its ruling Socialist leadership, inspired the Asian Socialist Conference first convened in Rangoon in 1953. Dutch Socialists brought Marxism to Indonesia as far back as World War I. It deeply affected the launching of the Social Democratic Party before 1917 and of the Communist party in 1920, and, as in Burma, it permeated to a significant extent virtually all postindependence nationalist movements.

In somewhat related fashion, Marxism profoundly affected the nationalist movement which ultimately led to the elimination of France from Indochina and to the creation of the two Vietnamese states in 1954. Marxism-
Leninism is the official state doctrine in Ho Chi Minh's domain. South of
the seventeenth parallel, the avowed Socialist Party, affiliated with the
Asian Socialist Conference, has practically no political or ideological influence and few members. Clandestine Lao Dong or Labor Party (Communist) elements undoubtedly retain some influence in the countryside,
but this is difficult to ascertain because of their underground status and
methods. Two additional factors, probably far more influential and also
difficult to assess, must be noted: in the leadership of the Republic there
are those who have been trained under the Communist Viet Minh and who
carry over into their propaganda and organizational methods aspects of
this training; second, the existence of a Communist state north of the seventeenth parallel that seeks to capture the loyalties of all the Vietnamese
people affects the policies adopted by the Republic to prevent this from
happening. The multiparty, mainly government-supporting parliament
does not move beyond the policy set forth by President Ngo Dinh Diem.
That policy, anticolonial, nationalist, and anti-Communist, embraces a
variety of industrial and agricultural programs which are at the least "stat-
ist," if not Marxist, in character.

The Communist party is outlawed in Thailand, and other Marxist-
tinged groups or parties are weak, both numerically and in terms of influence. Even more than the Republic of Viet Nam, however, Thailand
has instituted state-run and state-dominated enterprises. Though the philosophy motivating governmental control of industry, irrigation and water
supply, transportation and communications, distilleries, and tobacco, textile, and paper mills is not consciously Marxist, the current methods of
capitalization and operation of these industries suggest analogies with
"middle-way" Socialist governments rather than with what Wittfogel calls
the "Oriental Despotism" of "a more or less aloof hydraulic society."[1] Marxist influence is directly observable, though in attenuated form, among some
elements of the large Chinese minority in Thailand and in the electoral
activities of various "Labor" and "Socialist" groups. But the inclusion of
Thailand in this study is in the end justified largely on the ground that
it provides a "control case" in the light of which factors affecting the origin
and development of Marxism in the other three countries may be more
clearly understood.

Even as cursory a review as this indicates the diversity of development
within the area. That Marxism penetrated the area at all must be attributable to the impact of the West on indigenous social structures. But the
impact was felt in each of the countries at different times and under differ-

ent circumstances, and by individuals whose response depended on their particular careers and aspirations. The four chapters devoted to the selected countries describe the historical events which affected the acceptance and spread of Marxism in each country. Each chapter approaches the problem somewhat differently, in accordance with the nature of the events treated. Nevertheless, the four situations are not wholly dissimilar, so that the reader will discern comparable elements and processes, cultural and political, operating in the various cases.

Obviously, any attempt to superimpose Western meanings on Southeast Asian Marxist vocabularies and corresponding actions must necessarily issue in varying degrees of political error. The names of Marx and Engels, of Lenin and Stalin, of Mao Tse-tung, and of other avowed Marxists will appear frequently in these pages. But this is not a study of these men. When Marx and the others are mentioned, or where their presumed authority or words are used in Southeast Asia, documentation will be offered so that the meaning in the instant case may be clear. However, the disputes and development of the international Socialist and Communist movements did affect the groups and parties of Southeast Asia. The bearing of these events on Southeast Asian affairs will be identified and analyzed. Marxism in Southeast Asia is both derived from its European setting and naturalized in its new environment. Its Southeast Asian character is our focus.

We have little reason, though there is ample temptation, to debate the niceties of Marxist doctrine and its application. To identify and analyze the role of Marxism in the respective countries does not necessarily involve any evaluation of the doctrine itself, nor of the degree to which the practitioners interpreted the doctrine, strategy, and tactics "correctly" according to canonical texts. Variations in interpretation, misinterpretations, as well as unsuccessful applications are equally relevant for our purposes, provided they appear in the guise of Marxism. This is not so much a self-imposed limitation as a reflection of the actual state of Marxist ideology and action in Southeast Asia. Southeast Asian Marxists have not often used that type of Marxist argument which so largely gave rise to the European and, later, Chinese literature of the Marxist movement.

One example may suffice to illustrate the temptation to discuss Southeast Asian Marxism in terms of canonical doctrine and to point up the pitfalls of doing so. In his recent book,[2] Kautsky offers a "case study in the postwar development of international Communist strategy" as applied in detail to "the twists and turns of the Indian Communist Party since 1945." He has conceived his task as requiring "the setting up of a rigorous taxonomic scheme designed to isolate the essential features of each Communist strategy." Three such strategies are found. The "left" or "classical" strategy, in which capitalism is the main enemy, calls for an alliance of workers, poor peasants, and, when possible, petty-bourgeois elements (regarded as unreliable) against the bourgeoisie or capitalist class and their allies, using the device of the "united front from below." The second strategy is of the "right" variety. Here the main enemy is Fascism, feudalism, imperialism, or any combination of these. During a period when this strategy prevails, the revolutionary aim of the left strategy is subordinated to the defense of "democracy" or "national liberation" or to the war against Fascism and imperialism, and the Communist party works for a "united front from above." Kautsky holds that these left and right strategies "were essentially the only ones pursued by international Communism" until after World War II. Then because of the cold war and the emergence of Communist China, a third strategy, designated as "Neo-Maoist," appeared. Neo-Maoism is defined as that strategy which, like the right strategy, "singles out foreign imperialism and where applicable feudalism as its main enemy" and which, again like the right, embraces in its appeal a "bloc" of classes or groups resembling the alliance components of the Popular Front. As Kautsky insists, however, the "essential and unique characteristic of the Neo-Maoist strategy is its direct appeal 'from below' (*not* through the bourgeois parties) to sections of the bourgeoisie. This appeal is made openly and defended on theoretical grounds, and unlike [Maoist] reliance on the peasantry is startlingly new to Communists." Thus the Neo-Maoist strategy containing left and right elements emerges. Kautsky believes that the Neo-Maoist strategy has been "long applied in Indochina, Malaya, Burma, the Philippines . . . [and since] the second half of the postwar decade by the Indian and Indonesian Communists, and for that matter, by those in Western Europe and Latin America."[3]

The history and theory of Chinese Communism are clearly within the scope of any study of Asian Marxism. But Kautsky's attempt to isolate a "third" strategy "startlingly new to Communists" does not impress the present writer as historically accurate or logically consistent. All the elements of this third strategy, combining the right with the united front from below, can be found clearly expounded in Dimitrov's speech of August 2, 1935, at the Seventh Comintern Congress, on "The Offensive of Fascism and the Tasks of the Communist International in the Struggle for the Unity of the Working Class,"[4] in the course of which he commented specifically on India and China. It could be demonstrated that Lenin's *Two Tactics of Social-Democracy in the Democratic Revolution* (1905), together with his report on "National and Colonial Questions" to the Second Comintern Congress, and the theses of that congress are among the major ideological seedbeds for what is called Neo-Maoism.[5]

Insofar as Kautsky's work is an exercise in Marxist intellectual history, it does not serve our purposes. True, we should know what the doctrines and the strategies and tactics employed at any given time are, as well as the rationalizations offered for them. But from the viewpoint of political analysis and future decision-making, it is not important, it may even be misleading to become involved in the historical pastime of establishing the Marxist provenance of ideas. On the other hand, to establish the contemporary meaning of Marxism at the operative level in any given context may help us to understand better the newly independent countries of Southeast Asia.

Thus far, the word Marxism has been used in a generic and eclectic sense to refer to the phenomena commonly embraced by the words Socialism and Communism and by the doctrine associated with Marx and Engels and their followers, including Lenin, Stalin, and Mao Tse-tung. There is no reason to offer our definition of these individual doctrines apart from the meanings they acquire in the context of their Southeast Asian use. Our broad use of the terms Marxism and Marxist is not intended to imply that we regard Marx and all his followers as occupying an identical theoretical position. On the contrary, we are in full agreement with the many students who assert that subtractions and additions have been made to Marxism by many individuals from Marx to Mao. For the purpose of analyzing the impact of Marxism on Southeast Asia, however, it is useful to specify three major, logically separable aspects of Marxism in the broad sense. Asian Marxism has responded more significantly, as we shall see, to some elements of Marxism than to others.[6]

Marxist philosophy purports to answer several basic questions which have arisen in the course of Western civilization. These questions relate to problems of being, knowing, and valuing. The Marxist "system" begins with what Kant, speaking of Descartes, aptly described as a "crude" psychophysical and epistemological dualism. There is nature—the external, knowable world—and consciousness, which includes man. The relations of man and nature—*there is no supernature*—are the stuff of history. Values are the products and the choices arising from the interaction. The process or the changes in things, man, and society is the "dialectic."[7] Dialectic is universal; it characterizes all reality.

Methodologically, the dialectic uses the principle of contradiction to analyze relationships between things, events, and persons. Knowledge about these is an act (dialectic) which changes the knower and the thing or event known. True knowledge is a consequence of proved practice.

Marxists since Marx and Engels have felt called upon to discuss and defend the metaphysic and epistemology of this system, known as dialectical materialism. However, apart from formal advocacy and frequent but inconsequential lip service, dialectical materialism as the philosophical basis for Marxism has continued to decline in European Marxist circles. It is enshrined in Communist hagiographical writings.[8] Only rarely (e.g., Tran Duc Thao, *Phénomènologie et Matérialisme Dialectique*) has it had much significance in Southeast Asian Marxist writings. Because dialectical materialism, an inverted Hegelianism, is a Western philosophy, and because Western philosophical teaching and writing are, on the whole, foreign to the Buddhist, Confucian, Islamic, and animist cultural contexts of Southeast Asia and still largely foreign to the curriculum of its schools, there has been little response to Marxism as philosophy.

Marxism offers a philosophy of history. The eleventh thesis of Marx and Engels on Feuerbach is often quoted: "Philosophers [i.e., all those who preceded Marx] have only interpreted the world in various ways; the point however is to change it." Changing the world represents the essential element in all Marxism. It is the application of the dialectic to a special case, namely, society. Once we are beyond the aridities of dialectical materialism, we find Marxism represents primarily the theory and practice of social change. The key to the theory of the change is the conception of history; the practice is revolution. In a most significant sense, Marx's own effort may be said to be largely devoted to expounding and defending his view of history—what it is, how it moves, how its temporal values are transformed, and what its determined outcomes are.

Marx's preface to *A Contribution to the Critique of Political Economy* (1859)[9] not only offers a fragment of intellectual autobiography, it also provides one of the most useful brief statements of historical materialism. History is predictively or "scientifically" unilinear. It begins with men in society seeking to gratify their needs. The forms of production, the mechanisms of exchange for the goods produced, the relations which men involuntarily enter into in order to fill these needs determine the nature of every social structure or society. "The sum total of these relations of production constitutes the economic structure of society—the real foundation on which rise legal and political superstructures and to which correspond definite forms of social consciousness. The mode of production in material life determines the general character of the social, political and spiritual (i.e., intellectual) processes of life."

Except in the presumably harmonious conditions of early primitive society, history develops by conflict and opposition in the relations of production. Thus history exhibits the dialectic at work. The acquisition of control and ownership of property and the way in which wealth is distributed split society into warring orders or classes. History, then, is the record of the origins of societies, their distribution in classes, and their conflicts both within and between the classes. History is transformed more or less rapidly, peacefully or violently, by changes and contradictions in the economic foundations of society. The direction of the changes "can be determined with the precision of natural science," though the immediate issues must be perceived by men as a prelude to "fighting it out." The life-work to which Marx and Engels dedicated themselves was not only to prove their philosophy of history by their writings, but also to participate in the historical struggle.[10]

If the predictions of Marx and Engels did not always have the "precision of natural science," other Marxists, notably Lenin, took up the cudgels to explain away the instant failure while safeguarding the long-range *Weltanschauung*.[11] From the viewpoint of Asian ideological and political developments, this particular aspect of Lenin's development of Marxism, including its application at the above-mentioned Second Comintern Congress[12] are infinitely more important than any other Marxist effort since the *Communist Manifesto*. Since capitalism did not suffer its predicted collapse and make way for the immediate victory of Socialism, Lenin provided both an explanation and an extension of time for its demise. Imperialism, "the highest stage of capitalism," did not fully develop until "the period 1898–1914." "Moribund," "decaying," "transitional to socialism," imperialism nonetheless provided a respite for capitalism by the enlargement of monopolies, advanced the quantity and power of export capital, intensified the exploitation of oppressed nations and colonies, and even created "a privileged upper stratum of the proletariat" in the imperialist countries "who live at the expense of the hundreds of millions of members of uncivilized nations."[13] The Marxist ideology of historical materialism was thus "saved" by reinterpretation.

However much historical materialism may err by regarding "economic conditions" as the sole historical causal agents, it has created and maintained an enormous following since it burst on the world of 1848. Its concrete applications, particularly in the deserved "exposure" of the conditions of men under nineteenth-century capitalism and imperialism, served to arouse Europe and later helped to arouse Asia.[14] While its critics were successful in pointing out specific shortcomings, historical materialism nonetheless thrived as a whole view of social reality and development. Before World War I, it captured the loyalties of more Europeans than any other social philosophy of modern times precisely because it represented a system of thought, a vocabulary of exchange which transcended national cultures and boundaries. And it served as a satisfying "explanation" for anti-colonial nationalists in Southeast Asia (and elsewhere) who did not necessarily adopt the rest of the Marxist intellectual baggage.

The very nature of dialectical and historical materialism required that it proponents also serve as executive activists. Their theory, underscoring unity of thought and action, demanded their participation in the revolutionary movement and development of a revolutionary praxis. Out of this came the national parties, the several Internationals, the supranational movement of the Marxists, and all the factional variations. Revolutionary praxis rested on the "demonstration" that Socialism (or Communism) was inevitable; that a classless society with economic institutions organized to serve human needs would replace the polarities created by monopolistic capitalism;[15] that the proletariat, properly organized and led, would will this replacement and be the instrument for its accomplishment. Legality was a convenient but not a necessary political weapon to implement the change. Agitation, propaganda, and above all revolutionary-minded organization were indispensable prerequisites.

All this is seriously set forth by Marx and Engels in the *Communist Manifesto*, in a style which is often prophetic and sometimes poetic.[16] It carried throughout the world the Marxist message that revolutionary practice based on "objective conditions" would, despite "interruptions," "half measures, weaknesses and meannesses," bring about revolutionary change. The bourgeoisie and the bourgeois state would struggle violently against their inevitable successors, but the proletariat and the "semi-proletariat" (the peasantry) must in time triumph. The victory would require a period of dictatorship, but once power was consolidated, coercive, class instruments would "wither away."

Since Marxists were not pacifists, since they had experienced the violence of the bourgeois state, they were not in principle opposed to violence. But the proposed variations in strategy and tactics produced schisms in the Marxist ranks on the issue of democracy versus dictatorship both as means and ends. On these and other issues, Socialists and Communists came to regard each other as bitter, irreconcilable enemies.

The road to power became, as Lenin was to call it, one of the "burning questions of our movement."[17] Marx, and Marxists before Lenin, predicted that in the "collisions between the classes," the proletariat would hasten the revolutionary process and assist the "grave-diggers" among the bourgeoisie. But the proletariat requires the assistance of "the most advanced and resolute of the working class parties, that section which pushes forward all others, . . . [which has] the advantage of clearly understanding the line of march, the conditions, and the ultimate general results of the proletarian movement."[18] This Marxist party was one among other working-class parties. And so it remained until Lenin.

After his amplification of the theory of imperialism and its application to colonial questions,[19] Lenin's second major contribution to Marxism was his conception of the revolutionary party and its role in preparing for and winning the revolution. In his earliest writings he had already adopted the view concerning the unity of "theoretical and practical work . . . which

. . . Liebknecht aptly described as: Studieren, Propagandieren, Organi-sieren."[20] *Iskra* was launched in 1900 to give a "definite physiognomy and organization" to the Russian Marxist movement and was to exhibit "a strictly defined policy."[21] Lenin's polemical work, *What Is To Be Done?*, completed and published early in 1902, led to the first of the many "splits" in Lenin's political life, this one with Plekhanov who supported the Mensheviks. This did not deter Lenin from his basic conceptions of the party and its role, either at the time or during the next two decades of his life. The party is "the vanguard of the revolutionary forces, . . . an organiza-tion of revolutionists" whose members constitute a "profession" which "of necessity [will] be not too extensive and as secret as possible." It will "guide" the struggles of the working class because it knows the course of history; it will "utilize" all conflicts with the "exploiters" because it can diagnose objective conditions; it will "preserve its political independence." When Stalin reformulated and codified this conception of the party in *The Foundations of Leninism* (1924), he in no way falsified the original, how-ever ruthlessly he was to apply its "line."[22]

As is well known, the party, which was to lead to the transitional dicta-torship of the proletariat on the day of the revolution, became a dictator-ship *over* the proletariat; "democratic centralism," the name given to the theory of organization, became the centralism of the leadership and the leader. Whether this development was inherent in Bolshevism or merely an accidental concomitant of the biographies of Lenin and Stalin need not here concern us. What is important is the fact that this conception of a professional, vanguard party, determined to help make the always predicted revolution, profoundly affected the nationalist, anti-imperialist struggles of Asia, including, with the exception of Thailand, the countries of our study.

The party, conceived and organized by Lenin, achieved a revolution and successfully came to power. The success of the Communist movement in Russia gave a powerful impetus to the acceptance of its ideas concerning revolution and the anticolonial struggle. Victors in a conflict can often shape future doctrine and action because they appear to have won on the basis of the alleged past. Colonial Asians were inclined to accept uncriti-cally the Soviet rationalization of these events.

As Lewis Corey remarked more than a generation ago, Soviet expla-nations of the autocratic dictatorship represented the "totalitarian poten-tial" of Marx and Marxism itself. The specifically Communist additions to Marxism, whether they come from Lenin, Trotsky, Stalin, or Mao, have been well summed up by Trotsky: "The welfare of the Revolution—that is the supreme law." And those who acquire and then perpetuate the power of this revolutionary law are the sole legislators and judges of their law.

This perhaps more than any other issue divides the Communist world from all other worlds.

Of these three main aspects of Marxism—dialectical materialism, historical materialism, and revolutionary praxis—the last two especially have had, as will be seen, a continuing effective life in Asia. (Dialectical materialism, of course, is "official" doctrine in Communist China and North Viet Nam.) Modifications have been made. For despite the Leninist-Stalinist interest in the colonial and semicolonial countries, more often than not their theory and practice were based on data largely derived from the developments in the technologically advanced, capitalist countries, the other "camp." Neither the Communists nor the Socialists of the West had any intimate knowledge of Asian lands and peoples, though the former, especially after the formation of the Third International, were more ready to acquire such knowledge and, above all, to move into the colonial areas.

Beyond doubt, the Comintern line toward Asia was more influential between the world wars than any other Marxist or Socialist view. It was the most influential because it appeared to be the most concerned about Asian needs and aspirations. But because it arrived first in Indonesia and Viet Nam, the nationalists of those countries achieved all the earlier a measure of sophistication in distinguishing its characteristics and in formulating non-Communist, nationalist, and Socialist (Marxist and non-Marxist) views. By the time it reached Burma in the mid-1930's, Comintern influence had to be shared with varieties of Marxism and non-Marxist Socialism (e.g., Fabianism) sifted through the factions within the British Labour Party.

It must be repeated that an understanding of the acceptance and spread of Marxism in Southeast Asia requires an analysis of the indigenous cultural factors which existed before the Western impact was felt. Among such cultural factors are the vestiges of the Chinese patriarchal system found in Viet Nam, Koranic law as a possible basis for social justice in Indonesia, and Theravada Buddhism in Burma and Thailand. These factors—"imports" from the long-range historical point of view—have been fully naturalized and are regarded by the indigenes as authentic elements of their traditional culture.

We shall see that some individuals, organizations, political parties, and governments in these four Southeast Asian countries identify themselves and their aims with Marxist symbols. Despite this, the terms they employ and the programs they adopt and execute partially reflect indigenous historical and cultural patterns. A reading of The Burmese Revolution—a speech given in December 1951 by U Ba Swe, at that time secretary-general of the Burma Socialist Party—illustrates the point. U Ba Swe, a former Prime Minister and one of the five most important political leaders in

Burma, speaks of his comrades as "architects of revolution . . . building a Burmese Socialist structure . . . with Marxism [as] the guide to action . . . [but] only a revolutionary movement which is entirely Burmese, conforming to Burmese methods and principles can achieve any measure of success." He further asserts that "Marxist theory is not antagonistic to Buddhist philosophy. The two are, frankly speaking, not merely similar. In fact they are the same in concept."[23]

Whether or not such identifications of the content of Marxism with the content of indigenous culture patterns are later abandoned, the fact that they are made, at one or another period, has been characteristic of the development of Marxism in the area. Even the most doctrinaire Marxists have at times found it necessary, if only for tactical reasons, either to incorporate elements of indigenous value systems or to phrase their own ideology in terms that would avoid conflict with the indigenous ones.

Related in importance to the indigenous culture pattern or ideology was the existence, prior to the introduction of Marxism, of political trends arising in response to the impact of the West. For example, the most popular slogans in Southeast Asia are associated with anticolonialism or antiimperialism, which prevailed in the area before Marxism had begun to play a role. The Leninist variant of Marxism, when discovered by some Western-educated Southeast Asian elites, provided additional intellectual justification for their reaction against alien political domination. Its common usage, particularly between the two world wars, served to blunt political and organizational distinctions between Marxists—both Socialists and Communists—and revolutionary or "extreme" nationalists. However, the 1948 Communist insurrections in Burma and Indonesia subsequently caused the non-Communists to modify or drop the Leninist rationalization and vocabulary and sharpened inherent, earlier-perceived differences between Communism and nationalism, though the powerful theme of anti-Colonialism has been meaningfully retained.

Nationalism, no matter how it was conceived and how it led to organization and activity, came first on the political stage in Burma, Viet Nam, and Indonesia. In each of these countries, patriotic memories of an independent, dynastic past, free from foreign controls, were prominent. Such memories of recent or older vintage, depending on the history of the country before the advent of the British, French, or Dutch rule, were actively fed by Buddhism in Burma, the Confucian mandarinate in Viet Nam, and Islam in Indonesia. This first expression of political and social antagonism to imperialist sway did not succeed in any ultimate sense, but it never really disappeared. It began in these three countries at roughly the same time—the turn of the century.

Marxism came in ostensible support of nationalism. At the time it arrived, first in Viet Nam and Indonesia and later in Burma, it was regarded by the indigenes as genuinely supportive of nationalist and anticolonial aspirations. Factional fights, divisive maneuvers, fratricidal warfare, severe as these might be, were regarded not as signs of an ineluctable conflict between dictatorship and freedom, but rather as "family" squabbles.

The concluding chapter of this book will show how nationalists and Marxists start out on a common front in opposition to all forms of colonialism. They reject any and all arguments which, in the interests of economic development and social and political tutelage, would retain the substance or façade of imperialist power. The Communists acquired and retained prestige in the struggle for independence until gradually the non-Communists became aware, as Darsono, a founding and now ex-member of the Indonesian Communist Party, has pointed out, that "they were trying to capture the entire leadership of the nationalist revolution."[24] In essence, this issue split the Marxist-nationalist amalgam, dividing the Communists from the nationalists and Democratic Socialists. The splits occurred at various times in each of the three countries. The Communist bid for power in 1948, on signal from Moscow, sealed the issue in Burma and in part clarified it in Indonesia. In Viet Nam, the 1954 conference at Geneva divided the Communists from the others at the seventeenth parallel.

In all this it would appear that Thailand remains untouched. But the appearance conceals a slower variant of the above development. The forces which produced the 1932 coup that ushered in Marshal Phibun, like the related forces of 1957 which ushered him out, represent various degrees of constitutional nationalism tied strongly to the military elite of Thailand. The quarter century difference in time registers more than a mere change in the Palace Guard. But unlike the other countries of the study, Thailand's guarded steps in the direction of constitutionalism and, in part, military government do not exhibit much pressure from internal Marxist movements. The absence of such pressure does not mean the absence of such tendencies or other forms of "protest."

The complete analysis of Marxism in Southeast Asia thus requires attention not only to the incorporation of its ideology into the activities of organized political groups but also to its subsequent application to problems of national policy. For example, the "charismatic" role of former Prime Minister U Nu of Burma has profoundly influenced the content of any ideology professed by the group around him. The common experience of members of the ruling group in that country as "radical" students, political prisoners, defenders of the country against insurrection, and elected or appointed leaders gives to the members of the group a special relationship with each other and a position in the country which affects our understanding of their ideology. Similarly, the personal relations, both good and bad, among Sukarno, Hatta, Natsir, and Sjahrir have profoundly affected the course of Indonesian politics, though they represent not one but three parties each of which has consciously accepted an infusion of Marxism.

Finally, the analysis of ideology and leadership roles inescapably relates to political behavior. A prime example is the continuing Southeast Asian preoccupation with "national planning" and its execution. *Pyidawtha* is not only a set of plans for the welfare state in Burma, derived in part from the Marxist background; it is also a country-wide program of action which in the face of socioeconomic reality causes the planners to modify and otherwise alter or move away from Marxist theory. Conversely, principles of private enterprise and property in the Republic of Viet Nam are diluted or in part surrendered by the government as it seeks to implement nationally instituted and directed programs of land reform and resettlement. The effects of such reciprocal conditioning are to be seen not only in the arena of domestic development but also in the formulation and execution of policies designed to provide security in external relations.

Insofar as our historical analysis succeeds in disentangling and clarifying patterns of expression and behavior, it will have set forth the role of Marxism within the indigenous culture of the selected countries. The concepts or the contents of this Marxism may be compared with concepts of Marxism presumably operative elsewhere in the world. Whether or not such comparison is made, the domestic and international policies of these Southeast Asian nations should in the result be more intelligible to the West. The distaste that exists in the West for overt or covert forms of something called "Marxism" is understandable, but it does not necessarily serve as the most desirable basis for international relations. It is our hope that objective sociopolitical analysis, such as is here attempted, may contribute to facilitating present and future political discourse within the free world.

While this book was being written, Southeast Asian Marxism continued to develop, sometimes in unexpected directions or in response to unforeseen events. The authors cannot hope to have produced even a definitive history, much less an analysis of the current role of Marxism, which will remain valid indefinitely. They can hope to have contributed to a basic understanding of the phenomenon, and in particular to have helped indicate the scope and methods of study which are required for full understanding.

2

MARXISM IN BURMA

JOHN SEABURY THOMSON

Marxist slogans dominated the campaign speeches in Burma's 1956 national election. From Prime Minister Nu, leader of the Anti-Fascist People's Freedom League (AFPFL) to U Tun Pe on the democratic right and Dr. E. Maung, spokesman in Parliament for the Communist-dominated National Unity Front (NUF), Burmese political leaders relied on a Marxist appeal to the voters. "We are all Marxist now," Geoffrey Fairbairn quoted Burmese politicians as saying at the time.[1]

The 1956 election, however, probably marked the end of an era. It is possibly the last time that Mr. Fairbairn's quotation will apply. For the preceding twenty years Marxism and nationalism had been very nearly synonymous in Burma, particularly during the struggle for independence from Britain. Once independence was assured, however, Marxism appealed and applied less. Practical problems of national development dominated the thinking of major Burmese leaders and, from 1945 on, Burma's moderate socialists gradually began to remove from the coalition the Communist and left-wing socialist elements. Their aim, it was felt, could not be reconciled with real Burmese national goals. By January 1958 the process had gone so far that Prime Minister Nu, speaking to the third national congress of the AFPFL, specifically rejected Marxism as a guiding philosophy for the future of Burma.[2] As a matter of fact, certainly for the past ten years, Burma has been under the leadership of moderate democratic socialists whose programs, developed through trial and error to meet pressing Burmese needs, have been much closer to a "New Deal" approach than to Marxism.

Nevertheless, Marxism has played a significant role in the development of present-day Burmese politics and remains a part of the political heritage of the contemporary government. Marxist influence began in Burma in the 1930's and reached its height in the early 1940's. Its original impact came later than in most other Asian countries, as Marxist literature first became available to Burmese nationalists only in 1931. It was the Marxist explanation of imperialism and capitalism that made the strongest impression and it was a group of younger nationalists, the Thakins, from which have come today's national leaders, who were first stirred. But it was Marxism with a difference—a difference based on Burma's historical development and on contemporary conditions in the country. As Deputy Prime Minister Kyaw Nyein, who is also general secretary of the Burmese Socialist Party, chairman of the Asian Socialist Anti-Colonial Bureau, and one of his party's leading theoreticians, put it in 1954, he had seen Marxism develop in Asia originally as a reaction against nineteenth-century capitalism. However, in Burma at least, experience had led to the adaptation of Marxism to local circumstances and then to a critical evaluation of the reality of Marxism. Kyaw Nyein wrote:

[W]e find that in our typical Marxist analysis of society we have all along concentrated on a typical 19th century society. We have studied how society grew into feudal society and then again into industrial or capitalist society. . . . But what we have not analyzed is the other trend in the development of Soviet society. . . . As socialists we think we know how a typical capitalist society degenerates. We have ideas of how to turn this capitalist society into a democratic socialist society. Our line is clear. On the other hand, we have not studied how a great country like Russia took a very dangerous pill of communism. By taking the communism pill it is developing new symptoms of a very bad disease . . . [; it] is developing a new type of society which is equally imperialist and predatory and which is conquering the world gradually.[3]

THE BACKGROUND OF BURMESE NATIONALISM

To understand the place of Marxism in Burma, it is necessary to relate it to the other major factors which have shaped the development of modern Burmese nationalism. Extremely important as a background factor has been the widespread sense of a Burmese identity—a sense which far predates the arrival of Western influence and British rule and that was so deep-rooted as to survive the long periods of disunity between the three dynastic rules. The geographic isolation of the country from its major neighbors to the north and to the west also had its influence, as it meant the freedom of the peoples who drifted down from the Sino-Tibetan plateau in small tribal groups to develop their own culture, adapting what they chose from abroad but forced to accept nothing. Indeed, in challenging the thesis that modern Asian nationalism is a "response to the shattering impact upon Asia of the modern West,"[4] Dr. Htin Aung, Rector of the University of Rangoon, has insisted that Burma at least "became acquainted with the idea of nationalism many centuries before the British conquest of the country."[5] And although Burmese nationalism was at low ebb between 1890 and 1905, the spirit nevertheless survived, as it was during this time that political organizations—starting in 1897 with the Sasanadara Society—were developed.

Vitally important in giving content to the sense of Burmese identity and in reinforcing it against British efforts to maintain the separation of the different ethnic groups were two major factors. First of all, there was the matter of language: over 90 per cent of the Burmese people speak Burmese as either their first or second language, and all but the Indian, Pakistani, and Chinese aliens use the phonetic Burmese script.[6] In addition, the so-called politically advanced members of Burmese society speak English.

Even more important in providing a kind of cement for modern nationalism is the near universality of the Buddhist religion. Though it came originally from India, Buddhism has gone so deep in Burmese culture that the saying, "To be a Burmese is to be a Buddhist," is widely accepted, and the government of Burma is seriously considering making Buddhism the state religion. One may wholly agree with Htin Aung that Buddhism was not "the cause" of Burmese nationalism, but it is impossible to accept his view that Buddhism did not "affect" it.[7] For Buddhism is so much a part of the millennial history of dynastic and independent Burma that it has played an ineradicable role in the molding of the Burmese nation and the forms of its nationalism. The experience of the British is relevant here. Though warned that to ignore the Buddhist hierarchy would be to arouse Burmese antagonism, they refused to recognize its authority and consequently to grant it the administrative role the hierarchy had held under the Burmese monarchy. This unimaginative decision, inspired in part by unfortunate experiences with intervention in indigenous religious questions in India, drew the religious issue into the nationalist movement. As a result, Buddhist leaders—among them the Buddhist monks U Wisara and U Ottama—came to take an active part in the struggle for independence, and a number of Buddhist monks (*phongyis*) figured in much of the prewar violence against the government.[8]

The modern Burmese nationalist movement is rooted, then, primarily in a sense of national identity and in the unifying effect of Burmese Buddhism. But the driving force of the nationalist movement in modern times came from the impact of the West—and for Burma the "West" meant not only Europe but India. It is interesting to note that the initial Burmese reaction to British rule was not particularly hostile. Indeed, British rule, coming in three separate campaigns between 1824 and 1885 and culminating in the capture and exile of the last of the Burmese kings, had its not inconsiderable attractions at the outset. The economic development of the delta region of the Irrawaddy, the opening of new rice lands and markets, the development of communications, and the improvement of health conditions—all encouraged Burmese acceptance of the new regime. Thus, after an initial five-year period of "pacification," Burmese for some fifteen years on the whole appear to have accepted foreign rule as a mere change in leadership—and often a change for the better. The development of the Irrawaddy delta was, for example, described by a contemporary as "an unrecorded epic of colonization by the people of upper Burma," even though many died "clearing the rank jungle under a murderous sun in the malaria-ridden swamp."[9] Describing the direct impact of the British administration on the peasant's lot, the author showed the two sides of the imperial coin. On the one hand, he wrote:

Law and order had been established in a new way, more widespread and more uniform. Whereas my grandfather had formerly to trade with one eye on dacoits and river pirates, he could now travel with confidence, carrying large sums of money or merchandise over long distances. The main merchandise of the masses, rice, fetched higher and higher prices and internal trade prospered.[10]

On the other hand, the Burmese soon found himself unable to compete against the Indians, who had followed the British to Burma, either in business, in the government, or in finance, and he was forced to watch the economy move steadily into alien hands. The British government, pledged to the system of *laissez faire*, did nothing to intervene on behalf of the Burmese but rather, according to the same writer, provided " 'a fair field and no favour,' as the elephant said when he danced among the chickens."[11]

Central to all else was the fact that the Burmese were excluded from government leadership and participation. It has long been asserted that Lord Dufferin considered this unfortunate, the implication being that there were no loyal Burmese available to serve.[12] But it is also a fact that Lord Dufferin, even before the third Anglo-Burmese War, specifically rejected ruling through a Burmese monarch in favor of annexation.[13] Furthermore, very few efforts were made to adapt British rule to Burmese conditions, the British being satisfied to apply in Burma the governing arrangements developed in India to meet Indian problems. And, because India had reserves of personnel already acquainted with the British system and language, Indians rather than Burmese filled the administrative posts. Further, as Burma was made a province of India, most of the British personnel appointed to Burma gained their experience in the alien climate of India. Nominally, of course, the ranks of government service were open to Burmese, as were opportunities in business, but actually the opportunities to participate were not. On the lower levels of the administrative services, Burmese were able to enter directly; but it was not until 1920 that candidates could sit for the Indian civil service anywhere but in London, and not until 1923 that the first Burmese became a member of the Indian civil service.

It early became apparent that opportunities for advancement under the British were to come through an understanding of the British system of government and a knowledge of English. Government and private schools offering English and adequate for the training of clerical personnel soon developed in Burma. Even the traditional *Phongyikyaungs*, the monastic schools which every Burmese Buddhist boy is expected to attend, made efforts to adapt themselves to the new situation and to offer Western materials, but were discouraged through a lack of support from the government.

Perhaps most important, the schools modeled on the British rapidly developed to the point where they were turning out more graduates than the government could absorb. This situation led to the demand for higher educational opportunities and the development in 1920 of the University of Rangoon. But this expansion did not open for the Burmese the opportunities they sought. It produced instead an educated, largely unemployed, and discontented elite, which had by the mid-thirties grown to significant proportions.

The discontent of this elite was reinforced by the introduction of new ideas. In fact, the education which the British brought to Burma was vitally important in shaping the present forms of Burmese nationalism. First of all, the curriculum at the University of Rangoon was a close copy of offerings at British universities. By bringing the students into contact with ideas and conditions outside Burma, the University both broadened their outlook and broke into what has been described as their "extraordinarily self-complacent and parochial form of nationalism."[14] Over the long term, probably the most significant contribution of British education was that it instilled in the minds of the future leaders of Burma a deep and abiding respect for British legal institutions and a strong predilection for parliamentary government.

It is significant, too, that it was through the British educational system that the Burmese educated elite—today's leaders in both the government and the opposition—first came into contact with Marxist literature and ideology. Thus it was Burmese students returning from the United Kingdom in the thirties who introduced Marxist and Socialist writings into Burma. It was through the private collection of a retired British civil servant in Rangoon that Burmese students first had contact with the works of British radical leftist writers. And it was from England that the first full set of Burmese-owned Marxist classics was procured.

From the outset, Marxist writings produced a contradictory response in Burma. The chief attraction of Marxist philosophy lay in its explanation of colonialism and its attack on imperialism and capitalism. At the same time, Burmese Buddhists were repelled by its doctrinaire repudiation of religion. As Furnivall has pointed out,[15] Burmese readers of Marxist literature could see that Communism would have very little attraction for the Burmese people unless it could be reconciled with Buddhism. In the postwar and independence period, the attempt to effect such a reconciliation was to attract the major efforts of the Socialist leaders.

Before the war, then, the seeds of Marxism had already been planted, and Burmese nationalism had taken on a marked antiforeign tinge—both anti-European and anti-Indian. It was, however, the Japanese invasion which probably did the most to strengthen Burmese nationalism. U Nu himself has reported that when the Japanese invasion began, the Burmese generally looked forward to "liberation" from British rule and were ready to welcome the invaders. Interestingly, for the record, it was the few Communists among the nationalists of Burma, and Thakin Soe in particular, who preached the dangers of this course and urged Burmese nationalists to side with the British against Japan.[16] Though Soe was unsuccessful and was sometimes accused of being a British agent, his position was ultimately incorporated into a last-minute appeal—and threat—from the Burmese nationalists to the British, made as the Japanese were advancing into the country: "Grant independence, or the promise of independence, now," they demanded.

If you proclaim this now, we will help the English side against the Fascist brigands who threaten the independence of small nations. If you do not make this proclamation, we will do all we can to hinder your war effort in whatever way we can.[17]

U Nu's book *Burma Under the Japanese* and journalist Tun Pe's *Sun Over Burma*[18] give graphic accounts of the Burmese response to Japanese occupation and rule. Each from his own experiences illustrates the bitter hatred which grew up over Japanese face-slapping and looting and over the outrageous assumptions of superiority, and each shows how the callous disregard of the Japanese for Burmese sensitivities strengthened the nationalistic outlook of the Burmese people.

By the end of the war, as the Japanese withdrew and the British returned, Burmese nationalism was fully articulate. In a distinctive combination, its ingredients included indigenous nationalism; Buddhism; a background of Western political, economic, and educational institutions; a revulsion against foreign domination (British, Indian, or Japanese); and an intellectual bent toward Marxist ideology—the last having been added late and worked into the existing fabric. It is possible to suggest that where Communist propaganda in colonial areas customarily seizes upon the existing spirit of modern nationalism and rebellion against foreign rule and attempts to subvert that spirit to its own ends, in Burma it was more that the ardent non-Communist nationalists seized upon portions of Marxist philosophy and subverted them to the cause of Burmese independence.

BURMESE NATIONALISM TO 1939

As has already been mentioned, the first Burmese contacts with Marxism came in the early thirties. Before then, Burmese nationalists not only had no acquaintance with Marxism but did not appear to be concerned with developing or announcing support for any particular political philosophy, nor did they, except on an electorate basis, relate themselves to the mass of the people. At first the nationalist societies—starting with the Sasanadara Society—had to operate as religious and social groups or face British repression.[19] As British thinking on colonial issues became more liberal and change began to seem imminent, the Burmese nationalists grew more openly political, but even so they continued to emphasize practical rather than theoretical issues. Thus, in the twenties the major issue revolved around the degree of cooperation Burmese should give to the Legislative Council and to the government; in the early thirties it centered on whether Burmese interests would best be served by separation from India or not. In the twenties the General Council of Burmese Association (GCBA)—successor to the Young Men's Buddhist Association—under the leadership of the noted lawyer U Chit Hlaing and with the support of the leading *phongyi* U Ottama, stood for total boycott of the government. Dissidents who felt that their best contribution lay in the role of a loyal, nationalist opposition split off from the GCBA to form the Twenty-one Party. Stronger support for the government was expressed by the Golden Valley Party. No matter how much they differed among themselves, however, these parties stood for the return of Burma to indigenous control. Independence was not among their stated goals.

In many ways, the Burma in which these parties worked might have seemed a perfect setting for the merger of nationalism with some variant of Marxism. The growing Burmese desire for self-government and self-determination was being frustrated. The indigenous nationalists were almost entirely of an "oppressed" class; the capitalist and imperialist "oppressors," almost entirely alien. But no Marxist movement or ideological current became apparent in the twenties,[20] nor did any leader emerge who could definitely be classified as Marxist or even Socialist.

As it happened, the incident which may be cited as actually introducing Marxist materials into Burma was neither Marxist-inspired nor even Marxist-oriented. In 1931, following the fall in rice prices, the peasants of the Tharawaddy district revolted under the leadership of Saya San, who has been described as "a Burmese physician who dabbled in astronomy and astrology and who set himself up as the leader and the consecrated head of Burma."[21] Though this was one of the most serious revolts in the period of British rule, it is generally conceded to have had no external ideological orientation. Led by an ex-monk who utilized a variety of traditional Burmese appeals, including "magic," the uprising was primarily an outburst of peasant frustration against hard times and alien rule, much in the manner of a medieval peasant revolt.

Saya San was captured by the British in 1931, tried for treason, and hanged. But during Saya San's trial, Tun Pe prevailed upon him to bequeath the royalties of his book *Signs of Diseases* to the establishment of a library. The resulting 300 rupees (then about $100) were used by Tun Pe to buy books recommended in Pandit Nehru's *Impressions of Soviet Russia*, among them being, as Tun Pe listed them, "*Das Kapital, The State,* and *Revolution and Counter Revolution* [sic]." According to Tun Pe, demand for these books among the young nationalists of Rangoon was so great that he was himself never able to read beyond the introductions. "These books," he reported, "had a great influence over them and the ideologies they imbibed found expression before public meetings."[22]

The people among whom the Saya San books circulated were a new, younger, and more vigorously nationalist element just then emerging on the Rangoon University campus. At the time of the peasant revolt, they had been organizing the Dohbama Asiayone ("We Burmans" Association), which would, they hoped, change from a primarily student organization to one with a following in the countryside. It was members of the Dohbama who were to become known as the Thakins—the term by which the Burmese addressed their European "masters" under British rule. It was clear that the Thakins were resolved to be "masters in their own house." In contrast to the older nationalists, their goal was not accommodation with the British but national independence. Among the Thakins was much of the present leadership of Burma.

At the outset, neither the Thakins nor the Dohbama Asiayone had any set ideological tenets beyond their nationalist fervor. They were looking widely for ideas and weapons with which to forward their movement. They turned to Sun Yat-sen and the *San-Min-Chu-I,* to Nietzsche, to Marx, to the Sinn Fein, to the Fabians. They read voraciously and adopted freely. In addition to the rapidly circulating volumes from the Saya San legacy, another set of Marxist works was made available to the Thakins in 1932, when Dr. Thein Maung brought them back to Burma with him from the London Round Table Conference on the future of Burma.[23] Mr. J. S. Furnivall introduced British radical leftist literature through his Burma Book Club, Ltd., in Rangoon, and in 1937 Thakin Nu and Thakin Than Tun established the Nagani (Red Dragon) Book Club, which produced or translated a political work each month for its 217 members.[24] Among the works so made available were selections from *Das Kapital* translated by U Nu and a series of Marxist pamphlets translated by Thakin Ba Hein. On these sources of heady political literature, the Thakin leaders thrived. Discipline of thought was not a requirement, individual members adopting whatever attracted them and trying to apply their ideas in conjunction with the frequently contradictory ideas of others in the group.

The Thakins adopted the slogan, "Live dangerously," and—again unlike the older nationalists—spent much time and energy in agitation throughout the country. It should be remembered that in the thirties the reading public in Burma was both limited sharply and confined mainly to the area of Rangoon. The only effective way of reaching the mass of the Burmese population was to go directly to the people. Thus study groups—fundamentally Marxist in orientation—were organized by the Thakins to provide the meeting ground for discussion. In describing the Thakins' political activities in the thirties, the eminent journalist Dr. Maung Maung said:

The Thakins were beginning to force themselves on the attention of the public and the rather annoyed government. They were making their speeches after the fashion of Lenin or of Mussolini, Hitler or Kemal Ataturk, depending upon the latest book, or translation of a book, that they had read. Their speeches were fiery, their gestures were grand; the people were attracted to the new breed of native young politicians who wore native loom-woven clothes and clattered about in native wooden slippers, talking big and dreaming big whenever they could get an audience.[25]

Commenting from a Western viewpoint, John L. Christian said of the "extremist" Thakins that "the general Burmese criticism has been that . . . [they] should do something more than make speeches and hold demonstrations."[26] And the *Burma Handbook*, published during the war from the capital-in-exile in Simla, summed them up as follows:

The *Thakins* were violently nationalist and revolutionary; many inclined toward communist tenets and used the crossed hammer and sickle as their emblem but their only settled political principle was their intense nationalism. The *Thakins* opposed every ministry and avowed complete independence for Burma as their aim.[27]

In the wide search of the Thakins, it is not surprising that Marxist ideas, particularly on imperialism, received considerable attention. And the goals of Socialism, which, translated into Burmese terms, involved removing the country's wealth from Indian and British hands, struck a responsive note. Against this, it was probably the role assigned to religion which made it possible for observers to report that during the thirties no more than two or three of the Thakins actually considered themselves Communists.[28]

The first Thakin to come into direct contact with the Communist movement was Thakin Thein Maung, who in 1931 had been sent to England as a State Scholar. In London he met a self-exiled Burman, Ashin Kyaw Sein, who was a member of the British Communist party, and through him was introduced to the League Against Imperialism. When he became a member of this front organization, contact was for the first time established between the Thakins and the Communist party.[29]

It is interesting to note that in spite of this contact of Thein Maung's, Burma did not seem to come within the orbit of the Comintern offices in either Shanghai or Calcutta. Indeed, there is no record that the Comintern headquarters at Singapore made any contact with Burma from 1926 on, and if Tan Malaka or Alimin visited Burma between 1925 and 1927, there is neither record nor influence on the Burmese nationalist movement to show for it. The ties which might have been developed with Shanghai were cut off before they could begin, by the arrest of the bureau's chief executives in 1930–31. And, generally speaking, direct connection with Indian organizations was not popular in Burma.

Marxism's most important contribution to the Burmese nationalist movement in the thirties was not, however, in its international contacts nor in its ideological content, but in its emphasis on the organization of mass support—first among the younger intellectuals and then among other groups, especially labor and the peasants. It is worth while to note that though Burma sent no delegates to the Seventh Comintern meetings in 1935, the concepts of a Popular Front movement of anti-Fascism and anti-imperialism and of a movement for mass-organization support to the nationalist cause made considerable impact in Burma among the Thakins, who set out to organize and to agitate. Their first demonstrations took place at the University of Rangoon in the famous student striko of 1036.

Since 1935 the Thakins had been actively campaigning for seats on the Executive Council of the Rangoon University Student Union (RUSU). In 1936, they captured all of them and were ready for dramatic action. As so often happens, the immediate cause for the strike was trivial. As president of the Student Union, U Nu had delivered a forthright attack upon the teaching staff of the University, calling for an overhaul of the educational system and the faculty. The principal of University College, Mr. D. J. Sloss, immediately suspended him and demanded an explanation of his speech. This U Nu refused to give, and the Student Union walked out on strike.[30]

The situation was made more acute by the appearance in *Oway*, the student magazine edited by Thakin Aung San, of an anonymous article defaming an easily identifiable faculty member and entitled "Hell Hound at Large." When Aung San refused to name the author, he too was expelled from the University. Following this, seven hundred students went on strike and refused to return to classes until their demands for University reform had been met. The government temporized by appointing an investigating commission to look into the grievances. Most of the students then returned to their classes. When the report was completed, almost a year later, the students demonstrated again. It was in the course of these demonstrations that the nationalist movement gained a martyr—a student named Maung Aung Gyaw, who died of wounds inflicted by the mounted police. The student boycott was not finally settled until Ba Maw's government had been forced to resign in February 1939.[31]

Though Marxist influence was present in the student strike, the lasting significance of the demonstrations was in the fact that the University student body had for the first time been united for a political purpose by the Thakins. This point was generally missed by commentators. John L. Christian, for example, classified the 1936 strike as simply another in a long line of student strikes and did not even mention the names of the two expelled students.[32] G. E. Harvey also dismissed the strikes:

[There was not] much incentive to work when . . . university strikes, timed to break out just before final examinations, resulted not in the penalization of the strikers but rather the reverse—the examinations were invariably postponed, so that even the slackers got their chance.

He did, however, recognize that the RUSU was becoming a political force; though he added:

[I]t was largely run by law students, men who, after taking a poor degree, not good enough to get them a job, stayed on to study law (or rather they put their names down for the law classes) . . . and sometimes even the ministers, grown men, had to seek their permission before accepting office.[33]

And even in 1946, Harvey was still unwilling to give the student leaders the benefit of the doubt on the sincerity of their nationalist convictions.

Having gained control of the student body in 1936, the Thakins never lost it until the Japanese occupation. In fact, their control was so strong that they were able to designate the Student Union president, even going outside the student body for their choice. Ba Swe was a case in point. At the time of the 1936 student strike in Rangoon, he was still in high school in Tavoy, where he had organized student demonstrations and made contacts with the nationalist leaders in Rangoon. When they decided that he was needed for the leadership of the Student Union, he took his matriculation examinations, passed, came to the University, and assumed the office in 1938.

To a certain extent, Harvey's disparaging description of the RUSU leaders as students suited Ba Swe, though it is clear that in his case this was a matter of choice of activities and not of lack of ability. Thus, according to Dr. Maung Maung:

[In Ba Swe's first term,] the University became his operational headquarters. He lived and worked there, but not in studies. He went to classes at first just from curiosity, then stayed away. He took an exam or two just for the fun of it, failed and did not try again.[34]

Ba Swe's time and energies went to student politics. He was manager of the student magazine *Oway*, took part in a variety of nonstudent activities, and read Marx, Lenin, and Stalin on his own. In 1939 he "retired" from the University to help support two other Thakins, Ba Hein and Tun Shein, in their University careers[35] but was recalled by the Thakins in 1940 to serve as president of the Student Union for 1940–41. U Ba Swe's versatility has led to the often-repeated statement that he gave up a promising academic career for national politics. Though this may be true, his talents were clearly more suited to hard-hitting party organizing than to academic work.

While Ba Swe was at the University, the Thakin movement began to expand into other segments of Burmese society. Ba Swe, for example, took a special interest in the incipient labor movement, which he was later to lead. Although labor unions had been recognized by the government in the Trade Unions Act of 1926, their development as a significant factor in Burmese society had been extremely slow.[36] Strikes, of course, had occurred, and some progress had been made toward the development of an effective organization even before the Thakins took a direct interest in the movement, but it was not until they stepped in as leaders that labor developed anything like a national identity.

The Thakins moved into the labor movement in order to take over and reorganize the leadership. They worked, not through the shops and plants, but from the University. The outstanding example of the Thakin influence came with the oil field workers' strike in 1938–39, conducted under the leadership of two student nationalists, Thakin Ba Hein and Ba Swe. Both were by this time strongly Marxist-oriented, Thakin Ba Hein being "a complete convert to communism"[37] and one of the handful to be so known publicly. And Ba Swe, who considered himself a Marxist Socialist but not a Stalinist Communist, was so strongly attracted to the Russian leadership that he wrote at the time: "Let us respect and revere Stalin, let us pay our homage to him, for to pay homage to him to whom homage is due is a good deed."[38] Originally concerned with wages, the strike was deflected by the Thakin leadership to the nationalist cause. It culminated in a workers' march from the oil fields at Yenanyaung and Chauk to Rangoon.

The strike was put down with an iron hand. In an economic sense it was a failure. But the important development was that the labor movement had started to take on the nationalist and Socialist political orientation it was to hold from that time forward. This point was entirely missed by the government and undervalued by foreign observers.

While the strike was under way, the Thakins had called the first All Burma Labor Conference, to meet in July 1939. Even though it was a time of tense communal antipathies, representatives of both Burmese and Indian labor were included. From this conference came the organization on January 30, 1940, of the All Burma Trade Union Congress (ABTUC). In the words of Frank N. Trager:

The Thakins had achieved what no one else had been able to effect in modern Burmese history—a viable anti-British political instrument with its roots in something resembling a unified mass base of trade unions and related peasant organizations.[39]

Several months later, in August 1940, the ABTUC spelled out its objectives in detail: the establishment of a Socialist state in Burma; the socialization of production, distribution, and exchange; and the improvement of working conditions. The ABTUC called, too, for the promotion of civil rights, equality for all races and sexes, welfare benefits, and minimum wage and hour standardization; and it declared its intention to work for these goals through peaceful and democratic means, using strikes only as a last resort. A little more than two years after this declaration, Burma was invaded by Japan and all trade-union activity was suspended. It is not surprising, therefore, that the significance of the ABTUC was generally missed abroad, even in postwar years.[40]

At the same time that the Thakins were moving into the labor unions, they were also attempting to organize the peasants. Thakin Mya, an "older" member of the Thakin movement (born in 1897), who in 1936 had been elected to the legislature as one of the three Komin Kochin (One's Own King, One's Own Kind) representatives, presided over the first meeting of the All Burma Peasants Conference at Rangoon in 1939 and took an active part in organizing political-training classes for the peasant leaders. Out of the first conference developed the All Burma Peasants Organization, which has been intimately associated with the Thakin and nationalist movements ever since. In 1941, Thakin Tin became its president, a post he has continued to hold.

In other areas also, which attracted less attention, the Thakins were organizing and expanding their influence. In 1939, student organizations throughout the country were merged into the All Burma Student Union. In the same year, the Socialist party was formally founded as the People's

Revolutionary Party. It is also reported that in the same year the first pseudo-Communist cell—by description Marxist but not Communist—was founded in Scott Market (Bogyoke Market today) in Rangoon, including, among others, such future leaders as Aung San, Bo Let Ya, Goshal, Thein Pe, Ba Hein, and Thakin Soe.[41] And in March 1940 some fifteen of the Burmese nationalist leaders, among them Aung San and Thakin Than Tun, traveled to India to meet with the Indian National Congress Party leaders at their conference in Ramgarh. Dr. Kyaw Thet reports that the Indians, and Nehru in particular, made a tremendous impression on Aung San and the others, and that Indian Socialism and the Congress party from that time on strongly influenced the Burmese nationalist movement. The Dohbama Asiayone in its annual conferences of 1939 and 1940, for example, adopted almost verbatim the resolutions passed in the Indian Congress party conferences.

While the Thakins were gaining control of the growing mass movements as well as receiving considerable recognition in the vernacular press, they had made almost no positive impression on the government, and leadership was still far from their grasp. Their lack of national political importance was reflected, for example, in the "Who's Who in Burma" prepared by the government in 1943, while in exile in Simla. Of the seventy-five persons selected as "now prominent in Burma,"[42] only ten were from the Thakin movement, and little of their prewar activities was considered important enough for inclusion.[43] This inadequate listing was, however, no reflection on the knowledgeability of the British in Burma, for the Burmese members of the government-in-exile, as well as later British historians, from 1943 to 1945 completely underestimated support for the Thakins and continued to view them as "upstarts and extremists."[44]

The philosophy of the Thakins was still indeterminate in 1939, though the influence of Marxist literature—and of the Indian Congress party—was strong and growing. The membership remained divided in philosophy. In 1939, Thakin Soe, Goshal (Thakin Ba Tin), Thakin Ba Hein, and Thein Pe were Communists. At that time, Thakin Than Tun, who was later to become the leader of the Communists, did not consider himself one, and it was not until after the Japanese occupation that he became a party member. The Socialists were Thakin Mya, Aung San, Thakin Tin, Thakin Tha Khin, U Ba Swe, U Kyaw Nyein, Thakin Chit Maung, and many others. And, in addition, of course, there were some nationalists who refused to be aligned with any faction. Among these, of course, Thakin Nu remains the outstanding example. To his name should be added that of M. A. Raschid, Burmese nationalist from an Indian Moslem business family, who was to become an important policymaker in the independent Burmese government.

WARTIME NATIONALISM

The wartime period was important for Burmese nationalism in a number of ways. Japanese outrages hardened the nationalist movement and led to the quickened growth of the nationalist camp. Furthermore, because the Japanese insisted that the forms of "independence" be observed, Burmese leaders were appointed to government posts and thus had a chance to gain needed experience. Under the government of Ba Maw, Aung San served as Minister of Defense and Commander of the Burma Independence Army (BIA) (later the Burma National Army, the Burma Patriotic Force, and, after 1948, the Burma Army), Thakin Mya as Deputy Prime Minister, Thakin Nu as Foreign Minister and Minister of Information, Than Tun as Minister of Agriculture, and Kyaw Nyein as Secretary of the Cabinet and later as Vice-Minister of Information. Other Thakins served throughout the government and in the army. Furthermore, it was during this time that these leaders became widely known in Burma.

Also important were the effects of the military situation. To help meet their own needs, the Japanese organized and trained the famous band of "Thirty Comrades," who, under Aung San, formed the BIA. In 1945, Aung San took this force to the side of the British. Furthermore, disillusionment with Japanese promises led to the formation of guerrilla forces that proved rallying points for nationalists all over Burma.

At the outbreak of the war, the Thakins had had no fixed ideological goals. Their one interest was independence for Burma, and they would have supported whichever side promised them freedom. There was, however, some uncertainty as to the exact steps to be taken. When the Japanese early in 1940 finally negotiated an agreement with the Freedom Bloc—a coalition between Ba Maw's Sinyetha (Poor Man's) Party and the Thakins —the Thakin leaders were divided as to the desirability of accepting the Japanese offer. Later, in 1941, when Aung San returned to Burma with the Thirty Comrades to form the BIA, it was the ardent leftists like Thakin Soe and Thakin Than Tun—and even the Thakins' elder statesman, Ba Choe— who vigorously opposed aiding the Japanese and urged "everyone to help the democratic side without reserve."[45]

For a time the Burmese leaders thought—or hoped—that the Japanese would secure independence for Burma. The mistaken nature of such a hope quickly became clear, and a clandestine movement of opposition, led by government officials and cabinet members, soon developed. Thakin Soe, for example, fled Rangoon just before the Japanese arrived and sought out a Chinese military force with which to cooperate, in the process forming the nucleus of a Thakin (and Communist) guerrilla outfit. Others followed his example.

There was no set pattern of resistance among Burma's leaders. Unlike the Indonesian leaders, the Burmese did not consult together as to policy and attitudes but seemed each to follow his own best judgment, with the blessings of those comrades who chose different paths. For the most part, the Burmese combined resistance to the British, collaboration with the Japanese, underground opposition to the Japanese, and outright cooperation with the British in whatever proportions seemed desirable at any given moment. Aung San's role provides an outstanding example. He was organizer and leader of the BIA and Minister of Defense—all under Japanese sponsorship. Simultaneously he was the national hero and the leading figure in the anti-Japanese movement; as early as November 1943 he was in contact with the British authorities in India by radio.[46] Similarly, Than Tun, cabinet minister and adviser to Ba Maw, was a major figure in the development of the national resistance but stayed in the government until just before the Army and Aung San openly turned away from the Japanese in 1945. So, too, with Kyaw Nyein, who, when Ba Swe was arrested for heading the resistance in Rangoon, added to his role of Vice-Minister of Information that of stand-in for the imprisoned leader. In fact, almost all the important figures in the government of Ba Maw, with the possible exceptions of U Nu and Ba Maw himself, took an active part in the anti-Japanese resistance. And both Ba Maw and U Nu were informed of all developments and quietly supported the movement by providing the necessary cover for resistance meetings and by intervening in behalf of arrested guerrillas.

Throughout this period the nationalist independence movement was dominated, both within and without the government, by the Marxist-oriented Socialists and Communists of the Thakin movement. Power in the two groups centered on Aung San and Than Tun, friends and associates of long standing who were also related by marriage to sisters. Aung San was first and last a nationalist, with a Marxian-Socialist outlook. To him, Marxism was important as a vehicle for independence. Though starting from the same nationalist point of view, Than Tun moved slowly into the Stalinist-Communist camp to become ultimately a professed, full-fledged Communist and the leader of the Communist faction in the AFPFL. Just when Than Tun became a Communist is not clear. Burmese writers[47] make a strong point of the fact that he was not a Communist during most of his tenure of office with Ba Maw. It is estimated that sometime in 1943 he and Thakin Soe formally launched the Burma Communist Party (BCP).

Regardless of the specific date of the founding of the Communist party, on March 10, 1944, a preliminary agreement between the Communists and the Socialist party (known variously at this time as the People's Revolutionary Party, the People's Emergency Party, and the Burmese Revolutionary Party) was announced by Communist sources. In this agreement, the Communists and the Socialists stated that they had found common grounds for opposing the Japanese, that they would work together in a resistance front, and that they would plan for continued action against the British if necessary. At the conclusion of a general description of the problems facing the resistance front, the following instructions were issued "to all organizations for guidance":

1. Must organize, within two months' time, to be ready to launch resistance movement.
2. To fix the date of the resistance movement only after those two months of preparation and after a careful study of the world situation.
3. In launching the resistance movement we must regard the Fascist Japanese forces as our first and worst enemy.
4. When we are fighting the Fascist Japanese forces we must seek friendship of Soviet Russia and the Allied Forces.
5. After we have driven out the Fascist Japanese we must form organizations along democratic lines and start talks for independence.
6. We will fight any foreign power which presents itself as detrimental to the rights of the Burmese people.
7. We must separate the unfriendly nations whoever they may be from our democratic friends.[48]

Five months—not two months—later, in August 1944, the meeting was held. The scene was Rangoon, the Japanese stronghold. There, nine nationalist leaders came together in the home of Thakin Nu, cabinet member in Ba Maw's government. Their purpose was to draft the formal organization of the resistance movement. The Communists were represented by Thakin Soe and Than Tun, the Socialist party by Kyaw Nyein, Thakin Mya, and Ba Swe, and the Army by General Aung San and Colonel Ne Win.[49] It is significant that of the entire group only two, Ba Swe and Thakin Soe, held no official position with the government.

The leadership of the new organization, which was later known as the Anti-Fascist People's Freedom League (AFPFL), was divided between Aung San as president and Thakin Than Tun as secretary-general. It was immediately clear that, although the largest single organization in the AFPFL was the Socialist party, the best-organized element was the Communist party, which had the further advantage of having already established contact with the South East Asian Command of Mountbatten and the Indian Communist Party through two of its young members, Tun Shwe and Thein Pe. It was later charged by the AFPFL that the Communists spent most of the remainder of the Japanese occupation in organizing their own following and not in fighting or planning for the overthrow of the Japanese.

The AFPFL revolt against the Japanese came some eight months later, on March 27, 1945, a fortnight after Aung San had marched the Army out into the countryside with the full knowledge and approval of the British forces in India and Northern Burma. This action was an integral part of the Allied drive against the Japanese.[50] On May 7, 1945, after the Japanese withdrew from Rangoon, Colonel Ne Win (later the commanding officer of the Burma Army and Prime Minister) broadcast a declaration of war on the "Japanese Fascists," which had been drafted by the AFPFL leaders. This group had by then been expanded to include representatives of all the political and ethnic groups in Burma.

The manifesto set a first goal of driving the "Japanese Fascists" out "bag and baggage" and a second goal of establishing "a constitution for Independent Burma," which would guarantee civil liberties and a government dedicated to the social welfare of the Burmese people. It outlined a program for popular action in support of the "war effort." A note reminded the people that not all Japanese were Fascist and that the ordinary soldier should be persuaded "to come over to our side." The manifesto ended with a challenge:

Comrades: Do you want to be free? Do you want peace and security? Then drive away the Fascist Japanese Barbarians. Set up a People's Government. Destroy Fascism. Co-operate with the Democratic Allies.

ANTI-FASCIST PEOPLE'S FREEDOM LEAGUE
(Burma Patriotic Front)[51]

NEGOTIATIONS FOR INDEPENDENCE: 1945–47

The surface unity of the AFPFL against the British was, however, misleading. The persistent struggle for power and control between the Soviet-oriented Communists of Thakin Than Tun and Thakin Soe, on the one hand, and the national or democratic Socialists of Thakin Mya, Aung San, and the bulk of the present-day leaders of the AFPFL, on the other, actually began coming to a head in this period.

There is no doubt that the Burmese Communists were determined to take over control of the resistance movement. They were not in a bad position to make the attempt. As noted earlier, Than Tun was simultaneously secretary-general of the AFPFL and president of the Burma Communist Party, and in both capacities he commanded wide loyalty, respect, and admiration. Furthermore, active Communists held controlling positions in the mass labor and peasant organizations. And the surrender and expulsion of the Japanese had reopened easy contact between the Burmese and Indian Communist parties: Than Tun was rejoined by "the Indian mastermind,"[52] Goshal, who had retreated into India before the Japanese invasion. Directives and information were exchanged between the two parties. As a matter of fact, both directives of the Burma Communist Party and letters between the Communist leaders and the Socialist members of the AFPFL show a strong and significant assumption of superiority on the part of the Communists.[53]

It is charged that even before the surrender of the Japanese, the Communists planned to eliminate their Socialist colleagues. Kyaw Nyein, "whom he [Than Tun] early recognized as a future rival," was to be sent to the Communist stronghold of Pyinmina, to be liquidated in the confusion of the war. Ba Swe was to be left in Rangoon, where it was assumed he would be killed; if he survived, he was to be branded a collaborator. Meanwhile, Communist leaders Than Tun, Ba Hein, and Thakin Soe were to take to the countryside for safety, as indeed they did. In fact, U Maung Maung implies in an article that only the unexpected arrest of Ba Swe by the Japanese upset the Communist plan, for it meant that Kyaw Nyein had to stay in Rangoon to obtain Ba Swe's release.[54]

The Socialist faction of the AFPFL has also charged, with Communist letters and proclamations as support, that the Communists from the start of the coalition in 1944 "betrayed the trust of the people again and again."[55] They have also charged that the Communists played for power by vacillating and shifting positions and by backing actions which would weaken the Socialists in their relations with the British and in their attempts to gain control of the country. Specifically, the Socialists have charged that where the Army was too strongly entrenched to allow Communist recruiting, the Communists demanded its demobilization; that when, immediately after the return of the British, the Army was strong, the Communists advocated the surrender of Burmese arms to the British; that when, after agreeing to demobilize the Army, the nationalists were relatively weak and had to depend upon Aung San's negotiations to bring about independence, the Communists called for a revolutionary uprising; and that—this being the most serious charge of all—when the rest of the AFPFL was working directly for independence, the Communists were misusing the AFPFL label to recruit their own following and doing their utmost to undermine the leadership of Aung San and of the provisional government.[56]

In the period immediately after liberation, the Communists made considerable headway in building up their membership. From their leading positions in the labor movement and the peasants' organizations, they recruited a considerable following. They added greatly to their numbers also from the men of the demobilized Burma Patriotic Force (or Patriotic Burmese Force). Maung Maung reports that "PBF men, released from service and drifting through Rangoon, were easily caught. They came in their hundreds and attended short indoctrination courses. In a fortnight they became communists, more communist than Stalin. The communist menace," he adds, "was . . . more difficult to meet than Dorman-Smith and his crowd."[57] Belatedly, the Socialists, under the leadership of Kyaw Nyein and Ba Swe, began recruiting to counteract the Communist gains.[58] Besides bringing into the AFPFL the more conservative nationalists of the prewar period—under the leadership of Ba Pe, U Pu, and others—the Socialist leaders, in November 1945 under left-wing Socialist leadership, organized the Trade Union Congress (Burma). They also built up the All Burma Peasants Organization under Thakin Tin to counteract the influence of the older and Communist-controlled All Burma Trade Union Congress.

It is difficult to assess the degree to which ideology played a role in the internal disputes of the AFPFL and the degree to which the causes of conflict were personal ambition and personal antipathy. Though conditions in the country had been markedly changed by the war experience, all the leaders were still avowedly Marxist—that is, opposed to imperialism and capitalism, and working for a "people's democracy" and for independence. Even U Nu, who, as a member of no party beyond the AFPFL, attempted to act as mediator between the Socialists and Communists, in November 1946 said: "May the real Communist movement in Burma be successful and may the leadership by unscrupulous people, who are misusing the name of Communism . . . be quickly destroyed."[59]

The first rift which claimed to be on ideological lines came in 1946 within the Burma Communist Party. The ambitious and ruthless Thakin Soe had attacked the conservative Ba Pe as a "tool of the imperialists," without, as it happened, the support in this of Than Tun and the Communist party leadership. Deserted by the BCP, this fanatical man, who felt that his wartime guerrilla services had entitled him to leadership of the party, attacked Thakin Than Tun and Thein Pe for "Browderism"— certainly a unique charge for the Burmese political scene. He demanded that they admit that they were guilty of compromising with the "imperialists" and "opportunists" and that they turn over control of the Burma Communist Party Central Committee to him and his followers. While the accused admitted their guilt and apologized, they refused to make Soe the leader. Thereupon he withdrew from the Burma Communist Party to form his own Communist Party (Burma).[60] Soe's aim was to use the CP(B) to bring about a Marxist state in Burma by violent revolution.[61] Soe's following, however, has been so small that his party could almost be dismissed as a minor irritant.

The next split took place also before the constitution of the Union of Burma had been drafted or independence achieved. In this case it was the Burma Communist Party itself which split off from the AFPFL after a considerable history of conflict—a conflict inspired again as much by personalities and personal ambition as by ideology: Than Tun was apparently determined to wrest leadership in the AFPFL from Aung San and to direct the policies of the coalition himself.

The first outwardly visible step came in July 1946, when Than Tun was forced to resign the post of secretary-general of the AFPFL—a post which he had held from the founding of the coalition. Two explanations of the break have been given, both making clear the personal nature of the conflict. According to the first account, Than Tun publicly denounced two conservative members of the AFPFL, Ba Pe and Deedok Ba Choe, and was ordered to make a public retraction and apology. When he agreed to retract but not to apologize, he was forced to resign. The second account, which has something more of an ideological twist, is that, against the discipline of the AFPFL, Than Tun ordered a one-day strike to protest Sir Reginald Dorman-Smith's outlawing of Thakin Soe's Communists. Whatever actually happened, Than Tun had to hand over his post to Kyaw Nyein of the Socialists.

In July and in September, Than Tun again led the Communist-dominated All Burma Trade Union Congress on strikes, on these occasions specifically against what he called the "repressive measures" of the AFPFL. Simultaneously, in the name of the Burma Communist Party he demanded two seats on the Executive Council of the interim government which Sir Hubert Rance, the last British colonial governor, had invited Aung San and the AFPFL to head. His party received only one seat—and that went to his collaborator and, in a sense, rival, Thein Pe. In the Burmese view, this slight to his pride was more than Than Tun could or would take. Furthermore, he had also grossly overestimated the following of the Communist party in Burma. Than Tun then withdrew from all but token cooperation with the AFPFL. Thein Pe was later disciplined, stripped of Central Committee membership, and finally discarded by the party for his service with the AFPFL.

Unlike Thakin Soe, who resigned from the AFPFL with his following, Than Tun and the Burma Communist Party were ultimately expelled by the AFPFL Executive Committee on a motion made by U Nu on November 3, 1946.[62] In spite of everything, U Nu regretted taking the action.

Nobody wishes for unity between the AFPFL and the Communists more than I do. They themselves know it. When they were expelled from the AFPFL I had no hand in it. Their wrong doings brought it about. I saw that they would have to leave the AFPFL fold if they persisted in their wrong doings. Having no wish for such a split just then I went to their very doors to expostulate with them. After the split, how hard I tried to bring them back to the fold, their leaders know, especially the members of their politbureau, Thakin Than Tun, Thakin Ba Thein Tin and Ko Ba Tin. In my vain efforts I went to such lengths that the AFPFL leaders would have expelled me long ago as a Communist spy had they not the complete confidence they did have in my sincerity of purpose.[63]

From outside the AFPFL, Than Tun and the Burma Communist Party ran for the Constituent Assembly in April 1945, and, contesting twenty-seven seats, won seven. The AFPFL fully dominated the body.

The Constituent Assembly was responsible for two basic documents which are invaluable in showing the ideological bent of the leaders: the constitution and the *Two-Year Plan of Economic Development for Burma.* Based on a distinctive combination of Western parliamentary experience and Burmese historical and cultural patterns, the constitution was unanimously adopted in September 1947, after the most extensive debate. Though it is not a close copy of any other constitutional system, it naturally draws most heavily upon the British background and training of the writers.[64] The only section which might possibly be credited to "Soviet 1936" example is Chapter X, "The Right of Secession," Articles 201–206,[65] and even these provisions, which allow the hill states to secede after ten years if they wish, are better explained as assurances to the Shan, Kachin, and Karenni states to attract them into the Union.

In general, the governmental system provided by the 1947 constitution can be described as "parliamentary in form, liberal-democratic in political orientation, 'welfare-state socialist' in economic outlook (with the term 'socialist' employed in the sense of the British Labour Party rather than that of the USSR), and technically at least, federal in structure."[66] Its sections on Economic Rights (Article 23), Relations of the State to Peasants and Workers (Articles 30 and 31), Directive Principles of States Policy (Articles 32–44), and its General Provisions (especially Articles 218–220) spell out both the social welfare concept of the government and its awareness that without adequate preventive provisions, economic imperialism might stay on after independence to dominate the Burmese economy.

On the subject of private property, the constitution provided that "subject to the provisions of this section, the State guarantees the right of private property and of private initiative in the economic sphere."[67] At the same time, the rights of private property were limited, as the constitution also stated that (a) private property may not be used "to the detriment of the general public"; (b) "private monopolistic organizations . . . [,] calculated to injure the interests of the national economy, are forbidden"; (c) private property may be expropriated in the public interest with compensation to the owners; and (d) the state may nationalize or acquire by law "individual branches of the national economy or single enterprises . . . if the public interest so requires."[68] The constitution also forbade the development of large landholdings, while the government retained the right— which it has exercised—to determine the maximum size of private landholdings.[69]

In its general statement of Principles for State Policy, which can only

be enforced by specific acts of the parliament, the constitution stated that
the Union was to plan its economy to increase the public wealth, improve
material conditions, raise the cultural level, consolidate the Union and
strengthen its defensive capacity, as well as to provide the social services
of health, education, and welfare.[70]

In defense of the Union against foreign economic domination, the constitution provided essentially that the operation of public utilities must be
controlled by Burmese citizens; that the capital used in such operations
must be at least 60 per cent Burmese; that agricultural and mineral resources shall be developed by the Union of Burma or, with the approval of
the parliament, by private firms again subject to the 60 per cent limitation
and operating on a twenty-five-year renewable lease; and that, subject to
specific exemptions made by the parliament, no agricultural land was to be
granted to aliens for any purpose.[71]

Even such a brief look at these constitutional provisions makes it quite
evident that Marxism, which gave to the revolutionary period of the nationalist movement a kind of ideological framework, was second to British
tradition and practice in shaping the constitution.

The *Two-Year Plan of Economic Development for Burma,* which was
drafted simultaneously with the constitution, again shows a mixture of Burmese, British, and Marxist inspiration. But here the direction was toward
implementing the welfare-state program, and Marxism was drawn on more
heavily than in the constitution. Thus, for example, the drafters of Burma's
first economic plan assumed flatly that Burma was to be a Socialist state:
". . . the evolution of a fully Socialist economy in Burma," they declared,
"will ultimately remove the vast majority of the causes of friction and mis-
understanding between employers and employed."[72] "The profit motive,"
they said, at another point in the *Plan,* "and other considerations which
usually govern industries in capitalist economies shall not be allowed to
determine the development of basic industries in Independent Burma."[73]
Within the framework of a democratic constitution, the economy of Burma
was to be one of state socialism, and the evils of capitalism, as experienced
and interpreted in nearly a century of British colonial rule, were to be
specifically avoided.

After the severe shock of the state assassinations in July 1947, the political atmosphere in Burma became relatively quiet. The leadership of the
AFPFL passed directly to Thakin Nu. The Communists under Than Tun,
expecting that Than Tun might supersede Thakin Nu and possibly fearing
that outbreaks and disturbances might postpone the British withdrawal,
made a temporary show of cooperation. On September 25, 1947, the constitution was unanimously adopted. On October 17, Clement Attlee and
Thakin Nu signed the treaty in which the government of the United King-

dom recognized the Republic of the Union of Burma "as a fully Independent Sovereign State." On January 4, 1948, control of the Burmese government was formally relinquished by the British.

The new republic faced a number of serious problems. The war had damaged Burma fearfully. Reconstruction in the two and a half years of British postwar administration—notable as it was—still fell far short of restoring the prewar levels of the economy. Thus, when the British left, Burma was merely a shell of the prosperous colony of the prewar period. Education had also received a fearful setback, and trained administrators and public officials were in desperately short supply. Law, order, and respect for authorities—never a strong point of British colonial rule in Burma —had been undermined by more than six years during which it had been moral and patriotic to oppose the government by any means and violence against authorities had received public approval. Poised and ready, organized bands that had broken away from the AFPFL were preparing themselves to overthrow the government by force.

On the other hand, the war period and the negotiations had also brought certain benefits to the new nation. The hated Indian businessmen and moneylenders, the *Chettyars,* who had fled the country before the Japanese, were not returning, and the ultimate distribution of their landholdings rested with the new government. The major capitalists, both British and Indian, were also slow to return, and when they did, they came under the control of Burmese rather than alien legislation. The two main conditions of the prewar period—imperialism and alien monopoly capitalism—which had attracted the Burmese nationalists to Marxism were thus largely reduced or on the way to becoming historical memories. And the lack of opportunity for graduates of Rangoon University, which had been the source of so much prewar student discontent, was replaced by practically unlimited opportunity in the completely Burmanized government services. In a sense, as Burma started on its crusade for a democratic, Socialist state, it started in an ideal setting. For Burma essentially presented a classless or single-class society, with the "enemies" of that class impotent aliens.

DISINTEGRATION OF THE NATIONALIST COALITION: 1947–50

With independence, the government of Burma plunged directly into the task of providing the social and economic basis for a Socialist state. On January 27, 1948, the government announced its intention to nationalize one third of the teak extraction in the country. On April 20, the parliament passed the Inland Water Transport Nationalization Bill. On May 20, the government published the *Two-Year Plan of Economic Development* (re-

ferred to above), and on October 7 and 11, respectively, the Agricultural
Labourers' Minimum Wages Bill and the Land Nationalization Bill were
passed. Burma was well on the road, in its policy decisions at least, to a
Burmese-style Socialist welfare state in which all Burmese might participate, free from what was considered the interference of foreign capital.[74]

Indeed, at the start of independence, Burma's economic prospects appeared bright. Production levels continued to rise through the first three
months of independence, and it appeared highly likely that, given a reasonable period of peace, Burma could look ahead to a consistent rise in the
standard of living.[75] It was not long, however, before peace was ended,
and it was ended over a combination of ideological and personal considerations.

Although the Burma Communist Party had pledged its loyalty to the
constitution—and had in fact taken part in the constitutional debate and
the unanimous adoption of the basic law—the BCP's loyalty proved short-
lived. In December 1957, Goshal, the Burma-born Indian Communist who
was Than Tun's chief political adviser and a comember of the party's Politbureau, wrote his now famous twenty-seven-page thesis, "On the Present
Political Situation in Burma and our Tasks."[76] This violent denunciation
of the Nu-Attlee agreement was repeated in effect in a special interview
from Calcutta on December 20, in which Goshal expressed himself in the
following strong terms:

Though by the Anglo-Burmese Treaty, popularly known as the Second Nu–
Attlee Agreement, Burma is recognized by the British Government as a 'fully
independent sovereign State,' in fact permanent slavery is imposed on Burma
through this 'independence' which is fake . . . We Communists, and millions
of people with us, therefore, consider this Treaty to be a Treaty of national
humiliation and permanent slavery . . . Thakin Nu and his colleagues . . .
crossed over to the imperialist camp, becoming their completely subservient
tools.[77]

With this denunciation, Goshal called for the overthrow of the Nu government. Although the Communists stayed on in the parliament into March
1948, they were already stirring up trouble throughout the country in an
effort to undermine the government. On February 18, the Communist
party formally ratified the Goshal thesis.[78] In the same month, Than Tun
led a delegation to Calcutta, ostensibly to attend the South East Asian
Democratic Youth Congress, but in reality to take part in the Second All-
India Communist Congress. Than Tun's greetings to the Indian Communist party reiterated Goshal's charges against the Nu government. On the
same occasion, Than Tun announced his party's intention to take over the
government, without civil war if possible. Only in the last extreme, if
forced to it by the "national Bourgeoisie, backed by the Anglo-Americans,"

would the Communists fight, as he put it, to "smash the imperialist-feudal-bourgeois combine, establish real independence, a people's democracy and lasting peace."[79]

The AFPFL has charged that Than Tun was urged at this congress to launch an active revolt against the government in April. The coincidence of the successive Burmese, Malayan, and Indonesian Communist outbreaks of 1948 supports the charge. At any rate, while U Nu and the AFPFL leaders were attempting to reach a *modus vivendi* with the Communists and were in almost continuous negotiation, Than Tun had such a sweeping personal success at a mass meeting of the All Burma Peasants Organization, held in the Communist stronghold of Pyinmina early in March, that he was convinced he had the backing of the Burmese people: 75,000 peasants came to hear him, and they were—or seemed to be—wildly responsive to his words.

The resolutions adopted at the Pyinmina conference included, among others: "This meeting places on record its deep appreciation of the courage displayed by the Arakan Freedom fighters, who valiantly fought the British, the Japs, the Sir Paw Tun Government and the AFPFL Government to achieve freedom" (Resolution II); "This meeting fully supports the BOC [Burmah Oil Company] strike and other strikes which are prevailing in Rangoon" (Resolution IV); and "This meeting resolves to smash fascism (AFPFL) by all possible means" (Resolution VI).[80]

The government had its own comment on Than Tun's reception at Pyinmina:

This is credible. The time was March when all crops have usually been harvested, threshed and sold. It is a time for jubilation, for *pwes*, for pilgrimages for the peasants . . . [Than Tun's] egoism blinded him to the fact that for the peasants that conference of his at Pyinmina was the first opportunity for the display of their energy and their power and that the mass was as much for the AFPFL as for the first organizer Thakin Than Tun, the late Secretary General of the AFPFL.[81]

On March 27, the anniversary of the resistance movement, Than Tun delivered a threatening speech in the heart of Rangoon, calling for popular revolt against the AFPFL. Reportedly he said that "he would have the Bagaya—a Communist stronghold in Rangoon—overflowing with the blood of Socialists."[82] The next day, March 28, the Communist leaders left Rangoon for Pyinmina, where they went underground. On March 29, they began to lead the open Communist revolt against the government.

The next two years the government had to fight for its life. In rapid succession, in July and August, the People's Volunteer Organization (army veterans and others), sections of the army itself, and the Karen and Mon nationalists all revolted. Maps published by the government in August

1949 show almost the whole of the Irrawaddy delta from Rangoon north beyond Mandalay in insurgent hands.[83] Fighting occurred even in the suburbs of Rangoon. Nor was the trouble confined to military action. When the government's military strength was at its lowest ebb, in January and February 1949, the Ministerial Services Union went on strike, almost completely demoralizing the government and paralyzing its services. "Administration broke down," the government reported, "and in a few districts where a semblance of it was maintained it was only possible after the heart-breaking efforts of a few individuals. Law and order was no more. Guns and bullets held sway. But the Government did not crash."[84]

Any attempt to explain the insurrections must take into account the fact that ideological considerations were not their dominant theme. In fact, personal ambition played the major role in a number of developments. Soe and Than Tun both wanted to control the government. It was furthermore personal ambition on the part of Soe and Than Tun that forced the break between the Red and White Banner Communists, rather than their Marxist discipline or the government's lack of it. And the PVO's, who split into two factions even while attempting to mediate between the government and the Communists, appear to have been guided by personal ambitions and loyalties when they revolted. Basically these men were nonideological, disgruntled, and in search of greater personal power and influence. This was apparently true also of the Ministerial Services Union. The Karens and Mons, on the other hand, guided by loyalty to their separate ethnic groups and distrustful of the Burman majority, revolted in the hope of gaining an autonomous Karen state larger than anything which the government, in justice to the Burman majority, could and did offer.

While it was certainly the truly remarkable leadership, courage, and loyalty of the central core of the government strategically located in Rangoon that explained the government's survival, these personal clashes among the insurgent leaders and the obvious lack of a common objective were almost equally important factors. Despite repeated efforts among the insurgent leaders, there was almost no time when the full strength of the rebellious forces was directed against the government simultaneously. In fact, insurgent bands spent a good deal of energy in fighting one another, and as the campaigns wore on, many thousands surrendered individually to the government.

Another important factor in the government's survival was the non-participation of the peasants in the uprisings. After more than six years of war and disturbance, the peasant wanted peace and security above all else. And these the government provided, in the areas it held, far more satisfactorily than did the insurgents.[85] Furthermore, limited though the reforms of the AFPFL had been in the first two years of independence, the lot of the peasant had improved, rice brought a reasonable return in the market, and taxes and rentals had been reduced.

The relative unimportance the government itself placed on ideology, beyond its commitment to Burmanization and welfare-state reform, is evident in the lengths to which it was willing to go to end the hostilities. Even when the government knew that the Communists were planning to revolt and even up to, and beyond, the time when the Communists went underground, it continued to negotiate and to offer concessions. The government released captured leaders of the Communists, PVO's, and Karens in the hope they would serve as intermediaries to bring peace. It offered a general amnesty to the rebels and urged them to compete in free elections for control of the government—all without success.[86] Only on one point was the government consistently adamant in its negotiations, and that was that the insurgents lay down their arms before returning.

In April 1948, U Nu broadcast a dramatic appeal to the Communists, quoting Stalin to support his approach to a Socialist state in Burma through British democratic methods:

When Stalin, highest of Communist leaders, met a good will mission dispatched to Russia by the British Labour Party with Harold Laski as leader, Stalin said to them, "There are two roads to Socialism, the British road and the Soviet road. The British road attains it in slow but steady stages, the Soviet road attains it quickly, but involves bloodshed." I remember reading this. . . . [I]f the Government becomes vicious and you want to remove it, go to the people and ask for power by means of the democratic method . . . [Only] when it is made impossible to obtain power from the masses by lawful methods, when democratic remedies are denied and there is no alternative to seeking power by violence, then seek it by that method . . . [F]rom now onwards the people of the Burma Union will have to mark out two circles on the ground. Let those who like violence enter the circle of those who urge violence. Let those who favour the seeking of power by the method of democracy enter the circle of democracy . . . For myself, I have already chosen the circle of democracy, and in it I shall stand hand in hand with others who have chosen the same side, and together we shall exert our utmost efforts to protect this great Union of Burma from the dangerous threat of those who seek violence.[87]

It was, however, in June 1948, after the Communists had gone into open revolt, that Prime Minister U Nu made his most far-reaching concessions to the Communists. In a fifteen-point *Program of Leftist Unity*, he enumerated government goals in the following terms: nationalization of "monopolistic Capitalist undertakings," foreign trade, and land; transformation of the government and military forces of Burma into "people's" organizations; and the application of the weight of the government on the side of the worker and the poor "against the attacks which are being launched by the capitalists." In the international field he set two goals: to develop political and economic relations with the Communist states equal to those with the United States and Britain; and to refuse any foreign aid which would "compromise the political, economic and strategic independence of Burma." It was the final point of the program, however, which carried U Nu and the AFPFL the furthest they have ever gone toward the Communist camp. Though it was later dropped and the government now refers to the "fourteen-point" program, in 1948, U Nu proposed that a league be formed "for the propagation of Marxist Doctrine, composed of Socialists, Communists, *Pyithu Yebaws* (PVO's) and others who lean towards Marxism and to read, discuss and propagate the writings of Marx, Engels, Lenin, Stalin, Mao Tse-tung, Tito, Dimitrov and other apostles of Marx."[88] Reportedly the joint handiwork of Nu and Thein Pe, the one important Communist leader who had not gone underground, this program was utterly scorned by the Communists, vigorously criticized by portions of the AFPFL (especially on the final point), and so upset foreign relations that Foreign Minister U Tin Tut had to issue a special reassurance to foreign representatives, denying that the Burmese government was becoming Communist.

In April 1949, when there seemed to be some further hope of bringing the Communists out of insurgency, all the Socialist members of the government resigned from the cabinet temporarily, to ease the way for the Communists' return. At the same time, government leadership was taken over by such distinguished non-Socialist figures as General Ne Win, Dr. E Maung, and others. This effort, also, was of no avail. The government then returned to its old weapons against the insurrection—military force, appeals to individual rebels to leave their comrades, and a general countrywide program of economic and political reforms. The record has certainly been impressive. From the near depths of despair in late 1949 and early 1950, the government steadily advanced to the point where there was no significant challenge from its Communist and insurgent rebels.

Meanwhile, in addition to the divisions already discussed, from 1946 the AFPFL had to deal with still another internal conflict, this one between segments of the Socialist party itself. Since independence, the Socialists had been almost evenly divided between left and right, with control in the hands of a small group of "neutrals." In 1946 the left-wing leaders had the advantage of controlling the labor movement, as they headed the party's Trade Union Congress (Burma), which had managed to capture the Burmese labor movement from the Communist-dominated All Burma Trade Union Congress. Veering further and further from government policies, both domestic and foreign, the left-wing leadership by early 1950 openly urged the restoration of "Leftist Unity" with the Communists, on terms allowing the Communists to come back without laying down their arms. In foreign affairs the left wing of course approved the government's early recognition of Communist China—on December 19, 1949—but openly opposed the government's decisions in 1950 to accept aid from Britain and the United States and to go on record as supporting the United Nations in Korea.[89]

The division in the Socialist party was first made public in the 1950 May Day address of left-wing Socialist Thakin Lwin. In this decidedly pro-Communist speech, Lwin, in addition to lashing out against the government's decision to accept British aid, urged that the TUC(B) affiliate with the Communist - dominated World Federation of Trade Unions (WFTU). Apparently, this outburst was the direct result of the Asian and Australasian Trade Union Conference held in Peking from November 16 to December 3, 1949, where delegates from thirteen countries had affirmed that independence and social reforms were meaningless in ex-colonial countries unless they were carried out by governments under the direct control of Communist parties. At this conference, delegate Aung Win of the All Burma Trade Union Conference (ABTUC) had, in conformity with the Goshal thesis, roundly denounced the AFPFL government and Burma's independence as fraudulent and urged the completion of the revolution by the overthrow of Thakin Nu.[90] Thakin Lwin's outburst so closely paralleled this position as to suggest that he got his directives from the Peking conference.

Though the address upset both the right wing of the party and the government, no disciplinary action was taken for fear that, in a showdown, Socialist party president U Ba Swe, then classed as a "neutral," would move over to the left to preserve party unity. In the hope of gaining Ba Swe's support, the government immediately after the May Day address sent him on a tour of Poland, England, France, and Italy with Bo Set Ya (Than Aung). In his absence the right-wing Socialists put on a special drive to capture control of local party organizations from the left.

The next outbreak came in September 1950 when left-winger Thakin Hla Kywe, vice-president of the TUC(B) and an AFPFL member of parliament, vigorously attacked the government's policy toward Korea. This the government could not take. As punishment for breach of party discipline, it temporarily expelled the TUC(B) from the AFPFL, until such time as the TUC(B) had ousted both Lwin and Hla Kywe from office. It is also reported that the government was ready with plans to arrest the left-wing Socialist leaders if they went too far in opposition. On the surface, however, the party seemed restored to a semblance of unity. The TUC(B) demoted Lwin and Hla Kywe and returned to the AFPFL. In November and December the party Executive Committee sent Ba Swe on a six-week country-wide tour to reorganize and strengthen the party.

It was on December 8, 1950, while the reorganization was under way, that forty-three left-wing Socialists chose to break with their party, though not with the AFPFL. At the same time that they announced their withdrawal, they also made known the formation of a new party, the Burma Workers and Peasants Party (BWPP). In explanation for their action, they denounced the Socialist party for deviating from its proper course:

The original set policy based on Marxism and Leninism . . . has been supplanted with deviations and imitations of the doctrine . . . [D]emocracy is dying within the party . . . [and] the tasks of abolition of imperialism and waging a people's democratic revolution are now delayed.[91]

For the Socialist party this defection was of a serious nature. The defectors had held high posts in the party. Thus, though there was no loss among the top level of the AFPFL, one half of the Socialist party Working Committee and two members of the thirteen-man Executive Committee had gone over to the BWPP, as had five of the ten national officers of the All Burma Peasants Organization, all of the officers of the TUC(B)—including the men who had been put in to replace Lwin and Hla Kywe—and five of the fourteen national officers of the All Burma Women's Freedom League. These defections were to a degree counteracted by the nearly simultaneous rejoining of the Socialists by the pro-government segment of the PVO. However, in the few days before the Socialist party could mount a counteroffensive, it appeared that the defections had thoroughly destroyed Socialist support for the government policies.

It was three days later, on December 11, that the Socialist party answered—and that Ba Swe threw the weight of his influence on the side of the right-wing Socialists, who then became known as the "moderates." He denounced the BWPP leaders for going back on their word not to create difficulties while he was working on party organization. He insisted to the public that the party was not split, that members were free to resign as they liked, and that followers of the BWPP, who had, he said, left the Socialist party under misapprehensions, would be welcomed back. He concluded that the resignations were a blessing, a purification, and a strengthening of the party and signed his press release, "Yebaw Ba Swe, General Secretary of the non-deviationist Socialist Party."[92] The BWPP answered in a press conference that it would never deviate from Marxist-Leninist ideology and that, in the event of a third world war, it would side with "those who support our People's Democratic ideology."

The struggle turned next to the control of the mass organizations. The BWPP leaders in the TUC(B) ordered a strike of the Burma Army Ordnance Union to test the government's reaction. This reaction was immediate and severe. And Ba Swe again denounced the BWPP, this time in even stronger terms, saying among other things that complete acceptance of Marxist-Leninist philosophy meant the denunciation of religion, which was unacceptable, and that the Socialist party was adapting Marx to fit the times and conditions of Burma.

On December 19, the AFPFL took formal action against the BWPP, expelling both present and future members, withdrawing recognition of the BWPP-controlled TUC(B),[93] and simultaneously granting recognition to a "reconstituted" TUC(B), in which it installed new and loyal officers, with Ba Swe as president. It also withdrew recognition from the All Burma Women's Freedom League. Following these actions, U Nu, in a speech on December 23, denounced the BWPP members as pro-Communists and opportunists who had accepted the atheism of the Marxist-Leninists.[94]

The expulsion of the BWPP completed the reorganization of the wartime coalition. In the sifting and winnowing process the general orientation of Burmese political leadership had slowly but perceptibly shifted from the extreme left to a moderate Socialist position—the position officially adopted in the drafting of the constitution. The "international Communists," if they could be so called, had been eliminated from the government. The opposition groups had become ineffective. A nationalist coalition in which the relatively small socialist party provided most of the political leadership remained. It is in the policies of this socialist party that the role of Marxism in Burma since 1950 must be studied.

THE DEVELOPMENT OF AFPFL POLITICAL PHILOSOPHY SINCE 1950

Marxism until January 29, 1958, was still the professed philosophy of many Burmese leaders, but just what was meant by this profession was continually shifting, and therefore often hard to specify. This vagueness—and even confusion—is particularly evident in the Four-Year Plan for Economic Development proposed by U Nu on June 8, 1957.[95] Though not abandoning the goal of a social welfare state for Burma, U Nu declared that according to this plan, the government was going to rely even more heavily on private investment, both foreign and indigenous, and that it was going to withdraw as far as possible from direct participation in any except key industrial projects. Where the government was forced to participate, he said, the civil servants employed would be made shareholders rather than salaried officials—to be encouraged by the profit motive to devote their whole energies and abilities to the projects. In this plan, as in almost all other issues upon which Burmese political leaders write or speak, ideology played a very small role and was thoroughly subordinated to the realities of Burmese national survival and economic development.

Nevertheless, certain ideological trends can be discerned, particularly in the May Day addresses of U Ba Swe, as well as from government statements and the proceedings of the Asian Socialist Conference and its bureaus, in which Burmese leaders play a prominent part.[96] The Conference is clearly Marxist in origin, but it just as clearly disassociates itself from Communism of the Soviet variety. Its emphasis is on economic cooperation and development and on strong opposition to colonialism and imperialism.[97]

Perhaps one of the most interesting descriptions of the Burmese variety of Socialism is available in U Ba Swe's booklet *The Burmese Revolution*, first delivered as a speech to the TUC(B) in December 1951.[98] Here, a year after the defection of the left wing to form the BWPP, Ba Swe presented the four main tenets, as he saw them, of the Burmese Socialist movement. These tenets are as follows: ideology alone is the genesis of revolution, and Marxism is the guide to the Burmese revolutionary movement; Marxism must be adapted to the special circumstances of each country; Marxism and Buddhism are not incompatible but in fact "are the same in concept"; and Burmese Socialism is based upon the five fundamentals of People's Democracy, People's Economy, People's Education, People's Health, and People's Social Security.

As this was still in the Stalinist period, it is perhaps significant that, in denying that "the Burmese Revolution is being led by Thakin Nu or myself"[99] and in emphasizing that each person in the country was important in bringing the revolution to fruition, Ba Swe specifically denied what has since come to be called in Communist party propaganda the cult of the individual. Again, in the portion concerned with Marxism as a guide, he specifically ruled out duplicating the Russian or Chinese pattern in Burma. "In as much as Russian methods are not conducive to success in China," he said, "Chinese methods are out of place in Burma. Only a revolutionary movement which is entirely Burmese, conforming to Burmese methods and principles can achieve any measure of success."[100] Boldly, Ba Swe accepted the consequences of this kind of heresy, saying that if the Burmese were dubbed "opportunists" because of their position, they would "gladly accept this handle to [their] name."[101] In addition, Ba Swe made an important distinction between Marxism and Communism:

The acceptance of Marxism does not necessarily make one a Communist. To be a Communist, you have to observe certain set rules of conduct. Especially the so-called Communists believe that to become a Communist one must unequivocally accept Soviet leadership. It is therefore imperative that one must understand beforehand that not all Marxists are of the kind that the so-called Marxists define.[102]

Having thus disposed of the issue of alien direction of the Burmese revolution, Ba Swe ventured boldly into the far more difficult realm of reconciling Marxism and Buddhism. According to him, Marxism does not

reject religion; it merely rejects the theory of creation and is thus identical
with Buddhism in its outlook. Neatly dividing life into two spheres, Ba
Swe assigned one to Buddhism and the other to Marxism:

[We] can safely assume that Marxist theory occupies the lower plane, while
Buddhist philosophy occupies the higher. Marxist theory deals with mundane
affairs and seeks to satisfy material needs in life. Buddhist philosophy, however,
deals with the solution of spiritual matters with a view to seek spiritual satisfaction in life and liberation from this mundane world.[103]

Finishing with this ticklish subject, on which Ba Swe was at odds with
a large number of leading Burmese Buddhists and other authorities[104]
(and, by 1958, with himself), he ended on a note of personal faith:

In the beginning, I was a Buddhist only by tradition. The more I study Marxism,
however, the more I feel convinced in Buddhism. Thus I have become a true
disciple of Lord Buddha by conviction, and my faith in Buddhism has grown all
the more. I now believe that for any man who has deeply studied Buddhism, and
correctly perceived its tenets there should be no obstacle to becoming a Marxist.[105]

In his discussion of the five areas of the "Burmese Socialist structure,"
U Ba Swe also spelled out the goals of the government in the first four
years of independence and listed its successes and failures. Under "People's Democracy," he listed on the credit side legislation for democratizing
local governments but explained that real strides had to await the return
of peace and order in the countryside—as did the fulfillment of the Land
Nationalization Program.

In the field of "People's Economy," U Ba Swe was able to list real accomplishments, though he charged that too little progress had been made
in eliminating the "Imperialist Capitalists" and stated: "Economically we
still remain in bondage."[106] Rice marketing, timber, and the transport
system were already nationalized, and progressive nationalization was
planned for oil and mining activities. In addition, where private ownership persisted, U Ba Swe declared it policy to bring it under cooperative
ownership.

In the area of education, Ba Swe set the goal of free and compulsory
education throughout the country and noted that the government had already provided for free education extending through the University. The
State Scholar Program ensured that superior students would be sent abroad
for further, specialized training. And in the fields of health, social security,
and labor legislation, he pointed with pride to the government's plans and
its promising start in the improvement of the general welfare of the people.
Here again he admitted that Marxism had not entirely satisfied him.
"Marxism cannot provide an answer for spiritual liberation," he said.

"Neither can Science do [sic]. Only Buddhist philosophy can. Only where there is a satisfaction of spiritual needs can we find solace in life."[107]

Ba Swe closed his speech with a look at the government's enemies—who were still officially the capitalists. "All Capitalists," he said, "whether foreign Capitalists, or capitalist-imperialists or national Capitalists, or petit bourgeoisie are one-sided; they look only to their own rights."[108] But when Ba Swe actually listed the active enemies of the AFPFL and the Socialist party, it was not the right wing he named but the White PVO's, the Red Flag Communists, and the White Flag Communists of the extreme left (along with the Karen insurgents), who, he said, had been combining with the reactionaries to thwart the revolution. The reactionaries he left undesignated, however, and their inclusion appears to have been mainly a matter of ideological name-calling. In the name of his party, Ba Swe pledged to win the revolution by peaceful means, if possible, but added the warning that "if it can only be solved by force, we do not have any qualms about using it."[109] He ended his address with the slogan, "Towards a Socialist Republic of the Union of Burma."[110]

As this statement of U Ba Swe's has frequently been taken to be the definitive presentation of the Socialist party's position in Burma, it is fitting to see how the position has changed in succeeding years. Ba Swe's May Day address in 1952 adhered to much the same doctrinal position. By 1953,[111] however, some change was beginning to show. In international affairs U Ba Swe saw a struggle between capital and labor, colonial powers and dependent states, imperialists and anti-imperialists, and monopoly capitalists and Socialism. However—and this is important—he saw the great danger to world peace as coming from the two power blocs headed by the United States and the Soviet Union and pledged Burma by every means possible to remain free from both power blocs and to work for world peace and cooperation. On the internal situation he described the AFPFL in good Marxist terms as being composed of the workers, peasantry, trading class, and the "intelligentsia and patriotic bourgeoisie."[112] He quoted Lenin extensively to justify and support the government's policies—including the application of capitalist methods—in carrying on its struggle for Socialism. To his closing statement, "Long Live Socialism," he added: ". . . World Peace . . . Independence . . . Democracy" and "Workers of the World Unite!"[113]

By 1954, though the Marxist slogans of People's Democracy, People's Economy, and so on, were used as before, a change in outlook had become definite. Dangers to the state were no longer depicted as coming from the capitalists—in fact Ba Swe pointed with pride to the joint investment ventures of the Union government with foreign capital—but from "the imperialists and enemies of our State who launch political, economic and mili-

tary offensives against us with the aim of destroying our State."[114] Ba Swe's
line-up of government supporters still included the familiar four-class bloc
—the working classes, the peasantry, the trading class, and the intelligentsia
—still good Marxist terms, of course, but open to an all-inclusive interpretation. Nowhere in this May Day address was there favorable mention of
Marxism or Communism or of any Communist writer. In fact the only
mention of Communism was in relation to the "Red Flag and White Flag
Communist insurgents.[115] And the goal of the government's program was
given as the Socialist welfare state, to be achieved by democratic means.

Similarly in December, six months earlier, at the National Day celebrations, U Ba Swe had said that his government, following the Socialist as
opposed to the Communist approach, would carry out its programs with
an absence of cruelty and an absence of infringement on personal civil
rights and would make use of "democratic means to ascertain the will of
the people and to derive sanction from the *ludu* [common man]."[116] Here,
even more explicitly than in the May Day speech, Ba Swe showed the
change in his outlook, and in the government's outlook, on capitalism. In
discussing the methods of carrying out the economic development programs, he said:

The . . . programs will be carried out by the following agencies in the following
order of priority: 1. By Government if it is suitable; 2. By Government jointly
with indigenous or foreign Capitalists; 3. By Co-operatives; 4. By indigenous
capitalists; 5. Foreign Capitalists, independently or jointly with indigenous capitalists. *In all these cases, the Government will provide all necessary assistance.*[117]

This statement represents a marked departure from the position U Ba
Swe held two years earlier and, for that matter, from the original wording
of the constitution and the first *Two-Year Plan of Economic Development*.
By this time, it had become quite evident that the Burmese government
lacked both capital and trained personnel for its development programs—
and that reliance on Marxism could not be counted on to provide either one.
In addition, the nationalization of industries, where carried out, was not
bringing the industrialization and diversification Burma needed—and had,
in fact, in many areas led to greater difficulties. The Communist governments abroad had offered no assistance, despite repeated suggestions that
Burma would accept aid from whatever source, Communist or non-Communist, offered it. On the other hand, non-Communist nations—notably
Britain, India, and the United States—had offered aid. Beyond this, there
remained also the Red and White Banner Communist bands that continued
to terrorize the countryside.

So much for what Ba Swe has *said*. The test of theory is in its application. In its actions the Burmese government has never worried overmuch
about ideological basis. A realistic evaluation of the Burmese situation—

and Burmese government leaders are realists, for all the emphasis upon
U Nu's undoubted spiritual qualities—demanded from the beginning a
different approach, one which would encourage the development, and
make full use, of whatever resources could be found both at home and
abroad. This meant, among other things, the encouragement of foreign
and Burmese capitalists to take up as large a share of economic development as possible within the framework of the welfare state. Accordingly,
the government's ideological phrasing has shifted; for above all, nationalism and national welfare has dominated political thinking in Burma.

In 1952, a year after Ba Swe made the speech later published as *The
Burmese Revolution* and at a time when the insurgents had been beaten
back to a state of banditry, the government launched an ambitious eight-
year program of economic and social reform. The Pyidawtha movement,
as the program was named, grew out of a two-week conference held in
Rangoon from August 4 to 17. In ten separate resolutions, representatives
of the government and the mass organizations proposed plans for the passing of powers of government from national to local officials; the democratization of the country; the development of agriculture, industry, housing,
transportation, and communications; education; medical care; and public
health.[118] Essentially these proposals were based upon plans for a vast cooperative effort between the government and the people. Locally selected
committees were to plan and direct the work, and the government was to
provide financial backing and experts as they were needed, with revenues
from the international sale of rice providing the financial underpinning
for the program.

The Pyidawtha program, which started with a flourish of publicity—and
which has made some effective progress—has been seriously hampered by
the continuing lack of trained personnel, by personal disagreements and
political controversy, and, most disastrously, by the falling world price of
rice. By 1955 it was all too apparent that the ambitious programs adopted
in 1952 could not be completed by 1960 as planned, and the whole scheme
was re-evaluated and reshaped to meet the realities of the Burmese financial situation, with many projects of necessity postponed.[119] Even cut back,
however, the movement has brought real improvements to village life and
the Marxist terms such as People's Economy, etc., are being displaced by
Burmese equivalents. Thus, for example, *Pyidawtha*, which can be roughly
translated as "welfare state," has become the accepted term in Burma.

Following this trend, the government from 1954 to 1957 put a steadily
declining emphasis on anticapitalist vocabulary and came to accept and
encourage capitalist contributions. In contrast to the call for nationalization in the *Two-Year Plan*, the government has steadily turned to joint
ventures with foreign capital. Thus, for example, the Burmah Oil Com-

pany, the target of the major oil workers' strike in 1938–39, has become co-operatively owned by the British management and the Burmese government. Capital for the redevelopment of the refineries destroyed in World War II has come back into the country. U Nu has cited as the best form of joint venture the example of the Namtu (Burma) Corporation. Here, he says, "the Government is more or less a sleeping partner while the actual management and operations are done by experienced foreigners."[120] Similarly, the Burmese government has gone into partnerships with the Burmese business community to ensure a better quality of goods at lower cost to the public. And in May 1955, as an encouragement to foreign investors, the government of Burma announced a ten-year minimum guarantee against the nationalization of foreign investment, with the maximum length of the guarantee left open to negotiations.[121]

Perhaps the most striking statements of the new outlook have come from U Raschid, Minister of Trade Development and Labor. In a speech before the Union of Burma Chamber of Commerce[122] on February 22, 1956, Raschid explained that while it was the policy of the Burmese government to favor Burmese over aliens in issuing import licenses, it would not exclude foreign firms from such licenses. He also lectured the Burmese businessmen on their methods of doing business and warned them to prepare to stand on their own feet. "Self-help is important," he said:

We must teach our people the saving habit. They must learn to save money, they must learn to deposit their funds in banks or in Government saving certificates or in shares of companies, mines and plantations. They must go one more step forward. They must learn to trust one another in business so that they can combine and form big companies . . . May I ask you to consider how the foreign businessman in Burma has acquired . . . capital? Except for a few, none of the others brought their capital from overseas. Many of the big names in business were built in Burma. They started as hawkers or canvassers or petty shopkeepers. They worked hard. They saved their money over the years. They lived carefully. They did not waste their money. As a result of effort for years they built up their capital here. They had no Government support in doing this. If foreigners in a foreign country could build up capital through their own efforts and without Government support, there is no reason why Burmese businessmen with the same effort cannot do the same. In fact, this is exactly what many of the good Burmese firms have done.[123]

To Raschid, and to the government he represented, there was no special conflict between this advice and the Socialist orientation of the government's program.

Speaking a year later to the same audience, U Kyaw Nyein, Deputy Prime Minister for the National Economy, re-emphasized the goal of a mixed economy for Burma and again spoke of the government's eagerness to attract foreign capital:

I should repeat once more, Mr. Chairman, that Government welcomes foreign investment . . . Even now, we are considering what other positive measures can be taken in this connection . . . Some foreign firms established in Burma have already invested substantial capital in this country, and I believe they are making very good progress. It is hoped that other firms will follow the example of these firms and I am sure they will get all the encouragement they need from Government.[124]

Economic policies, then, have slowly been modified from a Marxist goal. Democratic procedures in Burma, on the other hand, owe nothing to Marx. Here, from the outset—in the elections for the Constituent Assembly, in the constitution, and in the two elections since independence—the Burmese have taken over the British pattern almost intact. The elections are open to all Burmese citizens eighteen years old and over. A multiple party system has developed. Democracy in Burma is far more advanced and secure than it is in Thailand, Viet Nam or Indonesia. Anyone in Burma is free to take part in the elections, and, insofar as the government has been able to do so, candidates of all parties have been equally protected. In both national elections to date (democracy on the local levels is not yet far enough advanced for judgment), the AFPFL has won overwhelming victories in the number of its candidates elected to the parliament and in gaining majorities that might well be envied in other democratic countries. The fairness of these elections—though both were marred by violence—shows in the scores of parties and candidates who campaigned actively and in the reasonably close divisions in the popular votes.[125] Essentially, however, despite the numerous organizations nominating candidates, the campaigns in Burma to date have been between the AFPFL coalition and its associated organizations in the hill states and an unstable coalition of opposition parties. In the 1950 elections the opposition was dominated by the Burma Workers and Peasants Party, and in 1956 by a similar organization, the National Unity Front.

Both the BWPP and the NUF have been accused of being the agents of the insurgent Communists. In campaign propaganda and otherwise, they have been charged with receiving foreign aid and with acting as the "stooges of foreign powers." Their programs from the formation of the BWPP in 1950 have been far to the left of the government and far more conciliatory to the insurgents. But essentially their spokesmen and leaders have been bound together, not so much by a common ideology, as by opposition to the government. The respected figure of Dr. E Maung headed the NUF delegation in the parliament. Lawyer, onetime Supreme Court Justice and cabinet member in U Nu's government, Dr. E Maung resigned from the government and the AFPFL in protest against what he regarded as its authoritarian tendencies and in 1956 organized his own Justice Party. He is so respected and so widely known as a believer in parliamentary democracy that he has been cited as proof that the NUF is not necessarily Communist. After the 1956 elections, when the government was attempting to explain why it had not done better, U Kyaw Nyein admitted that there were sound democrats in the opposition: "U Aung Than [elected on the NUF ticket] was not a Communist . . . U Aung Than is a Communist only to the extent that Dr. U E Maung is a Communist."[126]

The clear recognition that opposition at the polls is not a sign of treason is one of the most reassuring signs on the Burmese political scene. The AFPFL has appeared at times, with its massive majority in parliament, to dominate Burma completely, and it is sometimes suggested that free elections were allowed only because the government was sure to win. This appears the implication of U Ba Swe's statements in 1951 in *The Burmese Revolution* that the party would use force without "qualms" if necessary to carry out its programs (and, of course, when faced with violent insurgent efforts to take over the government, it has).

When the 1956 elections, even though successful for the government, indicated that this might not always be the case, U Nu resigned his post as Prime Minister with a year's leave of absence to devote himself to reorganizing and purging his party. He reminded his followers that in democracies all parties face the prospect of periodic defeats. When such defeat came to the AFPFL, he warned, if the party were corrupt and tyrannic, it would "fall like a dog," like the "great organization" of Chiang Kaishek, never to rise again. With strength, unity, and popular respect, however, the AFPFL would after such a defeat land like a cat on its feet, to regain control of the government through the democratic process.

In the same postelection period, U Ba Swe added the Socialist party's stamp of approval to the full acceptance of democracy as the route to the ideal society:

Life has proved conclusively that only Socialism, which is linked organically to democracy and to basic human rights and freedom, can assure a Socialist society which is both in control of its economic destiny, and which respects and enhances the human personality, its dignity and self respect.[127]

Burma, its Socialist party, and its Socialist leader stand here pledged to a program of social welfare based on democracy and the dignity of the individual.

This democratic orientation carries over into the field of foreign relations. Thus, Burmese Socialists early joined the Indian and Indonesian Socialist parties in announcing their opposition to both capitalism and

"Cominform Communism" and their intention to steer clear of both extremes.[128] Furthermore, Burmese foreign relations have been based on national interest, and not on ideology. Thus, the early recognition of Communist China resulted, not from the "appeal" of a Marxist state, but from recognition of an existing situation and from what was considered the absolute necessity of friendly relations with the colossus on the northern border. This statement is borne out by the fact that relations with the Kuomintang had been excellent up to the time of its defeat on the mainland. Indeed, the Nationalist government had been one of Burma's sponsors for membership in the United Nations. The underlying source of friction between Burma and both governments of China arises from the border situation. To deal with this, the Burmese government has needed diplomatic relations with both Chinese governments, as well as caution and tact.

Economic aid was accepted from the countries the Burmese Communists were branding imperialists, "because," U Nu said, "we needed it." And where it was used, it was found to be thoroughly to Burma's benefit. When American aid was declined in 1953, it was because, from the government's point of view, national security was more threatened by the presence of growing Kuomintang forces in northeastern Burma than it would be by the loss of the $20,000,000 American aid program—and the two seemed hopelessly intertwined. The cancellation in 1954 of the military agreement (the Freeman–Let Ya annex to the Nu-Attlee agreement) with the United Kingdom was intended to broaden the sources of Burma's military supplies. The original agreement had been signed in 1947 to ensure adequate arms and training for Burma's national defense forces, and its cancellation in 1954 was inspired by the same reason. By the free choice of the Burmese government, Britain has continued as one of the major sources of Burma's military equipment.

The Burmese method of ensuring this independence of choice has been to refuse any part in military alliances, such as SEATO, and at the same time to offer treaties of friendship and peaceful coexistence to nations that desire them. Burma has also taken an active part in all nonmilitary groupings for international cooperation which affect its part of the world: the United Nations and almost all its Specialized Agencies, the Colombo Plan, the Arab-Asian bloc in the United Nations General Assembly and, of course, the Bandung Conference (of which Burma was a cosponsor). Burmese material aid to the United Nations in Korea in 1950—400 tons of rice valued at $49,943—and Burmese sponsorship of the Bandung Conference in 1955 both had the same objectives: opposition to imperialism and the promotion of an international understanding in which Burma would be free to develop independently its own political and economic culture and society.

With the end in Burma of the United States Technical Assistance Program in 1953 (carried on through 1954 by a terminal agreement), the Burmese government adopted a policy of refusing all "gifts" from foreign governments and has insisted on paying for assistance with rice and other produce or through the repayment of long-term loans. In the 1955–56 period, when Burma was faced with a severe rice surplus, the government turned to a barter trade of rice for industrial goods. And because the Western powers were unwilling or unable to take the rice, the Burmese trade pattern shifted radically toward the Soviet sphere with China, Russia, and the satellites taking so much of Burma's export crop that there was not enough left to fulfill sales to the more valuable cash customers. The United States, perhaps disturbed by the bonds which such dependence on Communist countries could build, returned to the technical-assistance field in Burma in 1956 and 1957 with over $46,000,000 in long-term loans.

Both the barter agreements and the loans fell short of Burmese expectations. And perhaps quite naturally in their concern for Burma's freedom from political obligation, Burmese leaders would prefer aid through the technical-assistance programs of the United Nations, the Specialized Agencies, and the Colombo Plan. Thus in June 1956, U Ba Swe, speaking for the Asian Socialists and for Burma, said:

Although one must welcome the offers of increased trade and aid which have been made by the world's two giants—Russia and America—we yet feel that the countries in need of this aid would benefit more if it would be channeled through the United Nations.

Economic and technical aid given through the UN would remove all hints of political advantage or pressure, which usually accompanies the aid provided by any big power, and such aid through the UN would more easily fit into the framework of the receiving countries' industrial and economic needs, even of the most beneficial type.

Aid of this kind would become a symbol of disinterested international cooperation and the inspiring expression of an international community dedicated to the noble task of fighting poverty, disease and human frustration wherever it exists.[129]

The program U Ba Swe especially singled out was the proposed SUNFED (Special United Nations Fund for Economic Development), which he felt would best allow the underdeveloped countries to progress economically and carry out their internationally valuable program of neutrality:

The relaxation of international tensions, which we have described, the greater interest shown by the great powers in giving economic aid to Asia, the increasing respect which the nations of Asia are gaining in the world community by their mature and responsible approach to world problems, all these are the fruits of the independent policy of non-alignment and non-involvement, which these nations have pursued.[130]

Nevertheless, the "increasing respect" which rigid adherence to a neutral policy is supposed to have brought is sometimes qualified by doubts. Neutralism is open to the charge of opportunism, and it has been said in the West, and specifically of Burma, that an uncommitted nation is one that never commits itself against Russia.[131] It is a matter of record, however, that as early as 1953, U Kyaw Nyein warned his colleagues in the Anti-Colonial Bureau of the Asian Socialist Conference of the dangers of Soviet imperialism:

I need not remind you also, friends, that when we analyzed the origin and development of colonialism at our Rangoon Conference we included in our definition of colonialism, not only the typical 19th and 20th century colonialism or imperialism, which is the consequence of the growth of capitalism, but also included colonialism in another form. We may call it neo-colonialism or new-imperialism. I refer to the Soviet type of imperialism. To my mind, both types of colonialism are dangerous. In fact the Soviet type of imperialism is, perhaps, more dangerous, because it is more ruthless, more systematic and more blatantly justified in the name of world communist revolution.[132]

When the vital test occurred in the fall of 1956 with the double attack, first by the British, French, and Israelis upon Egypt, and then by the Russians in Hungary, the Burmese were fully prepared to condemn both instances of aggression and to accept the consequences. On the Suez issue the Burmese Ambassador to the United Nations promptly joined the efforts to force the invaders' withdrawal and offered Burmese troops for the United Nations Emergency Forces in the Middle East. After an initial delay of a few days, while awaiting instructions, the Burmese delegation also took the lead among the Asian neutrals in denouncing the Soviet intervention. Ambassador U Pe Kin supported the strongly worded Cuban resolution accusing Russia of "genocide," saying, "There—speaking of Hungary—but for the Grace of God, go we." In taking this stand, he had the full support of his government and the precedent of U Ba Swe's statement in Bombay of November 11. In this statement, U Ba Swe, speaking both as chairman of the Asian Socialist Conference and as Prime Minister of Burma, in effect charged the U.S.S.R. with "the most despicable form of colonialism":

We socialists have persistently urged that foreign troops should not be allowed to be stationed in a country without the consent of the government concerned, as they inevitably give rise to tension in the particular area. But for a big power to station its troops without the consent of a small country and, what is worse, to suppress people and impose on the helpless government its own puppets and stooges is the most despicable form of colonialism. Yet that is exactly what has been happening in Hungary, which has now appealed to the United Nations for help.[133]

This stand is the more courageous, or perhaps the more necessary, when it is recalled that Burma was at this time facing crucial negotiations with the Chinese Communists over the Sino-Burmese border.

MARXISM AND BURMA'S FUTURE

Nationalism is the guiding principle in Burma's politics today, as it was in the prewar struggle for independence. The independence of Burma, the economic and social welfare of the Burmese, and the promotion of Burmese control over all aspects of the Burmese society—these are the goals of Burmese nationalism. In the struggle for independence, anti-imperialist, anticapitalist Marxism of the Leninist variety had provided an organizing concept and a tool for the Burmese nationalists, perhaps the most effective they had. But with the passing of foreign political and economic rule, the appeal of this type of Marxism and its value to Burma have declined. In its place is a democratic Socialism in which the term "Marxist" is valued for its historical contributions and capitalism can within certain limits be encouraged without embarrassment. (The Pyidawtha, or welfare state of Burma, is now approaching the type of society normally associated with the mixed economy of Scandinavia.)

Kyaw Nyein, who, as Home Minister, Acting Foreign Minister, and Deputy Prime Minister, has borne the brunt of many of Burma's most difficult political decisions, in 1955 lightly passed off his own political development as following the traditional pattern of "revolutionary at twenty and conservative at forty."[134] And, to an extent, this description suits the course of Burmese politics also. Burma today is proudly Socialist, a nation built upon a combination of Burmese national identity, Buddhist philosophy, British political organization, and Socialist economic theories—both Marxist and non-Marxist. Marxism of the Communist variety is not likely to dominate Burmese thought and policies unless the Burmese political leaders fail to produce a rising standard of living through the democratic process or unless the surrounding countries—Pakistan, India, and Thailand—or Burma itself, by conquest, fall under Communist control.

3

THAILAND AND MARXISM

DAVID A. WILSON

Marx has had little influence in Thailand. During the last half-century the social and economic climate of the kingdom has not been salubrious either for the growth of an interest in Marxist ideology or for the development of a Marxist political movement. While other countries of Southeast Asia were yielding to alien penetration and domination, Thailand successfully maintained its formal independence. The result has been that the social and economic changes which followed in the train of Western influence developed in an indigenous and organic fashion.

The reader must be mindful of the differences in effect of the appearance of the West in Thailand and in colonial areas. In Thailand the traditional leadership was not deposed from power. Cultivators were not dispossessed of their traditional tenures. While Thailand shared with the entire South Seas the influx of proletarian Chinese immigrants—having today one of the most considerable minorities of any Southeast Asian state— the political and social, if not the economic, effects of this phenomenon have been under the control of an indigenous government. At no time has the Chinese minority been permitted a legitimate political role. This group has, furthermore, in recent years been simultaneously subjected to policies of assimilation and exclusion. As a result, it has either become Thai or has directed its interest, including a taste for Marxism, largely toward its homeland. Generally it has been alien and separate from Thai political life.

The management over the years of the nation's relationship with Europe also stands in contrast to that in the formerly colonial countries. Marxism has elsewhere crept in with the importation of the intellectual patterns of the metropolitan power. The Thai, approaching European thought pragmatically and selectively, did not become a reproduction of any European ideological model. Both the policy of sending students to a variety of countries and the policy of anticipating revolutionary ideas worked well, at least against Marxism.

Nor did Marxism offer any solution for the major political problems of recent Thai history. Since Thailand's relationship with the West was on the basis of diplomacy and treaties rather than war and revolution, negotiating skills were at a premium and revolutionary fervor at a discount. Moreover improvement of internal control, economic distribution, and economic surplus was needed to strengthen the negotiators. In diplomatic matters, both by coincidence and through the skill of Thai negotiators, foreign powers were passably amenable to Thai aspirations. Great Britain and France found it necessary jointly to recognize the independence and neutrality of the Čhao Phraya River basin in 1896 and to maintain Thailand as a buffer between their colonial possessions. At the same time, rich resources and an economy cushioned by a large segment of subsistence living protected the country against severe economic crisis.

Furthermore, Marxist political methods were and are altogether incompatible with Thai political style and tradition. Neither tightly disciplined organization nor mass-based ideological parties have a place in the Thai political system. Its most prominent characteristics are the maneuverings of individual political figures within a tiny, bureaucratic leadership group and the formation and re-formation of cliques and factions based on personal allegiances. At the same time, neither personal nor group loyalties are stable. However, these unceasing activities among the small ruling group were and are staged upon the foundation of a remarkably stable social life among the general population. One of the more interesting aspects of this life and of Thai society in general is the weakness of semi-public organizations and the fact that corporate bodies have no appeal. Political parties have been forbidden for most of Thai history. At those moments when open party activity was permitted, however, no popular or mass parties appeared.

On the level of ideology, as well, Marxism has lacked appeal for Thai intellectuals. Admittedly, it is dangerous and difficult to characterize a national mind; yet, certain modes of Thai intellectual life may be noted for the sake of argument. First it is evident that in Buddhism the Thai intellectual has a *Weltanschauung* which is both satisfactory and comfortable. This faith in traditional religion has saved him from heart-rending introspection and self-criticism and has preserved for him a matter-of-fact approach to life. The Thai intellectual is above all pragmatic rather than speculative. The architectonic intricacies of the Marxian theory are a small temptation. Moreover, the vitality of Buddhist ethics most certainly discounts the particularities of Marxian theory. The emphasis on violent revolution and social conflict, on materialist values, and on group loyalty runs counter to Buddhist concepts. Although the effect which Marxism has had in Thailand has been among intellectuals, the strength and vitality of tradition have greatly inhibited its impact.

THE SOCIAL BACKGROUND

The late John Embree with a felicitous bit of jargon characterized the society of Thailand as a "loosely structured social system."[1] By this phrase he meant to underscore the degree of independent action and the importance of the individual will among the Thai. Naturally, this degree and importance are relative to other Asian social systems, but the characterization etches one of the most striking qualities of Thai society. The Thai is an individualist. He carries the burden of social responsibility lightly. Within a structure of social obligation and rights, he is able to move and respond to his personal and individual inclinations without suffering a mortal social wound. Embree said:

The first characteristic of Thai culture to strike an observer from the West, or from Japan or Vietnam, is the individualistic behavior of the people. The longer one resides in Thailand the more one is struck by the almost determined lack of regularity, discipline and regimentation. In contrast to Japan, Thailand lacks neatness and discipline; in contrast to Americans, the Thai lack respect for administrative regularity and have no industrial time sense.[2]

This characteristic individualism of the Thai is supported by at least two fundamental social factors. Theravada Buddhism, the religious tradition from which Thai Buddhism springs, has as its central tenet "salvation" through individual accumulation of merit. The making of merit and progress along the eightfold path to enlightenment is viewed as a lonely and individual task in which, generally speaking, one may not look to others for assistance.

> By oneself is evil done;
> By oneself one suffers;
> By oneself evil is left undone;
> By oneself one is purified.
>
> DHAMAPADA[3]

This conception of the cosmic role of the individual surely reinforces the flexibility of permitted behavior and mitigates feelings of social obligation. Such a conception, it would appear, tends to contradict any ideological subordination of the individual to the mass or class. The significance of the relationship between this cosmic outlook and social behavior is, of course, neither easily measured nor demonstrated.

The second factor of importance in strengthening Thai individualism has been the very substantial luxury of resources in which Thai society has developed. Resulting economic satisfactions will be discussed more fully below. At this point it is sufficient to indicate the relationship between material plenitude and individualism. Since their arrival in the valley of the Čhao Phraya River in the thirteenth century, the Thai people have had a surplus of land resources, the fundamental form of economic wealth. To this day, population densities in heavily cultivated areas of Thailand are far below densities in comparable areas of China, Japan, Viet Nam, or Java. This surplus has encouraged something of the pioneering spirit and of economic self-reliance among the Thai.

Land surplus and low population density are correlated with geographic mobility and loosely organized villages[4] in an evaluation of the penetration of Marxism. Although there is little information available about rural Thailand,[5] there is a consensus among observers that patterns of cooperation and feelings of community allegiance and solidarity, such as are known in other parts of rural Asia, are relatively weak. Cooperative work, particularly harvesting, is common in rural areas, but the pattern of this work is one of personal reciprocity among individual members of fairly stable groups. It is not conceived of as duty to community, village, or any other corporate body.[6] While the significance of the correlation of land surplus and the characteristic Thai Buddhist ethic with this condition of rural mobility and community "looseness" may be questioned, it is sufficient for the present purposes to cite the fact of all three as aspects of Thai individualism and self-reliance.

The fluidity of social status characteristic of both traditional and modern Thailand is a natural correlative of the individualistic personality. Both social and geographic mobility are clear aspects of the social system. Mobility and its relationship with individualism contribute to the weakness of group and community institutions. Geographic mobility takes two forms: urbanization and rural migration. The population of Bangkok, the only genuine metropolitan center of the country, has increased substantially in the past thirty years.[7] The increase is statistically large enough to indicate considerable movement from the country to the city. This evidence is supported by impressions received in the city. Many people of all classes, born and raised in provincial areas, have come to the city for education or to seek their fortunes. This situation would not appear to be a development of recent years only. The ambitious individual has always gone to the capital to improve his lot. In addition to country-to-city migration, however, there has apparently at various times also been movement around the country. Although it is difficult to document, it is evident that the opening of new lands which has taken place in the past century involved substantial movements of people.[8]

Geographical mobility goes hand in hand with a tradition of mobility up and down the scale of social status. Old Thai society was made up of a system of social grades. At the bottom were slaves of two types (redeemable and unredeemable).[9] The remainder of the cultivators were freemen. Upon this foundation of cultivators and laborers was a complex structure of grades and offices which comprised the ruling group. This group was divided broadly into royalty and nonroyalty, each sector being subdivided into a large number of ranks. The ranks of nonroyalty were in fact nonhereditary commissions from the king and were more like civil service offices than noble ranks. A man might well hold several ranks during his life and his son hold none. Royal status was, of course, obtained through heredity. There was, however, in theory no continuity of this status from father to son. Rather, the passage of royal status from generation to generation was governed by a rule of declining descent, so that in five generations a family out of the line of royal succession returned to common status.[10]

In the face of this fluid system, any analysis of Thai society in terms of class structure is most problematical. On the one hand, social status was and still is graded to an extraordinary degree; while on the other, it is difficult to see any rigid lines of class division. Social gradation has been given substance in both law and language. A peculiarity of the Thai language is the fact that it is extremely difficult, if not impossible, to avoid the expression of the relative social status of speakers. That is to say, all terms of personal reference—pronouns, titles, and the like—carry with them definite connotations of social status. The linguistic function of social status in Thai is comparable to gender in English.

The traditional law of social organization in Thailand was designed to build society as a monolith integrated to serve the state, or more precisely the king. One of the guiding principles of organization was the uniquely Thai *sakdi na* system, whereby each man was allotted a degree of dignity and privilege measured quantitatively. This system of grades was part and parcel of the relationship of patron and client which integrated Thai society in terms of right, obligation, and justice. With the exception of slaves, whose rights and obligations were assumed by their owner, all people were bound together in social systems organized vertically. Each freeman had a *sakdi na* grade of twenty-five (historically related to the amount of land one man could cultivate); persons of higher status were allotted *sakdi na* numbers in terms of the number of their supposed clients. These systems of patron and clients were organized into royal departments, the functions of which were varied but inevitably included the collection of tax, or *corvée,* from the dependent freemen. These departments were both the social and administrative organization of the kingdom.[11]

There is a vital difference between grades of status and class. Insofar as these institutions, made up of legal and nonhereditary relationships of right and obligation and vertically organized social groups, had a genuine vitality, they worked against the development of class consciousness. It would be easy to overestimate the vitality of traditional institutions, of course, but, on the other hand, it would be a facile projection to read the Western Marxist dogma of class structure into traditional Thai society. There is little data available on the day-to-day conditions of a century or more ago, but there is no evidence of the kind of social unrest which would indicate class conflict. Social grades shaded delicately from one to another, and the Thai view of society was up and down within groups rather than over any impenetrable wall of class distinction. If aspiration to rise in society motivated a man, the next higher grade was never beyond the hope of attainment. Status among the Thai was, and as a matter of fact continues to be, conceived as a personal attribute. A man's social position is a consequence of his merit, either in the Buddhist or civil service sense of the word. As merit of men is capable of delicate gradation, so is social status. As merit is a result of volition rather than accident of birth, so is social status. In a context of this kind the Marxian appeal to class solidarity and conflict found sterile ground.

It is not surprising that, as an outgrowth of this tradition, the social system of present-day Thailand is also fluid. Although the *sakdi na* system and other aspects of the intricately structured legal forms of the old social system have been abolished,[12] social mobility and fluidity of social groupings are now, if anything, a greater reality than formerly.

This situation becomes apparent in any attempt to analyze present Thai society in terms of social classes or status groups. The most recent published analysis is that of Herbert P. Phillips.[13] Phillips notes first that the primary social division of Thailand is between country and city. The two are largely self-contained and tangential. Rural society in Thailand is remarkably homogeneous throughout the country in terms of economic status and occupational role. There are, of course, certain specialties other than the fundamental work of farming and fishing, but these are for the most part services for the producers. The significance of the social homogeneity is the conspicuous lack of any group of rural landlord gentry. The essential rural type is the small freeholder, operating his farm on a more or less commercialized basis. He makes up well over 70 per cent of the total population of the country.

The more complex urban, primarily Bangkok, society lives tangentially
to the rural society. It is here that both mobility and finely graded social
status are most apparent. Mobility and gradation are related to the variety
of criteria of status. Phillips notes five criteria—economic standing, political
power and connections, education, outlook on life, and family background[14]
—which in various permutations and combinations determine social status.
Thus, urban society may be analyzed into five social-status groups or
classes: old elite, new elite, upper middle class, lower middle class, and
lower class. In regard to this analysis, however, it is particularly necessary
to exercise caution. As Phillips notes:

The term [class] must be understood not in the sense of a restrictive and exclusive class but rather in the sense of a group of discrete individuals who by virtue
of various implied and arbitrary criteria have a common prestige status. . . .
[M]embers of a particular class do not have a strong sense of identity with other
members of their own class. Indeed, because of the "openness" of the system
and the general lack of class consciousness, of common class interests, Bangkok
society cannot be said to have a class system in the classical European sense of
the term. . . . Bangkok society is in no way marked off into static social com-
partments out of which people never move. Present urban society is characterized by an extraordinary amount of status (or class) mobility, both up and
down the ladder: people are constantly changing jobs, changing their statuses,
moving in and out of the city, and the like. As a result of this frequent movement, class lines tend to become blurred and unclear.[15]

The same caution applies to an analysis of Thai society in terms of
economic classes or occupation groups. Any generalized feeling of belonging to the working class or peasant class or ruling class is at most
incipient. The common attitude, which is consonant with the general
Thai attitude of individualism, is the more personal "I am a farmer," "I
am a taxi driver," "I am a government official." The opportunity for change
and advancement as well as the tie of many with the countryside and
families on the farm—all these factors work to dissolve class feeling among
urban people. And among farmers the strong traditions of the independent
freeholder have inhibited the development of a feeling of class membership. A final factor which retards the growth of class feeling is the rather
strong national feeling toward the large Chinese minority. This minority,
either native or China-born, constitutes perhaps 10 per cent of the population of the kingdom. It invokes a mutual attitude of ethnic solidarity;
at the same time, it cuts across certain socially significant occupational
groups such as free wage laborers and merchants, both large and small.[16]
    The four most important economic or occupational groups are (1)
farmers and fishermen, the basic producers of the country; (2) free labor,
primarily but not exclusively urban since it includes miners, forest workers,
construction workers, and transport workers; (3) the governing group,

including civil and military officials, politicians, princes, and the like, the organization of which links the city with the countryside; and (4) the commercial class, ranging from large import-export merchants to peddlers with a carrying pole—another connecting link between country and town, nation and world. The comparative sizes of these groups are shown by their respective percentages of the total labor force:[17] the rural producers constitute about 84 per cent of the total; the laboring group, excluding rural labor, is about 3 per cent; the governing group about 2 per cent; and the commercial group about 6 per cent.[18]

A peculiarly significant aspect of occupation groups in Thailand is the fact that economic class lines in some cases coincide with ethnic divisions. For example, the rural producers and governing groups are almost exclusively Thai; the commercial group is dominated by Chinese and other non-Thai nationalities, although the Thai, particularly in recent years, have by no means been completely excluded. Historically, free labor was largely Chinese, since much labor was recruited by the government from China in the last century in preference to paying the high wages necessary to attract Thai away from the farms.[19] In recent years it would appear, on the basis of impressionistic observation, that this situation is breaking down, both because of assimilation, over a generation, of Chinese workers into the Thai ethos and because the incentive of wages is becoming more compelling in certain areas of Thailand. Therefore the labor group, which might be expected to develop some approximation of class consciousness, is splintered into various ethnic groups.[20]

THE EDUCATED THAI

While the ultimate depth of the penetration of Marxism in a society will depend upon the success with which it may be used to explain and ameliorate crises in the social situation, its first appeal as an ideology must be to the educated members of society. Its penetration into a society as an alien idea will be through literary forms of one sort or another. Moreover, in Thailand the group which dominates the nation is distinguished from the general population most clearly by level of education. In order to understand the role of Marxism, therefore, it is necessary to examine in some detail the character of the educated leadership group and its relationship to power and to the general public.

As is peculiarly characteristic of bureaucratic societies such as Thailand, education, in the forms of bureaucracy at least, is a universal trait of the dominant group. Its ability to dominate depends in some measure upon superior know-how in the forms and methods of government and upon a monopoly of this kind of knowledge. The educational system of Thailand has been admirably suited to that end up to the present. It is now the primary recruiting agency for the elite. Recent broadening of the educational base[21] and increases in schools and enrollment from bottom to top reflect new complexities of government and a process of enlarging the top group. At the same time, because the educational system touches virtually every Thai, it serves both as an outlet for ambition and as a mode of winnowing candidates for leadership.

The educational qualification for leadership is a university degree or its equivalent. The bulk of responsible civil service positions[22] and commissions in the armed services and police are open only to university or military academy graduates. Knowing this, it is possible to infer two features of the leadership group: it is small, as the total number of university or equivalent graduates of all ages is probably at most 0.2 per cent of the total population; and it is characterized by a certain degree of Westernization. The educational system has been adapted from European and American models, and the curriculum reflects the source. At secondary level and above, a substantial part of the curriculum is devoted to the study of a foreign language—generally English. In addition, the ideal behavior of Thai students is an amalgam of Western and traditional Thai characteristics. Until World War II, the best secondary schools were administered by Europeans, and university deans were often Europeans. In the decade since the war, Europeans and Americans have again taken a considerable, although subordinate, place in upper secondary and university education. Their former leadership has been assumed by Thai educators schooled in Europe or America. At Čhulalongkọn University, the leading university, well over three-quarters of the faculty have had considerable education abroad. The same is true to a greater or lesser extent of the other universities. This pattern is continued in superior teacher-training schools and among responsible officials in the Ministry of Education. The educated group is, then, a tiny group trained in an atmosphere that is imbued with an adaptation of Western knowledge, spirit, and values, albeit still Thai.

A social fact of supreme importance in the history of modern Thailand is the absence of a frustrated, unemployed educated class. The traditional occupation of the educated is government and, because independence was retained, this field remained open to the Thai. Furthermore, the number of openings at the top of society has certainly increased in modern times, permitting the absorption of discontented elements into leadership positions. At the same time, control over the education system, the primary upward pathway and recruiting agency for new members of the elite, has permitted the maintenance of an approximate balance between qualified applicants for positions of responsibility and jobs. The gradual introduction of popular education, coupled with the development of a larger bureaucracy and the opening of top jobs to nonroyalty—a substantial result of the establishment of the constitutional monarchy in 1932—has prevented any significant frustration of ambition on the part of educated Thai. In concrete terms this means that the enlargement of the armed services and the police, the increasing need for schoolteachers as a result of the gradual expansion of the educational system, and the general enlargement of the civil service which has been consequent upon the new complexities of the role of modern government—jobs in the management of the economy, the improvement of agriculture, the construction of public works, and the variety of social welfare operations now assumed by the government—have absorbed the educated into positions of responsibility and prestige, if not wealth.

Because this is the case the Thai educated group as a whole has a peculiar bent.[23] Most educated Thai are officials faced daily with the stubborn facts of life. They are not therefore given to flights of imagination. They fit comfortably into an established structure of social organization. They are not stimulated by idleness and failure to an examination of the fundamentals of that structure or of the ultimate values upon which it is based. In a very real sense, the educated group is a class with a vested interest. Consequently it is conservative and pragmatic rather than radical and speculative. The range of serious modern literature in Thailand is symptomatic. In a very general way it may be grouped into three segments: poetry, fiction, and social comment of a didactic nature; narrative history and biography; and "how-to-do-it" and self-education books. Works of what might be called pure intellection are few.

The nature of university education is appropriate to this intellectual bent. At present there are five institutions which grant degrees in the country—Čhulalongkǫn, Thammasat, the Agricultural, Medical, and Fine Arts universities. The last three are training schools of professional level exclusively. The first two, Čhulalongkǫn and Thammasat, are more general and academic in their organization, but neither offers a course in philosophy or religion. At present the system of self-contained faculties effectively limits education to more or less specific professional and career courses. On the whole, training in these faculties is specific, practical, and applied.

Another opportunity for education is open to a minority of university-level students—education abroad in Europe or America. These opportunities are in the form of government scholarships for postgraduate study. The scholarships are generally awarded for further professional training and carry with them an obligation for a term of government service upon return. This procedure fits a potentially explosive group into the present social structure and provides it with an interest in the maintenance of that structure. While it is true that Western-trained Thai tend to suffer frustration in trying to implement new techniques in their work, they do not have the fundamental social frustrations which might stimulate revolutionary thoughts.

It must not, however, be overlooked that there is a tiny group of "pure intellectuals" among the educated people in Thailand. This group, which has little inner organization, is composed, on the one hand, of journalists and writers, and, on the other, of educators and a few leisured and aristocratic full-time intellectuals. In journalism there is, for example, a core of a few hundred newspapermen, surrounded by a large number of part-time writers. Journalism is not a particularly esteemed or stable profession in Thailand. Newspapers and magazines proliferate, prosper briefly, and die at a rapid rate. Many of the journalists are university students who failed to complete their degree. Perhaps the combination of low prestige and frustration with control of a large part of the national stock of literature has made this group the rather querulous and irresponsible critic of the government that it is.[24] This group of writers is a potential flaw in the structure of the educated class. The other segment of the intellectual group is made up of university professors and the few full-time writers, most of whom are of royal families or are former officials. University professors are actually government officials and, as such, in no position to exercise academic freedom. At the same time, they are few in number and burdened with heavy labors.

In sum, the educated leadership of the nation is a career group. Their place in society is made. They have opportunities for useful, responsible, and satisfying work, for which their training is designed to prepare them. It is to be expected that, having a substantial stake in society as it is presently arranged, they should, as a group, be conservative insofar as any fundamental social change is concerned.

With the exception of a general enlargement of the group and the internal power shifts involved in displacing royalty with commoners of the bureaucratic class, the leadership of Thailand has been essentially the same for centuries. This leadership is not faced with the necessity of justifying its legitimacy. Because the mass of people is not interested in rejecting traditional claims of right by the bureaucratic group, these claims provide support for the leadership. It is impossible to predict at what moment the population may be electrified and demand a new structuring of the rights of ruling, but indications are that for the moment this realization of need and power has not dawned.

Moreover, the leadership and the mass have been united not only on the level of political organization and legality but also in the Buddhist ethic. In Thailand, as in any other particular place and time, the ethical-religious system should not be confused with the rationalized philosophy of theoreticians. Buddhism in Thailand is a peculiar structure of ideas and value-attitudes which forms the ethical pattern of national behavior. Buddhism, in this sense, is a vital part of life. It is difficult to overestimate its importance, just as it is difficult, unfortunately, to analyze and measure its role. It is fully and generally accepted, and it is, without doubt, the keystone to the understanding of the failure of any other ideology to make a real penetration into the Thai *Weltanschauung*.

The Buddhist view of the cosmic place of man has been touched on above. This conception of man's individual responsibility for his own fate and the doctrine of rebirth, with its implication of a better life to come, metaphysically reinforce the sociological fact of social mobility and break up group or class solidarity. In contrast to the conception of men as equal before God or before the economic system, the doctrine of degrees of individual merit permits the structuring of society in levels of status.

Buddhism places the highest value on the nonmaterial and deprecates the material. In this it runs most clearly against the Marxist emphasis on material value—on labor and goods. Although it would be false to depict the Thai as uninterested in the acquisition of wealth, he puts great value on the accumulation of merit and on the making of merit through doing good in the infinite ways that good may be done. The most direct manner of merit-making is to participate in, and support, the faith. Thus a man's greatest opportunity to make merit is to become a monk, and a woman's is to support a man in this endeavor. The monk's life, in fact and symbol, is the mode of most merit and greatest value. It demonstrates the total denial of things of this world. The monk's role—celibate, half-starved, dressed in torn robes, and living as a mendicant—is a respected and valued symbol of the denial of desire, Buddhism's greatest value.

But no approach to an understanding of Thai behavior and attitude toward life is possible without consideration of the concepts of enjoyment (*sanuk*) and coolheadedness, or noninvolvement (*choei*). *Sanuk*, which is often misleadingly translated as "fun," is a quality which should be had in all experience. Its fullest meaning includes fun and more. Any activity can be and should be *sanuk*. Merit-making itself should be *sanuk*. Temple fairs and activities, elections, travel, and work should be *sanuk*. This seeking for enjoyment in all things is a fundamental part of Thai behavior, and for the Thai it may be said that what cannot be enjoyed has little value. Along with this seeking for enjoyment is an attitude of reserve and non-involvement in troublesome or novel situations. One should avoid having one's feelings hurt by keeping one's head, being cool in adversity, and remaining uncommitted emotionally. The concepts of *sanuk* and *choei* combine to make a lighthearted approach to life which discourages the acceptance of the great problems of the world. Interpersonal relations are built around the conception of elder and younger brother or parent and child. But in the Thai Buddhist view such relationships are not harsh and rigid. Perhaps the guiding concepts are benevolent and generous authority and diffident respect.

Thai culture also continues to be generally valid and vital for all groups and levels of society and serves to unify leadership with the general population. This continued vitality depends in large part on the traditional ethical system. Because of the cushion provided by a vigorously acting and successfully integrated social system, the Westernized Thai leadership has not been torn loose from its following, nor has it been intellectually dislocated from its faith and place in a system of values and statuses.

Concretely, Westernization of leadership, while it has gone forward rapidly since the reign of King Čhulalongkǫn, has not created a miniature and imperfect replica of any European nation. Čhulalongkǫn was sensitive to the peril of permitting the state or its leadership to fall under the influence of any particular nation. His policy was to take Western influence from various nations. This policy has been continued to the present. Students sent abroad have gone to virtually every nation of Western Europe and America. The advisers employed by the government at various times since the end of the nineteenth century have also been from different Western nations. As one result of this policy, there has been no insistent pressure of European Marxists in the country. In contrast to Viet Nam and Indonesia, where French and Dutch Marxists were on the scene, Thailand excluded such radically alien revolutionists. At the same time, the short term of the normal stay of the Thai abroad, the fact that they were closely supervised by Thai diplomatic officials, and the fact that returning Thai came from different nations apparently discouraged any possible ideological coherence among the members of this small group of returning intellectuals.

To sum up, Westernization has been important among educated Thai. Yet it is Westernization worn with a difference—a difference resulting from design and from milieu. Westernization was consciously chosen by Thai leaders, not thrust upon them by a politically dominant power. Westernization was taken selectively, both in terms of elements and sources. The result has been a peculiarly Thai form of Westernization which today many Thai do not recognize as such. It is in fact a Thai way of life.

ECONOMIC FACTORS

Certain elements of Thailand's recent economic history and present economic situation also contribute to an understanding of Marxism's slight effect in the kingdom. Two are particularly important. First, Thailand

has always had plenty of land available to accomplish the economic
objectives and maintain the standard of living of an increasing population.
Second, although the economy has changed considerably, such change has
been to a large extent a matter of quantity rather than kind. On balance,
the economic system has much the same shape today that it had a century
ago.

During this past century, however, under the influence of contact with
the West, a portion of the economy of Thailand has changed from a system
of self-sufficient subsistence production to a system of international trade
based on a rice-grain surplus, supplemented by forest products, rubber,
and tin. For two reasons the course of this change was, and continues to be,
most gradual. First, the government of the kingdom has by means of a
consistently conservative economic policy been reasonably successful in
mitigating the impact of new economic forces. In addition, the abundance
of land permitted both the absorption of increased population and the
realization of increased production without doing violence to social relations. Therefore, severe pressure of population on the land and the
related problems of peasant indebtedness, landlord tenant conflict, and
impoverishment of the rural population—so stimulating elsewhere to an
interest in social change and even Marxism—have not occurred in Thailand. At the same time, because of the very small-scale extent of industrial
development, anything approximating a working-class proletariat is lacking. In other words, the economic development of the country has not
produced that kind of economically depressed group—a desperate peasantry or an oppressed and depersonalized worker group—to which Marxism
offers a strong appeal.

During these hundred years of transition, three principal changes have
nevertheless taken place. These are the development of a partial money
economy, the change from self-sufficient production to specialization and
exchange in parts of the economy, and the appearance of an ethnic aspect
to the division of labor. The first two changes affect only part of the
nation, even today. The third developed as a result of Chinese migration
in response to new demand for free labor and merchants in an exchange
economy. The social effects of economic change and development have,
however, not been radical, and the social system of the greater part of the
population has not been seriously disrupted. Ingram summarized the history of economic change in this way:

The Thai population has largely remained in agriculture, and has neither improved techniques nor increased the proportion of capital to labor. Moreover,
most changes in the economy as a whole have been in volume rather than in
kind. New methods have not been used, new products have not been developed.
No product of any importance (besides rubber) is exported today which was
not exported in 1850.[25]

It would appear that this rather striking fact about the development of the Thai economy in one of the most dynamic, not to say revolutionary, centuries of human history reveals a great deal about the Thailand of today. When it is kept in mind that almost 85 per cent of the working population continues to engage in agriculture, and when it appears that the way of life of the cultivator has been little changed in a century, it is to be expected that the overwhelming proportion of the population would not be readily susceptible to a radically new and alien ideological appeal such as Marxism.

The lure of cash is a most potent force for social change in a subsistence economy, but some areas of the country, particularly in the northeast region, still have little contact with the world market. The average distance of farms in that region from a highway open six months a year or more is over 14 kilometers and from a railway over 84 kilometers. The national averages for the same distances are over 10 and 70 kilometers, respectively.[26] These figures merely illustrate the still incomplete penetration of the world into the Thai countryside. The large number of farms far from transport are operated almost completely in a self-sufficient manner, albeit with a rather low standard of living. Even in the more commercialized areas, farmers continue in a quasi-self-sufficient manner to produce their own food, fuel, housing, and tools.[27] The *Economic Farm Survey of 1953* revealed that the average cash expenditure of farm families for living expenses in the kingdom was *baht* 2,877 (one *baht* is about 5 cents U.S.), while it was *baht* 3,983 in the central plain, the most commercialized rice farming area.[28] The national average for farm operating expenses was *baht* 664, and the central plain's average 1,335.[29]

Coupled with the large element of subsistence farming in the economy is the small freeholder pattern of farm tenure. Both the agricultural census of 1950 and the farm survey of 1953 agree that over 85 per cent of the cultivated land is operated by the owner.[30] The small percentage of land operated on a rental basis is for the most part in terms of fixed rent, either cash or kind, so that the evils of sharecropping are absent from the Thai agricultural scene.[31] As might be expected in the light of the pattern of an independent peasantry operating in a quasi-subsistence manner, the problem of rural indebtedness is small.

These data indicate in a rough manner the economic status of the rural population of Thailand: it is in sound solvent condition and, in spite of increased commercialization, continues to follow a way of life rooted in tradition. Furthermore, its self-sufficiency to a great extent insulates it from the blows and disruptions of market instability. It is reasonable to conclude from this evidence that any expansive thrust of political or economic demand is for the moment negligible. The Thai peasantry must be considered a fundamentally conservative element in Thai society. When the relative size of this group in proportion to all other socioeconomic groups is considered, the conservative course of Thai history and the slight inroads of any radical doctrines, whether Marxism, liberal democracy, or even the simple but novel doctrine of progress, are not surprising.

Thai nonagricultural industry has its own socioeconomic peculiarities. In general it may be said that nonagricultural industry is organized in two ways: either as government or government-aided industry, or as private investment by aliens, primarily Chinese. Historically, this division has come about as a result of the reluctance of the Thai to enter into occupations on a purely cash basis other than government service. There may be several explanations for this situation. For one thing, agriculture has been sufficiently profitable and secure to retain a comparative advantage over the wage or profit incentives of labor or business.[32] The same is true of government service, which, in addition to being highly esteemed, has been sufficiently well remunerated and secure. But, whatever the explanation, the fact remains that the Thai are not involved in occupations which put them at the mercy of an impersonal cash economy.

The pattern of industrial organization is also a matter of social significance. Private investment in both nonagricultural and agricultural enterprise is organized as small family business. The home workshop, the home store employing largely family labor or a few wage workers integrated into the family pattern—these are the dominant forms of business activity. Ingram estimated that in 1952 there were not many more than a hundred factories in the country which employed over fifty workers, and this figure included at least twenty-five government-operated or -aided establishments.[33] On the other hand, a survey of the Bangkok Municipality in 1954 estimated that there were 36,520 business establishments with fewer than 10 workers in the city.[34] This type of organization involves, of course, an intimate pattern of interpersonal relations between employer and worker and probably includes a higher degree of social integration than is characteristic of large factories. Since the boss and workers are approximate social equals in a small shop, this pattern does not stimulate working-class solidarity and inhibits the appeal of the Marxist doctrine of class among workers.

The role of the state in the economy is a traditional one. Until the opening of Thailand to foreign traders about a hundred years ago, foreign trade from the capital was a monopoly of the king and probably one of the primary sources of royal income.[35] Liberal economic principles assumed a leading position in the commercial sector until the end of World War II, when the government took on a large role in the marketing of rice abroad. This, together with related control of collection and export, provided the government with an important new source of revenue as well as with policy control over the major item of foreign trade.[36] Such activities as irrigation, railway construction, electricity production, and water supply have long been the exclusive domain of the state. The government also entered early into manufacturing. The first government factory was built during World War I, and in subsequent decades the state entered the sugar, distilling, and tobacco businesses.[37] The state also plays a part, of undetermined importance, in the so-called private economic sector. In addition to owning shares in various corporations, the credit of the government guarantees the stability of such companies as the National Economic Development Corporation, Ltd., which was organized in 1954 to further industrial development.[38]

In those few industries where there are comparatively large organizations, the state also plays an important role. For example, the state railway of Thailand is the largest single employer among economic enterprises.[39] The largest manufacturing organization in the kingdom is the state tobacco monopoly.[40] Other government enterprises—sugar refineries, liquor distilleries, textile and paper mills—are among the few large-scale industrial establishments. This creates the peculiar situation that in an economy based on liberal principles, a large segment of the nation's industrial laborers are state employees—a situation perhaps somewhat confounding to those Marxists who would make nationalization of industry a tenet of their program.

The traditional economic role of the state, while ideologically distinct from Marxist economic organization, is somewhat similar in form. In recent times the development of state and bureaucratic capitalism has flourished in spite of the existence of a presumably free-enterprise system. This tendency, reinforcing tradition, has worked against any strong vested interest in a liberal economic system outside the community of Chinese and European entrepreneurs. As a result, there is no strong antagonism to the idea of state-organized and -operated economic enterprise which would present a barrier to Marxism in that area.

POLITICAL ENVIRONMENT

History has been generous with Thailand. Many of the experiences that have in the past century plagued and tormented other areas of Southeast Asia have passed Thailand by. It suffered neither the loss of political autonomy nor the internal disruption of stability and social order which have been the consequences of colonialism. The upheaval of the sudden intrusion and subsequent collapse of Japanese power in the area affected the kingdom mildly in comparison with its neighbors. Although it would hardly be accurate to say that the numerous alien forces left Thailand un-

touched, its experience with each of them has been entirely different from
that of other Asian countries. The key to this difference lies in the maintenance of Thai independence, an achievement which resulted from luck,
geography, diplomatic skill, and a political realism that is willing to pay
the necessary price. The price was the sacrifice over the years of certain
territory, certain territorial claims, and elements of fiscal and legal autonomy, as well as a readiness to change.

With the settlement of the demands of France and Britain in the first
decade of this century, external relations passed from a matter of survival
to a gradual unfolding of Thailand's role as an independent state. During
the past half-century the internal and external policies of the kingdom
have been inseparable. Through the whole is woven the thread of this
basic policy: to demonstrate the nation's political solvency and to avoid
any provocation for foreign intervention. In regard to European powers
this policy came to full flower in the mid-twenties, when treaty relations
with all major powers were renegotiated. Complete fiscal and legal autonomy was regained in principle. The final adoption of legal codes provided for in these treaties was completed in 1935.

The fact that the last overt restrictions on Thailand's autonomy were
wiped from the slate at a relatively early date is important in understanding the nature of Thai nationalism. At the same time, the fact that the
pressure of imperial France and Britain removed from Thai suzerainty
virtually all non-Thai national groups (with the exception of the small
number of Malays in the extreme south) gave the Thai state a cultural
unity which aided national integration. At least in part because of these
factors, modern Thai nationalism, while very real, is not on the whole
militant or aggressive and is largely restricted to the small educated group.
In fact, Thai nationalism originated as an attitude toward the Chinese
minority. This development may be ascribed to the simultaneous emergence of a national feeling among the substantial Chinese group in Thailand and the drawing together and integration of this minority as a
semiautonomous community with considerable economic strength in the
kingdom.

Although expressed nationalist feeling was, at least until recent years,
directed primarily at the Chinese,[41] there have also been a few anti-Western
outbursts. In the period of the late thirties, which saw the height of
nationalism under the leadership of Phibun Songkhram, the Thai government took several anti-Western actions. Most prominent among them was
the attack on France in Indochina and the reassertion of Thai claims to
several provinces which had been annexed by France in 1909.[42] These
actions were taken under the parasol of Japanese influence and were abandoned after Japan collapsed. In the past few years, new anti-Western

expressions have been appearing in the Thai press. These take a primarily anti-American line and are directed at American military aid, American oil companies, and presumed American dominance in the country's external relations. For the moment this new and enthusiastic sniping at America's rather prominent role in Thailand can be attributed to the exasperation of Thai opposition politicians who see the strengthening of the military forces that provide the organized base of the present government. It is not difficult to detect the financial and spiritual encouragement of Communist propagandists in this activity. The press, in the liberalized atmosphere of the past year attendant upon the "democratization" policy of the government, relishes its new role as critic. It seems unlikely, however, that this reflects any swell of public reaction against the West.[43]

As has been said above, Thai nationalism—in its mild but definite form —is largely an intellectual attitude and restricted to the educated group. This fact points up what is perhaps the most prominent contrast between Thailand and formerly colonial nations: the complete insulation of the vast majority of the population from the disrupting influences of alien peoples. The foreigner is still a curiosity in the Thai countryside because he has rarely been seen there. As a result, there is no evidence of anti-Western feeling among the rural population and no basis for any mass nationalist movement. Even against the Chinese there is little strong feeling of antagonism. On the whole the Chinese rice buyers and merchants appear to live in a symbiotic state with the Thai farmer.

The past half-century, which has seen the climax and downfall of colonial power in Southeast Asia—a process which has meant the weakening, and in some cases temporary destruction, of internal power in several states—has been a period of continuous internal peace and consolidation of internal power in Thailand. In fact, the present government can legitimately claim a continuity of regime extending to the foundation of the Chakkri dynasty in 1782. Nor has continuity meant lack of change; the government has been successfully transformed, first, from its traditionally loose administrative forms to a highly centralized, rationalized bureaucracy and, second, from the form of an absolute to a constitutional monarchy. As a result, the operative field of public power is today vastly broader, and its effective range greater than it was fifty years ago. During the entire period since the influx of Western ideas, the population of the kingdom has lived in a state of internal tranquillity and security, largely because of the strength and stability of a rather benevolent and paternalistic government.

The beginning of the process of consolidation of internal power coincided with the most insistent pressure from Britain and France. From the end of the eighties and continuing to the end of his reign in 1910,

King Čhulalongkǫn, with the aid of his brothers and other advisers, reorganized the administration of the kingdom, ended the role of petty princes in outlying provinces such as Chiangmai and Pattani, reorganized the army, established a gendarmery, and began an educational system for the training of civil servants. He also began the drafting of new law codes, in a most judicious manner brought foreign advisers into the government, and reorganized public finance.[44]

This reorganization of the government set in motion a political revolution of a most gradual kind, to match the slow economic revolution that began with the opening of the country to free foreign trade. In both cases the process of change has proceeded more or less steadily. The fact that the change has gone forward without internal violence on any considerable scale and without disturbing the politically passive peasantry in a radical manner has prevented the development of any considerable unrest. Thai political leadership has successfully stayed on top of the situation in such a manner that no substantial social group has lost its stake in society.

Illustrations of how this stability within change was managed may be drawn from the coup d'état of 1932 and the relationship with Japan during World War II. In the first instance, the change in form of government from an absolute to a constitutional monarchy was carried out without disruption of administration, foreign relations, or internal peace. A milestone in the Thai revolution, the coup was unusual in the history of power shifts in that the displacement of the monarchy's absolute power by the organized power of the new bureaucrats (including military officers) was carried out with a minimum of force applied to strategic people. The coup was over in a few hours. According to a contemporary view of the meaning of the coup:

The success of the revolution [was] explained by its character. There was no explosion but there was merely a readjustment. Capable men simply stepped into the shoes of the Princes and the thing was done. They called themselves the People's Party but the general public were spectators only. The King acceded quietly and the President of the new Senate complimented his party on having the King on their side. They recognize that the sovereign retains the love of the masses.[45]

The great feeling for continuity, as well, perhaps, as a feeling of insecurity on the part of the promoters of the coup, was demonstrated by the haste with which they turned to conciliate the king and at least elements of the royal party among the bureaucrats. Within two days of the coup, the king had been persuaded to give his blessing to the venture, and on the fourth day an old civil servant and royalist accepted leadership of the revolutionary government.[46]

This account is intended, not to diminish the significance of the *coup d'état,* but rather to emphasize the smoothness with which one group displaced another without internal disorder. The administration of the country did not falter, the bureaucracy on the whole accepted the change, and even the king avoided any appeal to outside groups to protect his power. At the time of the short-lived revolt of a section of the army and civil service in 1933 and also at the time of his abdication, the king condemned the use of force in his behalf and disowned any such efforts in advance.[47] Shifts or realignments of the ruling power group, as in 1947 and 1957, have been similarly smooth.

In the second example, Thailand successfully avoided a disruption of interior administration by Japanese World War II occupation and was lucky enough not to have fighting carried within its borders. At the end of the war, when Japan collapsed and the rest of Southeast Asia was embroiled in a chaos of power conflicts, Thailand quietly and successfully denied its role in the alliance with Japan and slipped into the postwar world with a minimum of difficulty.

The external maneuvering of the Thai government under the leadership of Phibun Songkhram in the late thirties and in the forties, when the power of Japan was insistently pressing on Britain, France, and the Netherlands, was rather ambiguous and has been characterized as most opportunistic. But from the point of view of the internal stability of the nation, the twists and turns of policy had a real consistency and were in the main successful. As one observer put it:

When trying nowadays to assess Phibun's, or Siam's motives, one must remember that all Asian countries saw the war according to their own light, as a chapter in the historical struggle of Asia for independence. The conduct of Phibun must be viewed together with the actions of such men as the late Subhas Chandra Bose, the late U Aung San, or Dr. Soekarno. Thus, it is interesting after the event to take from Phibun himself his own account of the drift towards an unwanted war. He claims that, even before he became Premier, he knew that Japan would go to war and come south via the land route, and that he warned the British and other legations repeatedly of Japan's aggressive ideas, and asked for military help from Britain. It was only when he was finally convinced in December 1941 that no help was forthcoming from Britain that he decided, for the good of Siam, to comply with Japan's requests.[48]

Although there is certainly an element of hindsight in this story, there is no denying the fact that collaboration with, rather than resistance to, Japan was in 1941 in the national interest of Thailand.

The reasonable evaluation of the realities of the situation by Thai political leaders at the beginning of the Japanese expansion into Southeast Asia permitted them to keep the quasi-occupation under their own control. This recognition was matched by a continuing re-evaluation of the progress of the war. The political tone of the government moved with the tide, so that, passing from Phibun through Khuang Aphaiwong and Tawi Bun-yaket to Seni Pramoj, the country met the Allied landings with an incon-testably pro-Ally government headed by the leader of the "Free Thai" organization.[49]

These two events in recent Thai history are cited to illustrate the suc-cessful continuity of power and administration in the face of challenging political problems. Such continuity is in contrast to the history of other nations of Southeast Asia, especially of those occupied by Japan. These two examples also illuminate the central and dominant fact of Thai po-litical history—that the government and the ruling group which controls it have been successful. The problems which have faced them have been adequately, if not dramatically, solved. The challenge of imperialism, Westernization, and war has been met. Political success breeds, or at least maintains, peace and consent, while political failure breeds revolution. Marxism has served politically dissatisfied groups as an alternative expla-nation of political and social problems which resist traditional solutions. But in Thailand the traditional methods have sufficed.

POLITICAL SYSTEM

Until 1932 the kingdom was ruled by an absolute monarch, advised mainly by the royal family and relying on the administrative skills and loyalty of a highly developed bureaucracy.[50] In the early thirties a coinci-dence of historical forces ended this rule. The fact that power had success-fully been centralized in the persons of the king and his family, the fact that the prestige of monarchy had been undermined by the education of many officials in Europe, and the fact that the economic difficulties of the govern-ment in the world depression had pinched certain elements of the bureauc-racy—all these converged to produce the *coup d'état* of 1932. The royal family, the nucleus of power, was forced out of power, and the throne be-came little more than a symbol of state. This effort was carried out by a group of bureaucratic factions centered in a number of army officers. Since 1932, power has been the monopoly of the bureaucratic group and has resided in the hands of whatever faction has for the time being been domi-nant.

Although ideological elements were certainly involved in the constitu-tional democratic setting of the *coup d'état*, the fundamental issue appears to have been the distribution of government resources throughout the bu-reaucracy.[51] The army was discontented over budget cuts, and the official services were disturbed by personnel cuts. The motive for the seizure of power was to end this process of reduction. A lack of any ideological com-mitment beyond constitutionalism has continued to be characteristic of Thai political styles.

The policy of the monarchy for fifty-odd years preceding the coup had been to maintain internal stability, solvency, and autonomy if not complete external independence. This policy, to which the bureaucracy as a whole was deeply committed for its own security, was continued by the constitutional government. The façade of government has passed through various styles—constitutional democracy, mild Fascism, reconstruction, and again democracy. The reality has, however, been in the maneuvering for places of power by cliques and individuals in the upper levels of the bureaucratic group.

In the constitutional period, as under the monarchy, the personal role of leading political figures has been very important. Since the consolidation of the *coup d'état*, there have been five men with the distinctive qualifications for a leading position. The earliest was Colonel Phraya Phahon Phayuhasena, first among the promoters of the coup and a man who could unite the various factions around himself for a period. As the central place of the army became clear, the dashing figure of Major (now Field Marshal) P. Phibun Songkhram, who was to succeed Phraya Phahon in the office of Prime Minister, came forward. As leader of the "radical" civilian faction in 1932, Nai Pridi Phanomyong (Luang Pradit Manutham) was at first forced to bow to the superior power of the army and Phibun before and during World War II, but came to a position of leadership after Japan's collapse. In the immediate postwar period the civilian faction split, with Nai Khuang Aphaiwong emerging as the leader of the conservative civilians. In 1957 the army split, with Field Marshal Sarit Thanarat, who was successful for many years in combining the loyalty of the army with the patronage of Phibun, emerging as the dominant figure. Of these five, Phraya Phahon is dead, Nai Pridi and Field Marshal Phibun are in exile, Nai Khuang continues to lead the conservatives' party, and Field Marshal Sarit is playing the benign protector of the peace as supreme commander of the forces.

The struggle for power in Thai politics is of the most intimate kind and is built largely around personal allegiances and ambitions. Thus it is possible and indeed common for a particular individual to move rapidly from faction to faction—for groups to form, dissolve, and re-form. In a general way it may be said to be a struggle among men who know each other as personalities, be they friends or enemies.

The looseness of allegiance and the flexibility of standards of status have permitted the group which circulates around the center of power to absorb new elements without difficulty. Since the removal of royalty from a position of special political privilege, there has been no barrier to keep any potential leader from joining the ruling group. As a result, the social group which dominates the nation has absorbed almost all available political talent and thereby has prevented the development of a threat from outside.

Although there is much struggling for advantage within the group, it has been, at least until recently, to no one's advantage to attack the group as such.

There is, however, one divisive factor in the political system which should be mentioned, namely, regionalism. There are three regions outside the central plain which, for cultural and historical reasons, have political importance. They are peopled by dialect-speakers, who are conscious of their difference from the central plain people. In the case of the Lao of the northeast, this linguistic and cultural difference is reinforced by some feeling of kinship with Lao in Laos and by the fact that the region is economically less rich and developed than central or northern Thailand. Political figures from the northeast seem to stand or fall on the vigor with which they oppose the government. Such opposition has often taken the form of more or less radical "leftist" ideology, although it has as often been pure oppositionism. The consistent ingredient has always been opposition, and it may be assumed that such an attitude is necessary for success in politics in the northeast. This situation has earned the region a reputation for breeding radical politicians. Whether or not such a reputation is deserved is difficult to say.

Thus, generally speaking, ideological commitment has, so far at least, been something of a hindrance in Thai politics. Personal relationships of participants in the political system provide the binding cement of group action which is elsewhere provided by ideological agreement and association. So long as the system of personal relationships functions satisfactorily, there is no need for the less flexible modes of ideological agreement. The successful functioning of the system is based upon the monopoly of power by the bureaucratic group. This monopoly in turn depends upon the political passivity of the public. For the moment, there is no large-scale political activity beyond the bureaucracy, and extragovernmental organizations are primitive and powerless.

Political parties have appeared only for brief intervals since the beginning of the constitutional period. The first party to make itself known was the People's Party, which carried through the *coup d'état* of 1932. Very soon thereafter, however, the government decided that political parties would be premature in view of the state of Thai politics. Thereafter the People's Party became a club, and no parties were permitted. The rather fluid situation at the end of World War II permitted various factions to express themselves publicly.[52] These were, however, little more than vehicles for the personalities of different leaders.[53] Following the return of the military in late 1947, they again tended to disappear.

At the end of 1955, the fad of the government again became democracy. Among other developments, an act dealing with political parties[54] was promulgated in anticipation of the general election in February 1957. This act authorized the formation of political parties, and the process went forward with great enthusiasm. Among the many parties registered were the main government party, organized by Phibun Songkhram; several other parties representing different cliques and supporting Phibun; the Democrat Party, headed by former Premier Khuang Aphaiwong and representing the conservative, semiroyalist faction; a number of left-wing parties, expressing some sort of Socialist feeling; and a good many other splinters representing local personalities making noise about themselves. Only two parties —the government party and the Democrat Party—nominated candidates on a nation-wide scale in the February 1957 election. Others entered candidates in the locality where their faction had some following.

The loose structure of party organization and the strength of the individual member's position was clearly demonstrated by the collapse of Phibun's big party after the September 1957 *coup d'état*. In the December election, however, more than half the parliamentary members of the party were re-elected as independents. The combination of the individual member's control over his own personal provincial organization with the personality orientation of the great bulk of the voters makes a substantial obstacle to the development of strong party organizations.

In addition, for the time being, other popular organizations, such as labor unions, cooperative societies, and similar extragovernmental pressure groups, are inchoate and virtually powerless. The history of associations of workingmen is a long one, but their political significance has been minor. Because until recent years the great majority of workers, and an even greater majority of organized workers, were Chinese, they were permitted no role in the political system.[55] Until the post-World War II period, labor organizations were apparently for the most part workmen's benevolent societies, which occasionally put pressure on employers by strikes, but primarily provided insurance and protection against complete economic disaster.[56] This form of organization is characteristic of Chinese associations, and it was to be expected that Chinese workers in Thailand would protect themselves in this manner.

Following the war, somewhat more elaborate labor organizations appeared. The first federation of workmen's organizations, the Central Labor Union (CLU), was formed in 1946 and claimed to represent fifty-one unions. Various writers have stated that the federation was founded with the backing of the political faction headed by Nai Pridi Phanomyong. At first dominated by Thai leadership, although the rank and file was Chinese,[57] it later came under Chinese leadership. Apparently influenced strongly, or even controlled, by Chinese Communists, the CLU in 1949 became a member of the World Federation of Trade Unions (WFTU).[58]

In the last few years the CLU has fallen on bitter days and is now apparently dissolved.

Meanwhile, in 1948, with the return to power of Field Marshal Phibun Songkhram and the military group, the government had taken the initiative in forming an all-Thai labor federation, now known as the Thai National Trade Union Congress (TNTUC). The federation was at first avowedly a government-sponsored and -led organization with a substantial number of army and police officers among its directors. At the time of its affiliation with the International Confederation of Free Trade Unions (ICFTU) in 1950, some effort was required to give it the air of an independent trade-union confederation, although its official connections necessarily continued. The TNTUC has a membership of Thai workers exclusively and has as a policy the promotion of the welfare of Thai workers over others, i.e., Chinese. The exclusively Thai nationality of the membership resulted in a heavy proportion of agricultural workers, fishermen, and tricycle taxi drivers, none of whom has the normal problems of wages and hours. The TNTUC has been most active in promoting patriotic and social interests among the membership and the public.[59]

The TNTUC having successfully stripped the older CLU of its Thai membership, the military group in power turned its attention to the remainder of the labor force. In 1954 the Free Workman's Association was established with the backing of the director general of the police. Going after the strongholds of the CLU—the rice mill workers and stevedores— and placing emphasis on the fact that workers of all nationalities were welcome,[60] the Free Workman's Association set out to destroy the CLU. Its real success is difficult to judge, since the dissolution of the CLU may be more apparent than real.

The consistent pattern of labor organizations has been, however, from the top down. It appears that the initiative for all three labor federations came from Thai government groups. This indicates that the political leadership is not unmindful of the potential role of labor in politics. The total passivity of the workers to the manipulation of their organizations, however, is the significant factor of the moment. Although the leadership of the country is able in some form to anticipate labor's power, the workers have not as a group a sense of this power. The result is that labor organizations as yet express the worker's interests only in the most particular "pork-chop" style of immediate demands for specific grievances. On the other hand, the labor federations are available to groups in political power for the dissemination of propaganda and the domination of worker opinion, such as it may be. Insofar as these unions may be said to have any ideology, it is that of social conciliation and respect for authority. For example, in a labor dispute in 1957, in which the Standard Vacuum Oil Company threatened to close its installation rather than yield to certain demands of the workers, the workers called upon the Premier for aid. He, in turn, assured them that "the Government [was] looking after their interests,"[61] and they went back to work. This looking to the sources of authority to settle disputes is characteristic of the Thai attitude toward conflict and revealing of the popular attitude toward the state and political authority.

The Labor Act, which became effective at the beginning of 1957, is the first law regulating the role of labor organizations as such. This comprehensive law was drafted and passed because foreign, particularly American, labor advisers urged it. The anticipation of the possible future social role of organized labor is as much a result of observation of labor in other nations as of concern for the real internal situation in the kingdom. When it is understood that the wage labor sector of the labor force is no more than one-eighth of the total, that of these no more than 15 per cent are claimed as union members, that of these a substantial part are agricultural laborers working for small proprietors, and that unions are in many cases sponsored by the state, it is reasonable to presume that the political role they are playing at present is a small one. The provision of the Labor Act which prohibits the spending of union funds for political purposes (Section 74) is little more than a supersafeguard against a possible danger.

Other extragovernmental organizations also demonstrate the paternalistic and bureaucratic nature of the Thai political system. For example, the cooperative movement, which is about forty years old, has been from the beginning a government-sponsored institution.[62] The rural credit cooperative is the most important type. These institutions, which are based upon government capital, have been developed in a most conservative fashion. They are small, cautious, and solvent; but because of these qualities, the membership is made up of the most conservative elements of the conservative peasantry. Ingram states that the greatest need in the cooperative movement is for what might be called the spirit of cooperation.[63] The members view the institution as a paternalistic organization, not as their own mode of self-help and expression. The government views the system as a stabilizing instrument of some importance, having recently raised the Department of Cooperatives to the ministry level. But the extent of the movement has been so limited that it should not be considered as either politically or socially significant.

An extreme example of the bureaucratic quality of extragovernmental organizations is the Teacher's Association. Organized by the Ministry of Education, the Association has all teachers as members. It is, in a sense, a transmission belt of information to teachers as persons rather than as officials. Its activities are paternalistic and informational, and enable the government to keep in contact with a significant group of social leaders.

Organization techniques in the milling and marketing of rice, while difficult to document, are sufficiently clear to be useful as evidence of the manner in which economic groups are integrated into the political system. Historically, rice milling and trading have been in the hands of aliens, mainly Chinese. In recent years, having found this arrangement somewhat unsatisfactory for both nationalistic and political reasons, the government has been moving into the business with such organizations as the Thai Rice Company, a semipublic corporation.[64] This movement is certainly designed to break the monopoly of uncontrolled interests in one phase of the country's major industry. At the same time, private millers and traders are associated with each other and often with Thai political figures, and so far as can be seen their relationship to the government is on the bureaucratic level. Negotiations are carried on between millers or associations of millers and the Rice Office quietly and without appeal to the public.

In sum, tradition—and success in fulfilling the demands of that tradition —has protected the bureaucracy from external popular pressure. There are two aspects to the traditional role of the Thai government and officials. On the one hand, the popular attitude has been, and continues to be, one of deference to the government and officials.[65] This attitude of deference has been strengthened by religious sanctions, while counterallegiances have been discouraged or nonexistent because of the total integration of society in the state. On the other hand, the tradition has a large element of benevolence and paternalism. Since the reign of King Chulalongkǫn (1868–1910), this aspect of the government's role has been revived and strengthened under severe external pressure upon the nation. At the time of the overthrow of royal power in 1932, the bureaucratic group, of course, made much of the benevolent role that it would play in the new democratic state.

This tradition is essential, but not sufficient, to explain the present security of the bureaucratic government from popular pressure. It is also necessary to point out again that in some substantial measure the bureaucracy has been successful in its role. Thai society as a whole has been protected and insulated from crisis. Independence has been maintained. Internal peace has been maintained. While it would be easy to exaggerate the positive benefits that the government has brought to the general population, there have been some advances. Public education has been spread throughout the kingdom. Transportation development has gone forward. Cooperatives, irrigation projects, and the like are under way. And the negative benevolence of the government is considerable. It rests lightly upon the general population. Direct taxes upon the rural population and the bureaucracy range from minimal to nonexistent. The villages of the nation know only the schoolteacher as a resident official. The demands of the state are felt primarily only in the conscription of young men into the military services. It is this conservative policy, successfully prosecuted, that has kept Thailand as serene as it has been.

MARXISM IN THAILAND?

There are, as we have seen, a number of important social, economic, and political reasons to explain why Marxism has in general had an unsympathetic and uncomprehending reception from the Thai. The emphasis upon class solidarity and class conflict, upon economic rewards and material values, upon discipline and revolution in politics which is the heart of Marxism—all this is alien to Thailand. Nevertheless, a few manifestations of Marxism, or more exactly Socialism in its broadest definition, have appeared. Through a somewhat detailed examination of the Thai application of Marxist or Socialist ideas, a further critique of the role of Marxist ideology in the kingdom will emerge.

Since, for all practical purposes, the Communists have been permanently underground, it is not possible to do more about their role than to connect a few isolated events with a web of speculation. Aside from the shadowy Thai Communist Party, whose activities are practically impossible to follow, Communism in Thailand has been almost a complete monopoly of Chinese and Vietnamese.[66] As such, the activities of the Communists have been bound up with the revolutionary situation in China and Viet Nam, and with the welfare of these national minorities in Thailand. At the same time, the anti-Communism of the Thai government has been linked and confused with the national policy of restriction and control of these alien minority groups.

The efforts of the Chinese and Vietnamese Communists in Thailand have been mainly among their own people, although from time to time there have been broad appeals for support among the Thai.[67] Apparently, the alien Communists, until recently, did not find it convenient or profitable to work with the Thai Communist Party, perhaps because their immediate purposes and strategies have been in conflict.[68] Thompson and Adloff (p. 52) have credited the fact that the Communists of Thailand have been almost exclusively alien as a potent factor in the Thai disinterest in Marxism. While there is doubtless some weight in this argument, it appears to be neither necessary nor sufficient. In other countries where similar national antagonism between groups exists, historical and social factors have overridden this situation, and Communism has flourished. Thailand's peculiar experience with the modern world, however, in which tradition has provided solutions to pressing problems, really defeated the Communists before they started.

Communist activities have unquestionably had their effect among the Chinese in Thailand. It is difficult to judge the extent or importance of these efforts because they have been so deeply clandestine. However, the fact that the big Chinese labor organization, the CLU, was affiliated with the WFTU and that the Communists have kept a daily newspaper in operation are indications of Communist activity. During 1951, 1952, and 1953 the Thai government cracked down on alleged Chinese Communist activity in schools and closed down *Chuan Min Pao*, the old Communist paper. There were also reports of money-raising operations in Bangkok in those years and efforts to encourage students to go to China to study. Indications are that, since the Bandung conference, agitational activities among the Chinese in Bangkok have been lessened.

Much more can be said about Socialism in Thailand, as its adherents have not been forced underground as have the Communists. Socialism made its first public appearance in Bangkok in 1932, in the national economic policy proposed by Nai Pridi Phanomyong, one of the important figures of modern Thai politics and the intellectual leader of the *coup d'état* of 1932. In sum, however, Pridi's career has been erratic, futile, and almost tragic. At no point was he able to organize a base of power sufficient to counterbalance the strength of his antagonists, the army group. And when his opportunity came, he failed to muster the decisiveness and direction required to rally the diverse elements to his support.

A brilliant law student in his youth, Pridi acquired his Socialism and also his first taste of political organization and conflict while studying in France on a state scholarship after World War I. Together with other Thai students in Paris, Pridi formed a club which took it upon itself to complain to the Thai minister that Thai students in France were being discriminated against as far as government allowances were concerned. This enraged the minister, who reported the matter to Bangkok. Apparently Pridi's scholarship was nearly canceled as a result of this matter. He was, however, permitted to finish his studies for the degree of Doctor of Law.[69]

This student escapade was a precursor of Pridi's career as a political leader. Upon his return to Bangkok, he was appointed lecturer at the Law Academy, and there he built a circle of friends and followers among students and faculty. This group, of which various members adopted somewhat leftist views, was one of the factions joining in the *coup d'état* of 1932.

Within a few months of the *coup d'état*, Pridi presented to the government an economic plan—the basis of his reputation as a Socialist. This plan was unquestionably radical in the solutions it proposed for the supposed economic problems of Thailand. Its alleged Communism became the rallying cry of the conservative-royalist group in the government, the threat of Communism being the ostensible cause for the dissolution of the first parliament. This in its turn furnished the provocation for the second coup in 1933.

During the hue and cry against Communism, both Pridi and the government found it convenient for him to retire from the scene, which he did by taking a trip to France. When the government of the second coup group was securely in power, Pridi was called home and the government convened a special commission to clear him of charges of Communism. This it did, while condemning his economic plan. During the remaining years before World War II, Pridi held high office, including the Finance and Foreign ministries. When in 1941 the government, under the leadership of Phibun, decided to adopt a pro-Japanese policy, Pridi was retired from active politics and appointed a regent. From this position he acted as leader of the anti-Japanese "Free Thai" movement within the country, recruiting members and aiding the Allied cause as he could.

With the fall of the Phibun government in 1944, Pridi's career entered a period of great opportunity which ended in disaster. In the role of Senior Statesman and also as Prime Minister, he was the acknowledged leader of the country. He found it difficult to get a grip on the complex postwar situation, however, and the mysterious shooting of the young king in 1946 damaged his career irreparably. He was driven out of power and into exile by the *coup d'état* of 1947, which returned Phibun to power. Since then, Pridi has remained in exile, with the brief exception of his abortive attempt to return to power by force in 1949. Meanwhile the core of his political group has been eliminated from the political scene by a series of mysterious deaths and disappearances. At present he is living in China as a political refugee.

From the point of view of ideological bent, Pridi's career indicates little rigid adherence to any particular mode. Following the discard of his economic plan, he appears to have abandoned any attempt at radicalism. He used none of his powerful positions, either before or after World War II, to forward any ideology, so far as can be told from the available evidence. In fact, his career indicates the kind of pragmatic outlook characteristic of the Thai bureaucratic class. Two events may illustrate this contention. In 1946, at the moment when his power was at its height, Pridi chose to abandon any effort to expand the play of democratic forces because he wanted first to safeguard his own position. Thus, he pushed through a revision of the constitution which established a second house in the National Assembly, to be elected by the lower house. While this action may have been motivated by a desire to protect himself from the military, it also limited the flexibility of the Assembly and the effectiveness of elections.[70] And in 1949, Pridi turned his back on the struggle to establish representative government in the kingdom by trying to meet the military on their own terms. He appears to have been instrumental

in planning and organizing the abortive coup in that year. The total effect
of this move was to make legitimate the use of force in the power struggle.

An examination of Pridi's economic plan reveals some of the peculiarities of his mind and also of his Socialism. In the first paragraphs of the
pamphlet which explained and justified his plan,[71] Pridi gave a brief account of the intellectual process which created it:

> In seeking a means to promote the welfare of our people I have taken into
> consideration not only their present mode of existence but also *those peculiar
> traits which characterize them as a nation*. I have come to the conclusion that,
> for the advancement of their well-being, only one course is feasible: namely, the
> government must undertake to administer a national economic policy by which
> the economic system will be subdivided into diversified co-operative associations.
>
> My conclusion is not the result of my adherence to any particular social
> philosophy. I have borrowed elements of value from various systems whenever
> I found in them *something appropriate to Thailand*. These ideas I have organized
> into a co-ordinated policy.[72]

Pridi's economic policy was based on the assumption that there were
two basic economic problems facing the kingdom. The first was the problem of personal insecurity—the insecurity of poverty, old age, and sick-
ness. In capsule form the solution for this problem was, as Pridi saw it,
for "all persons who are citizens by birth . . . to be insured by the government so that from birth to death, regardless of whether they are children, are ill or crippled, or incapacitated for work, they will have food,
clothing and shelter, in other words, the necessities of life."[73] In order to
provide this insurance, it would be necessary for the government to pay
"all of the people" a wage. "The plan to issue monthly wages to all of the
people is peculiarly well-adapted to the special character of the Siamese
people," Pridi wrote. "It is well known that all the Siamese want to work
for the government and that they like to receive regular salary."[74]

The second problem he identified as inefficient techniques of agricultural production and wasted labor. "It is apparent," Pridi said, "that the
peasants, who form a majority of the population of Siam, till the fields, on
the average, not more than six months out of the year (inclusive of plough-
ing, sowing, harvesting, etc.). Thus six months of their time is wasted."[75]
Pridi suggested as a solution for this inefficiency that the government buy
up all agricultural land and direct the national agriculture through state-
sponsored cooperative societies of which the farmers would be salaried
employees.[76] At the center, the government would take charge of general
planning,[77] protection against foreign competition,[78] and finance.[79]

It is clear, as Pridi made explicit, that the thinking behind this plan was
not Marxist. In political method, it was bureaucratic rather than revolu-

tionary. It combined authoritarianism with paternalism. "We may compare our Siamese people to children," Pridi wrote. "The government will have to urge them forward by means of authority applied directly or indirectly to get them to cooperate in any kind of economic endeavor."[80] In his economic analysis he specifically denied any influence of the "Surplus Value" theory.[81] His analysis was phrased in terms of insecurity and inefficiency. On the subject of class conflict, he had this to say: "There are prophets who say that class war may break out any time that the economic situation changes for the worse and poverty becomes rampant. We should take steps at the outset to protect ourselves from such an eventuality."[82]

Pridi was, of course, aware of Marxist thought, but he found it unsuited to Thailand. Instead, he relied upon an eclectic solution for economic problems as he understood them. "This plan is not Communistic!" he said. "It is a combination of capitalism and socialism. Communists reading it would find much to object to."[83] And further: "My policy includes points selected from many economic theories, which I have co-ordinated and adapted to fit the needs of Siam."[84] In the light of such statements, it is difficult, and unnecessary, to fit Pridi's thought into any strict ideological position. It is possible to admire his pragmatic effort to adapt some elements of socialism to Thailand in his economic plan.

Vague and incomplete as it was, Pridi's economic plan was the occasion for the enactment of specifically anti-Communist legislation, in 1933, shortly after the coup that eliminated royal power from the Thai political scene. The bulk of the participants in the *coup d'état* had been out of sympathy with any radical change in society. In the thrust and parry of factions in the early years, the straw man of Communism became a public issue. The first premier under the constitution, Phraya Manopakǫn, was not a member of the group promoting the coup and was not much in sympathy with it. He was offered the premier's office in order to conciliate the king and the conservative civil service. The task of forestalling any radical dynamic in the development of the coup fell to him. In the course of events, Phraya Manopakǫn was carried away by his enthusiasm or fears, however, and ended by proroguing the parliament over the issue of communism. At the same time, he enacted under emergency powers the Act Concerning Communism, which was designed in effect to outlaw Pridi's economic plan as well as the advocacy of "communism" or "Communist doctrine." These terms were defined in the act as follows:

Communism means the economic system or theory which rests upon the total or partial abolition of the right of private property, actual ownership being ascribed to the community as a whole or to the state.

Communist doctrine means any doctrine which implies the advocation of nationalization of land, or nationalization of industry, or nationalization of capital, or nationalization of labour.[85]

This rather broad act was more in the nature of declaration of government policy than the creation of a tool of repression, the penal code already providing adequate legal weapons against subversive or revolutionary activity. The policy was maintained by the government of Phraya Phahon Phayuhasena, the leader of the coup group, who came to power after the second coup in 1933. Upon taking office, he announced: "No element of Communism shall ever creep into Siam as long as I possess any influence in the government."[86] The policy continued through the thirties and during World War II. Although it is difficult to assess the effect of steady repression of revolutionary thought, it is clear that this policy has played its role in discouraging any lively interest in Marxism.

In the immediate postwar years, Thai policy toward Communism became something of an international issue. At that time the foremost diplomatic problem of the kingdom was to re-establish its position as a respectable member of international society. Initially this involved negotiating a settlement with Great Britain. This done, Thailand's next prime diplomatic objective became membership in the United Nations organization. In this process the Soviet Union made an issue of the Thai policy of anti-Communism, and it was felt necessary to repeal the Act Concerning Communism.[87] This reversal was carried out with some reluctance. Pridi, premier at the time, is quoted as having said in regard to this development:

Politics and diplomacy are two different things. Whether we agree with another country's beliefs has nothing to do with diplomatic relations. I wish to insist that Siam can never be a Communist country because our customs, conventions and history differ greatly from that of Russia. Before the Soviet revolution peasants and poorer classes in Europe were tools of the land owners and capitalists. The hardships which these poor people had to suffer gave rise to Communism. I have studied enough economics to be in a position to say that Communism can never happen in this country and that we have nothing to fear about that. I wish to make this point clear because I was once branded as a Communist.[88]

However, the repeal of the anti-Communist act, while opposed by some members of parliament, was more a gesture than a political reality. As has been mentioned, the penal code was adequate to meet any Communist threat from within. The political significance of the recognition of the Soviet Union in 1947 and the exchange of missions appears to have been slight. There is no available evidence that the Soviet embassy has provided any substantial help to local Communists nor carried on any undue activities. Soviet information activities have been small, as well. It is probably correct to conclude that the main overt Soviet interest in Thailand is, at least for the present, commercial.[89]

Anti-Communist policy began to come to the front again with Phibun's return to power. And after the victory of Communism in China, Phibun's anti-Communism became very useful both internally and externally. The anti-Chinese attitude of the government could now be most smoothly merged with its anti-Communist policy. This policy reached its climax at the end of 1952 when the government passed a new anti-Communist act,[90] this being accompanied by a general roundup of antagonistic Chinese, remnants of the Pridi group, and other opposition politicians and writers.[91]

Whether or not the policy of repression was effective against Communists is problematical, because the realities involved in the Thai Communist Party are hopelessly obscure. In 1932, during the *coup d'état*, leaflets and pamphlets appeared in the streets signed by "The Communist Party of Siam."[92] Although it is reported that this literature created consternation among Thai conservatives, nothing further was heard of party activities for some time. After the war, in one of the few legal Communist publications, it was stated that a group of Communists had been in existence for twenty years, that is, from about 1925.[93] It was not until 1935, however, that the group was organized as a party. Its initial purpose was to oppose imperialism and feudalism and, subsequently, specifically to oppose Phibun and the Japanese. In a peculiar attempt to assert the party's importance, the pamphlet claimed that in the decade 1935–45 over five hundred members had been injured or died in prison.[94] The remainder of the statement of the history of the party was devoted to self-criticism of the party's failure and a declaration of firm resolution to do better in the future.[95] The objective of the Communist effort was stated to be initially Socialism and then Communism. The level of the pamphlet's ideological sophistication was indicated by the definition of Communism in the classic apothegm of Marx—from each according to his ability, to each according to his need.[96]

The discussion then moved to a statement of the immediate party program outlined in the following ten points:

1. This party upholds democratic principles and is ready to cooperate with any political party or person who upholds democracy for the purpose of reconstruction of our country, to bring it perfection and happiness, and to make it truly democratic and independent.

2. To have the members of parliament elected directly by the people. To extend the election of local governments to districts, communes and rural areas throughout the country. To abolish the second category members of municipal councils in order to give to councils at every level the power to elect their own administrative organizations.

3. To give to all Thai nationals over 18 years of age the right to vote and to be candidates for election, regardless of sex, property, or educational qualifications.

4. To have local governments recognize the equality of national minorities and the right of these minorities to self-government.

5. To uphold the people's right to freedom of assembly, speech writing, publishing, advertising, religion, demonstration, establishment of political parties, association and organization.

6. (a) To improve the standard of living of the laboring class, through increasing of wages, fixing eight hours work, social insurance, relieving unemployment, and forbidding cruel treatment to apprentices.

(b) In order that soldiers, police and minor officials shall have capability, discipline and shall sincerely observe their duties, we must promote morality and raise their standard of living.

(c) Those who have independent occupations and cooperatives must be aided and protected.

7. To abolish heavy and troublesome taxes. Tax collection should be placed on a basis of social justice (surtax) and should protect national industry; and give to foreign nationals equal and reasonable opportunity for economic investment.

8. Agriculture must be promoted; farm rentals and the interest charged to farmers be reduced; help the farmers who have troubles; support the establishment of farmers' organizations, cooperatives of producers and consumers, throughout the kingdom. Poor farmers must be given implements and paddy seed free of charge.

9. The standard of living for teachers must be improved; primary education must be promoted, with special stress on social studies. Vocational training must also be improved. Education must be given to every uneducated person. Textbooks will have to be developed following democratic and scientific principles.

10. To have closer relations with other nations, especially Soviet Russia, China, England and America. Take the side of the UN. Punish war criminals. Get rid of fascists. To secure world peace. Give protection and rights to foreigners.[97]

The two years immediately following World War II were years of considerable political freedom, and there was active organization of political parties during that time. The Communists came into the open briefly to make something of a bid for public recognition and support. They published two newspapers and ran candidates for parliament under the label of Proletarian Party.[98] It was at this time that Prasœt Sapsunthon, described by one acute, but lighthearted, observer as Thailand's "one-man Communist Party,"[99] was in the parliament as representative from a southern province. There is no evidence that the Communist bid met with any success. After the coup of 1947, Prasœt retired to write a book about the new society and later fled the country, reportedly for China. From the immediate postwar years until 1953, the Communists maintained a publishing house—Mahachon—in Bangkok. Along with a fortnightly entitled

Mahachon, several Communist pamphlets are reported to have been published. These are no longer available. In the past two years, a few leaflets signed by the "Central Committee of the Thai Communist Party" have been mailed to students. The tenor of these messages is a general attack upon American imperialism, and to a lesser extent on the government, plus other standard Communist sentiments. Several daily and weekly newspapers are being published at present which may be aided by Communist money. Their major theme is anti-Americanism with no clear-cut domestic line.[100]

Aside from the Proletarian and Communist parties, which cannot be denied their Marxist orientation, the parties of 1945–47 are almost impossible to classify according to ideology. They were really appendages or manifestations of the various cliques and supported the clique leaders.[101] The return of the army to power in 1947 had little ideological meaning. Phibun's anti-Communism was well known.[102] This attitude, however, was more a matter of international relations and internal security than of ideology. Phibun has expressed himself at times as inclining toward mild Socialism and is reported to have said he was planning to organize a Socialist party in 1948.[103]

In the period between the *coup d'état* of 1947 and the end of 1952, there was a small but vociferous group of anti-government leftists active mainly in the Bangkok press. The focus of their work came to be the circulation of the Stockholm Peace Appeal and the organization of the National Peace Committee of Thailand. This sort of agitational work for peace, the abolition of atomic weapons, and similar sentiments came to an abrupt end late in 1952, when the government rounded up over a hundred suspects in what has come to be called the Peace Revolt case.[104] During the following summer, fifty-four defendants were tried as members of the National Peace Committee and the National Liberation Movement on the charge of conspiring to overthrow the government. During the trial it was revealed that there was a revolt plan which involved young military officers and intellectuals. Documents in the case showed the influence of Marxist-Leninist theories of imperialism, but its importance was difficult to assess.[105] There was also evidence that some Communists had played a part in the affair, although, in keeping with the times, the government doubtless emphasized this aspect of its case. After the trial, leftist politics largely lapsed. The prisoners were all amnestied in May 1957, in connection with the celebrations of the 2500th year of the Buddhist Era.

With the passage of the Political Parties Act of 1955,[106] the way was opened for the expression of political allegiance, sentiment, and ideology. This act, passed as a preliminary to the general election of 1957, encour-

aged the multiplication of parties by requiring only that five hundred
voters petition for registration. The result has been the appearance of
over twenty so-called parties. Among these parties, one or perhaps two—
the Democrats and Thammatipat—can trace lineage to 1947.

From the point of view of this study, the most interesting development
of the recent period of party activity has been the appearance of what
might be called the "new left." It manifests itself in the form of a number
of small parties and groups with a "Socialist" orientation and a so-called
neutralist or anti-imperialist foreign policy. The more important of these
groups are the Economist Party, the Free Democrat Party, and the Peace
Fighter (Santichon) group. Also involved are the Hyde Park Movement
Party, the Social Democrat Party, the Labour Party, the Socialist Party,
and several other tiny splinters. These groups are unquestionably trying
to obtain recognition on the basis of ideology rather than as supporters
of this or that active political leader. Their effort, however, has not yet
been a pronounced success, although the primary tune of anti-Western
nationalism and peace has struck a responsive chord in some small circles.
On the other hand, the traditional emphasis on personality and indifference
to ideology have required these groups to play the political game along
fairly usual lines.

For electoral purposes, a number of these groups in 1957 formed a
Socialist Front.[107] The Front is built around the Economist Party and
Thep Chotinuchit. He is a member of parliament from the northeast who
gained considerable fame in 1956 by a much-publicized journey to Communist China made more or less in defiance of the government. Upon his
return, this adventure landed him in jail and on the front pages. The case
was subsequently dropped.

Thep, while calling himself a Socialist, quite accurately denies being
a Marxist. He also repudiates the policies of Pridi Phanomyong as being
"state socialist." Thep's definition of Socialism is: "direct action by the
state in the economic realm for the economic betterment of the people."
The announced policy of the Economist Party places great emphasis on
full parliamentary government and local self-government in the political
realm. As for economics, emphasis is upon justice and efficiency promoted
by the state. The party policy as it has been published is vague about the
limits, if any, upon the state's economic role. For example, it is said that
"with regard to production, the state shall promote, advise, initiate and
assist or control production including transportation and distribution" and
that "family industry and large-scale industry will be organized in a big
way." The policy has none of the essential elements of Marxism—a view
of society consisting of antagonistic classes, a criticism of capitalism as a
system of exploitation, or a condemnation of private property.

The Peace Fighters are a deliberately unorganized group made up for the most part of graduates of the Peace Revolt case of 1952–53. It began to take shape soon after an amnesty in 1957 and entered an indeterminate number of candidates as independents in the December 1957 general election. In the Bangkok constituency, where the neutralist "peace" sentiment was most likely to attract the sympathy of student elements and other parts of the politically more alert urban population, the Peace Fighters entered a full slate of candidates in collaboration with the Socialist Front. The most prominent name was that of Uthǫn Phonlakhun, editor of *Khao Phap*, the leading leftist daily. The group received strong support in the leftist press for its anti-imperialist slogans, but ran head-on into public distrust of "Communists" and polled only a small vote.

The internal structure of this group, its size, and its strength are obscure. It is certainly numerically small. Members seem to be mostly newspapermen and writers. If, as is believed by serious observers, the group is a genuine Communist-supported front, its overt ideology is no more than tactical. Great emphasis is put upon nonviolence, friendship for all social groups and foreign nations, and social justice. The line of attack, however, is in keeping with contemporary Communist views on peaceful coexistence and international noncommitment.

The Free Democrat Party was formed by a small group of parliamentary members from northeastern provinces. Most of them were at one time left-wing supporters of Pridi Phanomyong. As such, however, the party tends to be on the right of the new left. The party policy is most interesting in its attack on the present political system: "We feel that in the conduct of political activities for the welfare of the people it is necessary to understand that principle or policy has a higher importance than personal relationships . . ."[108]

Even while cooperating with the Socialists, the Free Democrat Party policy explicitly endorses the value of private initiative and enterprise in industry and agriculture. The state is given a role in encouraging and aiding such enterprise both directly and by means of a sound fiscal system.

Two other parties of the new left are as clearly non-Marxist. The Social Democrat Party, under the leadership of Suthep Satčhakhun, has enunciated a policy of economic justice based upon political democracy. The party policy shows no theory of either class or property. Suthep attributes much of his Socialist inspiration to the "ideals of Buddhism and Christianity." His conception of economic organization is a mixture of agricultural cooperatives, private business, and state enterprise, combined for the purpose of the "progress and prosperity of the people and nation."

The Hyde Park movement developed, ironically, out of an inspiration of Prime Minister Phibun Songkhram after his return from a world tour in 1955. He was evidently impressed by the public speakers in London's Hyde Park as an institution of democracy.[109] He ordained that Thailand should have such an institution in the central park of Bangkok. The Thai public found the speakers' efforts well adapted to their taste for fun and slander. The movement prospered and became a vent for anti-government sentiment. Eventually it was suppressed, more or less. In the process, however, the Hyde Park Movement Party developed. This party is dedicated to the following aims:

1. For complete independence and democracy.
2. A state of the people, by the people, and for the people.
3. The people are supreme.
4. United we live, divided we die.[110]

This group is a member of the Socialist Front, but its Socialism seems to extend little beyond the claim that it is a party with the interests of the people at heart. A popular campaign slogan of Hyde Park speakers is "Only a farmer knows the problems of the farmer, only a worker knows the problems of the worker." The movement has no real organization, and some of its most prominent members have deserted to other parties.

The Socialist Party claims to be the extreme left wing of the Socialist Front. It is the only part of that alliance led by workingmen. The leadership has stated its general principle to be social and economic revolution by legal means. It is the only party on the political scene today which speaks even "off the record" of revolution in any form. The party views its program as a long-term one. The details of the program remain vague and obscure—whether naïvely or intentionally is unknown. One aspect of the party's thinking is clear—that Socialism must conform to the nation's temper. Its view of the Socialist revolution is a change of the total society and economy in accordance with Socialist thought, "in the Thai way."

The Labour Party seeks mainly to give political expression to the presumed desires of trade-union members. Prakǫb Tolaklam is the party leader.[111] He and the other officers are activists in the Thai National Trade Union Congress and the Free Workman's Association. It is therefore unique among left-wing parties in having a potential base of organizational strength. The quality of such strength is, of course, problematical because of the undeveloped nature of Thai trade-unions and the relatively small degree of influence that Congress leaders have in the unions. While the Labour Party subscribes to the anti-government and anti-imperialist policies which are associated with the Socialist Front, it is not a Socialist party. The Marxist element in party thinking is little more than a distant derivation. The first principle of the party policy is: "To assist all labourers to receive the just fruits of their labour and to give rise to a democratic society on the pattern of advanced countries."[112]

These parties and groups are all united in opposition to the present government and, to a large extent, to the present political system. They share a policy of condemning the role of the military institutions in government and the devices, such as appointed members of parliament, which forestall the development of popular participation in politics. They are also united in condemning the role that the United States plays in Thailand, particularly its support of the armed services and its restriction on relations with China. These two themes run through the public pronouncements of the Socialist Front, the Peace Fighters, the Free Democrats, and all leftist groups and individuals. Yet the fact that these tiny parties insist upon maintaining their separate identities is probably symptomatic of the individualistic and competitive nature of Thai politics rather than of ideological hairsplitting.

The actual political strength of the new left is difficult to measure because the significance of election results is impossible to interpret. Between the February and December, 1957, general elections the seats held by left-wing members dropped by one-third (from twenty-one to fourteen). There can be no question that this was in part a result of the removal of Field Marshal Phibun and his clique from the scene. Persons of different political complexion had been moved to cooperation by a strong current of opposition to the former premier and his reputation for corruption and cruelty. The leftists continue to try to rally similar feeling against the present government but without the cooperation of other groups. The orthodoxy of the Socialist, not to mention Marxist, element of these parties is for the moment questionable. It is questionable to such a degree, as a matter of fact, that a representative of the Asian Socialist Conference visiting Bangkok after the Bombay meeting in 1956 found it difficult to decide if the parties are "true Socialists."[113]

The meager influence of Marxism in Thailand is evident also in the very small number of publications to appear which are either avowedly Marxist or crypto-Marxist. Perhaps the most meaningful fact is, however, that there are no translations of Marxist classics into Thai. The basic Marxist literature is therefore closed to all but the most highly educated group in the society. The same fact also explains succinctly why such manifestations of quasi-Marxism as have appeared on a popular level have been vague and incomplete. Although it is impossible to be certain that no clandestine translations exist, the consensus is that virtually none has been made.

Efforts have been made, however, to bring some understanding of Marxism into the Thai language. The work of Supha Sirimanond, probably Thailand's leading Marxist intellectual, is the most important in this connection. Supha is a former journalist of some fame, Thailand's first international war correspondent, and a commentator upon world affairs. During World War II, Supha served in the Thai army as a private and later fled Thailand to join the "Free Thai" movement in India. After the war, at the time when his friend Pridi was in power, Supha joined the Thai diplomatic service and traveled throughout Europe and the U.S.S.R.

Supha explains that his interest in Marxism derived from his experiences as a private in the army and from his reading of John Reed's *Ten Days That Shook the World*. He then progressed to reading Marx and Engels, Lenin and Stalin, as well as Laski, Shaw, and other British Socialist writers. The basis for his interest in Marxism he describes as "sympathy for the under-privileged classes."

Supha's book *Khaphithalit* (*Capitalism*) appears to be the only serious attempt in Thai to explain Marxist theory to Thai readers. It is based on Marxist texts and amounts to a summary of Marx's critique of capitalism. The title is itself an indication of the author's opinion that Marxism is somehow alien and inapplicable to Thailand. His transliteration of a technical term in preference to seeking some approximate Thai equivalent is the result of a conscious decision that such equivalents would be not only inadequate but misleading. The book, published in a small edition in 1951, is now out of print.

Between 1949 and 1952, Supha was also editor and publisher of a monthly magazine called *Aksǫnsan* (*The Newsletter*). It was a magazine of news and comment into which was occasionally inserted an article on Marxist theory. The circulation of the magazine was small (less than 1,000).

Another Marxist book published within the last decade is Prasœt Sapsunthǫn's *Chi wa that* (*View of Life*). It is, however, not so much a theoretical work as a propaganda tract. The first third of the book is devoted to a formalistic, and not very illuminating, explanation of the Marxist theory of historical stages and social development. The remainder consists of a series of black-and-white contrasts between conditions in the "old society" and the "new society." In this context the author discusses such topics as work, economics, politics, religion, the monarchy, the family, sex, marriage, children, and so on. Since Prasœt is an avowed Communist and *Chi wa that* openly revolutionary in intent, the book was suppressed by the government and presumably had a very small circulation.

Class-conscious fiction is a genre of Thai literature dating from before World War II. Perhaps the first of such works was *Songkhram chi wit* (*Struggle of Life*), by Si Burapha (Kulab Saipradit). This novel, which was extremely popular, depicts the contrast between the luxurious life of the princes and the dismal life of the poor. Kulab is, like Supha, a jour-nalist. He was at one time the dean of the profession, having edited some of the greatest papers in Bangkok. Kulab has interested himself in politics as well as literature and is said by many to be a key figure in the confused scene of left-wing organizations. He was arrested, tried, and convicted on charges of Communist conspiracy in 1952.

This class-conflict fiction relies heavily on the simple opposition of wealth to poverty. The stories run to such either/or titles as "The Domain of Heaven and the Domain of Hell"[114] and "Darkness and Light."[115] Al-though it is impossible to assess the effect of this kind of literature, the fact that most readers are of the middle and upper income levels can be taken as indicating that these stories will not incite to rebellion very soon. In fact, it is likely that their appeal is based more on the high value placed on benevolence in Thai ethics than on class consciousness. As Supha Sirimanond said, they inspire "sympathy for the under-privileged classes."

It is this attitude of benevolence which explains the interest that certain Thai have taken in Marxism or quasi-Marxism. Their interest is most cer-tainly a matter of personality rather than a result of the logic of their ex-perience or situation. There is little consistency in the backgrounds of Pridi Phanomyong, the intellectual leader of a bureaucratic coup; Kulab Saipradit and Supha Sirimanond, journalists and personal friends; Thep Chotinuchit,[116] a lawyer and politician; Suthep Satčhakhun,[117] a business-man; Wisit Siphat,[118] leader of the Socialist Party, a worker.

CONCLUSION

The role of Marxism in Thailand is unimpressive because it has never been successfully adapted to, or associated with, any real social, economic, or political issue. The manifestations which have been examined have an isolated and individual quality which is out of the main stream of events in the country. Only recently did quasi-Marxists find an issue of some validity. That issue was opposition to the government of Phibun Song-khram and to the role that America played in the country in cooperation with that government. Whether this issue can be maintained or turned into a movement of any serious magnitude under present circumstances is questionable. It would appear that flirtation with Marxism by Thai politicians and intellectuals will continue to be a matter of personality.

This conclusion depends upon the persistence of the factors working against Marxism which have been here discussed. In recent history, the government of Thailand has been generally successful in coping with the problems of social, economic, and political change which have been a part of entering the modern world. It has been pointed out that this process amounts, in fact, to a revolution-in-process. But the pace has been so gradual that the necessary reintegrations of society have apparently followed in company. The characteristic Thai individualism and self-reliance have, no doubt, been important in keeping this process going smoothly. The Thai seems never to have been closed into a tight system of social organization and behavior. Rather he has traditionally had social room to move and accordingly the need to determine his own actions and attitudes. This characteristic has stood him in good stead in the face of change.

But the fact of the matter is that the degree of change has not actually been great. Social organization continues to be a system of personal statuses—a system which has over recent years perhaps become even more indeterminate and confused. The system of economic production and organization still rests on rice cultivation by the peasant proprietor. It is true that there has been an increase in specialization and in commercialization, but the cultivator still remains to a great extent self-sufficient. The village is still on the fringe of the political realm, largely untouched either positively or negatively by direct state action. In the background of this happy scene is a benevolent and luxuriant environment, a warm and wholesome climate, adequate land and water, and sufficient but not excessive population.

The fact that there is little discontent in Thai society is related to this situation. Particularly among the segments of society which provide leadership, continuing satisfaction (or at least belief in the possibility of satisfaction fairly soon) is important. It is reasonable to assume that on balance the satisfactions of the leadership or potential leadership gained in the present system are sufficient to outweigh discontent with certain aspects of the system. The demands of the articulate are within the limits of the system. Given such a background, the steady policy of repression, directed against whatever attempts have been made to express some more revolutionary demands, has been effective.

By a combination of geography, skill, determination, and luck, Thailand has been able to absorb the shocks of the past century. The penetration of alien, Western ideas and forces has been met with a successful process of adaptation and absorption. It is largely because of this success that Thailand has not needed to import the revolutions and revolutionary doctrines of the West to solve its new problems. It is this success that has blocked the penetration of Thailand by Marxism.

4

MARXISM IN VIET NAM*

I. MILTON SACKS

On September 2, 1945, the day of the Japanese surrender marking the end of World War II, the Democratic Republic of Viet Nam issued its Declaration of Independence.[1] The Republic proclaimed the reunification of Tonkin, Annam, and Cochinchina, constituting three of the five administrative divisions of French Indochina in prewar days.[2] This area, inhabited principally by Vietnamese,[3] is ethnically and linguistically separate from Laos and Cambodia, the other two divisions.

New nationalist states were coming into being throughout Southeast Asia, but it soon became clear that the situation in Viet Nam differed in one essential respect from that of Burma and Indonesia: in the new Viet Nam government, the commanding positions were held by a Communist minority. In fact, the very president of the new republic was Ho Chi Minh, alias Nguyen Ai Quoc, a veteran leader with twenty-five years of service in the international Communist movement.

In the next nine years, through peace and war, this Communist leadership in Viet Nam maintained its position and withstood French efforts to re-establish French sovereignty in Indochina. The Communist leaders

* The following chapter is adapted from my dissertation presented for the degree of Doctor of Philosophy at Yale University. Part of the necessary research was made possible through a Social Science Research Council Area Research Fellow Training award that enabled me to work in Paris for thirteen months in 1952–53 and support from the Yale University Southeast Asia Studies program. I must thank Harold R. Isaacs, Morris Watnick, and Irving Howe for their kindness in assisting me with advice that immeasurably improved the presentation. However, I bear complete and sole responsibility for the views expressed.

succeeded in keeping the support of many of the non-Communist nationalists with whom they had joined originally in 1945 to create the Democratic Republic of Viet Nam. In the end, it was only through the pressure of international negotiation and settlement that the Vietnamese Communists were denied the full fruits of their political and military victory by the partition of Viet Nam in 1954.[4] Even so, they became the undisputed masters of Viet Nam north of the seventeenth parallel, where they have since been building the Democratic Republic of Viet Nam as a People's Democracy—an integral unit of the Communist bloc of nations.

The unusual strength of Communism in Viet Nam bears investigation, since it serves as a case study of the influence of Marxism in a colonial area. The Vietnamese Communists have operated within a conceptual framework that is a Leninist-Stalinist variant of Marxism. In effect, the Vietnamese Communists combined the teachings of the Communist International with the Chinese Communist system of peasant-based military operations to win their eight-year war with France and consolidate their rule. It is only through an investigation of the historical influence of Marxism on the Vietnamese that present-day events in Viet Nam can be assessed. Such an investigation may lead to an understanding of the behavior of the leadership of the Democratic Republic of Viet Nam as it faces the problem of defining its relationship to neighboring Communist China. It may also help us to evaluate the factors influencing not only the Communist Democratic Republic of Viet Nam but also its southern competitor, the anti-Communist, American-supported Republic of Viet Nam.

THE INDIGENOUS ROOTS OF VIETNAMESE NATIONALISM

Before considering the development of the influence of Marxism in Viet Nam and the subsequent emergence of Marxism-Leninism as the official state doctrine of the Democratic Republic of Viet Nam, it would be well to give some attention to the political aspects of traditional Vietnamese society as it existed prior to the sixty years of French rule.[5] For it was then that the patterns of indigenous political thinking were shaped. Even though predominantly new institutions resulted from the impact of French rule on Vietnamese society, due weight must be given to the older political and religious conceptions that subtly influenced and pervaded the new structures.[6]

The French conquest did transform Viet Nam. It opened the door of a closed society to new ideas, notably such European concepts as individualism, social humanism, and Marxism. Yet, all of these new influences were absorbed into an ancient culture that had developed its own thought patterns. To this very day, the predominantly peasant population of Viet Nam reveals in its thinking the heritage of this historical past. Vietnamese nationalists who opposed French rule drew on this reservoir of ingrained political customs to gain popular support. And it is to these historical traditions that both contending Vietnamese regimes often turn today to justify their actions.

Another factor that should be borne in mind is the importance of Chinese influences in the development of Vietnamese society and its political institutions. For a thousand years, from the advent of the Christian Era, Viet Nam was directly under Chinese domination. During this period, Chinese cultural life left its mark on Vietnamese society, never to be erased, despite the achievement of Vietnamese independence in A.D. 931. The subsequent Vietnamese dynasties jealously guarded their separateness, but it was maintained by accepting a relationship of vassalage to the Chinese empire through a formal recognition of Chinese suzerainty. Although the Vietnamese developed an integrated national heritage of their own, they never lost their attachment to Chinese civilization, nor their awareness that it formed part of a broader culture that included Japan and Korea as well as their own country.

The Chinese successfully implanted the Confucian state pattern in Viet Nam together with its system of values. The governmental system in Viet Nam was characterized by the same convergence of political, legislative, and religious power, vested in a sovereign emperor who was assisted by a mandarin bureaucracy, as that which prevailed in China. Its principal units were the family system, the semiautonomous village, and the central state authority. The Vietnamese state, like China, was conceived of in magical and religious terms, as "the symbol of a world order and the expression of a system of proprieties in human and superhuman relationships."[7]

The basis of the social structure in traditional Viet Nam was the larger family unit. The extended family or clan was governed by the same patriarchal authority as was the smaller family unit. At the village level a council of elders, representing the principal families, exercised authority. The villages were fully autonomous in dealing with internal matters and had little to do with the outside world. The undeveloped communications system promoted localism.

Such relations as existed with the imperial court lay in the hands of a mandarin bureaucracy that acted as the agent of the central government with respect to the semiautonomous villages. The mandarins were chosen through an examination system that sometimes provided a means of upward mobility for gifted individuals who could qualify. The mandarin bureaucracy was the only element in Vietnamese society that represented economic privilege above the village level. The mandarinate's ability to exploit the peasantry stemmed from its governmental position, rather than from its possession of property.

The imperial court had several general tasks to perform. Chief among them were defending the national territory against invasion, furthering its expansion, maintaining internal peace, providing for the upkeep of the extensive canal systems and waterworks that protected the land against the ravages of floods and assured irrigation of the crops, and providing for the court and machinery of government.

The demand for taxes to meet these needs always produced friction with the localities, so that permanent tension existed between the local units of government and the political center. The entire economy usually operated on a subsistence level. The accumulation of great landed wealth and the corresponding growth of independent centers of political strength were impeded by military and tax powers of the government. Low production was guaranteed by sumptuary laws and all kinds of restrictions on liberty of exportation.

The intimate relationship between the forces of nature and the well-being of agricultural society found expression in unified and integrated political and religious concepts. Religious practices mirrored the necessity for a harmonious relationship between man and his environment, as well as among men, lest calamity befall all. The emperor at the apex of the system also combined both religious and political functions.[8] In good times, coincident with high crop yields, he enjoyed the mandate of heaven. Otherwise, his removal was dictated not only by obvious internal difficulties in his regime but by the apparent displeasure of nature itself.

Thus, religious or political dissidence involved challenging the total system. This interpenetration of religious belief and social ethics and behavior was one reason for the periodic persecution of Buddhism, Taoism, and Christianity. The mandarinate saw in these nonorthodox conceptions an eventual challenge to the holders of power. Buddhist and Taoist teachers, in response to governmental persecution of their beliefs, were often the chief organizers of secret societies.

The formation of secret societies was the only means by which dissidence could be developed, new followers recruited, and a new leadership created to struggle for control of the state itself. Since the secret societies grew in response to a situation created by an authoritarian society where religion was indissolubly tied to politics, they also tended to be hierarchical in their basic structure.[9] Prevailing religious customs pervaded the ritual of these organizations. The Vietnamese who joined these societies was an individual whose every act fitted into a cosmogony, whether it was well defined or an eclectic mixture of several religious practices. And the aim was always the same: to replace the existing dynasty by a new one that would allow the desired modification of the social, political, and religious structure in Viet Nam.

This was the Viet Nam which fell before the superior power of French arms in 1885. French administration and economic and cultural policies rapidly destroyed the traditional pattern of local isolation and self-sufficiency. A new economy reflecting the interests of the French settlers was superimposed on the older, rice-producing agricultural society which operated at the village level.[10] New French corporate enterprise took over and expanded rice production. It developed rubber plantations in the South (Cochinchina). It also established mining and textile industries. The top levels of administration were in French hands and served to buttress French economic development. Salt, tobacco, and alcohol monopolies were created. The population felt the impact of the new government through new taxes and through the ever increasing pressure to recruit labor for the new economic undertakings. The development of the communications system contributed its share to the changed rhythm of life. The disintegration of the old patterns of rule and the opening up of the whole country to foreign influences invigorated traditional national feeling and promoted nationalist organization. Vietnamese nationalists regarded the imposition of French rule as a sign of their own national weakness and began to seek ways to deal with the conqueror. French domination became the transcendent issue in the political thinking of the Vietnamese.

The subsequent activities and alignments of Vietnamese nationalists reflect a wide range of political efforts to find solutions to the problems that arose under French control. Nationalists repeatedly sought the aid of foreign states for their anti-French activities, and the strength of various political tendencies often fluctuated with the support they received from such external sources. Although all Vietnamese nationalists shared a common goal—the end of French rule—the means they chose for reaching it not only divided them in ideological allegiance but even led in some instances to fratricidal conflict.

Open resistance first came from elements of the mandarinate who attempted to use the institution of the monarchy as a rallying point.[11] Their military efforts were smashed, and they were deprived of their remaining power by having most of their administrative functions taken over by the French. These rebels out of the old tradition could not succeed against the French, but many of them became legendary heroes. The great emphasis on historical tradition that is a feature of Vietnamese culture led nationalists of a later time to claim direct links between their movement and these early efforts.

THE EMERGENCE OF MARXISM IN VIET NAM

Some of the earliest Vietnamese nationalists received their education in Japan in the years after 1905 and may have been exposed to Socialist ideas in their contacts with Japanese students,[12] but it was not until World War I that significant numbers of Vietnamese came into contact with Marxist ideology. Some 100,000 Vietnamese were sent to France during the war.[13] In the armed forces and industry, they met Socialists and trade-unionists who opposed the war and preached the creed of class struggle. Some of these Vietnamese returned to Viet Nam fired with the desire to transform their own country in the light of their newly acquired Western knowledge and determined to achieve the standards of democracy and self-government that they had seen applied in France. Although the French Socialists had done little until then to develop ideological contact with the Vietnamese, the new left-wing elements in the French Socialist movement were eager to do so. Thus, liaison was established with Vietnamese in France by the same people who shortly thereafter organized the French Communist Party.

In addition, there was the seminal influence of the events in Russia. The very fact that the Bolsheviks had seized power in Russia, a country which straddled Eurasia, would alone have sufficed to quicken other Asians' interest in the politics of Marxism-Leninism. Indeed, when the Communists emphasized the international implications of their victory in Russia and its particular meaning for the oppressed colonial and semi-colonial peoples,[14] a new program against colonial rule was provided for the nationalist-minded Vietnamese intellectuals and workers. Moreover, since the newly created French Communist Party promised to support the independence efforts of the Vietnamese, some Vietnamese nationalists saw that their own efforts could benefit from political support in France. The French Socialists were also now forced to take cognizance of the desires of the many peoples of the French empire whose demands for self-government were cruelly dashed at Versailles. From this time on, many Vietnamese looked to the French left for support.

Marxism offered an appealing synthesis to some of the Vietnamese who wanted to improve the situation in their country. Its emphasis on eliminating the contradictions of capitalism through the creation of an international Socialist order was seen as a direct successor of the older, religious-political, universalistic ethic of Confucianism as it had been developed in the Chinese cultural sphere. The Leninist doctrine of imperialism was regarded as an adequate explanation of the spoliation of Viet Nam by the French colonialists. The vanguard theory of a party and its conspiratorial features were easily grasped by those familiar with the hierarchical organization of secret societies in their own country. The belief that the

Russian revolution, occurring in a backward country, was the harbinger of a future world society in which all peoples would be free offered psychological compensation for their recognition of the backwardness of their own society. It seemed to promise that they, too, had the capacity to overcome quickly this backwardness. The emphasis in Marxist doctrine on racial equality of all peoples had a powerful effect on the consciousness of those who had been forced to accept the domination of the white colonial overlord. In these circumstances, it is not surprising that the first Marxist cadres among the Vietnamese were formed in France. It was there, in fact, that Ho Chi Minh first learned his Marxism and began his career as a Communist leader.[15] It was there that Ton Duc Thang, who was to become chairman of the permanent committee of the National Assembly of the Democratic Republic of Viet Nam, served his revolutionary apprenticeship. Later he participated in the Black Sea Revolt as a sailor aboard the *Waldeck-Rousseau* and served a seventeen-year sentence in the Poulo-Condore Prison for having engaged in revolutionary activities in Viet Nam.[16]

The significant acceptance of Marxism by a small group of Vietnamese coincides, then, with events in France in the period immediately following World War I. These Vietnamese nationalists found an outlet for their grievances and protests against French colonialism in the then French Socialist newspaper *L'Humanité*. Signed articles were submitted under the collective pseudonym of Nguyen Ai Quoc (Nguyen Who Loves His Country, i.e., Nguyen the Patriot). Adopting this name,[17] a young Vietnamese, later called Ho Chi Minh, became active in the Socialist party and is known to have been present at the Tours congress in 1920, when the majority split off to form the French Communist Party. Nguyen Ai Quoc enrolled in the newly created French Communist Party. During this period, a branch of the Chinese Communist Party was established in Paris, including in its membership Chou En-lai and Li Li-san.[18] It is probable that some of the Vietnamese revolutionists came to know them.

Apparently, however, Nguyen Ai Quoc became dissatisfied with the activities of the French Communist Party on colonial matters.[19] This mirrored the experience of other Vietnamese and other colonial subjects of France, who found that, despite the verbal declarations of support of the Communist International's program on colonial affairs, the French Communists did little to help form Communist colonial cadres.[20] This lack of interest and comprehension on the part of Europeans was to be a recurrent theme of the Vietnamese Communists, who often felt through the years that their interests were slighted by the bulk of the leadership and the membership of the French Communist movement.

Nguyen Ai Quoc's activities won him the favorable regard of the leadership of the French Communist Party, and he was sent to Moscow for further training. He left France in June 1923 and was enrolled as a student in the newly founded Communist University for the Toilers of the East.[21] Nguyen also acted as French Communist Party delegate to the Peasants' International, or Krestintern, meeting of October 1923, in Moscow. He was elected the Asian representative on the permanent directing committee of the Krestintern and served in that capacity for the next eighteen months.

During this period, Nguyen Ai Quoc also was a delegate to the Fifth Congress of the Communist International, held from June 17 to July 8, 1924.[22] At this congress he presented a series of five steps for immediate action by the French Communist Party. These proposals indicated the still tentative character of Communist activity among the Vietnamese in France. The proposals included (1) the publication, in the French Communist newspaper *L'Humanité*, of a regular column devoted to colonial problems; (2) intensified propaganda and recruitment among the Vietnamese residing in France; (3) the dispatch of Vietnamese recruits to the Communist University in Moscow; (4) the organization of Vietnamese workers in France; (5) the requirement that French Communist Party members interest themselves in colonial affairs.[23]

Despite the program proposed at the Fifth Comintern Congress, the French Communist press continued to treat colonial problems sporadically, and most of the party membership remained indifferent. Nonetheless, a base for Communist recruitment existed. Continuing work among the Vietnamese in France was conducted by a small group with which Nguyen Ai Quoc had collaborated. Prior to his departure for Moscow, he had helped formulate plans that led to the creation of the Viet Nam Hon (The Soul of Viet Nam) group. Under the leadership of Nguyen The Truyen, this group functioned from 1923 to 1925. From among its members, candidates were chosen for further training in Moscow. With the aid of Nguyen The Truyen, Nguyen Ai Quoc published the brochure entitled *Le Procès de la Colonisation Française* (*French Colonization on Trial*) in France in 1925.[24]

The *Procès* is now regarded as a landmark in the history of Vietnamese nationalism and Communism. It set forth the themes to be heard in varying measure in all Asia between World War I and World War II. Unevenly written, it consists of little more than a collection of bits and pieces that detail the purported French crimes during their colonial rule. Nonetheless, it was the first major work directly appealing in Marxist terms to the Vietnamese in this early period. It also shows the simple basis on which its writers hoped to win recruits to the Communist cause, since it is only in the concluding chapter, entitled "The Revolt of the Slaves," that we find direct references to Communist ideas and organizations. The chapter includes "The Russian Revolution and the Colonial Peoples," an extract from a manifesto of the Executive Committee of the Third International, a Krestintern (Peasants' International) appeal, an extract of an International Red Trade Union statement, and a manifesto of the Union Intercoloniale. An annex calls on the Vietnamese student youth residing abroad to emulate the Chinese in forming associations to liberate their country. The appeal is designed to shame the Vietnamese youth into manifesting their patriotism in contrast to their actual apolitical, and in many cases pleasure-seeking, life. It derides the obsequious behavior of Vietnamese who thank the French for governing Indochina.

The brief section entitled "The Russian Revolution and the Colonial Peoples" is of greatest interest since it probably represents the direct reasoning and experience of Nguyen Ai Quoc. In this section, capitalism is pictured as a "leech," draining the lifeblood of the metropolitan and colonial proletariat. The creature must be severed from its hold in both areas simultaneously, lest its continued life permit it to regenerate tentacles. The Bolsheviks truly understood this, he points out. Not content with making fine Platonic speeches and voting humanitarian motions in favor of oppressed peoples, they aided them morally and materially and taught them to fight along the lines outlined by Lenin in his colonial theses at the Second Comintern Congress. Moreover, the Communists had convoked the Baku congress, to which twenty-one nationalities of the Orient sent delegates. Representatives of the Occidental workers' parties had participated in the congress, marking the first time in history that the proletariat of the dominant nations and that of the subjugated countries met fraternally to formulate the means of fighting capitalism, their common enemy.

Revolutionary Russia, despite internal and external difficulties, has never hesitated in her support of the peoples whom she had wakened from lethargy. Thus was created the Oriental University at Moscow, offering advanced instruction to students of sixty-two nationalities who meet on a plane of equality. The facilities are described in glowing terms. The writer ironically refers to the so-called barbarism of the Bolsheviks, who, not content with treating these "inferior colonials" as brothers, have even invited them to participate in the political life of Russia. Students, who in their country of origin are "subjects" and have no political rights, are here granted full voting rights and send their own delegates to sit in the soviets. "If only my colonial brothers who wear themselves out in vainly begging naturalization would make the comparison between bourgeois democracy and a workers' democracy!"

After outlining the attractions of the University, the writer turns to a consideration of the peoples of the Near and Far East. Despite their great numbers, these oppressed peoples have never seriously tried to emancipate themselves, nor do they understand the value of national and international solidarity. The founding of the Oriental University marked a new era. In uniting active and intelligent younger elements of the colonial countries, the University undertook a great task:

1. To teach these future combatants the principle of class struggle, a principle which racial struggles on the one hand and patriarchal customs on the other had confused in their minds.

2. To put the vanguard of the colonial workers in intimate contact with the Occidental proletariat in order to prepare the road for an immediate and effective collaboration which alone will assure the international working class definitive victory.

3. To teach the colonial peoples—up to the present isolated from each other—to get better acquainted and to unite, thus laying the basis for a future Oriental Federation that will constitute one of the wings of the proletarian revolution.

4. To provide the proletariats of countries whose bourgeoisie possessed colonies the example of what they can and should do for their subjugated brothers.

It was in these terms that Nguyen Ai Quoc made his contribution to the necessarily limited efforts of the Communists to recruit among the Vietnamese in France. Early in 1925, he was called on to engage in a more serious enterprise. His assignment was to the Soviet consulate at Canton, where he served under Borodin as a "Chinese translator"—a euphemistic cover for his efforts to create an Indochinese Communist movement. Canton, in southern China, was not only the scene of heightened political activity by Chinese Nationalists and Communists which might be expected to influence political events in Viet Nam, but also a center for many young Vietnamese who, in answer to the appeal of veteran nationalist Phan Boi Chau, journeyed there to acquire an education in order to help liberate their country. Moreover, within Indochina itself, a parallel change of opinion gave promise of the growth of a revolutionary nationalism.

THE WEAKNESS OF MODERATE VIETNAMESE NATIONALISM

The changes in the outlook of Vietnamese in France were matched by an upsurge of democratic ideas in Indochina. New concepts of freedom of the press, of assembly, and of association were discussed and found favor among Vietnamese intellectuals. On all sides there arose demands for extending the educational system, for the large-scale admission of Vietnamese into government administration, for social legislation, and for rights for the Vietnamese equivalent to those enjoyed by the French settlers in Indochina. The impetus for these demands was provided by the new Vietnamese intelligentsia.

This intelligentsia represented a new force in Vietnamese society that had been created as a direct consequence of the French occupation. Replacing the old mandarinate, which had been either destroyed or devitalized as the leading class in Vietnamese society, there had arisen a new intellectual class formed by the transplanted French educational system. The education provided for the Vietnamese followed metropolitan models for reasons both of principle and of practical necessity. The French idea of cultural assimilation demanded a native elite thoroughly imbued with French standards acquired through French education. The needs of French colonial administration and the new economy it was building required at least some native personnel at lower and intermediate levels who could help in the success of the French enterprise.

This new intellectual class consisted of civil service employees, professional people, white-collar employees, returned college students, noncommissioned army officers, and skilled workers. Their ranks were swelled by remnants of the mandarinate and royalty and by a small number of wealthy Vietnamese (primarily landowners and businessmen in Cochinchina), who were set apart from the mass of the peasant population by virtue of their higher incomes and educational training. To a considerable extent, it was this new class that fell heir to the prestige and the responsibilities of the former mandarinate.[25] Like their predecessors, they rose essentially through what may be considered a merit system, depended on income from public or professional employment, and as a group could voice the collective aspirations of the Vietnamese people.

As the only part of Vietnamese society that had the necessary technical and administrative ability required for political organization, this intellectual class became the carrier of a new and invigorated nationalism. It was stimulated to move in this direction by its collective life experience under French rule. In the first instance, many intellectuals discovered that there was a freer atmosphere for them in metropolitan France than in their native land. In France, they could enjoy all the democratic freedoms which they were denied in Indochina. Second, the colonial civil service was clearly inferior to the same service in France. Worse still, it was characterized by unequal pay and unequal standards of eligibility for Vietnamese. This discrimination rankled, since many Vietnamese discovered that, regardless of competence, they were denied real positions of responsibility in their own country. Vietnamese businessmen found themselves chafing at administrative restraints. Finally, there were no representative institutions in which the intelligentsia could function. It was from among such people that leaders emerged to organize the new small working class, to give voice to the economic dissatisfaction of the peasantry, and, in so doing, to further their own national aims.

A significant reform movement arose among the Vietnamese associated with the colonial administration in Cochinchina. The peculiar legal status

of Cochinchina—a directly administered colony as opposed to the protectorates of Annam and Tonkin—afforded a greater measure of political
freedom. In 1923, Bui Quang Chieu,[26] Nguyen Phan Long,[27] and Duong
Van Giao[28] established the Constitutionalist Party. The three representatives of the Constitutionalists in the Cochinchina Colonial Council successfully opposed a proposal to create a port monopoly in the city of Saigon.[29]
As a result, the Constitutionalist Party gained influence in Cochinchina
among intellectuals, wealthy Vietnamese landowners, and government
officials. The party attempted, without challenging French sovereignty
in Indochina, to mitigate some of the less liberal aspects of French rule.
It campaigned for French citizenship, equality before the law, the transformation of the Colonial Councils into genuine legislative bodies, agricultural credit to improve the lot of the peasant, and other moderate reforms. The party's reform program was conceived of by its promoters as
a means of offsetting revolutionary attempts to oust the French completely
from Indochina.[30] At the end of December 1923, *La Cloche Fêlée* (*The
Cracked Bell*) made its appearance as a "propaganda organ of French
ideas."[31] It was published by Nguyen An Ninh.[32] He, too, sought in this
early period to evoke sympathy from the French both in Indochina and in
metropolitan France for a program of reform in the colony. Success of
the reform movement was dependent on the willingness of the French
colonial administration and the metropolitan government to grant their
demands. The failure of the French to do so tended to drive younger, more
impatient individuals to support revolutionary ideas that promised a short-
cut to freedom.

At this same time, a number of underground nationalist societies, composed primarily of Vietnamese youth imbued with Socialist and revolutionary convictions, sprang into existence. In Saigon an illegal group
called Jeune Annam was formed under the leadership of Ta Thu Thau,
who later became the most outstanding Trotskyist leader. In neighboring
Annam, in mid-1925, a number of young Vietnamese nationalists formed
the Phuc Viet (Restoration of Viet Nam).[33]

This accelerated political activity within Indochina coincided with a
period of liberalization of the French colonial regime. In 1924, the Cartel
des Gauches (Left Bloc) had won the elections in France. As a result,
Alexandre Varenne, a Socialist deputy, was named Governor-General of
Indochina in July 1925. His appointment excited Vietnamese hopes for a
new era in Indochina. In addition, after fourteen years of exile, the veteran nationalist Phan Chau Trinh had returned from Europe on June 26,
1925, and had begun to meet with Vietnamese to outline his views. Previously, while in Paris, he had come into frequent contact with the French
left, particularly the French Socialist Party.

Governor-General Varenne arrived in Indochina on November 18,

1925, shortly after the death of Emperor Khai Dinh (November 6, 1925), to find himself confronted by a number of pressing political issues.[34] The first dealt with the imperial court. The interim governor-general had transferred the few remaining powers of the Regency Council to the French Resident Superior. This was a blow to Vietnamese national pride. Varenne moved to assuage national feeling on this matter. The second issue was the touchy question of political prisoners. The famous nationalist Phan Boi Chau had been arrested in Shanghai by the French police on June 30, 1925, and sentenced to death on November 23, 1925. This action touched off a wave of national protest. A political amnesty was granted. Phan Boi Chau was pardoned along with many other nationalists. Finally, the Constitutionalists, led by Bui Quang Chieu, stepped up their political activities and petitioned the new governor-general for a series of reforms embodying the Constitutionalists' program. Varenne ordered a certain liberalization of conditions, permitting Vietnamese to enter the civil service in larger numbers. In addition, representative assemblies (of a limited nature) were created in Tonkin and Annam.

These events inaugurated a period of collaboration with the French administration. In Annam and Tonkin, a movement to create a legal party, similar to that of the Constitutionalists, was launched by Pham Quynh, an influential mandarin and literary figure. He was joined by veteran nationalists such as Huynh Thuc Khang and Le Van Huan. The latter, in fact, had benefited from the recent amnesty, and his participation in the moderate movement attracted the support of some of the younger people affiliated with the clandestine revolutionary nationalist organizations.[35] Even the veteran fighter Phan Boi Chau declared himself a partisan of Franco-Vietnamese collaboration.

But the hopes of collaboration were soon ended. French colonists, fearful of the loss of their prerogatives, began to call for Varenne's recall and to express in the local French press their opposition to his policies. On the occasion of the death of Phan Chau Trinh on March 24, 1926, a tremendous funeral procession was organized and Nguyen An Ninh wrote a "eulogistic obituary" for which he was arrested and his paper censored.[36] Students who wore mourning in commemoration of the patriot were enjoined from doing so by the school authorities. The arrest of Nguyen An Ninh led to sympathy strikes among postal and bank employees and workers at the Saigon Arsenal. A rash of student strikes broke out, leading to the expulsion of some five hundred students.[37]

The moderate nationalists were soon bypassed by events. When Bui Quang Chieu returned from a successful tour in France and called for a French charter of liberty for Indochina, he was met at the dock by local French settlers who demonstrated against him. The underground youth organization Jeune Annam organized a counterdemonstration in his favor. But the youth were becoming progressively estranged from the reform movement, which gave little promise of achieving its ends through peaceful reform of the colonial administration.[38] The failure of the French administration to recognize the reform movement in Tonkin and Annam, which in September 1926 had formally asked for recognition under the name of Viet Nam Tan Bo Dan Hoi (Viet Nam Peoples' Progressive Party), was a severe blow. The new party's offer of unity with the Constitutionalists had also come to naught. Moreover, the French authorities had cracked down on Jeune Annam, leading to its virtual dissolution. The younger intellectuals began to turn to new underground revolutionary organizations, while some of the disappointed leaders and their supporters in Cochinchina joined the new Cao Dai religious movement.[39] When Governor-General Varenne was recalled in 1927, hope for the reform movement faded.

It can be seen from the foregoing that the reform movement had little Marxist inspiration. Nationalists like Bui Quang Chieu, Phan Chau Trinh, and Phan Boi Chau had traveled abroad and come into contact with Socialist and Communist ideas, but these ideas had evidently left little imprint on their thinking. Only the younger students and intellectuals responded to the new currents, which moved faster as a result of the failure of the reform movement. More accurately, attempts to reform the French administration by a small group of nationalists—without links to the mass of the population and inhibited by a heavy-handed colonial authority—opened the way for the attempt to seek through revolutionary means the desired road to freedom. So we must again turn to Nguyen Ai Quoc's activity in southern China, which had become the center of a lively, functioning émigré organization. Moreover, the growth of the Chinese Kuomintang soon led to a parallel development among the Vietnamese.

THE NEW REVOLUTIONARY NATIONALIST AND COMMUNIST ORGANIZATIONS

When Nguyen Ai Quoc began his work at Canton in 1925, he had the authority of an assigned Comintern representative with Moscow training. However, when it came to specific application of Marxism to Viet Nam, his was a mixed legacy. In Marxist terms, there was no authoritative analysis of Viet Nam's social structure from which a corresponding strategy for building a native Communist movement could be elaborated. It was at the Second Comintern Congress that the first set of "Theses on the National and Colonial Question" had been formulated. Lenin personally defined the relationship to be observed between the Communist vanguard and the "bourgeois national revolutionary movement."[40] Communists could join in a "temporary alliance" with the national revolutionary movement but were enjoined to maintain the "independence" of the proletarian movement even if it was still at an embryonic stage of development. This general formulation concealed latent ambiguities in the definitions of what constituted "temporary alliance" and "independence" and did not provide clear organizational directives for building a Communist movement. Five years of subsequent experience amply demonstrated that Asian Communists were as divided among themselves as were the leaders of the Comintern on the manner in which Communists should participate in national revolutionary movements.[41] Varying strategies, ranging from the building of independent Communist parties to direct participation by Communists in the building of a "national revolutionary movement," were put into practice with mixed results. In effect, Nguyen Ai Quoc had little more than his mandate from Moscow to guide him in his choice of means for building a Communist movement in Viet Nam.

As shown in the pamphlet *Procès*, it is clear that Nguyen had a poor opinion of the political consciousness displayed by his fellow countrymen. His previous experience in France had taught him how much education was needed. His activity as a Communist in Moscow, aside from his studies at the University, was principally as a functionary in the Peasants' International (Krestintern), an organization designed to serve as an international alliance of revolutionary peasant parties and groups collaborating with the Communists. Hence it is not surprising that Nguyen's organizational efforts would be devoted mainly to building a broader national revolutionary organization instead of a strictly Communist movement among the Vietnamese.

Moreover, Nguyen Ai Quoc served with Borodin, whose specific mission was to supervise the reshaping of the Chinese Kuomintang with Chinese Communist support.[42] Given the many parallels between Chinese society and Vietnamese society, it is understandable that Nguyen was led to duplicate Borodin's organizational activity by building a Vietnamese national revolutionary movement similar to the Kuomintang. This strategy was also ideologically consonant with a Marxist interpretation of colonial evolution as consisting of two stages, held by some leading Comintern figures. Applied to Viet Nam, this theory envisaged the first stage as the "bourgeois democratic revolution," leading to independence and brought about by an alliance of all the revolutionary classes opposed to foreign domination. The second stage would be that of the "proletarian revolution," leading to Viet Nam's integration into a World Soviet Federation. The Communists in Viet Nam would organize their party as the situation matured and would move on independently of their former nationalist allies once the necessary tasks of the first stage had been accomplished. It was with these conceptions firmly in mind that in June 1925, at Canton,

Nguyen founded the association called the Viet Nam Cach Menh Thanh Nien Dong Chi Hoi (Viet Nam Revolutionary Youth League).[43]

This new organization published a weekly paper called *Thanh Nien* (*Youth*), of which eighty-eight issues were printed from June 1925 to April 1927. At first the paper was concerned primarily with appeals to nationalist sentiment and included material on the history of Viet Nam. Only in 1926, after a preparatory period of educational activity, including translation of Marxist terminology into Vietnamese, did Nguyen finally introduce the idea that "only a Communist Party can [ultimately] insure the well-being of Annam."

Selected members of the organization enrolled in the Whampoa Military Academy, where Chinese Nationalists and Communists were receiving training as the future leaders of the Chinese Nationalist state and army. The members of the Youth League also received special instruction under Nguyen's direction. In addition, the League sought to establish and maintain liaison with underground nationalist and Communist organizations in the interior of Indochina and with sympathetic organizations abroad. The center of the *émigré* movement was established at Canton, with authority over the training of new recruits from Indochina.

While it is clear that the major appeal of the Youth League was to nationalists and that it drew its supporters from among patriotic Vietnamese youth, the growth of Marxist influence was unmistakable. As indicated above, revolutionary propaganda began to have an impact in Indochina during 1926–27. The international Communist movement took notice of the Jeune Annam group and its revolutionary potential was appraised.[44]

However, events in China interrupted Nguyen Ai Quoc's activities. The split in the Kuomintang between the Communists and Chiang Kai-shek's followers forced Nguyen to leave Canton in April 1927 for Hankow and then Moscow. In Hankow, Nguyen apparently attended the Fifth Congress of the Chinese Communist Party and then participated in the May 1927 formative meeting of the Pan Pacific Trade Union Conference. Beyond its functions as a trade-union agency, the Conference, later known as the Pan Pacific Trade Union Secretariat, was set up to provide a cover for Communist International activities in the Far East.[45] Nguyen Ai Quoc worked closely with this organization in his role as Communist International representative in Southeast Asia.

In Moscow, Nguyen is reputed to have said in the summer of 1927, in summing up his Canton experience, that the creation of an Indochina Communist party was impossible at the time because "no one as yet understood the significance of the word communism." However, he continued, it was "possible to constitute an Indochinese nationalist-socialist and revolutionary party whose leaders would be responsible for bringing all its members step by step to orthodox Marxism." His presence in Moscow in 1927 and 1928 ensured liaison with the top Comintern leadership. Articles began to appear in *International Press Correspondence* (*Inprecor*) devoted to events in Indochina. At the Sixth Comintern Congress (June–September 1928), three Indochinese delegates sat with the French delegation.[46]

At the congress, the French Communist Party again came under attack for its inadequate activity in the colonial areas. Kuusinen, in delivering the report of the Colonial Commission, attacked the French Communists for the lack of independent parties in Tunisia, Algeria, and Morocco.[47] In the discussion that followed the major report, which was delivered by Bukharin, Ch'en Kuang, a Chinese delegate, stated: "The Chinese revolutionary masses, particularly the Chinese Communists, have always followed with great attention . . . the unfortunately inadequate work of the Communist Party of France in Annam . . ."[48] It may be observed that the work of the Vietnamese Communists had been closely coordinated with that of the Chinese Communists in the preceding period. The defeat of the Chinese Communists at the hands of the Kuomintang was far more significant to the Vietnamese than the lack of aid reasonably to be expected from the French Communists.

While Nguyen was in Moscow, the continuing split between the Kuomintang and the Chinese Communists caused difficulties for the Viet Nam Revolutionary Youth League. The Kuomintang authorities were basically anti-French. They were willing to allow the Youth League to exist as long as it directed its agitation against the French and did not mix in Chinese affairs. This tolerant attitude lasted until December 1928, when members of the Youth League who were secretly members of the Chinese Communist Party were arrested.[49] The Youth League's central office was transferred to Kwangsi province and then to Hong Kong. There, preparations were made for a congress of the League to be held in May 1929.

The Communist-directed Youth League had made marked progress in Indochina. An estimated minimum of 250 Vietnamese had received revolutionary training abroad, and the Youth League had approximately 1,000 members and sympathizers. The majority of the members in Tonkin belonged to the working class. In Annam and Cochinchina, the social composition was mixed, including workers, teachers, students, and peasants. The party machine was composed predominantly of teachers and intellectuals, and the important functions were carried out by the graduates of the Canton emigration. It was necessary for the Youth League not only to review past activities, but to formulate a program of action that would reflect the decisions of the Sixth Comintern Congress. Moreover, new developments were taking place in Indochina that demanded consideration by the Youth League Congress.

The growth of the Viet Nam Revolutionary Youth League was paralleled by the deterioration of economic conditions in the country. At the end of 1928, speculation in the rice market led to a sharp break in prices. This blow was succeeded by the general slump in grain prices and raw materials under the conditions prevailing in world markets in 1929—an economic dislocation that stimulated political unrest in urban and rural areas.

Before discussing the program adopted and the implications of the Hong Kong Congress, it is necessary to consider briefly some of the other nationalist-*cum*-Marxist organizations which sought leadership in the struggle against France. These included the Viet Nam Quoc Dan Dang (Viet Nam Nationalist Party), the Nguyen An Ninh Association, and the Tan Viet Nam Cach Menh Dang (New Viet Nam Revolutionary Party). All these political groupings, formed since 1925, conducted their activities under conditions of severe police repression. Recruiting was done on an individual basis to maintain the security of the underground organizations. This invariably made for the isolation of little cells within the larger structure. Personality differences were heightened by the strain of underground existence. Regional peculiarities flourished and the different groups varied in strength depending upon the locality in which they operated. The bond drawing these groups together was the common desire for independence from France. They gradually accepted Communist ideas, as the influence of the growing number of returned graduates of the *émigré*-directed Communist Youth League increased.

The first of these organizations, the Viet Nam Nationalist Party,[50] was the chief non-Communist rival of the Viet Nam Revolutionary Youth League. Formed in 1927, the Viet Nam Nationalist Party was modeled directly on the Chinese Kuomintang and sought its aid to help drive the French out of Viet Nam. It was this link and the benefits it promised that led to mutual hostility between the Viet Nam Nationalist Party and the Viet Nam Revolutionary Youth League. In 1927, the split between the Chinese Communists and the Chinese Kuomintang was reproduced in Indochina. Like the left Kuomintang, the Viet Nam Nationalist Party had a "Socialist" coloration and also talked in its program about the liberation of "oppressed peoples" through revolution. Its party organization was highly centralized, fitting Borodin's prescriptions for the Kuomintang. The Viet Nam Nationalist Party was conceived of as a vanguard party, an adaptation of the Bolshevik model in Indochina, and to that extent it reflected the impact of Marxism.

Two other organizations, the Nguyen An Ninh Association[51] and the New Viet Nam Revolutionary Party,[52] were attracted to the Communist doctrine of the Viet Nam Revolutionary Youth League. The Nguyen An Ninh Association was formed by its leader, Nguyen An Ninh, in 1927, following his return from France. It was secretly known as the Cao Vong Thanh Nien Dang (Hope of Youth Party). Its membership of from seven hundred to eight hundred was organized in the typical Communist cell structure. At the outset, its program was agrarian-socialist in character, but its supporters soon came under the influence of the Viet Nam Revolutionary Youth League. The Association membership was made up of minor functionaries and also counted a considerable number of ordinary workers in its ranks. With the arrest of Nguyen An Ninh in 1929, it was destroyed, though a large number of its members became Communists or joined organizations which the Communists controlled, i.e., trade-unions, mutual aid societies, and the like.

The New Viet Nam Revolutionary Party was significant mainly as an attempt to have a revolutionary nationalist party free of either Russian or Chinese influence. It failed, and thereby helped to ensure the pre-eminence of the Communists within the nationalist movement. In its lifetime, from 1925 to 1930, the New Viet Nam Revolutionary Party never counted more than several hundred members in its ranks. Most of its members were teachers, students, and petty officials in the administration of Annam. From the start, it was the meeting ground of a wide variety of nationalists, ranging from reformers to Communists. As a result, the organization suffered an unending series of quarrels. It changed its name frequently, either because of programmatic shifts resulting from altered views as it lost members to competitors or because of the desire to facilitate fusion negotiations, which never succeeded.

Though the initial program of the New Viet Nam Revolutionary Party favored revolution only after all other means had failed, it did seek to obtain military training for party members. The party was based on the idea that independent Indochina would "recreate its government in accord with republican principles" and "would only adopt Communist theories when the great powers had accepted them." It sought the "moral, intellectual and economic revival of Indochina." The party also accepted the typical cell pattern of Communist organization. Later this program was modified to accept statutes that were clearly Communist, calling for national and world revolution.

Dao Duy Anh, one of the leading theoreticians of the New Viet Nam Revolutionary Party, made an original contribution to Vietnamese political thought in his penetrating "Study of the Vietnamese Revolution."[53] The study systematically portrayed the economic situation and evaluated the role of social classes in Indochina; it used Marxist methodology to challenge the validity of the Communist class-struggle approach to Viet Nam. Since the Communists themselves later employed some of his themes whenever they emphasized the all-national character of their activity, his argument bears examination here. In his economic analysis, Dao Duy Anh called attention to the limited industrial development of Indochina, the domination of commercial activity by the Chinese and a few French firms to the virtual exclusion of Vietnamese, and the large numerical predominance of tiny peasant proprietorships which characterized agriculture. Communications were undeveloped due to the low state of modern commercial and agricultural activity. Investment was mainly in the hands of foreigners, with only one small bank organized by Vietnamese capital. As a consequence, he reasoned that Vietnamese social classes were at a precapitalist stage and not differentiated as in developed capitalist societies. There was no "true" Vietnamese capitalist class, and the small number of workers did not possess the class consciousness of the European proletariat. The same lack of differentiation could be observed among the peasantry, which constituted nearly the "entire population." The only other social formation in Vietnamese society was the "petty-bourgeoisie which comprised intellectuals, functionaries, employees, little businessmen, artisans, etc." It too was divided, was "without common interest," and had a multitude of views ranging from "reactionary" to "revolutionary." Dao Duy Anh concluded that a revolutionary party would have to "recruit its supporters among the advanced elements of all the social classes." As a consequence, its program "must be nationalist and not combat the interests of any one of the diverse social elements which would form the revolutionary front." He envisaged the creating of subsidiary organs of the party that would recruit workers, peasants, women, and students. It can be seen that Dao Duy Anh's analysis joined that of Nguyen Ai Quoc in emphasizing the need for building a revolutionary nationalist organization.

Their views did differ markedly in one respect: Dao Duy Anh denied the possibility of building a Communist party. In his interpretation of Marxism, such a party required a proletarian base on which to build, and this hardly existed in Indochina. In doing so, he failed to grasp the essential import of the Leninist theory of the party as a vanguard organization, as it came to be used by Asian Communists. The term "proletariat" came to be construed as an "elliptical reference to the leadership and cadres of the Communist Party itself,"[54] no matter what their class origin. For Communists in colonial areas, it became common practice "to deduce class affiliations from ideological tendencies"[55] rather than the other way around.

Not only did the New Viet Nam Revolutionary Party contribute ideologically to the subsequent evolution of the Communist movement in Viet Nam but it contributed leadership, for some of the outstanding Communist leaders and personalities in the Democratic Republic of Viet Nam received their early training in this organization. Prior to the dissolution of the party in 1930, it even gave rise, in 1929, to a separate Communist group called the Dong Duong Cong San Lien Doan (Indochina Communist Alliance), which was to help found the Indochina Communist Party.[56]

We are now in a position to understand the events which took place at the Hong Kong Congress of the Viet Nam Revolutionary Youth League. It occurred at a time when the organization was rapidly expanding its influence and membership. Yet this success belied the true state of affairs within the organization, which reflected the regional variations and personality differences that plagued all the clandestine organizations. In addition, there was a profound difference of opinion about the need for building an independent Communist party in Indochina. The delegate from Annam, Tran Van Cung, and the two delegates from Tonkin proposed that the organization adopt the name Indochina Communist Party. When the Congress refused to uphold their point of view, they considered their disagreement to be fundamental and split the organization.

The dissident delegates' views reflected the impact of the Chinese Communist-Kuomintang split of 1927 and their reaction to the new colonial program initiated by the Sixth Comintern Congress in 1928.[57] Their manifesto, in which they explained their break, called for a party that truly defended the interests of the proletariat of Indochina—a class which grew "more numerous and more enlightened from day to day." They attacked the leadership of the Viet Nam Revolutionary Youth League for its repeated fusion efforts with the New Viet Nam Revolutionary Party, since the latter party was a quasi-nationalist organization that consisted of a "bunch of fakers, advocating national and world revolution, who had never worked among the proletarian masses" and who had maintained liaison with a "revolutionary anti-proletarian party"—the Chinese Kuomintang. Tran Van Cung was here merely repeating arguments that he had leveled against the leaders of the New Viet Nam Revolutionary Party when still a member. These arguments were exactly contrary to the views expressed by Dao Duy Anh. Tran Van Cung resented the attitude toward organizing "coolies" that had been expressed in that party. In reply, the émigré leadership conceded the necessity of organizing a Communist party, but maintained that the Congress had no authority to take such action until the Youth League itself had adopted a Communist program. In reality, the leadership was unwilling to deviate from the political line previously set by Nguyen Ai Quoc, who had aimed at building a revolutionary nationalist party that would include Communists.

The Hong Kong Congress adopted statutes bringing the organization in line with the decisions of the Sixth Comintern Congress, while maintaining its quasi-nationalist character. It decided to continue fusion negotiations with the New Viet Nam Revolutionary Party. The Congress also decided to wage a struggle against the Viet Nam Nationalist Party, which it described as a "bourgeois party," presumably because of the latter's links with the Chinese Kuomintang. (The Communist International had attacked the Kuomintang as a "bourgeois" organization.) It also addressed a letter to the Comintern requesting recognition of the Viet Nam Revolutionary Youth League.

The dissident delegates, after their return to Indochina, won the Tonkin and Annam regional organizations of the Youth League to their point of view. They set up a new organization called the Dong Duong Cong San Dang (Indochina Communist Party), and their emissaries to Cochinchina established a section in that region. By November 1929, the Indochina Communist Party was sufficiently strong to rival in Cochinchina the Youth League regional organization that had upheld the *émigré* leadership. By this time, the *émigré* leadership, too, had secretly adopted the name Annam Cong San Dang (Annam Communist Party) for fear of losing its more militant members to its rivals within Indochina.

Thus, there were two competing Communist organizations whose programs were barely distinguishable from each other. Both the Indochina Communist Party and the Annam Communist Party sought to gain recognition from the Third International as its official section in Indochina. In Annam a third existing group, the Indochina Communist Alliance, added to the confusion.[58] Given this impasse, only the authoritative voice of the Communist International could impose a solution. For this, the services of Nguyen Ai Quoc as Comintern representative were needed.

In 1929, Nguyen Ai Quoc was in Siam, where he had been secretly working among the large Vietnamese colony, which numbered some thirty thousand *émigrés*. There he had succeeded in building another group of nationalist character called the Hoi Than Ai Nguoi Annam O Xiem (Annamite Fraternity of Siam). He left Siam, and after his arrival in Hong Kong in January 1930, Nguyen began the work of reconciling the various Communist groups. By the end of February, he successfully arranged the fusion of the three Communist organizations: the Indochina Communist Party, the Annam Communist Party, and the Indochina Communist Alliance.[59] The new party adopted the name Viet Nam Cong San Dang (Viet Nam Communist Party), transferred its Central Committee from Hong Kong to Haiphong, and asked for recognition from the Comintern.[60]

In 1930 the new Viet Nam Communist Party had clearly defined relations with the international Communist apparatus. Together with the

Communist organizations in Malaya and Thailand, it was directed and controlled by the Southern Bureau,[61] a subordinate unit of the Comintern Bureau of the Orient at Shanghai. It was linked through its trade-unions with the Pan Pacific Trade Union Secretariat and the Secretariat of the Confederation Générale du Travail Unitaire, thus tying it to the French Communist Party. Its anti-imperialist organization was a subordinate unit of the League Against Imperialism and for National Independence, with headquarters at Berlin.[62] The successful fusion negotiations ensured support from the international Communist movement and allowed the Vietnamese Communists to turn from internal squabbling to dealing with the developing crisis in Viet Nam.

A TIME OF CRISIS

By 1930 there was marked economic distress in Indochina. The most noticeable lowering of living standards occurred among rubber workers and miners (principally coal). The decline in foreign trade and commercial activity affected the petty employees of the large banking and trading firms, and forced economies in the government services. The greatest difficulties resulted from the fall in the price of rice, accompanied by a bad harvest in the North. The conditions of the impoverished peasantry plummeted to new lows. The deterioration in the economic situation stimulated political dissatisfaction with French rule in Indochina.

In December 1929, the French Communist Party had been alerted to developments in Indochina by instructions from the political secretariat of the Comintern.[63] Thus, in January 1930, the French Communist Party called attention to the activity of its brother party in Indochina.[64] Jacques Doriot, then a leading French Communist spokesman in the Chamber of Deputies, raised the issue of colonial rule in the budget debate,[65] and the French Communist newspaper L'Humanité began an almost daily coverage of events in Indochina.

Suddenly, on February 9–10, 1930, the Viet Nam Nationalist Party launched an armed uprising, with the complicity of some Vietnamese soldiers in the French forces stationed at Yen Bay. The Yen Bay move was quickly taken in hand by the French military. Small actions took place throughout the Tonkin delta, but they, too, were of little moment. Though the insurrection turned out to be ill prepared and resulted in the arrest and execution of the principal leaders of the Viet Nam Nationalist Party, it stirred others to restlessness and action. The underground cadres of the newly united Communist party were in an excellent position to provide leadership for the dissatisfied populace and to profit from this activity begun by the Viet Nam Nationalist Party.

The uprising also had a profound impact in France. The dramatic turn of events elevated the situation in Indochina to first-rank political importance. The French Communist Party undertook a press campaign in support of the Indochinese nationalists and revolutionists. Political support by the French Communists was important to the Vietnamese Communists since they could point to activity in France that complemented their own work. Moreover, the propaganda agencies of the Comintern began to call attention to the situation in Indochina.[66] Both the Comintern leadership and the Vietnamese Communists operated on the assumption that events in Indochina offered a substantial basis for the large-scale growth of their movement. The Communists indicated their solidarity with the insurrectionists at Yen Bay and called for support of the arrested members of the Viet Nam Nationalist Party.

The French Communist Party soon found itself under French government pressure for backing revolutionary activity in the colony. Subsequently, in March 1930, at the Seventh Congress of the French Communist Party, a resolution was voted which demanded that underestimation of colonial work be denounced and combatted "as being a manifestation of the worst opportunism and of a grave imperialist deviation" and which called for the development in the whole party of "the study of the Leninist position on the colonial question."[67] Doriot was personally friendly to *émigré* Vietnamese active in France and did much to get the Communist Party to create some sentiment and organization in the unions for aid to the Vietnamese and to mobilize French workers against the colonial policies of the French government.

In Indochina, the destruction of the Viet Nam Nationalist Party by the French police left the field virtually clear for the Vietnamese Communists. The Communists emphasized the need to end French rule in Indochina, as opposed to the more moderate demand of reform elements for amelioration of the French regime. A large number of new and willing recruits swelled the ranks of the Communist Party. These included former supporters of the Viet Nam Nationalist Party and other revolutionary nationalists who were encouraged by the then prevailing unity among the Communists.

But the rise in membership was not an unmixed blessing. The influx of young people, who barely understood the esoteric doctrines of Communism but could accept the call to revolutionary nationalism, swamped the organizations. Given the relative inexperience of the party leadership and the recently forged party unity that had been realized only through Comintern intervention, the Vietnamese Communists rushed headlong into a disastrous bid for power. They were abetted in their folly, for a "good many of the leaders of the Communist International already believed that democratic victory was in sight."[68]

In *Inprecor* at this time, the French Communist J. Berlioz wrote: "The influence of the Communist Party of Indochina is growing despite the sectarian tendencies of certain of its officials." He mentioned the strikes on rubber plantations, in the textile industry, and on the railways and also called attention to the mass demonstrations that had taken place on May 1, 1930, in Indochina for the "first time in history." He argued that "the Communist slogan, 'Free the Indochinese National Revolutionaries,' must be taken up everywhere. The protest action must be developed into a powerful campaign of solidarity on behalf of the heroic fighters in Indochina, who represent the most important connecting bridge between the revolution in India and China."[69]

The strike movement in the cities was reinforced by peasant demonstrations. By the summer of 1930, under Communist leadership, the peasant movement took on unexpected scope. From peaceful rallies which called for amelioration of the peasants' plight through agricultural credit and tax limitation, the demonstrations turned to more violent methods. Municipal buildings in local administrative centers were looted, tax rolls and land registers were burned, and local notables and landlords were forced to desert their rice fields. Elsewhere, strikes and demonstrations gave way to political killings and robberies as the wave of unrest spread.

A Communist source described the situation as follows:

A few months afterwards thousands of peasants in Cochinchina held demonstrations with red flags and the sign of the Soviets and for the slogans: the land for the peasants, against taxes, down with the imperialist terror, defend the Soviet Union! The revolt in Indochina thereby entered upon a phase of mass action under the leadership of the Communist Party. But later the situation became even more tense. In North Annam, the movement has assumed the character of a mass insurrection.[70]

The last reference to "mass insurrection" refers to the creation of soviets in Nghe An and Ha Tinh provinces, where some land actually was distributed to the peasants.[71]

The violent methods employed by the Indochina Communist Party met with an equally determined counteroffensive by the French colonial army in 1930 and 1931. French authority was re-established throughout Indochina in a campaign that led to an unprecedented number of arrests and used such brutal methods that the authorities later came in for criticism at home in France. The French authorities were able not only to suppress the Communist movement but also to try many of its leaders publicly as common criminals. Virtually the entire apparatus of the Indochina Communist Party was smashed. "The first of May, 1931, when the Party made a 'census of its forces' was only a feeble gasp testifying to the unrelenting agony of the Indochina Communist Party."[72] So wrote one of the Vietnamese Communist dissidents in surveying the wreckage.

ASSESSMENT OF DEFEAT

The Indochina Communist Party came under sharp attack from two quarters as a result of its failure in the 1930–31 period. On the one hand, it was berated for its shortcomings by the Comintern. The Comintern disassociated itself from activities that smacked of terror and pillage on the part of individuals since such activities were not consonant with the "organized violence" of Marxist doctrine. Though this theme had been stressed in the training of Vietnamese students in Moscow and southern China,[73] it was hardly to be expected that such admonition would be obeyed by revolutionary nationalists engaged in insurrectionary struggle with the hated French authority.

The Indochina Communist Party leadership was also criticized for the lackadaisical manner in which illegal activities had been conducted. Nguyen Ai Quoc was directly taken to task for not having taken greater security measures to safeguard the leading cadres of the Indochina Communist Party from surveillance and arrest.[74] The international leadership was directly compromised by the defeat in Indochina because the French authorities were able to seize documentation showing the external links of the party. Moreover, the apparatus of the Comintern in Southeast Asia was destroyed when Nguyen Ai Quoc, a Comintern agent known as Serge Lefranc (Ducroix), and other leading Communists were arrested by the British authorities in Hong Kong and Singapore raids in June 1931. As a result, the Indochina Communist Party also suffered a temporary severing of its own international contacts.

On the other hand, during this same period, internal difficulties developed with the emergence of a number of small groups which reacted to the party defeat by attributing it to faulty leadership. The policies of the party and the Comintern were repudiated. From among these critics came the cadres that formed the significant Trotskyist movement in Indochina. The first Trotskyist group emerged in western Cochinchina in May 1931, and was called the Lien Doan Cong San (Communist League). It was followed, in August 1931, by the founding of the Ta Doi Lap (Left Opposition), whose membership increased with the repatriation of a number of young Vietnamese who had studied in Paris and had come in contact with the French Trotskyists. Among those returning in 1932 was Ta Thu Thau, the most prominent leader of Indochinese Trotskyism.

Three distinct groups comprised this original nucleus. One retained the name Ta Doi Lap (Left Opposition); another, Ta Doi Lap Thang

Muoi (October Left Opposition); and the third, Dong Duong Cong San (Indochina Communism).[75] The principal issues dividing these groups were tactical divergencies arising from their collaboration with the Stalinists. They were in the throes of just such a discussion in August 1932, when some thirty of their principal members were arrested by the French colonial police.[76] They were all agreed, however, in accepting the line that Leon Trotsky had developed in his condemnation of the Communist International under the leadership of Stalin.

The central political doctrine around which the Trotskyist groups in Indochina organized was the "theory of permanent revolution" and its application to the colonial world—a theory first advanced by Leon Trotsky in the period preceding the 1905 revolution in Russia.[77] In this analysis of the prospects for revolution in Russia, Trotsky contended that the Russian capitalist class would be unable to play the progressive role that had been manifested by the rising commercial and industrial classes in the nations of Western Europe during their period of bourgeois revolution. Trotsky argued that the numerically small working class would have to take the leadership in the fight against tsarism and carry through the tasks of the democratic revolution, e.g., land division, separation of church and state, and the granting of democratic rights. The events in Russia of November 1917, which saw the accession to power of the Bolshevik party and the establishment of a proletarian dictatorship, were seen as a vindication of the theory. Subsequently, this theory was extended in application to the colonial world. It was Trotsky's contention that only the proletariat—although a weak and embryonic class in colonial countries—could successfully lead the struggle for national independence as well as solve the tasks of the democratic revolution. He argued that modern imperialism had given rise to a corrupt and comprador bourgeois class in the backward colonial lands. This class would display inherent weaknesses, as did the Russian bourgeoisie, in the struggle against imperialism.

It was in line with this conception that the Trotskyists bitterly attacked the official Comintern policy of alliance between the Communists and Chiang Kai-shek during the period 1924–27. They characterized the Kuomintang as a reactionary bourgeois organization. They predicted defeat for the young Chinese Communist Party at the hands of its reactionary nationalist allies, who, the Trotskyists claimed, would behead the revolution. When Chiang Kai-shek's nationalists broke with the Communists and suppressed them in 1927, the Trotskyists saw this as proof of the correctness of their criticisms of the Stalinist line in China. Subsequently, when the Chinese Communists embarked on a program of creating soviets, the Trotskyists attacked this as a manifestation of "ultra-leftism." They argued that the Chinese revolution had entered a period of decline and that this policy would expose the party survivors in the cities to complete suppression by the Kuomintang. Here again, the Trotskyists seemed prescient, as the Kuomintang completed its conquest of power and forced the Communists to retreat to the remote countryside.[78]

The Indochinese Trotskyists simply adapted the foregoing analysis to the events in their own country. They attacked the creation of the Indochina Communist Party as having been faulty, since it had been "formed for the most part of peasants and petty-bourgeois liberals, escapees from the ranks of the disintegrated Nationalist Party." They attacked the party leadership for having "mechanically adapted themselves to the 'theory' of the bourgeois and democratic stage" (of the revolution in Indochina). The Trotskyists pointed out that "terrorist activity had taken precedence over proletarian organization, brigandage over the economic struggle of the workers." The Trotskyists went on to claim that "opportunism degenerates here as elsewhere into adventurism. The formation of 'semi-legal' (?!) soviets in Nghe-Tinh, in the middle of a period of revolutionary decline constituted a little putsch on the style of the Canton insurrection, but of less breadth."[79]

In line with Trotsky's policy of seeking to reform the Communist International from within, rather than building a new rival International, the Indochinese Trotskyists indicated in 1932 a series of required steps to reshape the Indochina Communist Party. The recommendations were:

To put the proletariat into its rightful place in its own party; that is, at the head and not at the tail.

To reorganize the Party of the Indochinese proletariat conforming to the idea of communists' parties and not in accord with that of "workers' and peasants' parties"; that is, on the base of factory cells and not that of street cells and peasant cells.

To develop the almost nonexistent organizations of the proletariat: red trade unions, workers' aid, etc.

To dissolve the Anti-Imperialist League since it is the entryway into the Party of nationalist elements.

To reorganize the Red Aid on the basis of workers' aid and not as a charitable society. . . .

To base ourselves on the immense experience of the October Revolution, in order to clear our way for a line leading the proletariat toward dictatorship and socialism.[80]

Although numerically a small group, the Indochinese Trotskyists exercised a considerable degree of influence on the Indochina Communist Party's demoralized cadres in 1932 and in the years following. One factor contributing weight to their criticism of the Indochina Communist Party and the Comintern was the behavior of some of the arrested leaders of this party. Some of the principal leaders, who had received their posts at the insistence of the Comintern at the time of the fusion negotiations in February 1930, cooperated with the police after their arrest and denounced some of their erstwhile comrades.[81] Their weakness in the face of police pressure was seen as verification of the Trotskyist criticism of the party leadership as "petty-bourgeois."

In addition, some views of the Trotskyists at this time were indistinguishable from the official line of the Comintern. The Comintern was then in the throes of what had been designated as the "third period," in which a sharp "radicalization" of the masses was assumed to be taking place throughout the world. Discounting the Trotskyist criticism of past actions, there was unanimity of view in emphasizing the need for "proletarianizing" the Communist movement. In the case of the Indochina Communist Party, many of the Trotskyist proposals could easily be accepted as a basis for reconstituting the smashed organization.

Given this congruence and the desire to indicate to its followers that the revolutionary movement in Indochina still functioned, the French Communist Party reproduced sections of the aforementioned critique of the Indochina Communist Party in their theoretical journal *Cahiers du Bolshevisme* on March 15, 1932, and further referred to it in laudatory terms in their newspaper *L'Humanité* on March 25, 1932. Naturally, the French Communists excised those portions which directly indicated the Trotskyist bias of the author, but their use of it indicated the extent of actual agreement.

This view is also confirmed through examination of the new *Program of Action of the Indochina Communist Party*, issued in 1932. The leading role of the proletariat in the Indochina revolution is stressed throughout, even in a retrospective treatment of the events of 1930–31:

> The Indochinese proletariat, though young and few in number, nonetheless, directed the peasantry and the poorer classes of the cities. The Communist Party fought energetically in order that the working class assume leadership *because it is in this way only that the revolutionary camp—the proletariat, the peasantry, and the poorer classes—can vanquish the anti-revolutionary camp—imperialism, feudalism, the plantation owners, the functionaries and the fake reformist national capitalists.*[82]

In marked contrast to the foregoing stand of the French and Vietnamese Communists was the clearly divergent position taken by some leading Comintern circles at this time. This position is explicitly set forth in the form of a series of questions and answers which comprise a summary presentation of the advice offered to the Vietnamese Communists by a leading representative of the Comintern.[83] A glance at this important document permits a fuller appreciation of the ideological confusion that reigned in Communist circles attendant on the destruction of the Indo-china Communist Party. It covers the range of all the political and organi-zational problems faced by the smashed party. The questions often reveal actual doubts and differences afflicting the membership of the organiza-tion, and the responses often are concealed apologia for the mistaken acts of the past. Moreover, the document again underscores the difficulties resulting from the attempted application of Marxist-Leninist doctrine to Indochina.

The questioner is candid as to the plight of the party but asks if the party has suffered a serious defeat. The reassuring reply is that there is "no reason to speak of the defeat of the revolution in Indochina." By passing off the events as a temporary phase due to "unprecedented repres-sive measures by the French military authorities," the Comintern clearly refused to recognize the extent of its debacle in Indochina.

The key disputed problem of assessing the role of social classes in Indochina is posed. The preponderance of Communist strength among nonproletarian elements is dismissed as due to "unevenness in revolu-tionary agitation" and to the relatively more pauperized condition of the peasantry. This deficiency can be rectified if the party will "synchronize its actions" and augment thereby its proletarian character. But it is the attitude to be taken toward the native bourgeoisie that is most trouble-some. If the "native Bourgeoisie" is counterrevolutionary, "why should we not advance the slogan of overthrowing it?" The response is negative, since under such circumstances—

We shall have there an immediate socialist revolution instead of a bourgeois democratic revolution, but the nature of the forthcoming revolution is not de-termined by that. . . . [In Indochina it is necessary to] win the peasantry and urban petty-bourgeoisie over to the side of the proletariat. The peasantry in Indo-china makes up the majority of the population, whereas the proletariat represents an insignificant minority. . . . [Furthermore,] when the Communist Party raises the question of liberating Indochina from the French yoke, it will win over to its side the petty-bourgeoisie, and even part of the bourgeoisie which suffers from the import of goods from France which compete with the native manufacturers. . . . The most urgent task of the forthcoming revolution is to form a workers' and peasants' government in order to effect the tasks of the bourgeois democratic revolution and liberate the country from foreign domination.

Here, in direct contrast to the program that the Communist Party of Indo-china adopted in 1932, is the return to the formula of the two-stage revolu-tion. And again one can observe the same ambiguity that prevailed in previous years with respect to this problem.

Another principal theme barely touched upon is an echo of the great debate that preoccupied the Chinese Communist movement. Having re-cently undergone the experience of creating soviets in Indochina with disastrous results, the questioner asks when the creation of "partisan detachments" will be in order. He is assured that this activity will be mandatory only when there is a "rising wave of mass movement" in the country or a "big fight is in progress." The strategy later employed by Mao Tse-tung is proscribed at this time in Indochina and is not attempted until World War II.

Another difficult problem raised is the attitude the Vietnamese Stalinists should take toward the Viet Nam Nationalist Party and other nationalist groups, including Trotskyists. From the questions, it is clear that the Vietnamese Stalinists did not quite agree with the designation of their rivals as "social-fascists" and "counter-revolutionary" when in fact they, too, were being persecuted by the French colonial authorities. Here the policy of "united front" is advanced, with the proviso that the Vietnamese Stalinists must always seek to profit at the expense of temporary allies. In the case of reformist organizations tolerated by the government, the Communists should point out the treacherous character of the leaders and should contrast the persecution of the revolutionaries with the indulgence by the government of their opponents.

After many questions relating to the very minutiae of organizational activity under clandestine conditions,[84] concern is expressed about maintaining the democratic character of the party under conditions of illegality. In reply, it is stated that under such conditions there is no violation of democracy resulting from the appointment of a provisional central committee. The party bureau or center may be located outside the country, but the central committee must be inside the country. Since the party bureau was itself subject to the authority of the Comintern, it is clear that this reply ensured direct control from the top down in the reconstitution of the destroyed party.

In view of all the foregoing, it is not surprising that there were many Vietnamese Stalinists who doubted the advice they were given by the Comintern and who experienced real difficulty in choosing the proper interpretation of Marxist doctrine to apply in Indochina. Nonetheless, at the end of 1932, individual Communists, whether of Stalinist or Trotskyist persuasion, persistently set about the task of re-creating their organizations and carrying on agitation in Indochina. Although their movement had suffered a severe defeat, they had gained invaluable experience in leading large numbers of people and had established themselves as the pre-eminent leadership of revolutionary nationalism. Their principal rival, the Viet Nam Nationalist Party, continued to vegetate as a small group in exile. From this time forward to World War II, the Communist movement in Viet Nam dominated nationalism with its ideas, activities, and disputes.

REBUILDING THE COMMUNIST MOVEMENT

A short-lived attempt to reorganize the shattered Indochina Communist Party took place in 1932. Toward the end of the year, a provisional apparatus had been rebuilt in Tonkin, Annam, and Cochinchina. However, the French police were fully informed of these activities and destroyed the embryonic organization. Two hundred arrests were made. The French also apprehended émigrés returning home from Thailand and China who attempted to help reconstitute the Indochina Communist Party. By the end of 1932, the French authorities succeeded in virtually extirpating the underground revolutionary societies of nationalists and Communists.

In October 1932, Tran Van Giau, a former student at the Oriental University at Moscow, returned to Saigon with two other students and began to rebuild the underground Communist party. He was instrumental, early in 1933, in setting up a regional committee in Saigon, issuing a paper called Co Do (Red Flag), and circulating a theoretical magazine entitled Tap Chi Cong San (Communist Review). New efforts were made to re-establish the international connections of the Stalinist Communists in Indochina, and liaison was established with party centers in Nanking, Shanghai, and Hong Kong. In January 1933, Nguyen Ai Quoc, who had been detained by the Hong Kong British authorities for eighteen months since his arrest, was released. He went to Shanghai and then to Russia.

In April 1933, a conference of the Indochina Communist Party was held in Ban-Mai, Thailand, just over the Laotian border. The poor state of the party was clear, since not a single representative from Tonkin attended. The Central Committee was located in Thailand, contrary to Comintern directions requiring that the leading committee be inside the country. It was decided to re-establish liaison with, and rebuild, the Tonkin organization and to open an émigré school at Ban-Mai. Meanwhile, it was only in Cochinchina that the party was able to function with any effect.

Despite the revolutionary phraseology of the 1932 program of the Indochina Communist Party,[85] the party cadres became involved in the more prosaic and limited task of contesting the Saigon Municipal Council elections of May 1933. They did so through the medium of a legal, united-front organization called La Lutte, which included Trotskyists and other unaffiliated revolutionary nationalists.[86]

Given the general attitude of the Comintern toward the Trotskyist group Left Opposition, the Vietnamese Stalinists' decision to collaborate with them was clearly a peculiarity of the local situation occasioned by the weakness of the party. For the Trotskyists, by contrast, the policy of "united front" was an article of faith. In 1933, Leon Trotsky regarded

Germany as the "key to the international situation" and called for a united front of the German Socialists and Communists against the Nazis. This policy the Trotskyists tried to apply internationally. In Indochina, they were divided into two groups. The split in their ranks that developed in 1932 was to be a permanent feature of Vietnamese Trotskyism. One group, led by Ta Thu Thau, threw its full efforts behind the new La Lutte organization and was called Nhom Tranh Dau (Struggle Group) for this reason. The other group, known popularly as Nhom Thang Muoi (October Group), named after its illegal magazine (published 1931–36), was under the leadership of Ho Huu Tuong. The October Group supported La Lutte but criticized Ta Thu Thau and his followers for collaborating too closely with the Indochina Communist Party.[87]

In April 1933, a slate of eight candidates under the name of the "workers' list" was nominated. The electoral program stressed mainly a series of democratic demands (right to strike, right to form unions, voting rights, etc.) and a number of welfare measures designed to alleviate the condition of the Vietnamese workers (lighter taxes, housing, recreational facilities, etc.).[88] Through the good offices of a French resident who accepted legal responsibility for it, the newspaper La Lutte was published.

The distinguishing characteristic of La Lutte's participation in the municipal elections lay not in its program but in its candidates. These included, for the first time, a number of individuals who could by no stretch of the imagination be considered intellectuals. This ran counter to deep-seated Vietnamese beliefs about being educated, held in particular by the restricted electorate that could vote. An issue of La Lutte, appearing on the eve of the election, attacked voters who would vote only for the three "intellectual" workers. Moreover, since some of the candidates could not speak French, the paper also stressed that Vietnamese was the language of the country and that a knowledge of French was secondary since interpreters could always be used. In a striking phrase, the article pointed out that the elected representatives of the Vietnamese had a right to use their own language, which is "not that of Voltaire."[89]

By labeling its candidates "the workers' list," La Lutte sharply differentiated itself from the Constitutionalists and others. Moreover, it refused to accept the support offered by some prominent moderates. To the astonishment of many, including both the authorities and some revolutionaries, the first two candidates on the "workers' list," Nguyen Van Tao (journalist) and Tran Van Thach (professor) were elected. The success of these two candidates, apart from the appeal of their program to the predominantly lower-middle-class electorate of Saigon, was undoubtedly a measure of the genuine popularity enjoyed by the clandestine revolutionary movement. However, legal difficulties were raised which caused suspension of *La Lutte*, and steps were taken that led to the annulment of their election. In addition, "since illegal work was thought, at least by some, to be more important than legal activity, the La Lutte movement was temporarily shelved."[90]

In 1933, the principal activity of the Stalinists and Trotskyists was the defense of the many members of both groups who were brought to trial. They were aided by the French Communists, who waged a campaign against the heavy sentences meted out to their Vietnamese comrades and formed an Amnesty Committee in Defense of the Indochinese and Colonial Peoples,[91] which attracted the support of some prominent non-Communists.[92] The colonial administration found itself on the defensive in the face of the astute press campaign waged against it.[93]

A Workers' Delegation to investigate the situation in Indochina was constituted as a result of French Communist efforts and left for Saigon in January 1934. It included the Communist deputies Péri and Barthel. Their unannounced mission was to determine the best means of rebuilding the shattered Indochinese Communist movement. On his return, Péri wrote:

> The Communist Party of Indochina is subjected to fierce repression and persecution, but the blows which descended upon it have not crippled its fight. After every bloody orgy of French imperialism it has succeeded in mobilizing and organizing its forces to continue the struggle. The Party lives in close touch with the heroic Communist Party of China, whose glorious example serves as a beacon to the Communist Parties of the East, as does the Communist Party of the Soviet Union to the Communist Parties of the West.[94]

These words of ritual praise concealed the true state of affairs within the ranks of the Vietnamese Stalinists, at least as far as the estimates of both the Communist parties of France and China were concerned. The fact was that Péri had consulted with the revolutionary nationalist, Nguyen An Ninh, to determine what the prospects were for creating a legal grouping of revolutionaries in Indochina. The latter told him that it was only possible to do so together with the Trotskyists in a framework such as La Lutte had provided. The Vietnamese Stalinists believed that under the leadership of Nguyen Van Tao they could swing the organization in support of their views.[95]

While this tactical arrangement was approved, the Comintern was clearly dissatisfied with divergencies within its Indochina affiliate and with the criticism that was directed against the Comintern leadership itself. Within a short space of time, two heavy blasts directed against the Indochina Communist Party were made public.

The first attack, prepared by the French Communists, appeared in an unsigned article entitled, "Toward the Reinforcement of the Indochina Communist Party."[96] After carefully paying tribute to the beleaguered Vietnamese Communists, who were operating under "the most ferocious terror," the article became critical. The difficulty was that "young cadres have been substituted in place of former tested cadres that were equipped with great ideological strength." These new comrades, "while they look at the problems of the Indochinese Revolution in a generally correct way, have, on certain questions, leftist and non-Leninist erroneous points of view."

Only two such "erroneous" views were specified. Some Vietnamese Communists apparently were against the slogan of mere "expulsion of the French Army." They wanted to disarm it for "defense of the revolution" and to guarantee that its arms could not be used, if evacuated, against their "brothers, the French workers." In reply, simple "expulsion of the French Army" was deemed the best slogan, since "imperialism . . . could not maintain itself for one day without a strong army." The second error stemmed from the desire of some Vietnamese Communists to link the "right to separate" slogan with the "right of the Cambodian, Laotian and other nationalities to self-determination." In summary, the dissenters were told: "We must imbue ourselves with Lenin and Stalin's teachings and not pose the national question from the point of view of formal democracy."

But these lessons in Marxism-Leninism were hardly worth a special article in the theoretical journal of the French Communist Party. The anonymous writer gets down to cases on the key question of concern to the international Communist leadership: "Democratic centralism and iron discipline demand that inferior organs of the Party must submit to superior organs and carry out all the resolutions adopted by the latter." Freedom of discussion is not at stake since "the lower organs may discuss at length all these decisions" and even "demand explanations" on obscure points.

[What is not permissible is for] the lower organs . . . in the absence of a definitive reply from the superior organs . . . to correct these decisions or to make use of their press to enter into polemic with the superior organs. . . . We do not demand that the comrades execute blindly the decisions of superior bodies [Provisional Central Committee and the Comintern]. If they find that certain points in the program do not fit the concrete situation in the country, they can ask the Comintern to add or subtract something. But if they allow themselves to correct the Party program of action elaborated by the Comintern without asking its opinion, such action is incompatible with the principle of democratic centralism, with iron discipline, and with the Comintern.

This reading of the riot act to the Indochina Communist Party was underscored again when the Central Committee of the Communist Party of China wrote an open letter stressing the same themes to the members of their brother party in Indochina.[97] No mention is made of divergent views that are disapproved. Here, the harangue is directed toward the central notion which is to be grasped by the Vietnamese Stalinists, since their very future depends on it; i.e., "the gauge of victory is a disciplined and powerful Bolshevik Party." Moreover, the Chinese Communist Party, "whose glorious example," in Péri's words, "serves as a beacon to the Communist Parties of the East," itself modestly calls attention to this fact:

> Our Party under the leadership of the Communist International has strengthened itself successfully and bolshevized its ranks. And that alone explains the immense conquests that we registered in the present period. . . .
> The Party must be based on iron discipline. Under conditions of complete illegality, the least infraction of discipline, the tiniest struggle of faction or clique, the smallest divergence from the fundamental line of the party can have fatal consequences. Comrades, you must never forget your Party's history. You must remember that the six years since Communist groups first appeared in Indochina have been years of struggle and factional quarrels. You must remember that at the moment of party unification, sufficient care was not taken to demarcate and select the best elements from among the Communist groups which were united. That is why the Party must always be prepared for the possible resurrection of a factional spirit and of sectarian tendencies among certain groups or among certain party members and be ready to curb them with a violent reply. *Every Communist must guard the unity of the Party as the apple of his eye.* [Italics in original.]

In effect, the Comintern was demanding unconditional adherence to Moscow's line and the creation of a "monolithic leadership" within the Indochina Communist Party. The timing of these sharp attacks on the Indochinese Stalinists was dictated by the need to ensure unquestioning acceptance of a new Comintern policy that was itself a consequence of a major shift in Soviet Russia's diplomacy.

PEOPLE'S FRONT—VIETNAMESE-STYLE

In 1934, in response to the avowedly anti-Soviet policy of the Hitler government, the U.S.S.R. began a policy of *rapprochement* with France and joined the previously despised League of Nations. It became a major aim of Soviet diplomacy to create an anti-Fascist coalition directed against resurgent Germany. The French nation occupied a key role in these calculations. The ability of the French Communists to emerge from their political isolation and influence French foreign policy could seriously affect the possible success of this strategy.

In June 1934, the French Communists, under Comintern direction, adopted a united-front policy directed toward the French Socialists.[98] By the end of the year, the united-front concept was enlarged by the Communists to that of the People's Front to allow for the inclusion into a left

bloc of the Radical Socialist Party. These Communist efforts were successful and the subsequent People's Front electoral coalition met with victory
at the polls in the 1935 municipal elections and the 1936 national elections.
As part of the ruling governmental coalition in June 1936, and as a consequence of their own rapid rise to strength, the French Communists could
now exert some influence on French policy at home and abroad. These
events had great repercussions in distant Indochina.

The united-front policy of the Comintern was easily accepted in Indochina since the Vietnamese Stalinists had already had some success in
conducting joint activity with the Trotskyists and other unaffiliated national revolutionists in the Saigon municipal elections of May 1933. The
People's Front line created problems since it posed anew the question
of permissible collaboration with nonrevolutionary nationalists.

In this connection, Trotskyist influence was a factor to be considered
both in its impact on the cadres of the Indochina Communist Party and
in the relative popularity of its leaders among the more radical Vietnamese
nationalists. The Struggle Group Trotskyists were disposed toward a
united front with the Stalinists. The October Group, which had changed
its official name from Left Opposition to International Communist League
in 1934,[99] was also willing to participate in joint action, but was extremely
critical of the Stalinists. The Trotskyist groups mistrusted Comintern
policy, which, they believed, would lead the workers into opportunistic
collaboration with bourgeois elements.

The organization La Lutte was again reconstituted as a collective bloc
of Stalinists, Trotskyists, and revolutionary nationalists. Its newspaper
La Lutte was able to resume publication in October 1934. Despite a limitation on its potential influence due to legal obstacles that forced it to
appear in French and not in the vernacular, it achieved a substantial measure of popularity. To develop the class consciousness of the Vietnamese
intelligentsia and working class, the editors of La Lutte vigorously attacked the Constitutionalists.[100] They did so in order to destroy among
the Vietnamese any political tendencies favoring simple reform of the
colonial administration and to assure, by this policy, working-class hegemony in the coming struggle for Vietnamese independence.

It is also true, however, that within the rather rigid framework of
Marxist ideology, La Lutte addressed itself to problems which could and
did elicit the sympathy of many non-Communist and moderate Vietnamese. It carried on a campaign against the hard life of jailed Vietnamese
and called for amnesty of political prisoners. It directly attacked the
stereotypes which many French (and even some Vietnamese) held about
the character of the Vietnamese people; e.g., that the Vietnamese were
by nature "sly," "prone to frivolity," "submissive," "profoundly attached

to tradition," and "incapable of solidarity."[101] To replace the restrictive, unrepresentative institutions that functioned in Indochina, *La Lutte* called for a parliament to be elected by universal suffrage. It championed democratic rights and liberties for all. It called for universal and free education and favored a program of public works. As a result of this activity, the Stalinists and Trotskyists augmented the strength of their underground organizations.[102]

The growing strength of the People's Front in France raised hopes among the Vietnamese of a possible liberalization of the colonial regime. It also focused Vietnamese attention on this new strategy as a means of building a larger nationalist movement. As the Vietnamese Stalinists tentatively began to press for this policy, conflict ensued between them and the more extreme Trotskyists.

When, prior to the Saigon Municipal Council elections of May 1935, Duong Bach Mai, a leading Stalinist, was proposed as one of the nominees, a sharp fight broke out. Ta Thu Thau, the Trotskyist, had considerable difficulty in convincing many members of La Lutte that they should accept Duong Bach Mai as a candidate since they regarded him as much too "reformist." Ta Thu Thau felt that the united front must be maintained and spoke for Duong Bach Mai as the most capable representative of the Vietnamese Stalinists.[103] Subsequently, four of La Lutte's candidates, their leading representatives and intellectuals, Nguyen Van Tao, Duong Bach Mai, Ta Thu Thau, and Tran Van Thach, were elected.

The columns of *La Lutte* became a mélange of views, reflecting the fluctuating positions of Stalinists and Trotskyists within the joint organization. Thus, on May 18, 1935, the elected representatives of La Lutte stated:

> The Indochinese working class now is only at the stage of elementary organization. . . . Habituated to obey orders and to let themselves be maltreated, it is necessary that those who sell their labor power emerge from their submissiveness, raise their heads and claim their share of well-being and intellectual culture. It would be inexplicable, in the given political situation, for the elected workers to practice a systematic extremist policy apropos of anything and everything in the Municipal Council. . . . Modest demands are called for by the masses. . . . Marxists are not blind sectarians. Their doctrine does not exclude— far from it—supple and accurate tactics, constantly on the mark. We want to be constructive in our activity as representatives of the working class.[104]

This "constructive" policy was apparently carried so far that their Constitutionalist opponents now accused them of collaboration with the administration! They were forced to specifically deny that they were becoming "friends of the administration."[105]

The French Communists, despite their own domestic political behav-

ior, still approved of a policy of hostility to the moderate nationalist
elements in Indochina. G. Péri clearly favored such a Vietnamese policy
when he wrote approvingly of the "workers' opposition" which had "forced
a breach in the Constitutionalist Party."[106] Moreover, Chajan, the Indochinese delegate to the Seventh Comintern Congress, made the same point
in his address. He argued:

[The influence of the party has increased,] especially recently among those masses
which were under the influence of the National Reformists. This was shown by
the municipal elections in Saigon, Cochinchina. Our Party put forward its "workers' list" and, of the six native deputies to be elected to the Municipal Council,
secured the election of four of its candidates. This was the first experience of
broad mass work by our Party.[107]

His only public reference to dissatisfaction with the Vietnamese Stalinists
indicated that "many of them continue their old practices and pursue
sectarian methods of work." There was no reference to the participation
of Trotskyists in the "workers' list" and in La Lutte. The only formal
action taken at the Seventh Congress in regard to the Vietnamese was
to admit the Indochina Communist Party into the Comintern as a national
section on August 20, 1935.[108] It seems clear that the Vietnamese Stalinists
were at this point being granted special dispensation in the tempo at
which they introduced the policy of the Communist International in Indochina.

Nonetheless, the People's Front trend was unmistakable in the latter
part of 1935 and 1936. Gradually the Vietnamese Stalinists moderated
their line toward the Constitutionalists and the colonial administration.
But it was not until May 1936 that the Central Committee of the Indochina
Communist Party finally adopted the new line of the Comintern.

Right up to May, 1936, the Indochinese Communists were still demanding
of other groups and parties, as a condition for the formation of the People's Front,
the struggle for the immediate overthrow of imperialism, for the agrarian revolution, etc. The Communists appealed only to groups and parties long known as
anti-imperialist, forgetting that the People's Front should unite all the people,
that the people have immediate demands common to all parties.[109]

When the People's Front government came to power in France in June
1936, it became mandatory for the Vietnamese Stalinists to emphasize
to their members complete acceptance of the new policy. That is why
the commentator above goes on to say:

Last July [1936] is an historic date for the Communist Party. The Party
leadership sent out directives correcting sectarian mistakes and explaining the
political line of the Comintern. Sectarianism has not been completely eliminated.
. . . [There are] too sharp attacks on the Constitutionalists. . . . [The party]
can't formulate simple, concrete slogans.

Despite these criticisms, the fact was that the Vietnamese Stalinists had managed to take over control of La Lutte from the Trotskyists in this period.

The advent of the People's Front government in France did lead to a marked amelioration of conditions in Indochina. A number of political prisoners were released from jail. A greater measure of civil liberties was allowed, and the revolutionary underground organizations were able to build legal counterparts. In Cochinchina the Trotskyists and Stalinists created a movement known as the Indochinese Congress, whose final convocation was designed to prepare a set of popularly formulated demands to be presented to a long-awaited Commission of Inquiry from France. Many moderate nationalists were drawn into this activity, including Bui Quang Chieu and Nguyen Phan Long, of the now virtually moribund Constitutionalist Party, and Dr. Nguyen Van Thinh, of the newly formed Democratic Party. At the base of this movement more than six hundred committees of action were formed to organize the workers, principally in the Saigon-Cholon area and throughout Cochinchina. It was here that the Trotskyists were most active and most effective.[110] Whatever influence they had lost in La Lutte, they compensated for in the new mass organizations. They were instrumental in promoting union activity, and a large number of strikes occurred. In turn, their success in this activity strengthened their influence in La Lutte.

During 1936, there was also a rebirth of nationalist activity in Tonkin. The underground Communist party was able to create a legal counterpart in the Indochinese Democratic Front, led by their militants Vo Nguyen Giap and Pham Van Dong. The movement spread to Hué in Annam. A concomitant of this activity was the legal founding of a Federation Socialiste du Nord Indochine. In 1936 this organization included some five hundred members in the nine branches (Hanoi, Hai Phong, Ha Dong, Lang Son, Nam Dinh, Hong Gay, Thanh Hoa, Vinh, Tourane). From 1936 on, it accepted Vietnamese members, and about half of its partisans were Vietnamese. Some of them were Stalinists, like Vo Nguyen Giap. Other prominent Vietnamese members included Hoang Minh Giam, Pham Anh, and Vu Dinh Hoe.[111] A similar legal Federation Socialiste du Cochinchine was formed in October 1936 and had members in Cambodia, Cochinchina, South and Central Annam.[112] These federations were sections of the French Socialist Party, and to the extent that Marxism had any real influence in that party, it was reflected in its Indochina affiliates.

It was during this period that the full impact of the People's Front line as promulgated by the Stalinists became clear. In its application to Indochina, the policy indicated abandonment of the struggle for separation from the mother country.

In 1937, at the Arles Congress of the French Communist Party, Thorez summed up the colonial policy of the Party in the formula: self-determination, right to independence; but, making use of a proposal by Lenin, he added: "The right to separation does not signify the obligation to separate." The interests of the colonial people are in a union "free, trusting and paternal" with democratic France. To forge this union, so it appeared in his eyes, was "the mission of France all over the world."[113]

The application of this policy to Indochina by the Vietnamese Stalinists brought them into violent conflict with their Trotskyist allies. In the estimation of the Trotskyists, the Indochina Communist Party was betraying the Vietnamese to please the French Communists and ultimately the Soviet government, which had signed a mutual defense pact with France. They spoke against any approval of national defense measures against the Japanese on the grounds that the coming war was equally reactionary on both sides. Trotskyist propaganda was successful in attracting many who were thoroughly dissatisfied with French colonial rule. The failure of the French People's Front government to carry through an extensive program of reforms in Indochina was further grist to the Trotskyist mill. In contrast to the Vietnamese Stalinists, who had adopted a more conciliatory tone toward the colonial administration, the Trotskyists stepped up their campaign of strikes and their demands for more Vietnamese freedom. Now, the Trotskyist strength increased at the expense of the Stalinists in La Lutte, which was torn by a severe factional fight.[114]

The Stalinist faction recognized that they were at a disadvantage vis-à-vis their Trotskyist rivals in La Lutte. They were also subject to heavy pressure from the Communist International and the French Communists to end the bloc with the Trotskyists. In May 1937, they published the first issue of their own paper L'Avant Garde and attacked the Trotskyists therein as "professional agitators."[115] A split in La Lutte was now inevitable.[116]

On June 14, 1937, La Lutte was split when the Stalinists refused to support a motion, introduced by Ta Thu Thau, attacking the People's Front.[117] The Vietnamese Trotskyists gained popular influence at the expense of their rivals. They reproduced a copy of a letter in La Lutte from the French Communist Party to the Indochina Communist Party that clearly indicated that the order to split La Lutte had come from Moscow.[118] When Ta Thu Thau was arrested by the colonial authorities on orders from Paris, this action simply increased, in the eyes of his countrymen, his already great prestige as an outstanding leader in the fight for Vietnamese freedom.

The Indochina Communist Party line now closely paralleled that of the French Communist Party. In Tonkin and Annam, the Democratic United Front, which was under Stalinist direction but included non-Communist groups and parties, mirrored this development. In its program, it spoke of the "resolute soldiers who would struggle on the battlefield in the event of invasion by the Japanese fascists."[119] The Indochina Communist Party had rebuilt a strong organization, but it began to lose ground among its supporters. Internal schisms multiplied as the new policy led to a marked lessening of party militancy. In the next two years, the Indochinese Stalinists supported all the steps taken to bolster the French war effort, to the accompaniment of severe criticism from the Trotskyists. Stalinist participation in the Cochinchina Colonial Council elections of April 1939 resulted in a crushing defeat and a subsequent split in the party. Nguyen Van Tao formed his own faction, while Duong Bach Mai maintained leadership in the official party.

Toward the end of 1937, the legally published weekly newspaper *Le Militant* was issued by the Trotskyist October Group, only to be suppressed for its role in supporting the vigorous strike movement. In 1938 the magazine *October* again appeared as a semilegal magazine accompanied by the weekly newspaper *Tia Sang* (*Spark*), which became a daily at the beginning of the year. The Trotskyist Struggle Group continued to publish *La Lutte* and supplemented it in 1939 with an edition in Vietnamese, *Tranh Dau*. At the elections for the Colonial Council of Cochinchina on April 30, 1939, the three Trotskyists Ta Thu Thau, Tran Van Thach, and Phan Van Hum received 80 per cent of the votes, defeating three Constitutionalists, two Stalinists, and several independent representatives in the balloting. This was probably the high point of Trotskyist strength in Indochina in the pre-World War II period. A Trotskyist source claims that they had a Vietnamese membership of three thousand in 1939.[120]

The approach of war and the political situation in France indicated a new revival of the policy of repression by the French colonial authorities. The Trotskyists of the Struggle Group, who had thus far relied for the most part on their legal organization, began to construct an illegal apparatus. An underground organization limited to the Saigon-Cholon area was set up. But now, together with their Stalinist rivals and the other nationalist groups, the Trotskyists of both the Struggle Group and the October Group were caught up in the maelstrom of World War II.

A NEW BID FOR POWER

The Stalin-Hitler pact and the outbreak of war in Europe radically altered the situation in Indochina. On September 26, 1939, the French government decreed the dissolution of the now "antiwar" French Communist Party. This same decree was applied in Indochina. The French colonial police arrested some two hundred Stalinists and Trotskyists. The Indochina Communist Party and the Trotskyist groups were driven completely underground. Despite the arrests, an underground, tightly knit Stalinist organization prepared itself for action against French authority in Indochina.

The Indochina Communist Party's Central Committee in Cochinchina met in plenary session from November 6 to 8, 1939. A new policy, consonant with the "antiwar" position of the Comintern following the Stalin-Hitler pact, was adopted. The former Democratic Front was replaced by a new United Front of Anti-Imperialist Indochinese Peoples. With the help of the U.S.S.R., designated as "the fortress of world revolution," the new Front would oppose the "imperialist war, overthrow French imperialism and the native feudalists, recover the independence of Indochina, and install an Indochinese Democratic Republican Union."[121]

As it happened, however, the Communist party was hardly in a position to accomplish these objectives. The French colonial authorities, acting under a new decree of January 21, 1940, arrested more of their members and restricted the liberties of others. The Vietnamese Stalinists were in practice limited to propagandizing against all measures designed to aid the French war effort. However, when France fell in June 1940, the Vietnamese Stalinists, like other nationalists, felt that the time had come for decisive action against the colonial authority. The Central Committee of the Indochina Communist Party adopted a new policy:

[The Indochina Communist Party resolves] in view of the very critical internal situation in Indochina and of the imminent external danger which menaces this country, to prepare armed insurrection in order to install a republican government which will ally itself with the Resistance Front of the Chinese people, with the U.S.S.R., and with the world revolution.[122]

The French authorities seized numerous documents, in July 1940, which are said to have revealed the systematic preparation by the Central Committee for education of its militants on questions relating to insurrection, guerrilla warfare, and sabotage. All sectors of the population were called on to join in the struggle under the banner of the Anti-Imperialist United Front of the Indochinese Peoples. The Indochina Communist Party distributed literature in three languages (Vietnamese, Chinese, and French) which emphasized the weakening of the colonial regime occasioned by the defeat of France and which warned against an alliance of French imperialism with Japanese fascism.[123]

In the northern areas of Tonkin, bordering on China, bands of Vietnamese nationalists undertook unsuccessful military operations against the French in September and October 1940. These events and the colonial government's inability to withstand Japanese demands contributed to considerable unrest among the Vietnamese in Cochinchina. The agitation of the Indochina Communist Party began to achieve some success. The Stalinists were able to stage demonstrations in the provinces of Vinh Long, Tra Vinh, Bac Lieu, and Rach Gia. These meetings called for opposition to arrests, refusal to recognize the authority of officials, pillage of the wealth of rich proprietors, destruction of French imperialism, obstruction of the way to Japanese invasion, and realization of Indochinese independence. Though the external bureau of the Indochina Communist Party, located in Kunming and headed by Nguyen Ai Quoc, apparently counseled against premature insurrection in Indochina, the organization in Cochinchina, believed to number some three thousand members at this time despite the internment of some eight hundred party members the preceding year, was mobilized for a coming insurrection. The left wing of the faction-ridden party in Cochinchina pressed for this policy. The insurrection was probably also supported by other revolutionary nationalists who felt this was a propitious moment. It began in the Plaine des Jonco and spread through the western provinces. A number of districts were declared free of French authority. But the French, informed in advance of the attempt, reacted with dispatch and engaged in a thorough operation designed to clear all of Cochinchina of the insurrectionists. More than six thousand arrests were made, and French authority was quickly re-established throughout the provinces.

After this defeat, a regional meeting of the Indochina Communist Party was held from January 21 to 28, 1941. Those responsible for the insurrectionary movement were attacked and several expelled from the party, and several members (believed to be police agents) condemned to death. Provision was made for the immediate reorganization of the smashed party apparatus. Liaison with the Chinese in Indochina, as well as with the masses of Tonkin and Annam, was declared necessary. The new program called for concentration of forces in an army located in the region of Saigon-Cholon and western Cochinchina. This striking force would, after augmenting its ranks sufficiently, move into Tonkin and Annam. These plans remained on paper, however, since the movement had been effectively destroyed as a functioning organization. The Vietnamese Stalinists were forced to regroup in exile in southern China during World War II.

THE VIET MINH—A NEW STALINIST STRATEGY IN INDOCHINA

The Japanese occupation of Indochina from 1941 to 1945 brought great changes in Vietnamese political life. The weak French regime depended for its existence on the good graces of the Japanese. Both authorities looked for bases of support in the indigenous population. Many nation-

alists tried to curry favor with the Japanese in the hope that the latter
would dispense with the French colonial administration and install an
"independent" Vietnamese government. Other nationalists took advantage of the new opportunities offered by the French in their effort to
keep the allegiance of the Vietnamese; they accepted leadership in newly
created organizations (youth groups, educational associations, etc.) and
moved into the higher administrative posts now made available to them.
Indochina's isolation from metropolitan France forced the colonial administration, under Admiral Jean Decoux,[124] to develop local resources.
This situation and the events of World War II drew thousands of young
Vietnamese into political life and accelerated their political education.

Meanwhile, the defeated remnants of the Indochina Communist Party
reorganized in southern China. In May 1941, Nguyen Ai Quoc convoked
a meeting of his party's Central Committee in Tsingsi, a small Chinese
village in the border area of Kwangsi province near the Vietnamese frontier city of Cao Bang. The decision was made to found the Viet Nam
Doc Lap Dong Minh Hoi (Viet Nam Independence League), popularly
known thereafter as the Viet Minh, which would serve as a coordinating
organization for both individuals and affiliated groups in the struggle to
free Viet Nam.[125] The bulk of the Viet Minh membership was provided
by the Indochina Communist Party. Its leadership included tested Stalinist veterans like Vo Nguyen Giap and Pham Van Dong. In northern Indochina, henceforth, the Vietnamese Stalinists functioned exclusively within
the Viet Minh and formulated its policy. The principal affiliates were
a number of National Liberation Associations set up to enlist workers,
peasants, youth, businessmen, Catholics, Buddhists, etc. The program of
the League was summed up in three major points:

1. To drive out the French and Japanese Fascists and restore the independence
   of Viet Nam.
2. To unite with all the forces fighting fascism and aggression.
3. To build a Democratic Republic of Viet Nam.[126]

From the beginning, the Viet Minh asked for aid from the Chinese
Kuomintang government. It sought to capitalize on the Chinese interest
in striking blows against the Japanese troops in Indochina. This occupation had cut off a valuable supply line for China. The Viet Minh offered
the Chinese its services in gathering information in Indochina and creating a local military force for joint action against the Japanese.[127] The
Chinese, who had no love for the French administration in Indochina,
were quite willing to provide haven and aid to the various groups of
Vietnamese refugees in southern China.

However, the Viet Minh had competitors in southern China. Remnants of the Viet Nam Nationalist Party and other small revolutionary

nationalist groups vied with the Viet Minh for Chinese support by playing on the Kuomintang's antipathy to the Chinese Communists. Early in 1942, Chinese suspicion of the Communist character of the Viet Minh led to Nguyen Ai Quoc's arrest and imprisonment for thirteen months.[128]

The Chinese governor of Kwangsi province, Chang Fa-kwei, encouraged consolidation of the various Vietnamese groups. Representatives of the Viet Minh and all the refugee Vietnamese organizations in southern China met jointly at a congress in Liuchow from October 4 to 16, 1942. On October 10, the formation of the Viet Nam Cach Menh Dong Minh Hoi (Viet Nam Revolutionary League) was announced. The Central Committee elected included Viet Minh representatives. An organizational plan for southern China and Indochina was approved, and control of the organization vested in Nguyen Hai Than, a veteran nationalist and partisan of the Viet Nam Nationalist Party. The League's program was broadly equivalent to that of the Chinese Kuomintang and included Sun Yat-sen's Three People's Principles. It called for the liberation of Viet Nam and close cooperation between independent Viet Nam and China. Organizationally, the new League was constituted as a paramilitary formation that worked in close liaison with the Chinese Nationalist army. It was charged with setting up an espionage apparatus in northern Indochina.[129]

Although nominally a member of the League, the Viet Minh nevertheless carried on its own independent work in Indochina. It set up its own network in the villages, issued its propaganda independently, and presented itself as the principal organization uniting all groups in the struggle against French and Japanese domination of Indochina.[130] Nguyen Ai Quoc maintained contact with the Viet Minh from his prison cell, while Pham Van Dong headed the organization in southern China and Vo Nguyen Giap directed its activities in northern Indochina.

The Viet Nam Revolutionary League, however, met with little success in its efforts to set up an espionage network in northern Indochina, and the Chinese became dissatisfied with this failure and with the fact that the organization was plagued with internal quarrels. In jail, Nguyen Ai Quoc, apprised of these difficulties, wrote to Chang Fa-kwei asking for his release and offering to build an effective organization in northern Indochina to aid the Chinese war effort. This strategy succeeded. In February 1943 he was released, and to dispel the aura of his Communist past, he changed his name to Ho Chi Minh (He Who Is Enlightened, or Has Wisdom). He was installed as head of the Viet Nam Revolutionary League and received the financial aid that had formerly been given to its nationalist leaders. The work of the Viet Minh was promptly intensified in northern Indochina, and along with its other activities, it provided the Chinese with the military information they sought.

Viet Minh propaganda in 1943 was not only aimed at the Vietnamese but called upon the French in Indochina who were dissatisfied with the puppet administration to rally to their side in building a united anti-Japanese front. The Viet Minh followed with close attention events in Europe and associated itself with all the appeals of the French government-in-exile, then known as the Algiers Liberation Committee.[131] In its propaganda efforts the Viet Minh sought to present itself as the legitimate Indochinese representative of the Allied fighting forces.

However, on December 5, 1943, the De Gaulle government issued a statement on the future of Indochina. It promised reorganization of the Indochinese economy and large political reforms, but it clearly envisaged nothing more than an autonomous status for Indochina within a larger association of France and her overseas territories. The Vietnamese Stalinists reacted strongly to this proposal. Under their own name—and not that of the Viet Minh—they bitterly attacked the Algiers Committee's declaration. They called attention to the difficulties of the anti-Fascist French in Indochina and said that they were willing to unite with them against the Decoux administration and the Japanese. This united front was possible, however, only on two conditions: a jointly planned effort by the participants in the front; and acceptance by the French of the complete independence of Indochina. "The Algiers Liberation Committee is mistaken in believing that the Indochinese people will content themselves with flatteries, assurances, and promises. We want complete liberty." The Stalinist statement commented bitterly on the failure of De Gaulle's representatives to work together with them in Indochina. They argued bad faith on the part of the De Gaullists and pointed out:

[Their ambiguous attitude] probably puts them between two fires: on the one side, the Japanese militarists; on the other, the revolutionary peoples of Indochina. They [the De Gaullists] clearly hope the intervention of the Allied forces will get them out of this situation. But the Allied powers who denoted themselves as "liberators" at Teheran do not have the right to impose any kind of yoke on other people, even when this yoke is "humanized" and sweetened by the partisans of De Gaulle! The end of the Axis signifies at the same time the decline of imperialism. In the sacred struggle for their emancipation, all the people of the world have arisen. The freedom offensive, led by the U.S.S.R. and its allies, stirs up the millions of oppressed against all autocracy and all exploitation.[132]

In contrast, the Viet Minh League itself publicly emphasized the need for unity among the anti-Fascists of Indochina and did not attack the De Gaullists. Since the fall of the Vichy government plainly foreshadowed difficulties for the local French administration in Indochina, the Viet Minh called upon the anti-Fascist French to prepare themselves for a possible Japanese coup that would dispense with the local French administration:

> Republican France has arisen and calls on its children to strenuous combat for liberty and peace. The revolutionary peoples of Indochina are preparing for the overthrow of fascist domination. The Chinese Army is ready to cross the frontier of Tonkin in order to chase from Indochina the Nipponese invaders and their lackeys of every description. May all the forces of liberty and progress in Indochina unite together to parry in time an imminent political crisis![133]

The independent activity conducted with increasing success by the Viet Minh caused dissatisfaction among the other nationalist organizations functioning in southern China. Pressure was also brought to bear on the Chinese by the French intelligence services who pointed out the Communist character of the Viet Minh. The French were unwilling to lend prestige to the Viet Minh for fear of building up its strength in Indochina.[134] To meet these objections, Chang Fa-kwei had another congress of the Viet Nam Revolutionary League convoked in Liuchow from March 25 to 28, 1944. The outcome of this congress's deliberation was to again place control of the League in the hands of the Viet Nam Nationalist Party, which was deemed more reliable by its Chinese mentors. The Viet Minh continued its nominal membership in the League, which now set up a provisional Indochina Republican government-in-exile; in fact, Ho Chi Minh occupied a ministerial post. Nevertheless, relations between the Chinese and the Viet Minh became strained.

To offset the loss of Chinese support, the Viet Minh attempted to gain American aid in this period. Contact was established with the U.S. Office of Strategic Services (OSS). The Viet Minh received a small amount of support from that quarter for its agents in northern Tonkin.[135] In that region, the Viet Minh continued to function independently, and its propaganda took effect. Many Vietnamese began to sense that Allied victory was a certainty. The Viet Minh program seemed attractive as a means of realizing the long-sought independence of Viet Nam, and it won many new recruits.

On December 22, 1944, the Viet Nam Liberation Army was officially formed. Its aim was to conduct guerrilla warfare against the Japanese and French military forces and also to prepare the political and military bases for the future uprising that would free Viet Nam.[136]

Several months later, on March 9, 1945, the Japanese dispensed with French authority in Indochina. On March 11, Bao Dai, as Emperor of the court of Annam, declared that the French-Vietnamese treaty of 1884 had been abrogated and that Viet Nam was now an independent state. Under the watchful eyes of the Japanese, various nationalist groups began to mobilize support for their version of a free Viet Nam. The Viet Minh attacked the new Bao Dai government as a "puppet government which deceives the people on behalf of its Nipponese masters." It called on the Vietnamese to help drive out the Japanese by following "the glorious example of the Russian, Rumanian and Chinese peoples," and indicated that an invasion of Indochina by "Chinese, American and British troops" was imminent.[137] Viet Minh influence grew as many Vietnamese became aware that Japan was on the verge of defeat. In May 1945, the Viet Minh officially set up "a liberated zone comprising the six provinces of Cao Bang, Lang Son, Ha Giang, Bac Kan, Tuyen Quang, and Thai Nguyen."[138]

Meanwhile, the destroyed Trotskyist movement had resumed activity within Indochina. Beginning in August 1944, the first regrouping of adherents of the Fourth International took place in Saigon. Aided by several partisans from northern Indochina, these former supporters of the October Group reconstituted the International Communist League. Shortly after the Japanese coup on March 9, 1945, the League called on the "revolutionary Saigon masses" to prepare for a coming insurrection. Its manifesto of March 24, 1945, declared:

The future defeat of Japanese imperialism will set the Indochinese people on the road to national liberation. The bourgeoisie and feudalists who cravenly serve the Japanese rulers today, will serve equally the Allied imperialist states. The petty-bourgeois nationalists, by their aimless policy, will also be incapable of leading the people towards revolutionary victory. Only the working class, which struggles independently under the flag of the Fourth International, will be able to accomplish the advance guard tasks of the revolution.

The Stalinists of the Third International have already abandoned the working class to group themselves miserably with the "democratic" imperialisms. They have betrayed the peasants and no longer speak of the agrarian question. If today they march with foreign capitalists, in the future, they will help the class of national exploiters to destroy the revolutionary people in the hours to come.[139]

The program of the Trotskyists called for opposition to imperialism and for support of world revolution, a worker-peasant united front, the creation of people's committees (soviets), establishment of a constituent assembly, arms for the people, seizure of land by the peasants, nationalization of the factories under workers' control, and the creation of a workers' and peasants' government.

The Trotskyist Struggle Group also reorganized in May and June of 1945. The difference between the two Trotskyist groups, revolving mainly around the question of relations with the Vietnamese Stalinists, had not been reconciled, though their programs tended to be similar. Both groups were to play an influential role in subsequent events in South Viet Nam.[140]

Meanwhile in North Viet Nam, during June 1945, the Viet Minh consolidated its hold in the liberated areas under control of its guerrillas. It appealed to the Vietnamese under the rule of the Japanese-backed Bao Dai government for support by extolling the virtues of its own regime:

Revolutionary administrative centers have been set up in different localities. The people's Revolutionary Committees, directly elected by different organizations of the population, are using revolutionary methods to bring back freedom and happiness to the whole people.

The properties of the population in the Liberated zones are being effectively protected. Properties belonging to the invaders have been seized. They have become public property or have been distributed to the poor. Democratic rights and liberties are being translated into actual deeds. All citizens are equal before the law. The sick and poor are given assistance, robbery and banditry are completely stamped out. All taxes and impositions have been abolished, and land taxes reduced. The working hours are shortened. Boys and girls are either pursuing their studies or fight[ing] on the battlefields. Rich and poor, young and old, are working day and night to supply our armies. Over one million of our compatriots already enjoy revolutionary liberties and happiness. A "New Vietnam" has come into being![141]

This same appeal indicated that "although French rule in Indochina has been practically shattered, yet, De Gaullist elements are endeavoring to stage a comeback and to re-establish the French colonial yoke in our country." This was a perfect example of Communist duplicity, for the Viet Minh was already in contact, and desirous of negotiation, with these same De Gaullist forces. In fact, the Viet Minh had even communicated to the De Gaullist French a memorandum which accepted the principle of the temporary re-establishment of French sovereignty in Viet Nam.[142] These negotiations came to naught. The Viet Minh pressed its preparations for a National Congress and, after delays due to "transport difficulties," the congress "formally opened in the liberated zones on the day of Japan's capitulation."[143]

The Viet Minh reacted quickly to the news of the imminent surrender of the Japanese and the end of the war in the Pacific. On August 13, 1945, a Military Committee was established which ordered the units of the Viet Nam Liberation Army into action throughout the country and called for a general insurrection.[144] The Viet Minh asked that the Japanese army lay down its arms and proposed that the Japanese authorities hand power over to the Vietnamese people. Within three days, on August 16, 1945, the hastily convened National Congress met at Tan Trao, a city in Thai Nguyen province, which was part of the liberated zone set up by the Viet Minh. Policy was formulated, and a Viet Nam People's Liberation Committee was appointed. The Viet Minh's program at this time was designed to realize three essential objectives:

1. To disarm the Japs [sic] before the entry of Allied forces into Indochina,
2. To wrest the power from the hands of the enemy, and
3. To be in a position of power when receiving the Allied Forces.

In some areas the order for the general revolution was not received. Acting on their own initiative, members of the Viet Minh front ordered a general mobilization and led the population into the fight for power. Thus, on August 11, our compatriots of Ha Tinh took up arms against the Japanese fascists, while uprisings also took place at Quang Ngai.[145]

The Viet Minh leadership clearly recognized that it would be to their interest to establish their rule in Indochina before the arrival of Allied detachments to receive the Japanese surrender. They hoped, by presenting these Allied forces with a *fait accompli,* that their government would be accepted and their leadership confirmed. The tide ran in favor of the Viet Minh. Throughout Tonkin and Annam, the local populations demonstrated in favor of their newly found freedom. A genuine popular revolution took place that surpassed the wildest calculations of the Viet Minh, though they alone were prepared for the events as an organized force with a definite program. Claiming the support of the Allied powers and pointing to their previous activity, the Viet Minh won acceptance by the people, particularly in North Viet Nam. The Japanese authorities looked on benignly while Viet Minh partisans occupied the public buildings in Hanoi. They also turned over local stocks of arms to the Viet Minh.

At Hué on August 22, 1945, Emperor Bao Dai was prepared to call upon the Viet Minh to form a new government. This proposal would probably have been accepted by the Viet Minh, since Ho Chi Minh favored an arrangement in which the monarchy would remain and his provisional government be granted authority. This would facilitate acceptance of its legitimacy by the Allied powers. However, on the preceding day, August 21, a large meeting had been convoked under the auspices of the Hanoi General Association of Students. Some left-wing intellectuals, including Ho Huu Tuong, a former leader of the Trotskyist October Group, successfully moved the adoption of a motion which:

1. Called for the abdication of the Emperor of Annam, the installation of a republican regime, and the grant of power to a provisional government formed by the Viet Minh;
2. Asked the Viet Minh immediately to open negotiations with the other parties with an eye to forming a provisional government;
3. Called on all parties, all classes of the population, and the largest body of the people to support the provisional government in order to begin the work of consolidation of national independence.[146]

These demands were incorporated in a telegram that was sent to Bao Dai, who decided thereafter to abdicate on August 24, 1945. In his abdication act, Bao Dai specified:

We ask the new government to treat fraternally all the parties and groups which have fought for the independence of our country, although they did not associate closely with the popular movement; this, in order to afford them the possibility of participating in the reconstruction of the country and to show them that the new regime is built on the absolute unity of our entire population.[147]

The abdication of Bao Dai was a great windfall for the Viet Minh. In turning over the imperial seal and the lineaments of his office, Bao Dai effectively signified to the tradition-minded Vietnamese people that a great historical shift of power had taken place, and that the new Democratic Republic of Viet Nam now had the mandate of heaven.[148]

THE DEMOCRATIC REPUBLIC OF VIET NAM UNDER VIET MINH LEADERSHIP

Despite the clear desire of many Vietnamese nationalists to make the new government as broadly representative as possible, the Viet Minh was of a different mind. It was prepared to concede little in the way of real power until it could consolidate its hold. The provisional government of the Democratic Republic of Viet Nam that was sworn in at Hanoi on September 2, 1945,[149] was hardly more than a slightly modified version of the People's Liberation Committee chosen by the restricted membership of the clandestine Viet Minh congress at Tan Trao on August 16, 1945. On the propaganda level, the Viet Minh deliberately played down the dominant role of the minority of Stalinists in the government for both internal[150] and external[151] consumption and emphasized the "democratic" character of its government. The watchword was unity behind the new government so that it could successfully maneuver on the diplomatic front and win international acceptance as the legitimate government of Viet Nam.

The Viet Minh devoted its primary energies to building a new state apparatus. The new organ of power at the village level was the People's Committee, which destroyed the existing administrative and judicial structure. The People's Committees were linked at the provincial level and were hierarchically organized under the Interior Ministry directed by Vo Nguyen Giap. Where, as in many areas of North and Central Viet Nam, there was considerable local opposition to the Viet Minh, the Viet Minh cadres quickly moved to consolidate power in the name of the new central government. Its effort to establish full control of the nationalist movement in South Viet Nam is a clear example of its basic unwillingness to share leadership with the other nationalist forces.

Political conditions in South Viet Nam were markedly different. At the time of the Japanese capitulation, the Viet Minh had little more than a handful of constituents, principally the few loyal cadres of the Indochina Communist Party. Its support was augmented by the membership of a youth organization, the Thanh Nien Tien Phong (Advance Guard

Youth), headed by Pham Ngoc Thach. The nationalist movement consisted mainly of the two principal religious sects, the Cao Dai and Hoa Hao, and a number of minor groups and parties. These organizations were grouped together in a Mat Tran Quoc Gia Thong Nhut (United National Front), which had been legally established on August 14, 1945.[152] It included some of the formerly pro-Japanese parties, as well as the Trotskyist Struggle Group. This Front had wielded governmental power for a few days in Cochinchina when, beginning on August 17, 1945, the Indochina Communist Party and the Viet Minh asserted themselves.

The prestige of the Soviet Union was used as a means of augmenting Stalinist and Viet Minh influence in Saigon. A typical leaflet issued by the Indochina Communist Party stated:

[The Communist party and the Viet Minh disapprove of] all actions of provocation and violence among inhabitants of Indochina of every origin and every race; they will enforce by all means at their disposal the repression of disorder from any source. . . . The authorities and the French population of Indochina must remember that the powerful ally of their country, the U.S.S.R., is also the guide and hope of the Indochina Communist Party and the Viet Minh; that this community of attitude must be the guarantee of an exact understanding of the situation.[153]

On August 25, 1945, the Viet Minh formed a southern executive council, called the Provisional Executive Committee.[154] While presenting itself as the southern arm of the Hanoi government, this committee, dominated by Tran Van Giau, could hardly claim to represent the nationalist parties and organizations in the South. It was forced to meet with the United National Front and undertake to compose its differences with that more representative organization of the nationalist movement. Yet, the bargaining position of the Viet Minh was strong, since it could claim support of the Hanoi government and argue that the Allies would be more disposed to deal with it than the United National Front, which was tainted by the pro-Japanese character of some of its constituent organizations and which had received power from the Japanese.

Formal unity between the Viet Minh and the United National Front was achieved during the following week. On September 7, 1945, a new Southern National Bloc Committee[155] was chosen, and issued the following appeal:

In the face of the excessively grave situation now in progress, we appeal to all the groups and parties, as well as all the patriots of the South to uphold the Viet Minh Southern Committee as well as the Southern National Bloc Committee in order to resist and repel the strong invasion which now approaches us.[156]

This merger covered up real differences that existed within the nationalist camp on the issue of welcoming or resisting British troops charged with accepting the Japanese surrender.

In practical terms, this became a question of distributing or not distributing arms to the population. The Trotskyist International Communist League held meetings calling for "arms to the people." As distinct from the Trotskyist Struggle Group,[157] which participated in the United National Front and in the negotiations with the Viet Minh, the International Communist League denounced the Viet Minh as a coalition including bourgeois elements in Vietnamese society; the League called on the masses to complete the revolution that had brought independence, by building up People's Committees as organs of state power and by distributing land to the peasants.[158] They conceived of their role as equivalent to that of the Bolsheviks vis-à-vis the 1917 Kerensky government in Russia, with the Viet Minh government cast in the role of representative of the bourgeoisie. The International Communist League's agitation for arming the population did strike a responsive chord among other nationalist groups who mistrusted the British and feared loss of their independence.[159]

On September 7, 1945, the Viet Minh replied to these attacks in a statement signed by Tran Van Giau for the Viet Nam government's Provisional Executive Committee:

A group of persons have organized a meeting demanding that the population be armed. The Japanese and Allied authorities, informed of this, fear that new and more bloody difficulties will ensue. . . . According to international agreement, the Japanese Army must assure order up to the arrival of the Allied army of occupation and everyone cannot but know that the Japanese forces here are still intact despite the surrender. Japanese General Headquarters has therefore decided to: (1) disarm the national troops, (2) confiscate machine guns or other arms, (3) ban all political movements which trouble order and security, (4) ban all demonstrations without prior authorization of Japanese General Headquarters, (5) disarm the population. In the interest of our country we call on all to have confidence in us and not let themselves be led by people who betray our country. It is only in this spirit that we can facilitate our relations with the Allied representatives.[160]

On September 8, 1945, a further Viet Minh appeal asked:

Who are those who have provoked these measures [by the Japanese]? In this situation can they oppose a superior military force? Have they means with which to make diplomatic protests? Democratic liberty which we, the Administrative Committee, have given to the People, these irresponsible individuals have used to harm the people, to harm the country. So, for the people's rights, for the nation's life, the Viet Minh Executive Committee appeals to the population to unmask the egoistic provocateurs. This alone will permit us to surmount the difficulties of the moment and get the people out of the trap which has been set by their enemies.[161]

When, on September 12, 1945, the International Communist League, and the People's Committee under their control, issued an appeal which "denounced openly the treasonable policy of the Stalinist government, and its capitulation before the threat of the general staff of the English troops," Duong Bach Mai, then Saigon police chief, ordered the arrest of the leaders of the International Communist League and the closing of its headquarters. When his police detachment raided the headquarters of the People's Committee, where an executive meeting was in progress, they met with no resistance. The Trotskyist commentator says: "We conducted ourselves as true militants of the revolution. We allowed ourselves to be arrested without opposing police violence, even though we outnumbered them and were all well armed."[162]

It seems that these Trotskyists still considered that they were part of the same movement as the Stalinists. The Viet Minh, for its part, displayed no such tender concern for the "true militants." In the months that followed, the leadership of both Trotskyist groups, the Struggle and the October, was decimated.[163] The Stalinists were determined that their authority be accepted over the entire nationalist movement.[164]

Yet, though it moved with tenacity toward the goal of consolidating its power, the Viet Minh was subject to great ideological strain as a result of the situation it encountered. Its forces were limited in a country that was in the throes of popular revolution. The Viet Minh leadership was much more cautious than its supporters. From the beginning, Ho Chi Minh had stressed the need for moderate political tactics and the need to conciliate the major social classes. But the ranks of the Viet Minh organization had been swelled by the return of released prisoners, who, after long years of privation, were determined to re-establish themselves and settle old scores with their conservative opponents. They, together with the other militants of the Communist party, had received their training in an organization that stressed revolutionary tactics. Hence, it is not surprising that there was some confiscation of private property and land distribution.[165]

The Viet Minh leadership, however, took a calculated risk in its assessment of the internal situation and gambled on the principle that a moderate policy was preferable to class-struggle tactics. It attempted to mobilize the existing social structure behind its regime. Provincial committees were reminded that Viet Nam had a capitalist system that had not been changed by the Declaration of Independence. The owners of land and private property must be respected and protected by the authorities. "The rice fields, the agricultural lands, will not be divided as has been falsely reported."[166] In every area of public life, the Viet Minh moved to conciliate the largest population groups by adapting itself to their wishes. Its leadership moderated the policy of its militants and won support for its program. Through this policy, the Viet Minh sought to forestall the creation of a rival conservative nationalist bloc that would challenge its leadership. This policy also could calm the fears of foreign powers that the new Democratic Republic of Viet Nam was Communist.

The principal appeal of the Viet Minh was directed toward meeting the external danger to the independence of Viet Nam. In South Viet Nam, the Viet Minh government's authority was not recognized by the British, who arrived in mid-September 1945 and within a few days reinstalled the local French in power. The Southern Executive Committee was forced to organize the very armed struggle that their Trotskyist and nationalist opponents had agitated for with such disastrous results. Only now, the "resistance forces" were badly split. Worse still, the French government that had returned to Indochina had the support of the French Communist Party. Apparently determined to play the parliamentary game to the hilt, the French Communists were again applying the policy enunciated by Thorez in 1937 at the Arles French Communist Party Congress;[167] Viet Nam was to remain within a French Union. Little wonder that Vietnamese Stalinists spoke disparagingly of their French comrades in September 1945.[168]

In the North the greatest danger to the Viet Minh leadership resulted from the presence of the Chinese army of occupation, which arrived shortly after the establishment of the Democratic Republic of Viet Nam. The Chinese army had moved into Viet Nam north of the sixteenth parallel in accordance with Allied agreements that gave to it, and to the British in the South, the task of accepting the Japanese surrender. In the van of the Chinese army came the Viet Nam Revolutionary League and the Viet Nam Nationalist Party. This generated serious economic and political problems for the Viet Minh leadership and threatened the very existence of its government.[169]

Economically, the Democratic Republic of Viet Nam had to meet the staggering expense of maintaining the Chinese forces. The financial condition of the Hanoi government was precarious. In its move to gain popular support, the government had sharply reduced its own income by abolishing the bulk of the old French-levied taxes. Just prior to the arrival of the Chinese, the government had launched a successful nationwide popular subscription campaign to raise funds. The bulk of the money collected ended up in the pockets of the Chinese. It was the price of survival for Ho Chi Minh's government, which thus bought toleration by the new army of occupation. An additional financial appeal had to be made later, again to placate the Chinese.

Politically, the Viet Nam Revolutionary League and Viet Nam Nationalist Party had old scores to settle with Ho Chi Minh and his entourage.

In their eyes, he was guilty of duplicity, since he had set up an independent government and thus broken the 1944 agreements whereby he had accepted a ministerial post in their provisional national government.[170] In returning to North Viet Nam with the Chinese army, the constituent groups of the Viet Nam Revolutionary League systematically established new local administrations to replace the Viet Minh administrative committees in the villages. They gave every indication of having the same objective vis-à-vis the Hanoi government. The Viet Minh leadership quickly moved to neutralize its opposition.

On October 23, 1945, the Viet Minh signed a pact with a dissident section of the Viet Nam Revolutionary League in the interest of the "common struggle against the aggressive attempts of the colonial French, in order to defend the liberty and independence of the Democratic Republic of Viet Nam."[171] Other elements of the Viet Nam Revolutionary League and the Viet Nam Nationalist Party, not so easily pacified, kept up an insistent clamor for reshuffling of the Viet Nam government and for their admission to it. They also kept referring to the Communist control of the Viet Minh leadership.

The Ho Chi Minh government decided on a startling gesture. A three-day conference of the Indochina Communist Party was held on November 9, 10, and 11. At the end of the meeting, the party published a communiqué dissolving the Indochina Communist Party! This communiqué indicated:

1. Whereas, in consideration of the given historical situation, both internationally and internally, the present moment is precisely an exceptional occasion for Viet Nam to reconquer her unitary independence;

2. Whereas, in order to complete the Party's task in this immense movement of the Vietnamese people's emancipation, a national union conceived without distinction of class and parties is an indispensable factor;

3. Wishing to prove that the Communists, in so far as they are advance guard militants of the Vietnamese people, are always ready to make the greatest sacrifices for national liberation, are always disposed to put the interest of the country above that of classes, and to give up the interests of the Party to serve those of the Vietnamese people;

4. In order to destroy all misunderstandings, domestic and foreign, which can hinder the liberation of our country, the Central Executive Committee of the Indochina Communist Party in meeting assembled on November 11, 1945, has decided to voluntarily dissolve the Indochina Communist Party.

Those followers of Communism desirous of continuing their theoretical studies will affiliate with the Indochina Association of Marxist Studies.

CENTRAL COMMITTEE INDOCHINA COMMUNIST PARTY
November 11, 1945[172]

The opposition's persistent demand for a reshuffling of the government led the Viet Minh to schedule promised national elections.[173] Fearful that administrative pressure by the government would ensure their defeat at the polls, on December 23, 1945, the opposition parties wrested fifty seats for the Viet Nam Nationalist Party and twenty seats for the Viet Nam Revolutionary League from the Viet Minh in advance of the elections scheduled for January 1946. The elections were more of a plebiscite than a contest among candidates of competing parties. An inordinately large vote was claimed for a country where the parliamentary system was for the most part unknown. However, pressure from the opposition had forced the Viet Minh to replace a number of their own hand-picked candidates with more popular representative figures. Thus the National Assembly that emerged as a result of the voting was a fairly representative body. At its meeting of March 2, 1946, a new national coalition government was constituted which did include representatives of the Viet Nam Revolutionary League and the Viet Nam Nationalist Party.[174]

Nonetheless, the opposition's success was more apparent than real. The Viet Minh remained dominant and now could claim power on the basis of a popular mandate. Moreover, the presence of the opposition in the government forced it to take joint responsibility with the Viet Minh for negotiating with the French and for signing the March 6, 1946, agreement. This agreement permitted French troops to re-enter North Viet Nam, while the French government recognized "the Republic of Viet Nam as a free state having its own government, parliament, army and treasury, belonging to the Indochinese Federation and to the French Union."[175]

The rationale that led the Viet Minh to accept the return of the French was provided by Vo Nguyen Giap, head of the Democratic Republic of Viet Nam's army, at a monster rally of 100,000 persons in Hanoi on March 7, 1946. He traced the three alternatives which faced the Vietnamese people and its leadership: long-time resistance leading to complete victory; a short war of resistance leading to a better settlement; and, finally, negotiations.

The first alternative was dismissed because of the unfavorable international situation. The Democratic Republic of Viet Nam was completely isolated. Neither England, America, nor China could be depended on for help in a struggle against France. No mention was made of the Soviet Union or the Communist bloc in this connection.

As for the alternative of limited resistance to acquire a better agreement, Vo Nguyen Giap frankly admitted that this course of action might well lead to the complete destruction of such strength as the Democratic Republic of Viet Nam possessed. It would face the loss of not only its military cadres but also the largest part of its territory. In the course of a protracted war, many fainthearted people would desert the cause of national independence.

In justifying the acceptance of negotiations, he cited the example of the Soviet Union:

> Considering world history, one sees that many people have been able to overcome difficulties in bad situations by knowing when to wait for an occasion more favorable to their progress. Russia, for example, in 1918 signed at Brest-Litovsk in order to stop the German invasion, and by virtue of the truce was able to re-enforce its army and its political powers. Didn't Russia become very strong thanks to this treaty?[176]

Vo Nguyen Giap's language could be well understood by the militants of the Indochina Communist Party and the Viet Minh's revolutionary partisans who had been propagandized over the years to follow the Soviet example. His language clearly revealed his Marxist-Leninist training and the great attention paid to Soviet experience by the Viet Minh leadership.

As for the more nationalist Vietnamese, the Viet Minh leadership knew that dissatisfaction with the signing of the March 6 agreement was very great. Therefore, Ho Chi Minh also addressed the large audience and ended his remarks with a highly charged emotional appeal:

> I, Ho Chi Minh, have always led you on the road to liberty. I have fought all my life for the independence of our country. You know that I would prefer death rather than to betray our country. I swear to you that I have not betrayed you.[177]

From this point on, the Viet Minh leadership banked on the French left for a solution to its problems. As in prewar years, although now on the firmer base of state power, the Vietnamese Communists and nationalists had to await a more liberal policy on the part of the French government or alternatively embark on a total program of opposition to the French regime in Indochina.

One major consequence of the March 6 agreement was to allow the Viet Minh leadership to deal with the Viet Nam Nationalist Party and the Viet Nam Revolutionary League in peremptory terms. They accepted French military aid in re-establishing Hanoi's control over all the northern areas of Viet Nam dominated by the local committees previously set up by these two organizations. The departure of the Chinese troops[178] left these two parties without a protector, and they rapidly declined in the face of the vigorous effort made by the Viet Minh to limit their strength.

Characteristically, to offset its blows directed at the Viet Nam Revolutionary League, the Viet Minh intensified its propaganda efforts to reconcile the disaffected elements in the society and create the broadest possible unity in the face of mounting French pressure. On May 27, 1946, the Lien Viet (League for the National Union of Viet Nam) was created.

The twenty-seven founding fathers included prominent representatives of all the principal political organizations as well as independents. In addition, the Viet Minh kept collaborating representatives of the Viet Nam Nationalist Party and the Viet Nam Revolutionary League in leading governmental posts and permitted the rump remnants of their organizations to maintain themselves as officially sanctioned parties.

In July 1946, the Viet Nam Xa Hoi Dang (Viet Nam Socialist Party) was founded under the paternal eye of the Viet Minh government. The party manifesto of July 27, 1946, announcing the birth of the organization at Hanoi, clearly identified the organization as the Vietnamese equivalent of the European Social-Democratic Parties of the Second International.[179] However, the new Viet Nam Socialist Party was careful to disassociate itself from the prewar Indochina Socialist Federations that had been sections of the French Socialist Party.[180] The former organizations had been "ruptured in the ordeal of war," i.e., had split over differences between its French and Vietnamese members on the problem of Vietnamese independence and the attitude to take toward Marshal Pétain's Vichy government of France and General De Gaulle's movement.

The manifesto was signed by three members of the Viet Nam National Assembly, some prominent intellectuals, professionals, and some workers. It invited all those who had "remained faithful to socialism" to join the new party. In its organizational activity, conducted in August 1946, the party stressed the following program:

1. Cooperation with the present government's work.
2. Cooperation with other Vietnamese parties to defend Viet Nam against foreign aggression, to support national reconstruction, and to fight for democratic liberties.
3. Reliance on parliamentary means, peaceful organizational methods and propaganda.

Although its appearance was favorably received by the Viet Minh and Democratic Party, both organizations qualified their enthusiasm by warning the new party not to betray its program. This difficulty has never manifested itself. From the start, the Viet Nam Socialist Party has been a faithful supporter of the Communist leadership of the Democratic Republic of Viet Nam.[181] It also provided the Viet Minh with a means of emphasizing repeatedly the coalition character of its government.

It is not necessary to recapitulate here the history of fruitless negotiations accompanied by numerous violations of the March 6 agreement that finally led to the outbreak of war in December 1946 between France and the Democratic Republic of Viet Nam. It suffices to say that the Viet Minh was severely mistaken in its policy of relying on the French left; for, with both Socialist and Communist support at home, the French government pressured the Viet Minh into a situation that led to war rather than to peaceful negotiation. Only later, when they were in the opposition and no longer in a position to decide governmental policy, did these two parties clamor for negotiations. The Democratic Republic of Viet Nam was forced to fight the protracted war that Vo Nguyen Giap had indicated would be so ruinous to the interest of the Vietnamese people.

THE VIETNAMESE STALINISTS ADOPT MAO TSE-TUNG'S STRATEGY

Politically, the outbreak of war favored Ho Chi Minh's government. All of its critics, who had castigated it for not having been vigorous enough in opposing the French, were now forced to rally to the Viet Nam government and support its struggle. French reliance on a military solution and the failure to provide a political solution acceptable to Vietnamese nationalism left the Viet Minh as the undisputed champion of national independence.

The war severed the relationship between the cities controlled by the French and the hinterland that remained in the hands of the Viet Minh. The Viet Minh found its bases of support in the peasant villages that not only could survive as independent entities but also could provide an agricultural surplus, which could, in turn, be sold for the arms and matériel necessary for waging war against the French. The traditional centers of resistance to French rule became the bases from which the Democratic Republic of Viet Nam's army operated. One center was the mountainous region of North Viet Nam that had served as the Viet Minh's wartime retreat and now became the seat of the government. The southern part of the Tonkin delta, Thanh Hoa, Ha Tinh, and Nghe An provinces, famed for peasant rebellions and soviets in 1931, was another stronghold. In Central Viet Nam, south of Hué, the city of Vinh remained in Viet Minh hands. In South Viet Nam, the Plaine des Joncs and the Pointe de Camau harbored the southern detachments of the Republic's army.[182]

The Viet Minh divided its war strategy into a three-phase program designated as (1) defensive strategy, (2) period of equilibrium of forces, and (3) the general counteroffensive. This program was essentially a borrowing from the experiences of the Chinese Communists. The principal aim was to create a powerful army by operating from strategically located guerrilla bases in the countryside. This program required the continuing support of the war effort by the bulk of the peasant population. To facilitate the spread of its program, the Viet Minh developed an intensive educational campaign against illiteracy. The support of the more conservative peasant proprietors was won by instituting a moderate program of agricultural reform in the villages so as not to introduce sharp conflict which the French might exploit. The Viet Minh encouraged the greatest austerity among its leaders and won the admiration and respect of the Vietnamese (and of its enemies, too, for that matter). From 1946 to 1949, the Democratic Republic of Viet Nam's leadership continued to indicate a reasonable willingness to negotiate peace with the French. This policy afforded the French Communist Party and the French left generally a basis for opposing French military operations and for calling for peaceful negotiations.

During this same period, the Ho Chi Minh government carefully sought to maintain friendly relations with the Thai and Nationalist Chinese governments.[183] In addition, a determined propaganda effort was made to enlist the sympathy of the other Southeast Asian states for the Vietnamese struggle. In the developing cold war situation that polarized international relations, the Viet Minh leadership publicly refused to take sides and announced a policy of neutrality. Even when the Soviet Union and the world Communist press affirmed that Ho Chi Minh was a Communist or stressed that the Democratic Republic of Viet Nam was part of the "world Democratic Front" fighting against "American imperialism," the Viet Nam government itself maintained a discreet silence. The Vietnamese Communists did not feature the usual pro-Soviet, anti-American vituperative attacks so common to the world Communist movement. As late as March 1949, President Ho Chi Minh continued to denounce the charge of "communist domination" of the government he headed as "pure French imperialist propaganda."[184]

This policy of denying links to Communism conflicted with the Ho Chi Minh government's practice of strengthening the ties between mass organizations in Viet Nam and the agencies of international Communism. Supporters of the Viet Minh government claimed that this practice was the only way the Democratic Republic of Viet Nam was able to get some international recognition.[185] The conflict was there nonetheless, and such participation in front organizations raised difficulties: for example, when representatives of the youth organizations in the Democratic Republic of Viet Nam attended the regional meeting of the World Federation of Democratic Youth at Calcutta in February 1948. Since this meeting was used as a means of publicly emphasizing the new Communist strategy in Southeast Asia that led to Communist insurrections in Malaya, Burma, and Indonesia, the Vietnamese representatives were placed in an ambiguous position. They could and did point with pride to the "liberation struggle" that they had been waging. Yet, at the same time, they did not repudiate the avowedly successful policy of coalition with the "national bourgeoisie" pursued in Viet Nam. They simply avoided the issue posed by the new policy that stressed attacks on the "bourgeois nationalists,"

the need for Communist party leadership of liberation struggles, and the
necessity of direct ties with the Soviet world camp.[186]

This deviation from general Southeast Asian Communist policy during 1948–49 may be described as another demonstration of the tactical
flexibility of Ho Chi Minh's leadership. The Viet Minh was already leading a highly effective armed struggle against the French in Viet Nam and
enjoyed the support of many Vietnamese nationalists who believed the
non-Communist declarations of the spokesmen for the Democratic Republic of Viet Nam. Moreover, its government had a measure of sympathy and support internationally from non-Communist, anticolonialist
world opinion. To squander these assets simply to enunciate ideological
statements commensurate with Communist-bloc pronouncements would
have been a high price to pay at any time. Yet, the view may well be enter-
tained that Ho Chi Minh and some other Viet Minh leaders wanted the
greater measure of independence that nonalignment with either bloc
would afford, and hoped perhaps to escape thereby the inevitable polarization of the nationalist movement in Viet Nam with all its attendant
negative consequences.

However one interprets the above policy, it was the combination of
Chinese Communist victories and French efforts to set up a rival nationalist regime under Bao Dai[187] which led to a shift in Viet Minh strategy.
By their defeat of the Kuomintang, the Chinese Communists had created
a common border with the Democratic Republic of Viet Nam and could
now extend direct aid to its army. American intervention in support of
the French and Bao Dai governments was countered by the Viet Minh's
open affirmation of its adherence to the Communist bloc. From November
1949 on, the Democratic Republic of Viet Nam's propaganda agencies
completely coordinated their efforts with those of the Chinese Communists in the Far East. The process of transforming the Democratic Republic of Viet Nam into a People's Democracy proceeded apace. By February
1950, in its foreign relations, the Democratic Republic of Viet Nam was
recognized officially by the Soviet Union and the other nations of the
Communist bloc. Internally, the Viet Minh League was fused with the
Lien Viet to form a new United National Front of Viet Nam on March 3,
1951. On the same day, the Communist party was reconstituted as the
Viet Nam Lao Dong Dang (Viet Nam Workers' Party).[188] The Communists openly claimed the leadership and direction of the Democratic Republic of Viet Nam. Moreover, they retrospectively affirmed their leading
role in Vietnamese nationalism ever since the founding of their party
in 1930.

In the next three years, by virtue of the direct aid extended by the
Chinese Communists, the Viet Nam People's Army was able to realize
the last two phases of their program; i.e., from a defensive posture, they

moved to a positional warfare against the French, and then to the counter-offensive that led to victory at Dien Bien Phu. The war in Viet Nam became the subject of negotiations in a great power conference at Geneva in July 1954. The negotiations ended with the division of Viet Nam into two zones at the seventeenth parallel. North of the parallel was the Communist Democratic Republic of Viet Nam, which moved its government back to Hanoi. South of the dividing line, there was established at Saigon the seat of what is now the anti-Communist, American-supported government of the Republic of Viet Nam, the final outgrowth of the Bao Dai movement, today headed by President Ngo Dinh Diem.

MARXISM TODAY

The history of these years has been telescoped deliberately because it has been covered to some extent elsewhere and is not directly germane to the theme of this chapter. The interested reader can consult the numerous works cited. The concern here is with the influence of Marxism in its variant guises in Viet Nam. The creation of two Vietnamese states following the 1954 Geneva conference is a convenient point at which to stop and sum up the material presented in this study and make a tentative assessment of the impact of Marxism in Viet Nam.

In a curious way, the Geneva agreements duplicated the earlier March 6, 1946, agreement between France and the Democratic Republic of Viet Nam. Viet Nam was also divided in two at that time, and provision was made for a popular referendum. The difference was that the two protagonists then were French colonialism and Vietnamese nationalism headed by a dominant Communist minority. We have already seen that, faced with such an alternative, the popular choice was never in doubt. The Vietnamese people chose the nationalist camp even at the expense of strengthening Communism. To disassociate "nationalists" from "Communists" in order to assess the actual influence of Marxism was well-nigh impossible. After Geneva, the Vietnamese were given their real opportunity to select between alternative means of satisfying national aspirations, and our task becomes somewhat easier.

The fact that Geneva was a major international conference indicates the extent to which the settlement of Viet Nam's internal difficulties is inseparably bound up with the great power conflict that has split the world. The course of that struggle affects all political and philosophical systems, but such considerations are beyond the scope of this paper. In the same sense, tempting though it may be, it is not my intention to speculate on the "crisis" in the affairs of world Communism or even events in China which obviously have much bearing on the prospects for Viet Nam.[189] Suffice it to say that the partition itself and both contending Viet Nam states depend on external support for their continued maintenance.

A shift in international support might well tip the balance in either direction, through either internal subversion or an attempt to unify the country by military force. One thing is certain: the desire for unification is great, and neither side can afford to neglect this potent political fact. I propose to deal with the internal sources of support for each of the competing states insofar as they relate to the central theme of this chapter. To the extent that each of these states proves viable, it will correspondingly influence the other.

North Viet Nam

Popular acceptance of Marxism-Leninism in North Viet Nam is a result in large part of the leadership that Communists have given to Vietnamese nationalism for a quarter of a century. The Communists have shown themselves to be the most persevering, most cohesive, best-disciplined, and most experienced political group in Viet Nam. The Vietnamese people have known Communist political aims, techniques, and world connections only as they have been refracted through the prism of nationalism. This situation will continue as long as Viet Nam is divided and the Communists subordinate all their activities to the "struggle for unification." The Communists also have shown that they were capable of leading a war of eight years' duration against the white French colonial oppressor. To all Vietnamese, that war has deep emotional and meaningful significance. It is celebrated in song and verse. It is final proof that the Vietnamese were able to vanquish the colonial army through the use of their own manpower and regain thereby their national heritage. It establishes Vo Nguyen Giap as a pre-eminent Vietnamese military leader.

The Communists were successful in mobilizing a large number of intellectuals, professionals, technicians, students, writers, painters, musicians, etc., for devoted service during the war. It can be expected that the regime has a reservoir of talent on which to draw for the tasks of peacetime construction. These people have been indoctrinated for a considerable period by the Communist leadership. The Communists have turned out a literature of their own and have had considerable success in adapting the Marxist idiom to deal with cultural problems in North Viet Nam. Marxism-Leninism is the official state doctrine, and though this doctrine has been changed in certain essential features from that of its founding fathers,[190] other features have been retained, and it can be expected that the propaganda and educational activities of the government will reflect this commitment. In every respect North Viet Nam is a typical "people's democracy." This sets up a powerful cultural current that obviously exercises pressure on thoughtful people in the South.

It may be useful to specify briefly some of the major features of Marxism-Leninism that have been retained and comment on their applicability in view of Vietnamese history as described above.

First, the doctrinal influence of Marxism-Leninism certainly cannot be neglected since the Vietnamese Communists do insist that their practice is inseparably bound up with their theory. There is some sense in which ideology sets limits to the behavior of its believers. Yet to translate this theory into copybook maxims that can be consulted for answers to concrete problems would neglect the rich experience of the Vietnamese Communist movement that clearly shows how ideology has itself been manipulated to achieve practical goals.

Second, there is well-nigh universal acceptance of the theory of imperialism that clearly stems from the early teachings of the Communist International and its principal founder, Lenin. Whatever may be the fate of Marxism-Leninism, this may well be one of its most persistent features, for it is taken as an article of faith by many Vietnamese even outside Communist circles. This, because it can so easily be adapted to explain not only the past but the current position of an area like Viet Nam in world affairs.

Third, the belief that Socialism and finally Communism will redeem humanity can be expected to remain a major feature in the thinking of Vietnamese Communists and influence others in Viet Nam. This kernel of theory has a powerful appeal in terms of its call for rational purposive behavior on the part of man. Its final stress on egalitarianism can stimulate positive responses in a society that will for a long time to come be composed predominantly of a peasant and working class population which will have to labor very hard to achieve its goal of a society of plenty for all.

Fourth, the "role of the party" as *the* instrument of historical change looms large in the thinking of Vietnamese Communists. The privileged position in the society and access to power which party membership confers reinforces this belief. The social-psychological texture of party life is admirably suited to the needs of individuals torn from the security of their traditional beliefs and family relationships. Here, a warning note must be sounded, since there was a time when the Communist party was dissolved voluntarily to serve the vital "interests of the country," and the precedent remains for possible future use.

Fifth, there is the totalitarian potential inherent in the Marxist-Leninist view of the historical process. Unfortunately, despite the insistence of some on the inherently democratic nature of traditional Vietnamese society, there is a clear sense in which it can be described as a bureaucratic, elitist state. It is not too difficult to replace Confucian ideology with a new universal dogma which has so many points of similarity in its emphasis on control in every sphere of life. Certainly, despite the long campaign insisting on the coalition nature of their government, the fact is that the Communist regime has maintained singular uniformity on the part of all groups in the Democratic Republic of Viet Nam. Whatever political labels they carry, Vietnamese in the North are not permitted the luxury of deviation from the party line.

Sixth, in marked contrast to the foregoing, there is a repeated emphasis in Marxism-Leninism on "democracy." This itself is a standing invitation to its believers to put some real content into the formal ritualistic statements of belief in this matter. Despite the inherited authoritarian tradition, their experiences under French rule have developed in many Vietnamese a profound desire to obtain democratic liberties. The history of the party itself is replete with factionalism, and there is no reason to expect that it will be immune to such tendencies in the future. When, in the latter part of 1956, a measure of difference was allowed public airing, the unwillingness of many, including prominent Communist intellectuals like Tran Duc Thao, to accept the constricted state of affairs was manifested. The celebrated "Nhan-Van" (Human Knowledge) affair[191] showed that just as Mao Tse-tung unleashed the floodgates of criticism in Communist China in 1957 with his celebrated "Let a Hundred Flowers Bloom" remarks,[192] so this group of Northern Vietnamese gave vent to hitherto repressed criticism. If Marxism-Leninism as it is applied in Viet Nam does not demonstrate a sufficient degree of flexibility, it may succeed in alienating the very elite on whose support it depends.

Finally, the Communist regime in Viet Nam has, like Communist governments elsewhere, accepted the value of industrialization as an article of faith. Primary emphasis has been placed on rebuilding the war-devastated areas and developing new industry. There is a compelling economic reason for this, too. North Viet Nam is usually a deficit rice area and must export raw materials or manufactured goods to obtain food. The allegiance of the peasantry is important to the success of the Communist regime, and the agrarian problem remains to be solved. It is already quite clear that the Communist regime has experienced serious difficulty in dealing with the problem of land reform since Geneva.[193]

In all of the above matters, the Communist leadership must cope with the example set by the Southern regime. For, despite the propaganda of the official government agencies, the Vietnamese have developed their own means of communication. Since, in any case, there will be movement between the two hostile states, the capacity for judging relative accomplishments will not be suspended.

South Viet Nam

The Republic of Viet Nam began its life under the most difficult of circumstances. It had little real authority in the area that was nominally defined as its territory. Its leadership was inept and divided into hostile groups, each seeking exclusive leadership of anti-Communist nationalism. Worse still, the Bao Dai government was the prisoner of a French military authority that had been defeated at Dien Bien Phu and had been forced to negotiate at Geneva. The Bao Dai movement suffered the taint of having collaborated to a degree with French colonialism, while its competitors fought a war of resistance against the French.

Yet, despite these weaknesses, so powerful was the genuine force of nationalism which the young republic sought to tap that, once freed of the restraints placed on it by the French, and after internecine difficulties, it emerged in the form of a relatively strong, centralized state under the leadership of President Ngo Dinh Diem. The attractive power of this non-Communist nationalism was demonstrated at the very outset in the dramatic exodus of almost a million people from North Viet Nam to South Viet Nam after Geneva.

Despite the adopted presidential form of government supplemented by an elected national assembly that indicates the desire of its founders to establish a democratic state,[194] the government of the Republic of South Viet Nam in its trying period of consolidation has not always adhered to democratic practices.[195] The Republic is avowedly anti-Communist and, to counter Marxism, has made a determined effort to develop an ideology of nationalism. Yet Marxist influence persists nonetheless.[196] The National Revolutionary Movement, the largest political formation in South Viet Nam, is headed by some people who received their training from the Viet Minh. The Movement shows remarkable similarity in its organizational structure and propaganda methods to its Communist counterpart. Similarly, many other nationalists who worked with Communists in the past, but have since broken with them, have entered the service of the Southern administration. It is likely that the residue of their former experience influences their thinking and political behavior.

In South Viet Nam, there exist also the remnants of a number of political groups influenced by Marxism of the Social-Democratic variety. Some of these elements are clandestine; others are barely tolerated as long as they are known to be unsympathetic to the Viet Minh. The latter include ex-Trotskyists who remain Socialists by conviction and are active in the trade-union movement of South Viet Nam. Among the former are individual Socialists, earlier partisans of revolutionary nationalism who are to be found among the Cao Dai and Hoa Hao religious groups. They now find it expedient to camouflage their identities for protective purposes. A small Viet Nam Democratic Socialist Party existed from 1946 to 1948. It was a coalition of Socialist-minded elements in Saigon with some provincial support and included in its leadership some sect figures. It was persecuted by the Viet Minh, and some of its leaders killed. Finally, there is in existence in South Viet Nam a tiny Socialist Party, headed by Pham Van Ngoi, which is an affiliate of the Asian Socialist Conference. It publicly opposes President Ngo Dinh Diem's regime, which it attacks as dictatorial and inept in dealing with major problems.

It is probable that some of the continuing demands for improvements in the South Viet Nam regime are stimulated by intellectuals and others who have been exposed to the ideas of social democracy. These demands usually are concerned with three major areas of political importance: the area of democratic liberties, the problem of agrarian reform, and the emphasis on industrialization. Significantly these are the same problems that concern the regime in the North.

The pressure for democratic rights is constant from all disaffected groups,[197] who insist that unless the Southern government is mindful of this problem, it will not only alienate supporters in the South but also eliminate a strong point in its favor in competition with the North.

There is a constant demand for agrarian reform, since South Viet Nam is an area where land reform can have real significance.[198] It can be expected that there will be repeated emphasis on this point until the Saigon government satisfactorily deals with the problem.

Finally, in terms of the continuing emphasis on industrialization that exists in South Viet Nam, we can again see the influence of Marxism. This emphasis is not so much the result of pressure from a class of entrepreneurs anxious to maximize their opportunities, but rather the desire on the part of the intellectuals who have come to accept the creation of an industrial society as a desired goal and who are prepared to use the instrumentalities of the state to realize this ambition.

In conclusion, mention must be made of underground supporters of the Northern regime in South Viet Nam. They probably are still significant and can be expected to lend their support to activities that are contrary to official government policy as established in the Republic of Viet Nam. But they themselves are subject to the influence of their environment. To the extent that South Viet Nam is a viable regime[199] based on democratic practices, and offering a real alternative to the Communist North, their extremism, assuming they are not hard-core members of the *apparat*, can be not only moderated but turned into an asset for the South. Marxism of whatever brand can be expected to play an important role in Viet Nam for the foreseeable future.

5

MARXISM IN INDONESIA

JEANNE S. MINTZ

Indonesian experience with Marxism recalls that of both Burma and Indochina in a number of ways. In all three countries, awareness of Marxism came largely through influences from the colonial power itself; it was through Dutch literature, in contacts with Dutch radical politicians, and in Dutch universities that Indonesians were first attracted to Marxism. As in much of contemporary Asia, there are in present-day Indonesia few, if any, political groupings that do not bear the imprint of Marxism. The situation is aptly put by the Socialist leader Sjahrir when he says, "We in Indonesia are all socialists, or at least, socialistically inclined."[1] Writing from a somewhat different vantage point, Ruslan Abdulgani, a leading figure in the Partai Nasional Indonesia (PNI), has described the position of socialism in Indonesia as "an essential ingredient of nationalism, since we believe that socialism offers our people the quickest escape from the poverties of their national heritage."[2]

It may well be that few Indonesians who call themselves Marxists have actually studied Marx; many of the ideas which they frequently attribute to Marx are essentially those of Leninist doctrine.[3] The brand of Marxism which first made its way to Indonesia found a ready reception because of its explanation and description of colonialism. For those Indonesians who did read Marx, his characterization of Dutch colonialism as "undisguised looting, enslavement and murder"[4] had considerable popularity and appeal, as did the Marxist-Leninist definition of imperialism. In Indonesian experience, colonialism had come to be regarded as the child of capitalism. The view that foreign rule was not an expression of an immutable relationship between white and nonwhite peoples but a mere historical phase in the development of Western European capitalism was intellectually and emotionally satisfying to the restless, partly Western-educated elite.

THE SETTING: TRADITION AND CHANGE

The influence of Marxism in Indonesia understandably took special forms under the impact of certain indigenous conditions and of the nationalist movement.[5] The cultural traditions linked to communal landholding and *gotong rojong*, mutual help, the unique role of Islam in Indonesia and especially of Modernist Islamic doctrine, and the class structure of Indonesian society, particularly during the colonial period, all helped to mold the Indonesian view of Marxism. Superimposed on these elements in the twentieth century were the general Asian awakening, the emergence of a Western-educated elite, a growing social and economic unrest, and a burgeoning nationalist movement; these factors helped to create an atmosphere receptive to Marxism.

One of the relatively constant elements in the social climate was the primitive communism of a prefeudal, precapitalist variety that held sway in much of rural Indonesia. Until comparatively recent times, exclusive private ownership of land was a concept strange to most Indonesians; land belonged to the community. While a kind of permanent family leasehold gradually emerged in the last century, land, according to *adat* (customary) law, could not be sold without the consent of the village; if a family moved away, after a specified period of time the land reverted to the community.[6] Although in the past thirty years the amount of communally held land has diminished sharply, especially in Java, the constellation of ideas and the general social outlook engendered by a village society organized on the basis of communal ownership of land still prevail throughout much of the countryside.

The traditional political organization of the villages, the *desa* system, is another significant element. The most important aspect of this system is the emphasis placed upon mutually acceptable decisions arrived at by compromise of all viewpoints expressed.[7] *Musjawarat*, the deliberations of the villagers, and *mufakat*, the unanimous decision which emerges from these deliberations, are the essence of social relations and community action. The concept of majority rule, of the majority point of view being imposed upon and accepted by a minority, is thoroughly alien to village society. While final responsibility rests more or less in the hands of the village elders, agreement is reached through discussion and compromise; hence, responsibility as well tends to be shared. Important in such a context is the concept of *gotong rojong*, mutual help, the recognition of the common responsibility of the members of the community toward each other and toward the community as an entity. *Gotong rojong* is the motivating force behind village projects embarked upon by all able-bodied members of the community after agreement has been reached on the need.

Mufakat and *gotong rojong* are in fact the key words which express the ancient and still valid principles of social organization at the village level. When President Sukarno, in December 1956, used these terms as the slogans for his proposal for a new governmental structure, he was invoking some of the most hallowed concepts in Indonesian life.

While these characteristics of the social landscape remained more or less constant, other aspects of Indonesian life were undergoing basic changes, from the beginning of the twentieth century. An increase in education, in contacts with the outside world through the introduction of cash crops, wage labor on plantations, and the gradual replacement of a barter economy with a money economy all resulted in new attitudes whose net effect was a loosening of family and village ties. Accompanying this process was a slight but significant shift in social values toward individualism. This same period was also marked by the beginnings of the modern nationalist movement and the revitalized role of religion as a force for change in Indonesian life.

Islam in Indonesia does not have a close resemblance to Islam as it is practiced in other parts of the Moslem world. For one thing, especially in Java, Islam is but the latest addition to a body of ancient religious beliefs and practices on which layers of Hindu-Buddhism had already been superimposed. Therefore, while religion was and is one of the most important elements and binding forces in Indonesia,[8] it has been a flexible and dynamic force, not rigid in its adaptation to modern life. At the same time, Islam in Indonesia has never been a potent political or economic force on a national scale, although on the local level the *kiai*, the religious scholar or leader, generally enjoys considerable influence. There is, however, no powerful national church entwined with the repositories of nationwide political power.

The unique quality of Islam in Indonesia was further emphasized when, in the early years of this century, Indonesia's Moslem leaders were attracted to the Modernist Islamic movement then developing in Cairo. Intended to reform much of the current doctrine and practice of Islam while introducing some knowledge of Western science and history into its educational system, the movement also incorporated principles of political and social justice into Islamic teachings. In Indonesia, it was the teachings on political and social reform that received special attention.[9]

Because of the flexible nature of Islam in Indonesia, and especially because of the impact of the Modernist Islamic doctrine, religion has played a significant role as a vehicle for Indonesian nationalism and social development. Arriving at a time when Indonesian life was undergoing fundamental changes, the impact of the new doctrine was enhanced, its spread from village to village ensured by religious leaders through channels of communication long maintained. In turn, it was fed by the changing attitudes then beginning to emerge in rural Indonesia.

The turn of the century also saw the gradual emergence of a modern nationalist movement in Indonesia, a movement initiated by some of the small number of Indonesian students being educated in Dutch schools in Holland or Indonesia. These students were almost all members of families descended from the feudal aristocracy. Vis-à-vis the masses of the Indonesian people, they represented a social and intellectual elite by virtue of their Western-style education as well as their social heritage. But the roads to success were blocked to them under the colonial regime. Economic life in all spheres was dominated by the Dutch and other Europeans; the minor functions of the middle class were performed by Chinese, Arabs, and Indians. There were practically no indigenous landlords of significance, nor was there any Indonesian middle class to speak of. The university students therefore had no more reason to be tied to a "status quo" economic outlook than did the peasants and laborers. Furthermore, the students' advancement above a certain level in the colonial civil administration was practically impossible.[10]

As part of their Westernized education, the students had been absorbing ideas associated with nineteenth-century European nationalism and liberalism. As their views took shape, they began to evolve an articulate version of their own nationalism, and to advance beyond the simpler, largely negative ideas animating the earlier revolts against Dutch rule. The inspiration of Western education was greatly strengthened by two other factors in contemporary Asia. The first of these was, as Furnivall has pointed out, the stirring of the East:

> The Chinese and Japanese went to war like Europeans; the Filipinos rose against Spain; the Chinese in the Boxer Rising braved the power of Europe; there was trouble in British India; events in Turkey were shaking the Moslem world; and in 1905 the victory of Japan over Russia started an impulse which was to transform the peoples in Netherlands India, as in other tropical dependencies, from the extreme of acquiescence to the extreme of self-assertion.[11]

In addition, there was the influence of Dutch educators and liberally inclined members of the Netherlands East Indies government, who, in their local capacity or upon returning to prominent positions in Holland, served to spark the "Ethical colonial policy" (1900) which expressed official and popular Dutch conscience about the welfare of Indonesia.

Meanwhile, significant changes were also appearing in the villages. In the late nineteenth century, sporadic outbreaks of agrarian unrest had begun in Java. They continued to erupt periodically until after World War I. While these peasant movements coincided in time with the first stirrings of the modern nationalist movement, they were more the result of social disorientation that followed on the forced labor and crop system, the "Culture System," than of the nationalist fervor motivating the students. It is against the background of a village democracy increasingly disturbed by the pressures of indirect, and later of direct, rule, and of a society whose members shared an increasing common poverty, that these peasant movements should be viewed.

The most significant of these movements was the Saminist, which, starting about 1890 in central Java, was considered by more than one observer as a manifestation of the natural communism of the Indonesian people.[12] By 1907 this movement had some three thousand family heads enrolled in it. Led by Samin, a religious scholar, or *kiai*, it was fundamentally a negativist peasant reaction to government interference. Members refused to pay taxes in kind or in labor, avoided contact with government employees, and generally wished "to be left free to lead their own lives."[13] In 1907 the government arrested Samin and eight other peasant leaders and sent them into exile, but the movement apparently continued in strength until 1920.[14] The motivation and the techniques of Saminism and the other popular movements of the pre–World War I and wartime era have a certain resemblance to the peasant uprisings of the early twenties led by dissident leaders of the official Communist party who preached a doctrine of "religious Communism."

Another change reshaping the Indonesian scene was the appearance of a degree of popular resentment against the Indonesian aristocrats who had been absorbed into the Dutch civil service. In the growing bitterness against foreign authority, these men were assumed to be guilty of the sins of their employers. Though many students were themselves of the aristocracy, their nationalist sentiments led them to identify themselves, if only in a paternalistic fashion, with the peasants and their grievances. They were joined by a handful of Indonesian merchants, whose resentment, initially directed against the growing power of the Chinese traders, came to embrace as well the feudal Indonesian rulers in the Dutch civil service.

The Chinese, since the last decade of the nineteenth century, had also become the object of indigenous grievances. Second only to Europeans, they had thrived in the capitalism of the colonial economy and received special privileges from the colonial rulers. Merchant, trader, miller, pawnbroker, middleman, as well as craftsman and farmer, the Chinese, for a period after 1900, came to be regarded as "a main cause of the diminishing welfare of the Javanese."[15] And the Chinese could and did serve also as scapegoats for inexpressible but nonetheless real anti-Dutch feeling:

anti-Chinese riots broke out in 1911–12; and the first Indonesian party of mass proportions and genuinely nationalist character, Sarekat Islam, had its origin in a trade association formed by Javanese batik merchants in 1909 in an attempt to halt Chinese incursions into the few areas of Indonesian commercial activity.

The intellectual ferment stirring the small educated class, the outbreaks of peasant defiance of governmental authority, the rising tide of resentment against the indigenous aristocracy and against the alien middle class —all these elements combined to make the atmosphere in Indonesia highly charged in the period under discussion. Marxism, then, did not burst upon the Indonesian scene as a revolutionary doctrine disturbing a tranquil tropical paradise, but arrived at a time of significant change and growing tension.

THE INTRODUCTION OF MARXISM

It is generally agreed that Marxism was formally introduced into Indonesia in 1914, with the founding there of the Indies Social Democratic Association (Indische Sociaal Democratische Vereeniging). However, it is clear that some Indonesian leaders had earlier become acquainted with the development in Holland of a Socialist party that was interested in Indonesian affairs and that specifically opposed the extension of Dutch rule by force to those parts of the archipelago not previously subdued. This was the Social-Democratic Workers Party (Sociaal-Democratische Arbeiderspartij, or SDAP), founded in Amsterdam in 1894. This party had from the outset campaigned for an improved standard of living for the Indonesian people and had, as early as March 1901, while supporting the welfare provisions of the new Ethical colonial policy, adopted a program advocating the development of the Indonesian people toward ultimate self-rule.[16] In the lower chamber of the Dutch parliament, the party's representatives championed increased political rights for Indonesians, an improved judicial system, an easing of the islands' tax burden, better labor conditions, and the establishment of some industries to speed up Indonesia's economic evolution. Some knowledge of these activities reached Indonesian intellectual circles through the Dutch press and, more frequently, through contacts with the handful of Dutch Socialists residing in Indonesia, several of them members of the SDAP.

The first Indonesian nationalists to be drawn into the orbit of the SDAP in Holland were the exiled leaders of the Nationale Indische Partij,[17] Dr. Tjipto Mangoenkoesoemo and Soewardi Suryaningrat; the latter is better known as Ki Hadjar Dewantoro, the name he later adopted.[18] Both these men had been arrested for nationalist activities in Indonesia in 1913 but were permitted to go to Holland, where they found a sympathetic welcome from the SDAP. Typical of the nationalist leadership of their times—and indeed of the decades that followed until the social upheaval brought on by World War II—they were both members of aristocratic families with no previous inclination toward Socialism.

It was, however, with the founding of the above-mentioned Indies Social Democratic Association that Socialism first took firm root in Indonesian soil. This was both an active political organization and the first Socialist organization to be established in Southeast Asia. The founders were a group of Dutch socialists under the leadership of H. J. F. M. Sneevliet.[19] They were soon joined by some of the former members of the suppressed Nationale Indische Partij, along with other Eurasians, Dutch, and a few Indonesians. It was this group which later developed into the Perserikatan Komunis di India (PKI), or Indonesian Communist Union.

THE INDONESIAN COMMUNIST PARTY: FIRST PHASE, 1920-27

During the early twenties the PKI was the largest and most significant Marxist party in Indonesia.[20] Its history is filled with problems, arising primarily from the dichotomy between Marxist ideology as represented by the Comintern on one side and the realities of Indonesian life on the other. Since these problems form the essential background not only to the development of the PKI itself but also to the role of ideas of Marxist origin in the larger stream of Indonesian nationalism, certain aspects of early PKI history bear examination here.

Originally composed of a handful of Indonesians working with the Dutch leaders of the Indies Social Democratic Association, the PKI grew from a small revolutionary faction, operating within the country's first large-scale nationalist party, the Sarekat Islam (SI), to a mass-based party, which by 1923 claimed to have some fifty thousand members[21] and controlled a significant portion of the country's trade-union movement.[22] Even before the official founding of the PKI in May 1920, the Communist leaders had tried to gain control of the SI by forming workers' groups within its branches. This technique succeeded to the extent that the PKI was able to rally to its banners a significant number of SI branches, but in many instances the victory was a hollow one because many of these branches soon lost much of their peasant membership. Nevertheless, the PKI was able to build up a substantial following, primarily through the trade-unions. Encouraged by this rapid rise, a faction of the PKI leadership attempted a coup late in 1926. This proved to be a crucial error. First of all, the PKI did not have enough organization and power to carry it off successfully. Furthermore, the coup was staged without taking practical account of the political and military realities of the time. The severity with which the authorities dealt with the party and its supporters destroyed the apparatus of the PKI and drove it from the Indonesian scene as a political party for nearly a decade.

There were other reasons as well for the collapse of the PKI, aside from the gross misjudgments that had led to the coup. From the outset, the Communists faced difficult problems in trying to adhere to a fixed Comintern line no matter what its relevance to the domestic situation. In addition the Communists failed to take sufficient account of the vigor of the prevailing mores, and in particular of the significance of the role of religion in Indonesian life. It was not a question of religious heresy; the Indonesian people are remarkably tolerant on matters of religion. But the peasants were alienated by the Communists' refusal to give religion any place in their world view; this appeared to many of them as an attack on one of the most important elements in Indonesian life.

It is true that on issues of the day there appeared to be few differences, in the eyes of the average peasant, between the Marxist-Leninist doctrine of the Communists and the Modernist Islamic socialism preached by Tjokroaminoto, Hadji Agus Salim, and other members of the SI's central leadership. In a society where capitalism and foreign rule were regarded as one and the same thing and considered the main enemy, it was not too difficult for religious nationalists and Communists to work together, at least in the initial stages. In any case, the central leadership of the SI, whose nationalist sentiments had originally been clothed in respectably religious terminology, was gradually drifting toward a more secular view of the world. In addition, as the Communist faction within the SI grew stronger, the central leadership was forced to take a more radical stand on current issues, in an effort to maintain a hold on the rank and file. All the same, the moderate SI leaders, adhering to their personal convictions, continued to appeal to moral and ethical standards based on religion and to rely on religious terminology to phrase their appeal.[23]

Throughout the struggle between the moderate central leadership of the SI and the Communists, which raged from 1916 to 1924 and occupied the center of the stage at each SI congress within that period, the SI leaders placed an emphasis on the role of religion which indicated their recognition of this issue's importance in the fight for control. Certainly the SI leaders were willing to exploit their opponents' formal atheism, and did so on many occasions with conspicuous success. At times the religious question appeared as a genuine issue dividing the leaders of the PKI and the central leadership of the SI; at times it seems to have been primarily a matter of tactical behavior. Although the SI's central leadership was ultimately to lose much of its popular support because of an undue reliance on the appeal of religion alone, it is also true that the PKI's stand on religion was in large measure responsible for alienating much of the mass support that the Communists had hoped to gain by utilizing the SI and its organization.

The problem of reconciling the fundamental and pervasive influence of religious beliefs on the majority of Indonesians with formal Communist atheistic ideology dogged the PKI throughout its existence in the twenties, and still hampers it today. The party's leaders tackled the question in various ways: at first they firmly and openly repudiated religion; then, in one of their final efforts to keep from being expelled by the SI, they offered to take a neutral stand on the subject;[24] and on occasion they tried to utilize religion for the party's own ends. Much as the SI had been expected to supply a mass organization through which the Communists could carry on their work, so Islam was tried in various times and places as a likely vehicle for Communist mass propaganda. For example, in the period after his exile but before his break with the PKI, the outstanding Communist, Tan Malaka, specifically recommended religion as a means of propaganda.[25] And for some time before this recommendation, it was evident that religion and religious leaders were being used to good effect by the Communists, especially in the Minangkabau area of Sumatra.[26]

That the struggle between the Communists and the central leadership of the SI extended down into the membership at large and that the root of the problem was at the base, if not at the top, the role of religion was made clear in Tan Malaka's speech at the Fourth Comintern Congress at the end of 1922. There he stated with some eloquence the dilemma facing the Indonesian Communists in their efforts to apply the directives of the Third International to their domestic problems. Pointing out the difficulties raised for the PKI by the Second Comintern Congress resolution of 1920 opposing Pan-Islamism, he said:

> The Sarekat Islamists believe in our propaganda. They are with us "with their stomachs," but with their hearts they remain with the Sarekat Islam—with their heaven which we cannot give them. Therefore they boycotted our meetings, and we could not carry on propaganda any longer.[27]

After describing the then current *rapprochement* with the central leadership of SI, Tan Malaka warned that the question of Pan-Islamism was not settled and that it remained an important problem. He described the difference between historic Pan-Islamism and its current ideological content in the following manner:

> At present, Pan-Islamism is a nationalist-liberation struggle, because Islam for the Moslems is everything: not only religion, but also the State, the economic system, the food, in fact everything. Thus, Pan-Islamism now means the fraternity of all Mohammedan peoples and the liberation not only of the Arabian, but also the Indian, Javanese and all other oppressed Mohammedan peoples.

This fraternity is called the liberation struggle against the British, French and Italian capitalists, consequently against world capitalism . . . This is our new task, and just as we are willing to support the national war, we shall also support the liberation struggle of the very active and energetic 250 million Mohammedans, who are subject to the Imperialist Powers. Therefore, I ask once more if we should support Pan-Islamism in this sense, and in how far we are to support it.[28]

Nevertheless, whatever tack the Communists adopted, suspicion of their stand on religion still caused them heavy losses among their peasant following. Indeed, the antipathy aroused by the PKI's religious views was so strong in some areas where the party had taken over the SI organizations that the local religious leaders were able to form rival organizations, known as Sarekat Hidjau (Green Association), which harried the Communists in the villages and in some instances engaged in armed clashes with the PKI's local affiliates.[29]

Having failed to win strong popular support within the SI, the PKI was frustrated in its attempts to wrest control of the organization from its original leadership. Thereupon, the Communists altered their strategy and began setting up Red SI branches in competition with the older organization. In 1921 these branches were re-formed into a new organization called Sarekat Rakjat (SR), or People's Association. This organization was originally intended to supply the mass base from which properly trained and approved candidates could "graduate" to membership in the PKI. In 1924, however, in what was to be a nearly fatal error, the PKI decided to abandon the predominantly peasant Sarekat Rakjat and to focus attention on building up strength within the labor movement.[30] This policy represented the leaders' interpretation of what they understood to be the current "trade union emphasis" of Communist doctrine. However, since the party was already having difficulty in maintaining its following among the peasants, the new policy left the PKI leadership marching at the head of a revolutionary movement which lacked the mass peasant support formerly provided by the SR's. At the same time, the party rebuffed the renewed efforts of other nationalist organizations to reunite forces and to seek a new basis for cooperation.[31] Both for abandoning their peasant supporters and for failing to form a united front with the bourgeois nationalist parties, the PKI not only suffered setbacks in its struggle for power, but also incurred the wrath of the leaders in Moscow.[32]

Having narrowly escaped disaster through its mishandling of the religious issue and its abandonment of the SR's, the PKI proceeded to destroy itself by the coup in 1926. Despite the loss of much of its peasant following, the party had managed to rebuild its strength, principally through control of a significant part of the labor movement. Misled by the appearance of strength suggested by the size of the unions under its domination, and swayed by the revolutionary ardor of a faction which had risen to prominence within the party in 1924–25, the PKI in October 1925 laid plans for a revolution to take place the following June. This was the fateful Prambanan decision, taken at a meeting of the party's Executive Committee together with the leaders of the major Communist-controlled unions—a conference at which the revolutionary faction, led by Dahlan, Soekra, Alimin, and Musso, dominated the proceedings. However, increasingly severe measures by the authorities removed several of the leading participants from the scene; meanwhile, at a meeting in early 1926, a number of party leaders from Java and Sumatra decided to drop their plans for revolt. This left the PKI with a leadership split on the issue of revolt and with a mass backing much smaller than the Prambanan conferees had counted on. The grandiose plans for revolution crumbled away into a poorly organized uprising in Java in November 1926, followed by a similarly weak attempt in Sumatra some two months later, both crushed within a matter of days.

Yet the events that led to this abortive coup are important, because they resulted in the schism that has divided the Communist movement in Indonesia ever since. The essentials of the significant story, as told by two leading contenders, are these:[33] Tan Malaka, one of Indonesia's leading Communists, who had been exiled some years earlier by the Dutch and was currently the Comintern's agent for Southeast Asia and Australia, opposed the Prambanan decision, as he had earlier opposed the party's abandonment of the SR's. Failing to carry his point in the months before the revolt was to take place, he had had circulated in Indonesia a document giving his reasons for opposing the plans. Tan Malaka's efforts to dissuade the local PKI leaders from supporting the revolution were apparently quite successful; his arguments are generally assumed to have been a decisive factor in causing a sizable number of PKI leaders early in 1926 to drop the plans for a revolt. Thus, when the attempted coup ended in disaster, Alimin, Musso, and the other leaders who had pushed through the Prambanan decision and tried to carry it out over Tan Malaka's opposition, laid the blame for failure principally at his door. It was not until some time later, however, that this became the official Comintern version of the reasons for the revolt's failure.[34]

It was largely disaffection among the peasants that had led Tan Malaka to warn the party against such a drastic step as revolt. The burden of his arguments, contained in *Massa Actie*, a pamphlet printed in mid-1926, was that the leadership of the party no longer enjoyed sufficient mass backing to risk a major revolt and that the result might well be chaos.

He pointed out that Moscow would be unlikely to offer any aid for a venture that had so little chance of success. He also questioned the strength of the Marxist training of PKI members who would have to assume positions of leadership in any attempt at revolt.[35] Earlier, when the PKI's mass support had been stronger, Tan Malaka had taken a more optimistic view of the party's chances for successful revolt, provided proper attention was given to consolidating its support;[36] however, by the time the Prambanan decision was communicated to him, Tan Malaka felt that the PKI had missed the opportunity to strike with a possibility of success.

What kind of men were the Indonesian laborers and peasants who rallied to the PKI's banner and made their bid for power in that disastrous coup of 1926? Some 13,000 Indonesians were arrested in the days following the uprising, 4,500 of them being imprisoned and over 1,000 interned. Although the internees, who were concentrated at Boven Digoel, the camp in New Guinea, were labeled Communists by the authorities, it was clear even then to many observers that their crime and their motivation were essentially nationalist rebellion and not necessarily Communist revolution. Sjahrir, a later arrival in Boven Digoel, remarked of these prisoners of the 1926–27 uprising:

[The majority were men] who followed the command of the PKI at that time . . . with the same sort of disposition that they would have followed any prince or venal quack or lunatic. The largest number of them were undeveloped villagers, and the percentage of illiterates was high . . . [E]ven if a large majority of them were not Communists, they were still in favor of rebellion. However, I think that they did not even quite know what they wanted to represent thereby. . . . They are, simply and fundamentally, Indonesians. If one wishes to understand them, one must regard them in this light first of all, and only then can one really evaluate the so-called Communism that many of them profess . . . One finds that it is a strange sort of Communism indeed, a mystical Hinduistic-Javanese, Islamic-Menangkabau, or Islamic-Bantem sort of Communism, with definite animistic tendencies. There are not many European Communists who could recognize anything of their Communism in this Indonesian variety.[37]

While Sjahrir's description was accurate as far as it went, other writers have shed additional light on the prevailing cultural dislocation and on some of the specific reasons which had started many of Sjahrir's fellow prisoners on the road which ultimately came to Boven Digoel. It is apparent from these analyses that the propaganda disseminated by the Communists had come to have a special meaning and had found a special place for itself in many parts of Indonesian society. True, as Sjahrir wrote, there was little resemblance to European communism, but the appeal made by Communist leaders had clearly given a new tone to the dawning self-consciousness of Indonesian nationalism.[38]

Certainly the PKI leaders had not planned to depend for support on a following whose political orientation was practically limited to the negative slogans of anti-imperialism and anticapitalism. This was, however, the inevitable outcome of the leaders' attempt to build a mass party by seeking support without discrimination. There had, of course, been some attempts to school the rank and file in Marxist-Leninist teachings, and some sporadic gestures in the direction of holding party membership to relatively small and well-instructed cadres. But none of these efforts— from the Dutch Communist leader Baars' lecture courses on "agit-prop" work to the program, adopted in 1924, stipulating the training that aspiring party members would have to undergo before acceptance—really took precedence in the eyes of the leaders over their drive for members. It is difficult to determine whether the PKI leaders were dizzied by the rapid success of their appeal to the masses or whether they were guided by their belief that the proper role of a colonial Communist party with a mass base was, as in China, to move toward revolutionary action because "conditions were ripe." Certainly the PKI policy of seeking wide support fairly indiscriminately brought some strange figures into its ranks and caused the leaders considerable difficulty. For example, some unique "deviationists" became members of the party, including groups calling themselves "religious Communists." In fact, some of the deviationists, among them Hadji Misbach at Solo, Soediro in Semarang, and Datuk Batuah in Sumatra, were even able to threaten the party's control in a number of local branches.[39]

While these groups were operating on the fringes of the PKI as well as harassing its central leadership, an attempt was made by the PKI leadership to give a more clearly identifiable Marxist-Leninist tone to the party's program. Thus, starting with the congress of June 1924, the symbols of international communism were utilized more fully at public meetings. In addition, the program put forth at that meeting detailed plans for the establishment of a Soviet Republic of Indonesia, including the use of the techniques of "agit-prop" and the extension of the party schools, still known in that pre-1926 era as Tan Malaka schools.[40] Such measures did not, however, resolve the issue of the kind of party organization the PKI leaders sought during this period, or to what extent their actions jibed with their expressions of views on the organizational question. In its earliest days, the party was clearly intended to be a small elite group, operating as a cell within the mass-based SI.[41] However, the battle to gain control of the SI led the Communists to vie with the SI leaders in seeking mass support, and hence to subordinate the issue of the Marxist-Leninist training of these supporters. The brief experience of the PKI with the SR's does not appear to have altered this organizational pattern.

The fact that the Communist leadership of the local branches could be threatened by Hadji Misbach or Soediro and by other manifestations of non-Communist programs indicates that the party's "intake" procedures were far more lax than its leaders were willing to admit at Comintern meetings. Thus, for example, in his report to the Sixth Comintern Congress, Semaun claimed that the 1926 uprising had failed in part because of the elite nature of the party organization; he maintained that the PKI had only 9,000 enrolled members at that time, contrasted with the 100,000 or more in the SI.[42] This account of the party's size contradicts earlier boasts by PKI leaders about their strength and probably represents Semaun's effort to recast the history of the PKI and its errors in order to fit a new Comintern mold.

The PKI and Its Foreign Links: 1920–27

Reference has already been made to the links between the Indonesian and Dutch Communists and between the PKI and the Comintern. These merit further consideration. There is no doubt about the prime importance of individual Dutch Communist leaders in the establishment and first years of the Indonesian party. However, as these men were in turn exiled by the Netherlands Indies government, the link between the PKI and representatives of the Dutch party weakened. Meanwhile, the tie between the Indonesian Communists and Moscow was strengthened in a variety of ways. The PKI was represented in the Comintern, and it participated in various Comintern agencies operating in the Far East and Southeast Asia. It was also of some importance that a number of Indonesians attended the Communist University of the Toilers of the East in Moscow.

The original quadrumvirate of Dutch Communists—Sneevliet, Brandsteder, Baars, and Bergsma—were in a sense the true fathers of Indonesian communism. They provided the radical wing of the nationalist movement with a theoretical framework and a definition in Marxist terms of tendencies which had been developing in Indonesia for some time before their arrival. They also introduced their pupils to Communist strategy and tactics. And it was through Sneevliet that the PKI first established formal contact with Moscow in 1920.[43] Despite the importance of these men and their vital contribution to the birth of Indonesian communism, it is interesting to note that their subsequent disappearance from the scene worked to the advantage of the PKI. As Semaun put it, "The very fact that the leadership of the party was in the hands of native comrades still further raised the prestige of the party in the eyes of the masses, for we must not forget that in a colonial country like Indonesia, the masses are somewhat prejudiced against the Dutch comrades."[44] This comment suggests one of the main reasons why the PKI's links with the Communist Party of the Netherlands (CPN) were never as strong as those with the Comintern. As Semaun indicated, the intensity of anti-Dutch feeling which permeated much of the nationalist movement, and especially its more extreme elements, automatically made any Netherlander a suspect figure, no matter what his political convictions or behavior. This was not the case in Holland, where Dutch and Indonesian Communists worked well together. By associating continually with a variety of Dutch people, Indonesians in Holland were more likely to distinguish between those Dutch who were regarded as political friends and those who were seen as foes. In Indonesia, however, the racist aspects of colonial rule diminished the possibilities for any real mass confidence in a leadership in which Dutch participation was visible. Semaun was highly conscious of this racial problem; in a pamphlet apparently intended for distribution to Dutch comrades and sympathizers, he noted that "a revolution in Indonesia without Communist leadership will develop into racial warfare" and that the Indonesian Communist Party had tried to solve this problem by attempting to "create affection for our white fellow-Communists."[45]

Two other reasons may be advanced for the relative weakness of the tie between the two parties. One was the lack of regular communication. There were few channels by which Indonesians below the top ranks could learn of the Dutch party's activities and how these related to Indonesia's interests; in addition, the internecine warfare within the CPN during the twenties served to confuse the picture, even for those Indonesian Communists who were informed on developments in Holland. Communication with Moscow was not without its difficulties, but at least the Comintern bureaus and organizations operating in Asia were a good deal closer than Holland.[46] Furthermore, these Comintern bureaus were all seen as Asian groups, dealing with Asian problems, even as Moscow had the advantage of not being regarded as a Western capital.[47] Even where white Westerners were found on the Comintern staffs, the curse of paternalism, which always hung over the Dutch party and its members in the view of most Indonesians, was apparently not felt, or at least not felt as keenly.

Finally, Indonesian relations with their Dutch comrades were severely damaged in the developments arising from the 1926–27 revolt. When news of the revolt first reached Holland, the initial reaction of the CPN was regarded as extremely weak, both by the Comintern and the PKI. Moscow immediately issued a strong denunciation of the Dutch government and the Dutch Social-Democrats.[48] The Dutch Communist party's representative in the Netherlands parliament, however, joined with the

SDAP in backing a motion to send a committee of investigation to Java
to inquire into the mass arrests and internments that had taken place in
the wake of the revolt. Although De Visser, the representative in question, was Moscow's man, having come into power the previous year after
the purge of the former leaders Wynkoop and van Ravesteyn, he obviously deviated from Moscow's position in his initial reaction to the Indonesian revolt. When attacked in the Comintern for his stand, De Visser
claimed that the first reports of the revolt to reach the Dutch Communists
had indicated that it was merely another "provoked struggle." However,
he continued, "just as soon as the party recognized that the Javanese
workers had gone over to an armed uprising, it did everything in its power
to support them."[49] Nevertheless, the Indonesian Communists, who had
already had their heated disputes with the former Communist leaders
in Holland, accused the current leadership then and later of having failed
to support the uprising in a proper fashion.

If relations between the Indonesian and Dutch Communists were not
noticeably good, they were at least reasonably clear and public.[50] The
same could not be said for the Comintern-PKI relationship during the
period and over the events in question. The Prambanan leaders had
sought the support of Moscow for their planned revolt and had timed
the outbreak of the revolution to allow for that support to be received
beforehand. After sifting the events and noting that Moscow never made
public its reaction to this request for support, Kahin writes: "Not only
does the published advice of Russian and Comintern leaders to Indonesian Communists in the months preceding Alimin and Musso's arrival
in Moscow suggest that the reaction was negative, but Alimin's silence
as to their attitude when he is defending himself and attacking Tan
Malaka also tends to support such a conclusion."[51]

There is no doubt that before the PKI revolt the Indonesian Communist leadership had been criticized by Moscow. Stalin had accused it of
"a deviation of the left" for the failure to apply properly the "united-front-
from-above" tactics of the Fifth Comintern Congress.[52] This criticism certainly lends credence to the view that the Comintern supported its agent
Tan Malaka, who had been in Moscow in 1925 and who subsequently
condemned the plan and the leaders of the proposed revolution. But
Alimin and Musso, representing the "revolution-now" faction went to
Moscow—probably in mid-1926—to plead for support. On this specific
point, as Kahin indicates, the Kremlin is silent. That silence, and Alimin's
later reticence about the event, however, do not necessarily justify the
interpretation that Moscow's reaction to their appeal was negative. Quite
the contrary; the evidence suggests that the Comintern probably did not
oppose the plans for rebellion. Reference has already been made to endorsing actions taken both by the ECCI and the Profintern. And Bukharin,

speaking at a session of the enlarged ECCI in late November 1926, proclaimed: "From this rostrum we greet the proletarians and peasants of
Indonesia, the broad working masses of this Dutch colony who are like-
wise engaged in a bloody struggle against capital. Our full support to
the Indonesian people!"[53] Nor did this support end with the suppression
of the revolt. Had Moscow wished to be negative or to repudiate the revolt, it could easily have done so after the arrest of members of both factions. Instead, the ECCI turned its attention to building up the importance
of the revolt and defining the "tasks of Communists in Indonesia."[54]

Why the Comintern took this stand is not as clear as the fact that it
apparently did so. During the second half of 1926—the period of Musso
and Alimin's visit—Stalin was publicly still optimistic about events in
China, which could either aid or be aided by similar events in Indonesia.
It may be that the Indonesian revolt was considered as reinforcement for
the "revolutionary upswing" which he was still expecting or even that
it might provide a hedge in Indonesia against failure in China. In either
case, the ECCI was to submit "the lessons of the Indonesian revolt to an
extremely careful investigation,"[55] and perhaps to find the scapegoat when
it was ready. It is important to note that Musso, in particular, retained
the support of Moscow until his death in 1948.

This issue of the Indonesian coup was still very much alive at the Sixth
Comintern Congress in August 1928, at which Musso, Tan Malaka, Semaun,
and other Indonesians were present. The bitter and irreconcilable division
which had split the Indonesian Communists almost immediately after the
Prambanan decision continued to be ignored in Moscow. Though one
delegate felt the failure of the uprising to have resulted largely from the
split in the leadership,[56] Semaun, a founding member of the PKI, analyzed
the abortive coup and found the reason for its failure in less partisan and
more "correct" Marxist-Leninist terms.[57] The Congress ended its sessions
by refusing to pass judgment on the rival factions and by taking pains to
list "the uprising in Indonesia, the deep ferment in India, the great Chinese
revolution, which shook the whole Asiatic continent . . . [as] links in
one and the same international revolutionary chain, constituent parts of
the profound general crisis of capitalism."[58] Indonesian comrades did not
rate as high as the Chinese, but they were still in excellent Comintern
company.

MINOR LEFT-WING GROUPS BEFORE 1927

While the PKI dominated the left wing during this period, there were
also several minor exponents of socialism on the scene. Although none of
these smaller parties or groups of leaders was as significant as the PKI,
they too were precursors of some of the groups that were to come into
their own in the years after the disappearance of the PKI.

The scene of much of their activity was the Volksraad, the advisory body for the Indies established in 1916 and convened for the first time in May 1918. Here these parties had the opportunity of cooperating with the Indische Sociaal-Democratische Partij (ISDP), a Dutch Marxist group, led by Cramer and other Dutch Social-Democrats.[59] Although these smaller nationalist parties did not really belong to the left wing of the nationalist movement, their contacts with the ISDP and especially their experiences in the First and Second Radical Concentrations, the two blocs formed successively under Cramer's leadership, helped to give a Marxist flavor to the liberal nationalism of many of these leaders. Although the program of this coalition was essentially nationalist rather than Marxist, it seems worth a brief discussion here because, among other things, it is one of the earliest attempts to apply the traditional Indonesian principle of agreement through compromise to the facts of modern political party life.

The First Radical Concentration was formed during the second session of the Volksraad at the end of 1918, when news of revolution and revolt was streaming in from different parts of the world and there was a growing unrest in Holland. As Cramer put it,

. . . the current situation makes a concentration of the outspokenly democratic native and European elements in this country necessary. The basis of this concentration is an urgency program of reforms which are necessary because of the recent events in Europe.[60]

The members of the bloc were the ISDP, the SI, Insulinde, and Budi Utomo.[61]

Cramer attempted to use the Radical Concentration to force the conversion of the Volksraad into a provisional parliament. His motion, introduced on November 25, 1918, came almost simultaneously with the news of a revolutionary outbreak in Holland; and, very shortly thereafter, without waiting to consult higher authority, the governor-general promised far-reaching reforms. However, when the long-awaited revision of the colonial government's laws appeared in 1922, they proved a grave disappointment and led to the death of the First Radical Concentration.

Recognizing the need to direct the disillusioned nationalists into some channel that offered hope for success along parliamentary or at least constitutional lines, and conscious of the threat posed by the increasingly militant stand of the PKI and the ardent nationalists operating within the SI, Cramer, at the beginning of 1923, formed a Second Radical Concentration. This organization had a broader base than the original bloc and sought to include the entire nationalist movement, bringing in parties not represented in the Volksraad, as well as the labor movement. Leadership was still primarily in Cramer's hands, but members now included representatives of the PKI, who, not unexpectedly, came to play a major role in the bloc shortly after its inception. The bloc still continued to have as its goal constitutional reform; to this end, it published a militant manifesto in January 1923, demanding an end to the exploitation of Indonesia by capitalists and a revision of the constitution along the lines originally proposed by the governor-general.[62]

The Second Radical Concentration was even more short-lived than its predecessor. Almost from its inception it was divided, with Cramer, the ISDP, and the more moderate Indonesian parties ranged in opposition to the PKI and the parties and unions which leaned toward the Communists. This cleavage was distinguished, however, by the effort of several smaller Indonesian parties to seek some basis for cooperation on the traditional Indonesian grounds of compromise. Aware of the value of a unified organization which could work both within and without the Volksraad, these minor parties attempted, in the words of one of them, to play the role of "a party of compromise between socialism and communism."[63] However, any basis for cooperation among such disparate groups was destroyed when Semaun published a pamphlet which did not meet with the approval of the bloc's non-Communist leaders. The Second Radical Concentration then began to go downhill until its demise in June 1923.

From these two attempts to seek reform by constitutional means, Indonesian nationalists learned several lessons. For one thing, the experience helped make it clear that tactics of cooperation and parliamentary action could have only limited results, if any. This lesson was to be of some significance when these same nationalists faced the central issue after 1927: the debate over cooperation or noncooperation. Another set of lessons had to do with Marxism and its interpretation by the Social-Democrats. In the course of their cooperation with the ISDP, the nationalist leaders were exposed, to some extent, to the views and activities of the Second International and, more than that, to the thought that Marxism could travel more than one road. Finally, the parties in the First Radical Concentration were largely upper-class intellectual organizations whose leaders were firmly committed to the principle of legal, parliamentary procedure. When the Netherlands Indies government failed to realize the concessions wrung from it by these leaders, the moderate group lost its chance of winning popular support even from the SI, much less from the more radical nationalist parties.

Meanwhile, another current was at work in the Indonesian scene. Operating outside the realm of political activity, but developing and broadening contacts at the mass level which would ultimately make it a major factor in the nationalist movement, was the Mohammedijah. In an attempt to practice the principles of social justice expounded in Modernist Islamic doctrine, the Mohammedijah emphasized education and social and eco-

nomic welfare activities. It also indirectly encouraged the growth of nationalist sentiment in the many areas it reached.[64] Ultimately, of course,
Mohammedijah was drawn directly into the political arena, first as a participant in the wartime Islamic federation established by the Japanese
and later as a member organization of the Masjumi (Madjelis Sjuro Muslimin Indonesia, or Council of Indonesian Moslem Associations), the major
Islamic political party of the postwar era.

THE NEW GENERATION OF LEADERS: 1927—

In 1927 a new set of leaders and a new group of parties began to emerge.
They represented colonial nationalism and were free, for the most part,
of ties either to official Islam or to official communism. Many of these new
leaders who remained in the forefront during the 1930's are still among
the principal figures of independent Indonesia today.

The new generation of nationalists differed from most of its predecessors in several ways, all of them representing a general widening of
intellectual horizons. For one thing, a majority of the new leaders were
university-trained and, as such, formed part of a new intellectual elite
that was gradually becoming an important and respected element in the
Indonesian social structure. For another thing, most of these new leaders
were Marxist-oriented in their thinking; but their Marxism, while dominating their outlook on economic and social matters, was in the political
sphere, subordinated to their nationalist principles. While the independent
society they envisaged was based on some generalized Socialist principles,
the new leaders were unwilling to be deflected from their nationalist goals
by either the Comintern or the Second International. Furthermore, the
socialism embraced by these leaders, while tolerant of the views of the
Islamic radicals, indicated a comparatively sophisticated acquaintance
with the various schools of Western Socialist thought.

The era after the collapse of the PKI also marked the first time that a
significant number of the present generation of Indonesian leaders became
acquainted with non-Communist European anticolonialists. This broadening of contacts, as well as much of the new leadership's experiences with
the Third International during this period, in many instances took place
while a number of the young nationalists were studying in Holland. Particularly important in this connection were the activities of the Indonesian
student association, Perhimpoenan Indonesia (PI), the League Against
Imperialism (Liga), and the Dutch Socialist movement.

Contacts Abroad: PI and the League Against Imperialism

Whether they joined Perhimpoenan Indonesia (PI) or not, the majority
of Indonesian students in Holland were deeply influenced by the organi-

zation.[65] While the flavor of PI's politics was strongly Marxist, most of its members did not join the Dutch Communist party but sought support for their nationalist goals from any anticolonial group. Nevertheless, the exiled PKI leaders as well as many Dutch Communists had a strong influence on the association and, up to a point, the non-Communist PI leaders worked closely with the PKI representatives. This cooperation culminated in the political accord signed on December 5, 1926, by Mohammad Hatta for the PI and Semaun for the PKI. It was intended to serve as a preliminary to the establishment of a new nationalist party in Indonesia, to be led by returned PI members.[66] The agreement stated that PI was to assume top leadership and full responsibility for the nationalist movement in Indonesia, while the PKI and its affiliates were not to oppose PI's leadership as long as it continued to seek independence for Indonesia. The accord was intended to forestall any disputes over control of this new party, but it was a short-lived agreement. Semaun repudiated it the following year, stating that he had committed an error in signing this political contract and had come to the conclusion that an obligation of this sort would mean the liquidation of the independent role of the PKI.[67]

Although firm evidence is lacking, it is possible to speculate with some degree of assurance about the factors that precipitated Semaun's repudiation of the accord at this particular time. The most probable explanation is that his repudiation was an early application of the new Comintern line eschewing cooperation with nationalist groups—a reaction to the defeats in Indonesia and in China and a prelude to the line laid down at the Sixth Comintern Congress. In any case, despite the repudiation of the accord and until the hardening of the new Comintern line late in 1929, the non-Communist PI leaders continued to maintain their contacts with the Indonesian Communists in Holland, with the Communist Party of the Netherlands, and with the Third International's subsidiary organs.

PI's principal line of communication with the Third International at this time was through the League Against Imperialism, which had been set up by the Comintern in 1926. As a front organization, it was at first a heterogeneous collection of persons and parties which had attracted to its ranks a number of Asian nationalists of various political persuasions. The tie between the League and Moscow must have been fairly obvious despite the membership of numerous Social-Democratic parties and groups. This tie, however, and the League's obvious connections with various Comintern organs, such as the International Red Aid, were, if anything, probably regarded with some approval by the Asian nationalists, since the International Red Aid especially had so vociferously advertised its support for the colonial nationalist movements. Even among those Indonesian nationalists who may have felt some uneasiness over the League's tie with the Comintern, support from any source was still welcome, and, at the outset, the League had a respectably large number of non-Communist affiliates.

Cooperation between PI and the League was therefore extremely close at first. Hatta was a member of the League's Executive for some time, and together with other PI delegates as well as Semaun, who represented the PKI, Hatta took an active part in the League's first major conference in Brussels in February 1927. Responding to his speech outlining the situation in Indonesia,[68] the League adopted a resolution expressing sympathy and support for the Indonesian liberation movement and calling upon the Dutch government to give the Indonesians the right of self-determination, to annul the expulsions and death sentences arising out of the recent revolt, and to accord a general amnesty.[69] The League also proposed sending a delegation to Indonesia to make contact with the nationalists there—a proposal which came to nothing because of the Netherlands Indies government's refusal to permit the League's representatives to enter the country. When, late in 1927, the Dutch authorities arrested and imprisoned the leaders of PI in Holland, the League vied with the Dutch Socialists in energetic protests, although it was the efforts of the latter which reportedly made a deeper and more widespread impression on the Dutch people.[70]

Meanwhile, the divergent tendencies within the League were leading to the splitting of its leadership into two camps: the Communists, on one side; and the non-Communist nationalists from a variety of colonial countries, together with the European Social-Democrats, on the other. This division in turn sharpened the dissension between the non-Communist PI leaders in Holland and the PKI representatives. The showdown came after the Sixth Comintern Congress in 1928, when the League, applying the new doctrine of united front from below, renounced cooperation with the bourgeois nationalist movements in the colonial countries. As a result of this new policy, the non-Communist members began to withdraw. Relations between the League and PI deteriorated rapidly, and PI left the League in the summer of 1929.[71]

Contacts Abroad: The SDAP

While it did not alter the essentially Marxist orientation of PI's non-Communist leaders, this experience did tend to turn the attention of some of them to the other major Socialist body in Holland, the SDAP. As noted above, this party had a long history of activity on behalf of Indonesia, and, during the twenties and thirties, was increasing its activities in the colonial field. In 1933 the SDAP set up a Colonial Bureau and a colonial press service, Persindo, headed by L. N. Palar, an Indonesian nationalist who had been active in the SDAP.[72] While going much further in their demands for the abolition of colonialism than did the Second International as a whole, the SDAP still failed to win much favor with Indonesian national-ists. This was in part because it was difficult to give a moderate Socialist program the appeal necessary to win mass support. For example, the reso-lution on colonialism adopted by the SDAP in January 1930, while de-manding independence and the right of self-determination for all peoples, recognized the "realities" of the existing situation. Basing its demand for colonial independence on Socialist principles, the party's resolution then stated that, *as long as* foreign authority continued to exist, this authority should be conducted on the basis of a policy directed toward national independence for colonial peoples.[73] This tacit recognition of colonialism, contrasted with the Comintern's appealing and militant slogans demand-ing the immediate abolition of colonialism, was denounced vigorously by most Indonesian nationalists as well as by the Communists. So was the next point in the resolution, which recommended that foreign rule be exer-cised under the supervision of the League of Nations, in which the domi-nated nations would have their representatives. In the minds of most Indo-nesian nationalists, these points overshadowed the resolution's uncondi-tional recognition of the right of national independence.

In any case, however much the approach of the SDAP may have ap-pealed to moderate Indonesian intellectuals, few nationalist leaders would have been willing to risk the loss of popular support that siding with the SDAP would have meant. Nevertheless, after the Seventh Comintern Congress in 1935, when the Communists ceased stressing the fight for colonial independence in favor of collective security, it was the SDAP which was, in vain, the major protagonist of the Indonesian cause in the Dutch parliament and press. Earlier, the SDAP had carried on a vigorous campaign in Holland over the *Zeven Provincie* incident in 1933,[74] while it concurrently sought, through the non-Communist trade-union federation, to establish a basis for cooperation with Indonesia's organized labor move-ment.[75] Thus, while few Indonesian nationalists were openly affiliated with the SDAP, there is no doubt that the party and especially some of its leaders in the fight against colonialism, like Troelstra and Stokvis, had a strong influence on the political orientation of many Indonesians in the post-1926 generation of leaders.

SOCIALISM, INDONESIAN-STYLE

Nevertheless, the Marxism which came to Indonesia via returning PI members was for the most part not the Marxism of the SDAP. Instead, the leaders of the new parties, study groups, and clubs which began to emerge in this era developed a new brand of socialism which was a synthesis of the ideas absorbed in Holland, reformulated in terms derived from, and relevant to, Indonesia's social traditions. At the outset, some of the mass-based parties reflected in their membership and their programs the fact that there was still considerable sympathy among Indonesian nationalists for the now disorganized PKI. The disillusionments arising out of the shift in the 1928 Comintern line and the PI's experience in the League Against Imperialism were still to come. Some returning PI leaders, including Sjahrir and Hatta, were convinced that one of the essential lessons of the 1926–27 revolt—a lesson which constituted the heart of Tan Malaka's opposition to the timing of the revolt—was the need to educate a cadre group in depth. Without such provision, they felt, a mass party for independence could be destroyed whenever the colonial authorities chose to remove the usually thin layer of top leadership.[76]

Reflecting on this period a quarter of a century later, Sjahrir offered a plausible explanation for the Communist content and orientation of nationalist doctrine in that era and in the programs of the Partai Nasional Indonesia (1927) and its successor parties such as Partai Indonesia (1931). In his opinion, the outlawing of the PKI, the lack of any openly Socialist or Communist party in Indonesia from 1926 until 1945, and the persistent suspicion that European Social-Democracy was not genuinely committed to anticolonialism favored the influence of Moscow.

The brand of socialism which gained influence in politically awakening Indonesia was of the radical and revolutionary type, which was generally considered to be represented by the Third International . . . Hence, from its very beginning the Partai Nasional Indonesia was infused with revolutionary minded socialist tendencies, and in its propaganda, this party freely borrowed from the concepts and terminology of official communism: the Comintern . . . it adopted almost entirely the theory on Imperialism of the Communist International.[77]

Indonesie Klaagt Aan! *and the Mainstream of Nationalist Activity*

The eclectic nature of the socialism of the Partai Nasional Indonesia (PNI) as well as its strong reliance on the Comintern for the theoretical framework of its views on capitalism and imperialism are best seen in *Indonesie Klaagt Aan!* (*Indonesia Accuses!*), one of the major pieces of nationalist writing of that era. This was the famous defense speech made in 1930 by Sukarno, the founding leader of the new nationalist party.[78] In addition to indicating the extent of his borrowings from Marxist-Leninist theory, the work also shows the far broader background of Sukarno's knowledge of Socialism and contains one of the first expositions of the doctrine of Marhaenism, which in recent years has been incorporated into the philosophy of the postwar PNI and utilized by other parties as well. The importance of Sukarno's speech lies not only in what it suggests about the political orientation and resources of its author but also in the fact that his views represented as well the views of a good part of the nationalist leadership of that era.

Recognizing the hopelessness of avoiding further imprisonment, Sukarno in his defense speech was clearly dictating a document that he fully intended to be widely disseminated among the Indonesian people. One of his major points was to emphasize that his attacks on capitalism and imperialism were not attacks on the Netherlands Indies government as such, because, he said, "capitalism and imperialism are not synonymous with Dutch or Dutchmen or other foreigners. Capitalism and imperialism are systems. Capitalism and imperialism are not identical with a regime. We have often stressed that both capitalism and imperialism are international in character." In explaining why it was necessary for his party to develop a theoretical framework within which to operate, Sukarno quoted at length from Kautsky on the education of the masses and then pointed out that "a mass action without theory . . . is a mass action without soul, without will, while it is this will which is the motivating power of such an action."[79] In addition, he stated:

The Partai Nasional Indonesia is convinced that national independence is the most important condition in the efforts to reconstruct Indonesian society; thus all efforts of the Indonesian people must be directed toward achieving national independence. . . . The proletariat can break the resistance of the capitalist classes against the turnover of private property into public property by acquiring political power. Essentially, according to our convictions, the same applies to colonized peoples, to peoples dominated by foreign imperialisms. And it is the acquisition of this political power which the PNI advocates.[80]

In attempting to show that the PNI was neither Communist nor the heir of the PKI,[81] Sukarno pointed out that, while like the PKI in opposing imperialism and considering mass action the means by which to acquire power,

[the PNI] is a revolutionary nationalistic party and her mass-character, her kromo-ism, her marhaen-ism, are not the result of any communistic principles but exist because the Indonesian community makes it necessary for the PNI to subscribe to such a marhaenism. It is a necessity, just as European society makes it necessary for European socialists to adhere to proletarianism. The Indonesian community is a kromo-istic community, a community which consists of small peasants, small wage-earners, small seamen, in short . . . in all fields, a kromo or a marhaen.[82] A national bourgeoisie strong enough to take up arms against imperialism does not exist as yet. The Indonesian movement must be oriented toward the kromo, the marhaen. In their hands lies Indonesia's fate, and from the organization of the kromo and the marhaen must we draw our strength. The movement which keeps apart from the common people, which merely carries on "salon" politics, etc., cannot conduct politics seriously.[83]

This speech soon became the bible of the nationalist movement. It was in this speech that Sukarno staked out the ideas basic to his philosophy and built the strong foundations for the succeeding decades of his national leadership. At the same time, he gave to this PNI a tradition and an out-look which were to be of considerable value to the party of the same name organized after the war.

To a large extent, the launching of the PNI as a mass party initiated and dominated "the second wave" of the nationalist movement. Up to World War II, the PNI principles of nationalism and Marxism served as the ideological norm for political activity. However, no one sector of the nationalist leadership attained exclusive hegemony over the movement. A number of subissues, which could not properly be described as either left or right and which were at the time integral to Indonesian politics, brought into existence ardent nationalist organizations which deviated in program and structure from the model set by the PNI. These variations on the basic theme of independence are too numerous to allow for detailed discussion here;[84] however, the essential differences among them should be noted in typical examples.

Tributary Streams: Cadre Parties

One set of variants was represented by those who based their activity on cadre rather than on mass membership. Such was the Club Pendidikan Nasional Indonesia (Indonesian National Education Club), to which Hatta and Sjahrir devoted their efforts from the time of their return from Holland until they were arrested in 1934. In their opinion, a limited, trained mem-bership party could avoid the fatal blow that governmental suppression usually dealt to mass-based parties with a small leadership. Hatta and Sjahrir chose to work slowly and carefully, building up an elite group, thoroughly trained in nationalist principles, that would be able to continue to spread their doctrine in ever widening circles even after some arrests occurred.

It has been suggested that this organizational concept was the product of its authors' adoption of the Leninist concept of a vanguard revolutionary party. However, in discussing this period, both leaders have maintained that their plan of organization was derived from the situation in Indonesia rather than from any external, doctrinaire sources. Whether or not Lenin influenced these men in this respect, their ideological equipment from that time on arose largely from Socialist roots acquired initially in Holland. Their party very soon gave evidence of a Socialist orientation, and its program was based on the principles of "sovereignty of the people and collectivism."[85]

Another example of cadre structure was the Partai Repoeblik Indonesia (Pari), founded in Bangkok by Tan Malaka in early 1927.[86] This crypto-Communist organization functioned originally as an underground appa-ratus, with its leaders engaged in infiltrating mass nationalist organizations. During the first years of Pari's activity in Indonesia, Tan Malaka was still a Comintern representative despite his opposition to the policies and the leaders responsible for the PKI failure in 1926–27. His aides, who built up the organization in Indonesia, were apparently able to attract considerable personal support for their leader among the men they recruited. Later, during the Japanese occupation and in the first years of the Indonesian revolution, the leaders of Pari, among them Sukarni and Adam Malik, were clearly committed to Tan Malaka's national-Communist views. They were firmly opposed to the Third International's representatives on the numerous occasions when the two groups battled each other politically and physically during this period, although in program there were actually few basic differences between them.

Similar in almost every respect to Pari was the Communist underground organization established by Musso in 1935.[87] Generally referred to as the "illegal PKI," this party instructed its members to join the non-Communist nationalist parties and to encourage the formation of an anti-Fascist front.

In the years following the PKI debacle of 1926–27, there had also been a few brief and more open attempts by the outlawed Communists to re-enter political life. The first of these short-lived revivals was the Sarekat Kaum Buruh Indonesia (SKBI), or Association of Indonesian Workers, established in 1928 allegedly as a nonparty group which was to confine its activities to the economic field and specifically to union organization. Despite Communist protestations about the nonpartisan, nationalist character of this organization, soon after its founding the SKBI's leaders were embroiled in a struggle for control with a group of "revolutionary nationalists"—a battle in which the latter lost out.[88] Actually, the SKBI was apparently established by a group of Surabaya Communists led by Soenarjo and Marsoeki. Their aim was to infiltrate the various unions in order to gain control[89]—a return to the early PKI strategy used in the attempt to take over the SI. SKBI had some success in its single year of operation, and, among other things, became affiliated with the League Against Imperialism. In July 1929 the government arrested the leaders and outlawed the organization.[90] Other attempts to re-establish the Communist movement during the "third period" of the Comintern were equally unsuccessful.[91] Nevertheless, it was apparent that a large number of PKI sympathizers was still to be found, particularly in and around the major cities on Java. As Kahin notes, much of Sukarno's following in PNI and Partai Indonesia (Partindo) probably came from former members of the SR's and the trade-unions in which the Communists had previously played a dominating role.[92]

These three cadre organizations under one guise or another, but with a relatively stable leadership, survived the thirties, played a role during the Japanese occupation, and emerged during the revolution and after as the Socialist party (PSI), the Communist party (PKI), and the Murba Party, respectively.

Cooperation vs. Noncooperation

Another major issue which divided nationalists during this period hinged on certain strategic conceptions necessary to achieve independence: could independence be gained by working with or opposing the Dutch colonial and home government, by parliamentary or extraparliamentary means, or by a combination of both? Some parties, among them Budi Utomo, and some of the regional parties, such as the Pasundan and the Serikat Sumatra, favored cooperation with the colonial government and hence were willing to participate in the Volksraad. Other parties, such as the PNI, its successor, Partindo, and the PSII (discussed below), advocated a policy of noncooperation. In addition, despite the fact that the issue of cooperation is necessarily one of fundamental and usually divisive import in indigenous nationalist movements, there were parties, like the Surabaya Study Club, which had a mixed membership of those for and against cooperation.[93] The cleavage on this question did not parallel any left or right division in socioeconomic or political philosophy, nor did all the parties maintain their respective positions unchanged throughout the period under examination.[94] The foundations of the debate over cooperation underwent a metamorphosis in the late thirties for a variety of reasons, but the issue remained a major one up to the time of the arrival of the Japanese.

The debate over the strategy of cooperation versus noncooperation and the desire to build a mass party also affected the religious nationalists. Sarekat Islam had survived its earlier conflict with the Communists. In 1929 it changed its name to Partai Sarekat Islam Indonesia (PSII), but its influence as a nationalist organization had gradually diminished while its emphasis on religion increased. Five years later two opposing camps of leaders split the organization. One group, led by Sukiman and Abikusno Tjokrosujono, insisted on a policy of noncooperation while seeking to rebuild the mass-based organization with the aid of the religiously conservative local leadership. The other, led by Hadji Agus Salim, rejected this policy for one of limited cooperation while retaining the Modernist Islamic socioreligious program.[95] The latter emphasis tended to restrict the membership of the party, although it was not intended to resemble a cadre organization.

In spite of these differences, Indonesian leaders nonetheless drew on other Indonesian resources in efforts to advance the cause of independence.

Three times during this period—the last time just before the arrival of the Japanese—Indonesian nationalists, utilizing traditional patterns of compromise, succeeded in bringing about large-scale nationalist unity. The first of these federations was the PPPKI (Permufakatan Perhimpunan Politik Kebangsaan Indonesia, or Union of Political Associations of the Indonesian People). It was formed in late 1927 by six nationalist parties—including some for and some against cooperation—and through the initiative of PNI and SI (later PSII). The price of this unity, however, as Hatta later wrote, was that "in the PPPKI it was forbidden to touch upon principal differences of opinion between its members such as religious belief and noncooperation."[96] Though the federation was doubtless weakened by these differences among its component members, such differences were not considered a deterrent to continuing the united effort for independence on the basis of compromise. PPPKI was suspended in 1933 mainly because of Dutch action against the noncooperating parties in the federation.

Six years later a substantially enlarged federation was again organized, this time principally on the initiative of Parindra. Known as Gapi (Gabungan Politik Indonesia or Federation of Indonesian Political Parties), it included eight major nationalist parties. Gapi adopted a four-point program calling for self-determination; national unity based upon political, economic, and social democracy; a democratically elected Indonesian parliament; and cooperation between the Indonesian people and the Netherlands in face of the Fascist threat. In the next two years, Gapi succeeded in unifying the largest assemblage of nationalist groupings ever to take place; its final effort was the all-embracing Indonesian People's Council (Madjelis Rakjat Indonesia). The war, not the Dutch, then interrupted this surge toward independence.

THE COMINTERN AND INDONESIAN NATIONALISM: 1927–42

As we have seen, the nationalist movement in the late twenties and in the thirties developed in response to peculiarly Indonesian issues. It was supported by a generalized political philosophy drawn from both wings of European Marxism, and from Western secular and Islamic religious nationalism. It remains to note more specifically the relationship between the Comintern and Indonesian nationalists during this period.

With the exception of such manifestations as the SKBI and Pari, there seems to have been little Comintern activity in Indonesia during the early years following the Sixth Comintern Congress. However, the abrupt shift in policy introduced in 1935 at the Seventh Comintern Congress by the so-called Dimitrov doctrine had important repercussions in Indonesia and, ultimately, in Indonesian political circles in Holland as well. Actually, the revision of strategy to accommodate to the change in the party line had begun in Indonesia, as elsewhere, some months before the official promulgation of the "People's Front" doctrine. Much of what went on from 1935 to the outbreak of the war has been obscured by the clandestine nature of the establishment and activities of the "illegal PKI." There is some evidence, however, in official PKI postwar statements and publications to the effect that the illegal PKI was the beginning of their party's participation in the Popular Front.[97] It now appears that members of the illegal PKI did, in the prewar period, penetrate into various nationalist parties, where they were largely successful in cloaking their political loyalties while advancing their program. Few Indonesians then or for some time after World War II seemed to be aware of the link between these individuals and international communism.

The Communists found the task of building up an anti-Fascist, anti-imperialist front in the years after 1935 simplified by the developing character of Indonesian nationalism itself. Legitimate nationalists of whatever inclination could and did argue the merits of cooperation with the Dutch government without losing nationalist standing. The Soetardjo Petition,[98] introduced in the Volksraad of 1936 by a group of moderate nationalists espousing cooperation with the Dutch government, serves as a case in point. This petition, a mild document, sought to win Dutch consent for a conference to plan Indonesian self-rule within the boundaries provided by the existing Netherlands constitution. (The PI in Holland, already under a large measure of Communist control, supported this parliamentary move.) The petition was passed by a majority vote in the Volksraad, but, though the official rejection was not formally delivered until 1938, it was soon clear that neither the Dutch government nor parliament would approve it. This stubborn policy weakened the status of the moderate nationalists, who had in this instance been led by Parindra, and helped further to convince other nationalists of the superior merit of a noncooperative policy. The net effect of this episode was to encourage all sectors of the nationalist movement to seek greater unity and to adopt a more militant—in this sense a leftist—nationalist program. A campaign for internal consolidation along the national front was begun; a nationalist press bureau was established, and steps taken to unify the nationalist school system.[99]

While the militant nationalists who had opposed cooperation in the past now resumed the leadership of the movement, they did not employ the strategy of noncooperation that might logically have been expected. Instead they reacted against another political current which had gradually been growing in significance on the Indonesian scene during the early thirties: the expanding Dutch Nazi movement and its offshoots.[100] The Dutch organizations most prominent in Nazi and Nazi-oriented activities were also those most vehemently opposed to the nationalist movement and its social welfare ventures. As a result, there were wings of the nationalist movement whose programs coincided with the objectives of the Communists in building up an anti-Fascist front. While some nationalist leaders were undoubtedly apprehensive over the growing threat of international Fascism, it would have been rather difficult for them to win popular support for an anti-Fascist front which required cooperation with like-minded Dutch individuals and organizations, had it not been for the visible evidence supplied on the scene by the Dutch Fascist organizations.

When a new party, Gerindo (Gerakan Rakjat Indonesia, or Indonesian People's Movement), was established in the spring of 1937, it took the stand that cooperation with the Dutch was necessary in the present international situation since, in this time of crisis, "the most important fact is . . . the crisis of democracy."[101] This new party obviously reflected both the revolutionary-nationalist and the Communist strains, including in its leadership a number of prominent nationalists: Sartono, who had been active in the PNI and Partindo; Wikana, who was closely connected with the "illegal PKI";[102] and Amir Sjarifuddin, who, at a later date, claimed to have been a Communist since the mid thirties. Certainly, Gerindo's program bore a strong resemblance to the Comintern line, from its demand that the East-West controversy be abandoned as the basis of colonial nationalism and replaced by a demarcation line based on democracy versus antidemocracy, to its declaration of willingness to participate in the Volksraad in light of the current international situation.[103]

Gerindo, while powerful, proved a relatively short-lived organization. It faded from the scene after a decision to join Gapi,[104] reached at the party's second congress (August 1–2, 1939), led many of its leaders to concentrate their efforts on the latter organization. Thus far there is no evidence that Communists in Indonesia publicly espoused the line which Western Communists adopted between August 1939 and June 1941, in conformity with the Nazi-Soviet pact.

On the other hand, Gapi, like Gerindo, stressed two themes which made it possible for revolutionary nationalists and Communists to remain in the same organization: the formation of an anti-Fascist front and the demand for commitments from Holland for increasing measures of self-rule and self-determination. Anti-Fascist sentiment, certainly on the elite level, could win a following more, perhaps, in reaction against the vigorous Dutch Nazi movement in Indonesia than out of sympathy for the fate of Holland as such, though there were numerous evidences of support for Holland's predicament after May 1940 from noncooperative parties of the right as well as from moderate parties of the center.[105]

However important an influence may be assigned to the Communists in this period, there is no question that there were other elements in Gapi and in other parties as well which feared the threat of Japanese aggression and supported the policy of an anti-Fascist front for their own reasons. For example, Mohammad Natsir, writing in the Mohammedijah paper *Pandji Islam* in March 1941, commented on Gapi's statement to the Visman Commission[106] as follows:

There is only one thought in the hearts of the [Indonesian] people: the Dutch and their kingdom are in danger. In the midst of this situation, we are being badgered constantly . . . by slogans of Greater East Asian Co-Prosperity Sphere, etc., . . . and hints that Japan has to fulfill its sacred mission . . . At the time that the Japanese were sending up their trial balloon, Gapi was meeting with the Visman Commission and there emerged from that meeting a strong statement that Gapi backs the Dutch. Therefore, Indonesia's nationalist movement has shown to the outside world that its ties with Western people are stronger than those with certain other Asian peoples . . .[107]

It was on Indonesian circles in Holland, more than in Indonesia, however, that the policy of the Seventh Comintern Congress had a marked effect. As the Communist Party of the Netherlands (CPN) developed the local variation of the People's Front line, it decided to drop its demand for Indonesian independence. As noted above, many leading nationalists, members of the Holland-based Perhimpunan Indonesia (PI), had broken with Communist front organizations such as the League Against Imperialism after the Sixth Comintern Congress. But despite this experience, ardent nationalists in and out of Holland had for the most part retained some sense of respect for, if not identification with, the CPN. The party's forceful anti-imperialist and anticapitalist slogans and its early—and, for a decade or more, its unique—militant stance for Indonesian independence had an appeal to nationalists which no amount of disappointment or political sophistication completely destroyed. But when the CPN gave up its demand for Indonesian independence, its contention that "unity" in Holland was necessary to protect Indonesia from "Japanese imperialist Fascism" found little favor among Indonesians who were neither party members nor fellow travelers.

Some time after Sjahrir and Hatta left Holland (1932 and 1933), fellow travelers had succeeded in gaining control of PI, which after 1935 dutifully reflected CPN policy and was used by the CPN, where possible, to recapture lost ground. In 1936, PI and Dr. Sutomo, head of the moderate Parindra, drew up a joint program, which was described in the PI periodical *Indonesia* as a step toward unity within the nationalist movement, "to be based on a limited program of constructive activity which would have the approval of all participants . . . a unity which sought to join all the people of Indonesia without differentiation between left and right."[108] The draft program, which started with cultural, social, and economic planks, had as its first political goal "dominion status [for Indonesia] with national-democratic rights for the people."[109] It also contained an appeal for the establishment of an Indonesian militia—a point which was echoed in the programs of several Indonesian organizations, including Gerindo and Gapi.[110]

Through such tactics, PI was able to hold some of its non-Communist rank-and-file membership, doubtless for many of the same reasons that induced non-Communist nationalists in Indonesia to espouse a similar program of cooperation with the Dutch. However, it is interesting to note that it was left to the Dutch Socialists, in cooperation with Gapi,[111] to carry on the fight for Indonesian independence in the Dutch parliament and press. Meanwhile, of course, the Indonesian Communists in Holland had joined with their Dutch comrades in denouncing the war as an imperialist struggle, once again reversing their policy to accord with the Nazi-Soviet pact line.

In Indonesia the Communists apparently did not openly renounce the Popular Front during the twenty-two months of the Nazi-Soviet pact. It is difficult to determine whether this was, as in China, a response to Comintern directives and hence an officially endorsed "deviation" or whether it offers just one more example of a failure in communication between Moscow and its agents in the "illegal PKI." At any rate, the Indonesian Communists' continued espousal of the Popular Front policy paid dividends in the long run: during and after the war, when Japanese political manipulation and brutality had thoroughly alienated the Indonesian people, the earlier anti-Fascist stand of the Communists and the left-wing nationalists seemed thoroughly justified.

THE JAPANESE OCCUPATION

Whether or not the Communists and their fellow travelers were the decisive element after 1935 in shaping the left-wing nationalists' stand on international affairs, it is clear that they played a significant role in internal nationalist politics. By 1942, however, all nationalists, of whatever political coloration, had almost uniformly arrived at a common outlook: either the Dutch government-in-exile in England would make some commitment as to the kind of self-determination which Indonesia was to have, or the nationalists would forever be confirmed in their view that nothing was to be gained from dealing with the Dutch. Few nationalists expected the former, and only the Communists stood to benefit from the latter, as they could fight against the Japanese while collaborating with and receiving support from the Allies—a pattern resembling the role of the Communists in Burma.

For the non-Communist nationalists, there remained two alternatives:

to fight on two fronts, against the Dutch and the Japanese—which some nationalists elected to do—or "to welcome" the Japanese for opportunistic reasons or because the Japanese might become the instrument of eventual liberation. This decision with respect to the Dutch and the alternative decision with respect to the Japanese made for three kinds of response to the Japanese occupation: fighting the Japanese while carrying on the struggle against the Dutch by whatever means possible, collaborating with the invader, and using the Japanese to further nationalist ends.

The details of the nationalists' activities during the Japanese occupation have been related elsewhere.[112] For our purposes, the Japanese occupation had three interesting consequences: the underground movements formed during the occupation emerged as contestants for power in the postwar period; the Marxist education sponsored by the Japanese increased Indonesian susceptibility to that doctrine; and Japanese policies led to a sharpening of the race issue into a major element in Indonesian social attitudes.

Four major underground organizations were formed under Japanese occupation. They were led by left-wing nationalists, including avowed Socialists, or by Communists of both the Stalinist and national-Communist factions. As the Japanese rapidly succeeded in turning the bulk of the population against themselves, the resistance leaders gained prestige and popular support. This made them figures to be reckoned with in the postwar period, as against other leaders who had risen to the top ranks in the Japanese-run administration.[113]

A subject that remains to be explained satisfactorily—and one that is possibly related to the role played by Tan Malaka and his followers throughout the occupation—is the purpose behind the establishment by the Japanese of Asrama Indonesia Merdeka (Student Quarters for a Free Indonesia). This supposedly nationalist educational institution offered courses in nationalism, politics, economics, sociology, and Marxism. Among those invited (i.e., ordered) to lecture at the Asrama schools were members of the "illegal PKI," former Comintern workers, Hatta, and Sjahrir—a curious combination indeed. Kahin has recorded the various possible explanations for this strange Japanese maneuver, but, as he notes, these still leave the picture somewhat obscure.[114] Whatever the original Japanese purpose, the net effect of the courses must have been somewhat ambiguous, given the variety of political viewpoints represented by this unusual faculty.

Also significant among the many changes wrought by the Japanese occupation in Indonesian social attitudes were those concerning the matter of race. At the start of their occupation, the Japanese had a definite advantage in their relationship to the general populace because of the sense of racial identity. In addition, the bulk of the Indonesian people, as so many other Asians, took pride in the success of Japanese armed forces against the West, much as the Japanese victory over Russia at the turn of the century had served as an inspiration. Furthermore, however delicately it may have been dealt with by most nationalist leaders, the question of race had clearly been of major significance throughout the nationalist movement. Some of the most bitter experiences of Indonesians under colonialism could be traced more or less directly to this fundamental problem. Although the Dutch recognized Eurasians as Europeans for legal purposes—a relatively enlightened attitude for prewar days—the socially discriminatory policies and attitudes characteristic of any colony were prevalent throughout their reign. These were supplemented by the legal and economic barriers that stood in the path of the Indonesian and were reinforced by a strong element of paternalism. In the civil service, for example, Indonesians by and large never obtained posts of genuine responsibility; this situation was reversed under Japanese rule. The Dutch who were caught in Indonesia were interned, and their posts taken by the Indonesians who had previously been kept in subordinate positions. This change gave a boost to Indonesian morale comparable to no other experience in their modern history.

As has been pointed out, in spite of its malignant character the problem of race had, before the Japanese occupation, been treated with considerable tact and moderation by the various nationalist groups. Since educated Indonesians were generally freely accepted in liberal Dutch circles and since students in Holland were usually treated without prejudice, there was a firm bond of friendship and understanding between the Western-educated Indonesian leaders and their Dutch friends. This mutual tolerance, however, did not usually extend beyond personal social contacts. The race issue, which was to become such an important factor in the wartime and postwar era, had manifested itself before the coming of the Japanese in less violent fashion than was the case in some other Asian colonies. Resentment was certainly present, but, partially because of the skillful handling of the question by most of the nationalist leaders, the race issue as such had not been allowed to play a dominant role in the major nationalist parties.

The Japanese consciously and deliberately fostered racist feelings, especially among those who may have suffered prejudice and discrimination at the hands of the Dutch. In selecting members of the Peta, the Volunteer Army of Defenders of the Fatherland (Soekarela Tentara Pembela Tanah Air), they reportedly gave preference to those locally influential Indonesians who were victims of such experience.[115] Such devices might have served Japanese purposes better had the occupying forces not exhibited their own prejudices about the superiority of the Japanese over the other Asians. Their insistence upon Japanese supremacy alienated most of their potential friends. Since the war, Indonesia has manifested elements of xenophobia, attributable in part to the experiences of the revolutionary years and in part to this experience under the Japanese.

THE IDEOLOGICAL CONTENT OF THE REVOLUTION

Pantja Sila

With the collapse of the Japanese, the rising tide of Indonesian pressure for national self-determination burst the dikes that had restrained it with ever diminishing ability, and culminated in the proclamation of Indonesian independence on August 17, 1945. Even the promulgators of the declaration of independence had little hope that this gesture would accomplish more than demonstrating to the world at large the true nature of Indonesian feelings. They were, however, favored by a constellation of events which included the complete demoralization of the Japanese forces in Indonesia and a delay of some six weeks before the victorious Allied troops could return to Indonesia. In this brief interim, the Indonesian Republic grew from a gesture of defiance to the outside world to a national state with a government which, despite many weaknesses and inadequacies, represented the former territory of the Netherlands East Indies. The ensuing struggle for survival,[116] which lasted until the end of 1949, drew the masses of the Indonesian people into the political arena and, to an infinitely greater extent than any previous period in the country's history, set the lines for the shape and structure of contemporary Indonesia.

The Indonesian revolution was fought on the basis of nationalist principles strongly flavored with socialism. Both the leadership and the major political organizations of the revolutionary period were predominantly left wing. The dominating philosophy of the times was a synthesis of three strains: nationalist-revolutionary principles in the tradition initiated by the 1927 PNI and summarized so eloquently in *Indonesia Klaagt Aan!*; the eclectic socialism propounded in the early thirties by Hatta and Sjahrir; and the religious socialism rooted in Modernist Islamic doctrine as it had been developed over the years from Sarekat Islam to the Mohammedijah. The principal deviations from this philosophy were those of the Stalinist Communists and the Tan Malaka national Communists on the left and that of the orthodox, conservative Moslems on the right.

The essence of the predominating political outlook is to be found in the Pantja Sila, the five principles first enunciated by Sukarno on June 1, 1945, some weeks before the declaration of independence[117] and still regarded as the cornerstone of the nation's political and social philosophy.

The first principle Sukarno stated is nationalism, not, as he carefully explained, a narrow chauvinism, but one which, transcending tribal and regional ties and based on "the unity between men and place," sought to place the state of free Indonesia in a family of nations.[118] The second principle he laid down is internationalism, or, as it later came to be translated, humanitarianism. This principle is not, he said, "cosmopolitanism, which does not recognize nationalism . . . Internationalism cannot flower if it is not rooted in the soil of nationalism. Nationalism cannot flower if it does not grow within the garden of internationalism."[119]

The third principle is representative government, the details of which Sukarno left for future discussion. In his speech, however, he did seek to forestall critics among the advocates of a Moslem state by pointing out not only that representative government offered the Islamic religion the best opportunity to prosper, but that Moslems and Christians would work best together in a nation dedicated to representative government. The fourth principle, introduced as "the principle of prosperity," was developed in the speech along the line that the democracy Indonesia needed was not that of the West "where capitalists bear sway" but rather a political-economic democracy able to bring about social prosperity. This concept he then redefined as social justice, basing it not on a Western use of the term but on an ancient Indonesian reference to Ratu Adil, the god of justice. The fifth principle, belief in one God—not any specific deity but rather the worship of God according to individual religious tenets in a spirit of mutual respect—summed up the traditional Indonesian attitude in the sphere of religion.[120]

The concepts embodied in the Pantja Sila have been echoed, in one form or another, with or without reference to the basic document, in all the major statements of principle that form the core of Indonesia's political philosophy. They guided Indonesia's leaders during the years of the revolution. The essence of the five principles is contained in the preamble to the constitution drawn up in 1945 and is listed in more concise fashion in the preamble to the provisional constitution adopted in August 1950.

The Views of Hatta and the Sjahrir Socialists

While the Pantja Sila—and especially the principle of nationalism—very likely represented the sum of the average Indonesian's revolutionary credo, there were other writings at that time which, while reaching a considerably smaller audience, nonetheless became classics of the revolution. In this category is Vice-President Hatta's brief statement entitled *Indonesian Aims and Ideals*. Writing late in 1945 and primarily for foreign consumption, Hatta declared that the Indonesian people "are opposed to all forms of autocratic or fascist rule [and] are desirous of building up a national life on a firm basis of mutual cooperation, in order that there may be full social security. What we Indonesians want to bring into existence is a 'cooperative commonwealth.' "[121]

The Political Manifesto of November 1, 1945, written by Sjahrir but representing the views of the government of the time, was also directed principally at foreign audiences. It was this reasoned and moderate document summarizing the experiences that had led the Indonesian people to make their stand for independence, with its offer, among other points, to restore the private holdings of foreigners as soon as formal recognition was achieved, that first evoked widespread sympathy for the Republic abroad.[122] Another classic of the period is a series of articles devoted to a much more detailed analysis of the substance of Indonesian nationalism. First appearing in the Ministry of Information magazine *Het Inzicht* in early 1946,[123] these articles acknowledged and took to task the reactionary and negative elements participating in the revolution, but also made clear that the significance of these elements was peripheral when contrasted with the spirit motivating the bulk of the Indonesian people. The *Inzicht* articles show a keen insight into the mental processes of the nationalist intellectual from the time when nationalism was "a reactionary resistance to a life in servility and submission to Western countries" through the period when Asian intellectuals were obsessed with the philosophy of positivism, while at the same time they demonstrated an "inner cultural seclusion" that led them to reject the cultural background out of which Western technical progress had emerged. This dichotomy was eased when it became evident that "the movements for freedom in India and Indonesia [had] broken the contradiction between East and West . . ."

The essential task for the modern man today, whether he may come from the West or the East, is . . . to fix again his own position, the re-establishment of his absolute presence, his destination in the cosmos . . . [he must be] led by the ethical standards of truth, beauty and kindness, which form together the components of human dignity . . . This universal value is today no monopoly of the East, neither that of the West; it is the task for the fundamental man.

The second article in the series dealt with the economic problems of the country and specifically with what it defined as the fundamental problem of colonial economies—distribution. Beginning with the statement "Freedom doesn't mean anything if we fail to give it a social content," the writer analyzed the development of the Indonesian economy under Dutch rule and drew the following conclusions:

It is evident that mere absolute increase of production and welfare is not of sole importance. It is also paramount that as many groups as possible of the community involved should have their share in the increase of production . . . [T]he political liquidation of the colonial system should be accompanied by a change in social economic conditions. The distribution of the social product should no longer be left to the forces of a free market. A planned economy, led by the so-cialistic idea, is the organization of economic life which we bear in mind. Because only in the atmosphere of socialism is a just distribution of the social product conceivable, which would fulfill the demands of human dignity.

While the *Inzicht* articles included a somewhat more academic analysis of Indonesia's economic prospects than did the usual run of statements by political leaders on that subject, their approach reflected quite accu-rately the general views of the majority of nationalist leaders on the future economic organization of the state.

The most complete exposition of the Socialist content of Indonesian nationalism in the days following the declaration of independence is to be found, however, in a pamphlet written by Sjahrir at the end of October 1945 called *Perdjoeangan Kita (Our Struggle)*. It is a searching analysis of the mental and emotional climate of the country in the first weeks of independence. With his characteristic realism, the author frankly outlines the shortcomings as well as the strengths of the infant nation while he presents the tasks ahead with no attempt at minimizing them. Sjahrir characterized the revolution as one that "outwardly . . . resembles a na-tional revolution; when seen from within, it resembles a revolution of the people."[124] He also carefully developed the many domestic and interna-tional reasons why this particular revolution must necessarily have a social orientation. He castigated not only those guilty of excesses against for-eigners and other minority groups and those who had blindly followed the Japanese, but also those who would place nationalism above the social goals of a democratic revolution. The new Indonesia, he wrote, must be built by men free of any taint of collaboration with Dutch or Japanese Fascism—a statement that was not designed to win him many friends among the recent collaborationists then seeking high office in the Republican government. Many of those whose sole object in politics was nationalism, he reminded his readers, had not been deterred from seeking this goal along Fascist roads. Indonesia's revolution, he proclaimed, was "a demo-cratic revolution, of which the national revolution is only an offshoot. Not nationalism but democracy is the number one aim."

The pamphlet also examined the meaning of the struggle for inde-pendence as it affected specific groups of the population: labor, farmers, the youth, and the army. The passages devoted to labor exhorted the workers to remember that their present fight, in defense of an independent Indonesia, was but a part of the total battle that must be waged by labor internationally against imperialism; the farmers must emerge from the revolution free of the feudal structure that had kept them in poverty and bondage; the youth, who were playing such a vital role in the struggle, must keep in mind the social foundations of the revolution and avoid the misconception that this was a military struggle to be waged by military leaders; and the army, despite its importance, should not supersede the organs of the state in the democratic revolution. The two evils to be avoided at all costs were those of militarism and Fascism.

This document, while never as widely circulated as the Pantja Sila speech, became a kind of bible in the intellectual and student circles it did reach. Unlike most of his colleagues in government, Sjahrir did not seek to compromise sharp differences of opinion for the sake of unity when those differences touched at the heart of the principles of the revolution.

The Religious Socialists

The third dominant strain in the political thought of the Indonesian revolution was expressed by a group called the Religious Socialists, who drew upon the teachings of Modernist Islamic doctrine for their principles. This group was inspired by such Moslem leaders as Hadji Agus Salim, who had been a proponent of a philosophy combining a liberal or progressive view of Koranic doctrine in religion with related attitudes toward socio-economic and political issues. Within the Masjumi (Madjelis Sjuro Muslimin Indonesia, or Council of Indonesian Moslem Associations), these leaders provided a base for contemporary Moslem political thought, akin to the foundations provided by Sukarno, Hatta, and Sjahrir in other parties. The most vigorous exposition of their views is found in such works as Sjafruddin Prawiranegara's *Politiek dan Revolusi Kita* (*Politics and Our Revolution*)[125] and in the formulation of the party's political program.

The Religious Socialists defined their concept of "social justice" or "socialism" as one which "has no spiritual connection with Marxian socialism," which they associated with force or imposition; for them, Religious Socialism "does not abolish individualism, individual initiative and individual responsibility." It is opposed to "the elimination of a certain class or groups." It guarantees the freedom of the individual and the nation "without closing the door for possible nationalization or socialization of vital enterprises." The latter coexists with "private initiative." Both are necessary.

Such views were incorporated in the Masjumi party statement of principles and program. These were designed "to bring about greater political consciousness among the followers of Islam in Indonesia, to organize and strengthen the unity of Islam, to guide the people towards humanity, socialism, brotherhood and equality in accordance with the teachings of Islam [in a republican state] based on Moslem teachings [and] a guided economy."[126]

The ideas cited in the foregoing political spectrum represented in

varying degrees the philosophy of the majority of the Indonesian people
and their leaders in the years from 1945 to 1950. These formulations either
preceded or emerged from the platforms on which the political parties
were organized. Sukarno's general statement of nationalist-revolutionary
sentiments was largely adopted by the newly created PNI.[127] Two Socialist
groups, led by Sjahrir and Sjarifuddin, respectively, combined to form the
Partai Sosialis, or Socialist Party, but later, in the months immediately
following the organization of the Cominform, split once again. The latter
joined the Communist forces (see below), and the former reorganized
this group as the Partai Sosialis Indonesia (PSI). The Masjumi, long
regarded as the majority party, reflected the views not only of the Religious
Socialists but also of the Nahdatul Ulama, the conservative Moslem group
which formed one of its original component organizations. These three
were the major parties, in terms of popular support, prestige, and the
power of their leaders, during the early years of the revolution. After the
rupture in the Partai Sosialis, the PNI and the Masjumi continued to dominate the scene. In addition, there were a number of smaller parties, most
of which traveled in the orbit of one of the three major parties or of those
now about to be discussed.

There were other points of view which motivated certain leadership
groups and led them into political behavior which jeopardized the existence of the young republic. As noted above, the most important of these
dissident elements during the revolution were the Stalinist Communists
and the National Communists; they are perhaps better understood in terms
of their behavior than in terms of their professed programs.

THE ROLE OF THE PKI IN THE REVOLUTION

The Stalinist Communists entered the revolutionary period with certain
decided advantages. From the days of the "illegal PKI" in 1935, they had
played an able political game: they had cooperated with the nationalists
in an anti-Fascist, anti-imperialist front; they had refrained from publicly
espousing the Stalinist line during the era of the Nazi-Soviet pact; their
leaders in Indonesia had, with Dutch support, been active in a reputable
underground movement; and their leaders in Holland had been widely
praised for their very active role in the anti-Nazi underground. The dissolution of the Comintern in 1943 and the "right" united-front line pursued
by the Kremlin during the war and the first postwar year enabled the Communists in Indonesia to command a role in the revolution despite some
preliminary confusion.

This initial confusion arose on two counts. In Indonesia the PKI was
first re-established in October 1945 under the leadership of an individual
of questionable political background and dubious ability, Mohammed

Jussuf. Meanwhile, the Indonesian Communists in Holland and elsewhere outside of Indonesia had followed in the footsteps of the CPN, denouncing the revolution as a "Japanese time-bomb," and labeling Sukarno and Hatta as "fascist collaborationists." Encouraged by this attitude, the Netherlands government flew a number of PKI leaders back to Indonesia, in the full expectation that, once there, these men would present the Dutch case. However, within a very short time, the returned Communists had grasped the scope and significance of the revolution and switched to support of the Republic.[128] From that point on, the confusion disappeared, the party line straightened out, and both sets of old-time Communists—those who had been abroad and those who had remained in Indonesia—showed no further hesitation about re-embracing the wartime strategy of united front from above, this time in the presumed interests of independence. In pursuit of this goal, some joined the Partai Sosialis or one of the minor left-wing parties in the same orbit; others, notably Sardjono and Alimin, took control of the PKI and reorganized its central command.

The political haze created by the united-front policy enabled Communists and crypto-Communists to reach positions of high power within the Republican government, extending up to the post of Premier, held by Amir Sjarifuddin. It also made possible their participation in a left-wing coalition of Socialists, Stalinists, and National Communists, the Sajap Kiri (Left Wing). This coalition gradually developed into a new front, which was to become a mass instrument for the PKI in the prelude to the Madiun uprising of 1948.

Almost from its establishment this awkward alliance was rocked by disputes, which increased in vehemence after the "Zhdanov line" was laid down in September of 1947 and Cominform policy hardened into its new mold. The Communists' decision to oppose the Indonesian revolutionary government did not, however, take place until February 1948. At that point the Partai Sosialis split, the Sjahrir Socialists forming the Partai Sosialis Indonesia (PSI), while Sjarifuddin's group took the lead in transforming the Sajap Kiri into the Front Demokrasi Rakjat (FDR), or People's Democratic Front. The FDR made little attempt to cloak its true political color; purged of the Sjahrir group, the FDR denounced the Renville agreement (which had been negotiated under Sjarifuddin's leadership), and when its parliamentary maneuvers to join Hatta's new cabinet were rebuffed, it used that treaty as a convenient excuse for opposing his new administration. Through the spring and summer of 1948 there was growing evidence that the FDR was preparing for a showdown of some kind with the government.

In August, Musso, Communist leader from Moscow, arrived on the scene, unheralded and incognito, in the company of Suripno, the Republican envoy to Eastern Europe.[129] Armed with what he termed his "Gott-wald Plan"—a reference not without pertinence in the rapidly developing situation—Musso threw off his disguise, assumed command of the PKI, and briskly set about whipping that organization into shape for the challenge it was to give to the central government.

In the Communist plans, it was the FDR which was expected to provide the mass organization and backing that the PKI counted on in its bid for power. The strength of the FDR came principally from two sources: the loyalty of certain army officers to Sjarifuddin—a loyalty nurtured in the days when he had been Minister of Defense; and the support of the Sentral Organisasi Buruh Seluruh Indonesia (SOBSI), or All-Indonesia Central Labor Organization, the largest labor federation in the country. When the conflict finally did break out, at Madiun in September 1948,[130] neither of these sources of support proved to be as strong or as dedicated as the PKI leaders had anticipated, and the Communists suffered a disastrous defeat.

There can be no doubt about the origins of the Madiun coup. Although the popular discontent and the deteriorating position within the Republic might have encouraged such an adventure, there is sufficient evidence to show that the coup followed upon decisions reached in top Soviet circles abroad.[131] It can be cited as one more example either of the Kremlin's failure to assess properly the political and military realities of the situation in Indonesia or of its willingness to engage in expendable actions for "larger" purposes.

It has been suggested by both Kahin and McVey that the outbreak at Madiun may in a sense have forced the hand of the PKI leadership before it was ready to go into action, and that the uprising came when it did because local Communists were feeling the pressure of the government's campaign to disarm them and remove from crucial areas military figures whose loyalties it had reason to suspect.[132] However plausible this interpretation may be, there are a number of other considerations which lend support to a view that, while the revolt may have been off schedule by a matter of days, it had been planned for a time very closely approximate to September 18, 1948, the actual date it began. For one thing, Indonesian Intelligence had acquired Dutch documents detailing plans for a new attack on the Republic scheduled for the fall of 1948. This information also became known to the PKI. While the captured plans came as no surprise to many Indonesians since tangible evidence of the Dutch military build-up was on hand in many quarters, these documents presumably indicated, among other things, the relative imminence of the date set for the attack. It is reasonable to suppose that under the circumstances the PKI might have felt that its bid for power would either have to be executed before the Dutch action or else postponed, perhaps for an inordinate length of time. Second, there was the Indonesian reaction to the so-called Cochran proposals, submitted privately to Indonesian and Dutch representatives in early September.[133] The Cochran proposals were regarded in Indonesian quarters as favoring the Dutch at the expense of the Indonesians and thereby served to weaken the Hatta government.[134] In addition, economic conditions in Java had deteriorated sharply as a result of the Dutch blockade. The defeat of Indonesian attempts at the United Nations to force the lifting of the blockade made it clear that conditions would continue to grow worse. The reaction both to the Cochran proposals and to the blockade situation intensified sources of disaffection among the Indonesian people. Fourth, there was the significant timing of the return of Musso with his "Gottwald Plan." Finally, there was the sudden and dramatic shift in the attitude of the Soviet delegation to the United Nations toward the Indonesians. After having championed the Indonesian cause at the UN with a degree of vigor that was sometimes embarrassing to the Indonesian representatives, the Soviet delegate to the Security Council on September 1, 1948, abruptly "dropped" the Indonesians and their cause.

The defeat at Madiun, the execution of many of the rebellion's leaders, and the storm of popular reaction against this attack on the central government drove the PKI from the scene—but only for a short time.

The second dissident movement which ran counter to the general ideological temper and behavior during the revolution was that of the followers of Tan Malaka, who, for want of a more precise term, are called here the National Communists. As will be remembered, Tan Malaka had himself been called a Trotskyist by Bukharin during the Sixth Comintern Congress. It is certainly questionable, however, if Tan Malaka was ever any kind of Trotskyist; his views and conduct throughout three decades of political activity show a kind of internal consistency even when he was serving as an official Comintern agent before and after the 1928 Comintern congress. Tan Malaka was a Communist; he was at home in the Marxist-Leninist tradition; he was obviously a man who attracted a dedicated following. But perhaps the single most important element in his consistency and thereby in his ability to attract a following was the fact that he was almost always—if not always—a nationalist first, an Asian regionalist second, and a defender of tactical Pan-Islamism third, as well as a Communist. As Indonesians would say, and often have said, he was first of all an Indonesian.

There is some obscurity about Tan Malaka's role during World War II, but, as indicated, his followers remained in Indonesia and were active in an underground apparatus of sorts. Many of them made their first postwar appearance in a mass organization led by Subardjo.[135] Subardjo's party had originally been organized during the Japanese occupation, supposedly as an underground force, but its members included, besides many graduates of the Asrama schools, a number of Indonesians who were working in the Japanese-run civil service. Within a few weeks after the declaration of independence, his party had grown to massive proportions because other political leaders were at first unwilling to organize parties. When this problem was resolved by the Republican government in favor of a multiparty system, Subardjo's organization faded out of existence and a majority of his following joined one or another of the various organizations led by the followers of Tan Malaka.

Tan Malaka, strongly opposed to the Republican government's policy of negotiations with the Dutch, tried to establish himself and his lieutenants in controlling positions in the government and in the numerous parapolitical, paramilitary popular organizations which sprang up throughout the country in the first months of the revolution. He even attempted, through a rather elaborate scheme, to supplant Sukarno as leader of the state. In January 1946, frustrated in his series of attempts to wrest power from the Republic's central leadership, Tan Malaka established a coalition known as the Persatuan Perdjuangan (PP), or Fighting Front, which initially encompassed members of all parties and organizations. The PP's program demanded not only the dissolution of all political parties but the abandonment of any negotiations with the Dutch until all foreign troops had left Indonesian soil. The first point in this program alienated much of Malaka's support from the major parties in the government, and his uncompromising stand on negotiations ultimately led the authorities to arrest him along with several other leaders of the PP. Nevertheless, his organization continued to grow in strength, possibly because its extreme position on negotiations appealed to certain elements in the population. Encouraged by this support, the PP leaders, upon their release from prison, attempted a *coup d'état* in June 1946 which included the much-publicized incident of the kidnaping of Sjahrir. The leaders involved in the coup, Tan Malaka included, were reimprisoned, and the PP, after a few uneasy days when it appeared that a civil war might well break out, ceased to be a factor in domestic politics. In a way, the PP was a classic example of the curious amalgamations which arise on the Indonesian political scene. Besides Tan Malaka and several of the key figures from his prewar organization, Pari, its leadership included Abikusno Tjokrosujono, leader of a faction in the Masjumi; Suprapto, of the PKI; Subardjo, whose wavering political orientation has already been discussed; Iwa Kusumasumantri, whose previous activities included a year of teaching in Moscow; and

Mohammed Yamin, who is consistently listed as an independent, nonparty man and has a voting record in the parliament which, while generally leaning to the far left, is sufficiently confusing to support that designation.[136]

Despite the disappearance of this strange coalition, Tan Malaka's adherents continued to be active in a variety of smaller Marxist-oriented parties and especially in the leadership of small armed units. In June 1948 a number of these groups banded together in a new federation, the Gerakan Revolusi Rakjat (GRR), or People's Revolutionary Movement. While following in the footsteps of the defunct PP in opposing any negotiations with the Dutch, the GRR was nevertheless able to reconcile this position with support for the current Republican government, in contrast with the FDR. Indeed, its opposition to the Stalinist-oriented FDR seems to have been one of the GRR's principal reasons fer existence. The GRR, like its postrevolution successor, the Partai Murba, espoused essentially the same program as the Stalinist Communists but renounced any tie whatsoever with the Soviet Union.[137]

The GRR fought bitterly against the PKI-led troops at Madiun—as did Tan Malaka and the other PP leaders released from prison shortly before that event—and hence emerged from the revolution with a reputation considerably better than that of the PKI. However, this record of loyalty to the Republic in its darkest days was not enough to place the Murba forces in the front rank of Indonesian parties, as the 1955 general election results showed.

These two groups—one led by the PKI, which followed conventional international Communist policies, and one led by Tan Malaka, whose consistency is clear but whose rationale of political conduct is yet to be discovered—were the principal forces on the left which ran counter, in political behavior and program, to the major themes of the revolutionary era. Despite the very grave threats posed at different times and places by both these forces, the Republic fought its war with the Dutch to a successful conclusion, and the Sukarno-Hatta government was duly recognized in the transfer of sovereignty on December 27, 1949.

POSTREVOLUTIONARY INDONESIA

The political atmosphere in Indonesia at the time of the transfer of sovereignty was far from healthy.[138] While most of the Republic's leaders regarded the actual transfer of sovereignty at the end of December 1949 as a victory, despite the shortcomings of the Hague agreement and the general dissatisfaction with the federalist form of government it imposed, the popular reaction was quite different. For one thing, however much Indonesia's leaders maintained that the Hague agreement represented the final treaty in the war for independence, it appeared to large masses of the population to be no different from the two previous agreements that were to have brought peace and independence, Linggadjati and Renville. Twice burned, the Indonesian people were a good deal more skeptical of the finality of the new agreement than was generally realized abroad. For another thing, within days after the formal transfer of sovereignty, the first of a series of armed attacks in which Dutch units were involved broke out in Bandung, followed not long after by similar eruptions in Makassar and Ambon. To many Indonesians it began to look like a repetition of the previous pattern of truce, negotiations, and political agreement only to be followed by further military attacks. Finally, the continued presence of Dutch troops increased the general sense of uneasiness and contributed to the feeling that a new explosion was impending.

To the leaders in Djakarta it was clear that the Republic would not be openly challenged again by Dutch arms, but the understanding of the international situation and of the role of the United Nations on which this optimism was based was, of course, not shared by the masses. The tension inherent in such a situation was but one aspect of the general confusion and chaos that prevailed throughout the country after eight years of military occupation and warfare. In a far worse position than the European nations at the end of World War II, the Indonesians had not only to rebuild the most basic economic facilities, restore their transportation and communications systems, secure adequate food supplies, textiles, medicines, and other necessities; they had also to create a civil administration that would function on a permanent footing in place of the makeshift wartime services that had operated on an emergency basis. Here, the drastic shortage of trained personnel was a problem of the first order of magnitude. Added to these difficulties were the other special problems that characterized the postwar scene in Indonesia: the social upheaval that, in the course of eight years, had wrenched loose from their traditional moorings all but a small part of the country's population; the widespread disappointment and discontent with the seemingly blurred outcome of the revolution; and the rancor that embittered relations between the majority of the people and the minority who had collaborated with the Dutch.

The entire fabric of Indonesian life had been torn apart by the experiences of the revolutionary years, and with it had gone many of the old traditions, patterns of authority, and ties of family life. Guerrilla bands roamed the countryside, as they had since 1945. In some instances, their refusal to lay down their arms and settle back into civilian life arose from disgust with the final result of the revolution; in others, it was motivated by disbelief in the finality of the Hague agreement. Cer-

tainly the continued presence of Dutch troops and the series of major
armed clashes in 1950 in which the Dutch were involved encouraged
this belief. Finally, the lure of sheer banditry should not be overlooked.
Encouraging many Indonesian youths in their drift away from society
was the dimly sensed feeling that the caliber of their individual contributions and sacrifices should have culminated in something more than
the dubious advantages of settling down into a village life that many of
these youngsters scarcely remembered. These young people still form
the core of the numerous armed gangs operating today in various parts
of the country, sometimes under the name of Darul Islam (DI), sometimes under another banner chosen to indicate some local grievance with
the central government.

This sense of disappointment and resentment was not confined to the
youth, or to any one section of the population; within a few weeks after
the transfer of sovereignty, there was a general miasma of disillusionment, as the revolutionary *élan* faded and no single equally inspiring
force came to take its place. From the masses of the Indonesian people,
who had played an active role in achieving their independence, there
came a rather inarticulate but nonetheless real demand that independence bring in its wake something positive and tangible, some visible
difference from the poverty and hardship of their daily lives. As some
of their leaders had anticipated, the Indonesian people soon made the
discovery that independence is not enough. At the same time, these
masses were now receding from the political arena, and their leaders,
isolated in the halls of power, began the seemingly interminable political poker game that would ultimately decide which factions would survive and hence what the content of this new freedom would be.

Reactions to the International Scene

The elements of Indonesian life noted in the opening pages of this
chapter—the traditional social values, the role of religion, the *desa* system—had been undermined, and in some cases destroyed, by occupation
and war. This left a largely disoriented society open to the changing
winds of doctrine. In many ways, the cards seemed to be stacked
in the Communists' favor from the outset, despite the fact that the domestic Communist party was still in disrepute as a result of the events
at Madiun. A number of factors were involved. The residue of ill-feeling
for the Dutch naturally affected Indonesian attitudes toward the entire
Western bloc. Furthermore, the feeling that Indonesia's fight for freedom was part of a general postwar struggle against colonialism was more
widespread than foreign observers might have anticipated,[139] and helped
to exacerbate the sense of hostility toward Holland's allies. Spilling over

from this reservoir of bitterness into the economic sphere was a strong reaction against Western holdings in the country; this reaction in turn fitted into the pattern of the nationalists' historical stand against Western capitalism. The depth and range of this antipathy toward foreign capital can be judged from the fact that no Indonesian party has really dared to challenge this attitude in any consistent fashion. It is true that on occasion a few leading political figures have publicly proclaimed their view that this inclination toward xenophobia should not be allowed to stand in the way of reaping the advantages to be gained by Western, especially American, capital investment, but these moderate and measured statements have been all but lost on the domestic scene in the deluge of denunciations of foreign capital and nonspecific demands that Indonesia's economy be freed from any taint of colonialism.

This generalized anti-Western reaction of the Indonesian people at the end of the revolution continued to be nourished by a variety of incidents. The Indonesian farmer may be remote from world affairs and often only vaguely aware of the real issues at stake in the national political scene, but a considerable number of generalizations about world affairs have nevertheless trickled down to the village level and helped to form fairly widespread attitudes. Among the issues on which popular opinion was thus formulated were the struggle in Viet Nam, the war in Malaya, and the Korean war. Many Indonesians seemed to have an undifferentiated picture of these situations, seeing them in terms of their own revolution—a fight of Asians against Western imperialists. There was no lack of sympathy for the Vietnamese in their fight against the French, however noncommittal the Indonesian government's stand may have been on that prickly question.[140] Although knowledge of the Malayan situation was less widespread, the impressions formed about it seemed to be much the same; the fact that the Malay insurgents were labeled Communists did not impress the average Indonesian, since it was assumed that this was just one more Western attempt to justify an attack against an Asian people in revolt.

Finally, the prestige of the United Nations and the United States, which had been damaged in Indonesian eyes during the revolution, received a telling blow from the Korean war. In the first place, the original news of the attack, as it came through to Djakarta and spread out from there, did not make clear the fact that the attacking force had undeniably been North Korean. It was some time before the entire story was accurately recounted, even in the capital. In any case, the basic reaction in many quarters was resentment at the contrast between the prompt response to the violation of the Korean agreement and what most Indonesians regarded as the halfhearted, ambiguous reaction of the

United Nations to the second Dutch attack in 1948. Many Indonesians in government circles, who were in a position to know that the United Nations was in a stronger situation with respect to Korea than had been the case in regard to Indonesia in 1948, still persisted in their claim that this was simply proof that the United States and Britain would never take strong action against a nation which they regarded as "wearing the same school tie" (i.e., the Netherlands) but would only react with such vigor to the contravention of a United Nations truce by the other side in the cold war.

It was also obvious, both at the outbreak of the Korean war, when the badly outnumbered American forces were being pushed back, and later, when the war finally reached its dusty conclusion, that many Indonesians took a certain pride in what they regarded as the apparent success of Asian troops pitted against the West. In Indonesia, the popular view of the Korean hostilities was that of a well-equipped, highly trained, well-fed American force being held at bay by the sheer determination of North Korean and later Chinese peasants, mobilized to fight with little more than their bare hands. All the resentment toward, and disillusionment with, the United States that had started to snowball after the breakdown of the Renville agreement was expressed in this reaction. It pervaded many circles not in sympathy with the Communists on political grounds.

The natural inclination of much of the population to accept this picture of current world tensions was fortified by the heavy inflow of propaganda designed to capitalize on this general outlook. With the arrival of the first ambassador from Peking, in August 1950, the quantity and distribution of this material expanded tremendously.[141] The traditional dislike of the local Chinese in Indonesia—which had been vastly increased during the revolution, when a substantial portion of the Chinese population sided with the Dutch—made many Indonesians wary of this representative of the new China, but this suspicion did not carry over to the new supply of reading material in Indonesian, which was seized upon eagerly, especially by the younger students.[142]

This world view, which was to a large extent a projection of Indonesia's recent experiences onto the global scene, was enhanced by the continuing tangible evidence of the blurred outcome of the revolution: the continued presence of Dutch troops for more than a year after the transfer of sovereignty; the employment of Dutch civil servants in the administration for two years after the war, as arranged by the Hague agreement; and finally the thorny question of Irian which, left unsettled in 1949, is still the one issue on which all parties and political leaders agree—at least in public.[143]

Thus the attitudes formed during the revolution, coupled with these other factors, continued to give Indonesian politics all across the political spectrum an anti-imperialist, anticapitalist, anti-Western—indeed, a Marxist—tinge.

CONTEMPORARY INDONESIA: THE DOMESTIC POLITICAL SCENE

This background conditioned all of the significant elements animating the domestic political infighting which has been characteristic of Indonesia since the transfer of sovereignty. These elements, not given in any normative order, are the Presidency and President Sukarno, the position of the army, the role of the trade-unions, the state of the economy and its relation to the armed bands and to regional disaffection, and the structure and character of the political parties themselves.

The President. The first and the last of these elements—the role of the President and the nature of Indonesia's political party system—are rather closely related. Both reflect the highly personalized character of Indonesian politics—a phenomenon often encountered in, though not limited to, societies in an early stage of political development. To a degree which by Western standards appears unusually high, personalities supersede programs in the political arena, and personalities rather than ideology or program are often the deciding factor in determining political allegiance. The personal prestige of President Sukarno far transcends that of any other political figure; until a very short time ago, there was no political organ of any consequence openly opposed to him.[144] As a result, much of Indonesian politics since 1949 has consisted of efforts to curry favor with the President and of the President's manipulation of different groups for his own ends. Examples of the latter include the brilliant fashion in which the President in 1952 utilized the October 17 affair to achieve a firmer grasp on the army and once again place himself in a role above the petty internecine warfare of the parties, while all the time denying vigorously that he sought to become a dictator. Subsequent incidents involving the armed forces, including the air force affair in 1955, were all resolved in much the same fashion.

Sukarno is one of the phenomena of modern political history, in that he has thus far managed to straddle two chairs—or at least to jump back and forth from one to the other—without losing his balance. In his public stands on various issues, he has consistently managed to embody the traditional Indonesian principle of compromise, right up to the promulgation of his famous "conception" at the end of 1956; the conception itself was, of course, presented as a full-blown application of the principle of *musjawarat* to the solution of national problems. More recently, however, with the hardening of the opposition to the central government, particularly outside Java, reliance on Sukarno's name has ceased to be the magic formula for political success. An interesting question of the coming months in Indonesia is whether this time, too, Sukarno will be able to pull back from the tacit alliance he has entered into with the PKI and the left-wing elements in the PNI.

The armed forces. The Indonesian army is another major factor influencing domestic political developments. Composed of a variety of units that sprang up in response to the revolutionary situation—units nominally tied to a central military command but in reality largely accustomed to operating on their own—the army contains a number of officers who tend increasingly to play political roles. Part of the heritage of the army's wartime experience is the loyalty of many troops to their leaders of that era—a loyalty usually unencumbered by any personal political convictions on the part of the troops involved. The lack of a tradition of firm central command of the armed forces and the inability of the government to provide enough facilities to restore surplus troops to civilian life have made it easy for several political parties to use the discontent of various military units for their own purposes. Efforts to cut down the armed forces to a workable peacetime force, as originally attempted by the Sultan of Jogjakarta when he was Minister of Defense, have become political footballs, while the problem of reducing the army's size and modernizing its organization goes unresolved. Regional loyalties, struggles within the army high command, and independent action by local army leaders have made the armed forces an ideal fishing ground for political opportunists.

The labor unions. Indonesia's labor unions, several of which represent some of the largest mass organizations in the country, have historically been primarily political organizations, functioning as arms of political parties, though without wholly ignoring purely trade-union issues.[145] This political orientation has been as marked in the postwar years, with its proliferation of trade-unions and federations of unions, as it was in the twenties, when the SI and the PKI battled to win control of the first labor-union federation. All union activity was suppressed during the Japanese occupation, but within a few weeks of the founding of the Republic in 1945, new unions were formed and soon became a potent force in the internal politics of the nation.

Trade-unions in Indonesia are recognized by the provisional constitution and receive government subsidies for educational activities. There are from 175 to 185 national or regional federations of workers organized in a half-dozen confederations, each of which parallels a major political party or group of parties. The first such confederation to develop after the war was the Barisan Buruh Indonesia (Indonesian Labor Front), organized by Iwa Kusumasumantri in September 1945. The major labor-political organization in Indonesia, the Sentral Organisasi Buruh Seluruh Indonesia (SOBSI), took shape during 1946. From its founding congress in November 1946,[146] it was led and controlled largely by known and crypto-Communists. SOBSI's president, Sardjono, who was chairman of the PKI, and its general secretary, Harjono, a prewar leader of the Railroad Workers Union (VSTP), had both been active in the Australian wartime Communist movement; its vice-president, Setiadjit, was a crypto-Communist, while serving as the chairman of the Indonesian Labor Party and as a minister in the Sjahrir cabinet of 1946. All three participated in the Madiun rebellion.

From its founding in 1946 to 1948, SOBSI represented a high-water mark of "united frontism." In this sense, it reflected the success of the PKI in executing its rightist line during the early postwar nationalist-Socialist-Communist "honeymoon era." Scarcely six months after its founding, SOBSI, at its May 1947 congress at Malang, voted to affiliate with the World Federation of Trade Unions (WFTU) and dispatched its newly elected president, Setiadjit, and a commissioner, Oei Gee Hwat, to attend the WFTU's Prague conference in June. SOBSI also played a significant role in the revolutionary parliament, in which it held forty seats out of four hundred and in which it could usually count on the support of thirty-five delegates of the Indonesian Labor Party (Setiadjit) and the forty delegates of the Indonesian Peasant Front (Barisan Tani Indonesia); at first SOBSI operated as a part of the Sajap Kiri and later as a part of the FDR.

In May 1948 the first of the subsequent rival trade-union confederations was formed by the National Communists led by Tan Malaka. Known as Gabungan Serikat Buruh Revolusioner Indonesia (GASBRI), the new confederation broke with SOBSI on the question of going into opposition to the government. Those portions of SOBSI which remained loyal to the Communists supported the Madiun rebellion. Despite internal splits, highlighted in the objections of some of its non-Communist affiliates to the stand of the FDR just before Madiun, and despite the loss of several of its key leaders in the Madiun revolt, SOBSI slowly but steadily emerged from the revolution with its national reputation as a genuine workers' organization virtually intact. It was the largest, best-known, and best-organized standard-bearer for labor; moreover, its leadership's militancy during the revolutionary years stood the organization in good stead in the wave of disillusionment that swept over the Indonesian masses soon after the transfer of sovereignty. Although other political parties, including PNI, Masjumi, Murba, and PSI, have invested considerable effort in establishing rival unions and union federations to combat SOBSI's domination of the labor sphere, none of these organizations has thus far challenged SOBSI's pre-eminent position.[147]

Economic problems. With the exception of the brief rubber boom during the first years of the Korean war, Indonesia's economy has been in bad straits since the transfer of sovereignty. Again, the key elements involved have rarely been dealt with in their own terms but primarily as an extension of party politics. The need for a new foreign-investment law, the carefully mapped-out (but still unimplemented) plans of the Central Planning Bureau, the imposition of exchange controls that have veered back and forth as cabinets fall and are replaced, have all been the victims of the central struggle for political power with which the current leadership is almost totally involved. Smuggling, corruption in the handling of licenses, constantly changing demands on foreign firms operating in Indonesia have increasingly become the norm. The limited progress that has been made toward industrialization has had little impact beyond the immediate locale concerned in each case. At the root of the disaffection outside Java is resentment over the fact that some of these areas at the same time furnish most of the country's foreign exchange and receive the smallest returns on that exchange. In this chaotic situation, few national figures have had the courage to declare publicly what many of them privately feel to be true: that Indonesia's economic future for the next few years depends on vastly increased raw materials exports if new industrialization is to be financed. It is true that small-scale industries are being introduced slowly, but politically it is still considered expedient in most quarters to speak in terms of heavy industry—the mark of the advanced nation—as the national economic goal.

There has been some degree of improvement in the daily living standard of the average villager over the past seven years, but not enough to counter resentment at the central government for failing to provide the new standard of living so eagerly expected in 1950. Nor has the slight rise in the level of living been sufficient to encourage many peasants or laborers to withstand the blandishments of political figures who, during the election campaign, promised a whole new world of material goods that would arrive on the heels of their particular party's victory.

Disaffected elements. The armed bands, and in the past year the more highly organized armed opposition to the central government, form another key to the political picture. They are, in turn, increasingly the object of political penetration by different parties seeking local support. The ultimate solution to the problems both of the armed bands and the rebellious elements in Sumatra, Sulawesi, and elsewhere lies largely in the realm of economics. The terrorist bands cannot be put down by sheer force; their dissolution requires a positive program of rehabilitation that would give these discontented rebels a means of livelihood and a stake in the general economy, but this requires a sufficiently stable regime to create and carry out such plans. The areas outside Java demand not only a realignment of their political and general administrative relations with the central government but a reallocation of the resources of the national budget. In both cases the essential economic issues involved await a solution of the political power struggle in the capital. There are, of course, many more aspects to the organized opposition to the central government both in Java and in the other islands— aspects which lie beyond the scope of this study; nevertheless, it could be said that whatever the ideology espoused by the groups leading these opposition elements, their popular appeal has been greatly enhanced by the conditions created by the economic hardships besetting the population.

The political party system. Finally, there is the blurred character of the political party system and the way in which it has operated in Indonesia thus far. The plethora of parties,[140] the weakness of party structure (with the exception of the PKI), and the lack of party discipline (again excepting the PKI and perhaps to a lesser extent the PSI) are all symptomatic of the extent to which personalities supersede programs. This is a very real, if intangible, factor; it can be seen in the ability of various parties and politicians to work together, however unlikely such cooperation might appear in the light of the professed stands of the parties and people involved. It can also be seen in the bitter strife that divides parties and figures who would seem, logically, to be ideal political bedfellows.

It was not until the last months of the election campaign of 1955 that the lines of division separating the major parties began to be expressed in terms that indicated basic divergencies among their respective programs. Before that time, there was a good deal of truth in the jokes circulating in Djakarta to the effect that one had to read the title on the masthead in order to tell whose campaign platform was printed below. For the bulk of the population in any case, the debate over national issues, which became explicit in the closing period of the election campaign, was largely irrelevant. Votes at the mass level, particularly in the villages, were garnered on the basis of loyalty to local leaders, who in turn generally gave their support to a particular party on the basis of allegiance to individuals rather than on matters of substance.

Personalities rather than programs motivate not only the electorate at large but in many cases the leading political figures themselves. It is a matter of personalities, for example, that to a large extent divides the Wilopo wing of the PNI from the Natsir wing of the Masjumi or from the PSI. Indeed, a significant part of Wilopo's current following is made up of former PSI members who decamped from Sjahrir's party either because of personal dislike of Sjahrir or, at a later date, because of their realization that the political future of the PSI might not be too rosy. In the same way, men whose political views are in outright opposition often have a sympathy for each other that derives from their joint struggle as comrades-in-arms during the prewar and revolutionary years. This sometimes adds to the haze enveloping the leadership group, as does the tendency in circles beyond the inner clique of party leaders to equate social relationships with political affiliations.

Because of the predominance of personalities over programs, a final point to be kept in mind when considering the role of the different political parties since 1950 is the outlook of many of the older nationalist leaders, most of them veterans of the movement during the thirties. By the time undisputed independence was achieved, these men had spent the better part of their lives fighting against colonialism—a battle against an identifiable foe. Suddenly they found themselves catapulted into a world they could not fathom, where the negative politics of opposition were useless and where the need was rather for a positive approach. Yet few of them, in the years of struggle, had had the opportunity to develop in more than a hazy fashion any concept of the independent state they were fighting for or to consider in detail the many problems this hard-won freedom would bring. For many of these men, the experience of being uprooted from the familiar role of opposition has come too late in life; their mental and psychological processes are too rigid to make the abrupt transition that the new situation requires. As a result, many political leaders, perhaps dazed by the dimensions of the task before them, have turned their backs on these seemingly insurmountable problems and have devoted their energies to grappling for the tangible and familiar elements in the scene: the trappings of personal power and prestige within the limited arena of party politics. Many of these leaders are astute enough to sense the hollow character of the foundation on which their authority rests, but they are slow to formulate a response to the problems which confront them. As a result, the political atmosphere in Djakarta from the time of the transfer of sovereignty until the results of the first general election were available had a curious air of unreality. This translated itself into a generalized uneasiness and a continuing expectation of an impending showdown.

THE 1955 ELECTION RESULTS

At first glance, the elections in September 1955 seemed to have cleared the air somewhat. It was soon evident, however, that the fundamental instability plaguing the country and its leadership had scarcely been diminished.[149] The victors were obvious: four parties emerged as the strongest forces in the Republic; several parties which had been presumed to be second-rank contenders achieved a bare foothold in the parliament; and a number of small splinter parties were eliminated from the political arena.[150] Although the election results did not resolve the question of the basic political direction of the vast electorate, the election itself did bring about a sharpening of the issues, and the lines of demarcation separating the major party alliances became more distinct.

Despite much reluctance to admit it, the key factor in domestic politics today is the attitude taken by political leaders and parties to the strength and role of the PKI. This is not wholly surprising. Yet, during the years in which the PKI was rebuilding its strength, political leaders of all parties, with a few notable exceptions in PSI and Murba, continued to deny stoutly that the issue of communism versus anticommunism[151] played a significant role in Indonesian political life. The fundamental problems the Republic faced, these leaders said, were "Indonesian" problems: problems of reconstruction and rehabilitation of a devastated country and a weary populace; problems of economic development to sustain a nation of eighty million; problems of education, health, and all the other fundamentals necessary for a life of freedom and dignity. These problems, they claimed, would exist whatever the international situation—would continue to call for solution if the Kremlin and Peking were to vanish from the globe tomorrow.

There is no question that a good deal of truth underlies these assertions. Indonesia's basic economic and social problems are largely independent of the cold war; many of its political difficulties, rooted in the peculiarities of Indonesian social organization and institutions, would doubtless be the same whatever the situation beyond its shores. Nevertheless, this refusal to admit that communism posed a problem of genuine relevance to Indonesia's development was, in the face of the facts, a surprisingly strong and widespread viewpoint. To some extent, it may have been a projection of vain hopes that this would indeed prove to be the case and that Indonesia would be allowed to pursue its efforts at development unhindered by subversion or counterrevolution. To a certain degree, it may have been a reaction against Western warnings which were regarded either as ill founded or as special pleading. Whatever the origins of this attitude—and they were many and extremely varied—it is significant that the rapid comeback of the PKI since its defeat at Madiun was only belatedly recognized in many quarters (and may not be fully recognized even today) as a threat of major proportions.

Before turning to an examination of the resurgence of the PKI, it

will be relevant to glance briefly at the other parties which emerged
from the 1955 elections in strong positions, and at some of the minor
ones as well. Foremost among the major parties was the PNI. Its impressive showing demonstrated the effectiveness of its steady campaign
to broaden support and to reach beyond the ranks of civil servants which
had been its initial source of strength. Still drawing heavily on the reservoir of government officials, who, by virtue of the status traditionally
associated with rank in Indonesia, commanded considerable support
among the peasants, the party also increased its village support by a judicious handling of the appointments of new headmen from 1953 to 1955,
the period when Ali Sastroamidjojo first headed the government. The
party's prestige was further enhanced when President Sukarno, finding
his path blocked in other directions and especially after his break with
Vice-President Hatta dating back to 1950, began to work more and more
closely with PNI leaders. The popular impression that this PNI was
truly the successor to the prewar PNI was once again affirmed when
it took over, as the foundation of its party principles and program, the
philosophy of *marhaenism* so eloquently expounded by President Sukarno.

The PNI program shows no striking differences from those of the
other nationalist parties, nor, for that matter, does it differ radically from
the programs of such religious parties as the Masjumi or of several of
the Marxist parties. The PNI defines its basic guiding principle as social-
national-democracy or *marhaenism,* which it explains in the following
terms:

Indonesian society is still a poor and feudal society. The majority of the
Indonesian people are small peasants. Marhaenism wants to achieve a society
with equality and happiness for all. Thus, marhaenism is the principle which
fights for the achievement of such a society, a socialistic society brought into
accordance with the principles of *gotong rojong.*

The ideals of marhaenism can only be realized in an independent democratic nation. Therefore, the marhaen's struggle is based on social-nationalism
and social-democracy, and it rejects all forms of dictatorship.

An individual's actions are always determined by his needs and these needs
are to some extent determined by society. Thus the individual and society are
interdependent. All events in history are manifestations of man's and society's
needs, economic needs as well as ideological needs. Sometimes economic needs
are more strongly felt, but sometimes ideological needs take precedence. The
principles of historical materialism contain much truth but are not entirely true.[152]

The party's program is a mixture of recommendations for helping
labor, aiding farmers, fostering economic development, nationalizing vital
industries, and organizing youth "as the new pioneers of society"; its

foreign-policy planks call for an independent and active (neutralist) foreign policy and opposition to imperialism and racial discrimination.

The second party in the elections was the Masjumi, originally formed in November 1945 from a merger of a number of Islamic organizations which included groups as far apart in principle as the welfare-oriented Mohammedijah and the conservative Nahdatul Ulama (NU). With the withdrawal of the latter group from the Masjumi in 1952, the Religious Socialists within Masjumi—led by Natsir, Rum, and Sjafruddin together with Sukiman, the leader of a somewhat more conservative wing of the party—were confirmed in the leadership of what is still the largest single religious party in the country.[153]

The Nahdatul Ulama made a showing at the polls that indicates the existence of a large body of conservative Moslems strongly influenced by local religious teachers who adhere to a fundamentalist interpretation of Islamic theology. As a political party, it is a fairly amorphous body whose orientation and direction are still somewhat unclear. So far it continues to suffer from a lack of leadership of national reputation or sufficient experience to conduct the necessary parliamentary maneuvering. Its tendency has been to vacillate rather weakly among the more dynamic forces in the political constellation. Its popular following and its weak central organization undoubtedly make NU a tempting base for any politically sophisticated group.

Of the minor parties which emerged from the election with a handful of seats, two, the Protestant Parkindo and the Catholic Party, acquitted themselves about as well as could have been predicted on the basis of their assumed support from coreligionists. Both of these parties have supplied the Republic with leaders whose personal prestige, as for example in the case of Parkindo's Dr. Leimena, have often brought them into the government without too much regard for party strength or politics. On the whole, both parties lean in the general direction of the Natsir wing of the Masjumi and, to a lesser extent, of the PSI. Among the parties whose weak support at the polls virtually wiped out their parliamentary strength, Murba has been dealt with briefly above. The PSI, ideologically close to the Natsir-Rum wing of the Masjumi, has, since its disastrous defeat in the election, initiated a program designed to rebuild the party as a mass organization with a program clearly committed to democratic socialism. It calls itself a Marxist party but, like some of its European counterparts, has set about redefining Marxism in humanistic terms.

Of no formal party affiliation, there is the personality of Mohammad Hatta, who could and, when he so chooses, does command a following

which cuts across the Masjumi, NU, and PSI. Not as powerful as Sukarno, Hatta is nevertheless a figure to be reckoned with in any discussion of Indonesian political parties and programs. His own economic
program is still based upon an approach which is closest to Scandinavian
cooperativist socialism.

THE REAL WINNER: THE PKI

These are the parties which, with varying fortunes, have held leadership in Indonesian politics since the Republic was proclaimed by Sukarno
and Hatta in 1945. Though the PKI was present at these beginnings,
it had to retrieve a position of influence after Madiun. It has been successful in this task and has made its presence in Indonesia today one
of the most important issues—if not the most important—in political life.

At the beginning of 1950, the PKI had a long way to go to re-establish itself as a political party and to wipe out the opprobrium that still
clung to its name as a result of the Madiun revolt. By 1951 it was clearly
to be counted among the stronger parties in the country; by 1954 it
claimed a membership of 150,000; and in September 1955 the election
results revealed not only that the PKI was the fourth-largest party in
Indonesia but also that, with its trade-union affiliate and the splinter
parties in its orbit, it had attained an unpredicted high level of political
strength and maneuverability.[154]

The Communists restored themselves to this position by a variety
of techniques: by extending their control and influence first in the trade-
union movement, then in the peasant and youth organizations, and in
several minor parties which represent special local or racial (Chinese)
issues; by careful wooing of, and playing on, the factions in the PNI's
leadership; by campaigning ceaselessly to isolate the Masjumi while attempting to blacken the name of the PSI; by exploiting the numerous
crises and divisions that beset the national leadership, including the
upheavals in the armed forces; by nurturing a relationship with President
Sukarno until he could no longer afford not to weigh the advantages and
disadvantages of their support; and by pursuing for general public consumption a propaganda line which, subsequent to the 1952–53 Cominform shift to the right, adjusted itself neatly to the prevailing sentiment
on major domestic and foreign issues, especially anti-imperialism and
"world peace."

The PKI's first postwar victories were achieved in SOBSI, where Communist leadership largely continued to dominate despite the Madiun disaster and where the PKI was able rapidly to resume control of those
portions that had temporarily slipped from its grasp because of the uprising. The general unrest in the first months of official "peace" following

the transfer of sovereignty manifested itself in the defiant attitudes, wild-cat strikes, and disorder prevailing in many of the labor unions. It took little effort on the part of SOBSI's leadership to consolidate this situation into one of more carefully planned and organized strikes; by the summer of 1950, labor disorders had reached a point where the Natsir government felt obliged to arrest a number of union leaders. Nevertheless, the SOBSI unions continued their pattern of strikes until, in February 1951, the government placed a temporary ban on strikes in vital industries. At this point the PKI-SOBSI strategy turned to sporadic strikes, sabotage of plantation crops and cargoes at the ports, and similar incidents to maintain and feed the unrest in the country and to dislocate the economy, especially in the more remote areas to which the government had difficulty in dispatching troops. The unions meanwhile increased their wage demands and pressed for shorter working hours and larger bonuses for *Lebaran* (the most important Moslem holiday in Indonesia) and other benefits which, in the light of the decrease in production in most industries, placed unreasonable demands on the economy. Resentful of decisions by the official arbitration units established by the government, the union members' loyalty to SOBSI increased and its leadership's hold on labor was tightened.

Guaranteed a good-sized mass following through its manipulation of SOBSI, the PKI next turned its attention to the various peasant groups and the rump youth organizations still clinging to their wartime associations. In both instances, the party was able to gain effective control of the central command of the most important of these groups, among them the Barisan Tani Indonesia (Indonesian Peasant Front) and the Pemuda Rakjat (People's Youth), the successor to the wartime Pesindo, the Socialist youth group.[155]

Meanwhile, the PKI's representatives in the parliament had been active almost from the start in utilizing the disagreements between the Masjumi and the PNI to initiate cooperation with the PNI at the parliamentary level. The first such instance was the Communists' support of the PNI motion in October 1950 demanding that the Natsir cabinet be replaced by a broader coalition. Although the PNI maneuver was a failure, the support it received from the PKI helped to improve relations between some of the PNI leaders and the PKI. This was a strategy which the PKI continued to use profitably on various occasions.

In addition, although still denouncing the major nationalist and religious parties as members of the imperialist camp, the PKI in mid-1951 attempted to achieve a consolidation of forces by advocating the adoption of a National Unity Program in cooperation with PSII, Partai Buruh, and Partai Rakjat Indonesia. This attempt at establishing a limited united front collapsed rather quickly. Thwarted in some measure by the governmental ban of February 1951 on strikes in vital enterprises such as plantations and shipping, and hampered by the Sukiman government's arrest of large numbers of Communists and their associates in the summer of 1951, the PKI began to set the stage for its next gambit: the public defense of the PKI role at Madiun undertaken in order to erase this issue from future politics. This the party attempted to achieve by issuing a "White Paper" on Madiun.

This document[156] is an interesting exercise in the rewriting of history. The rebellion became the Madiun "provocation," a provocation which was described as the "climax of imperialist attempts to destroy the Indonesian Democratic Republic . . . , it also gave courage and solidarity to an oppressed people in their fight against the white terror."[157] The background of Madiun was related to the establishment of the Republic by "revolutionary groups which, due to their weakness and lack of understanding, were infiltrated from the start by pro-Dutch and pro-Japanese elements." Hatta, whose cabinet replaced that of the "democratic cabinet of Amir Sjarifuddin," was accused of carrying on secret negotiations with Van Mook, by which "the reactionaries gained in their attempt to stem the tide toward a People's Democracy and the influence of the Communists." Mass demonstrations at various centers against their government's policy —which "violated democratic rights," illegally introduced "censorship" and other repressive measures, and removed "revolutionary and progressive elements from the military," turning the army "into a loyal instrument for the suppression of the people's movement"—were "ignored." The Republican leadership was also called to task for permitting foreigners to participate in the politics of the Indonesian Republic.[158]

The Paper further claimed that the incidents leading up to Madiun included attacks on PKI men and kidnapings and executions by the Siliwangi Division. The readiness to attack the Siliwangi Division, at the time the most revered and respected force in the army, suggested considerable confidence on the part of the PKI, as did the attack on President Sukarno that followed. The document alleged that the final straw had been supplied by Sukarno himself, who "precipitated" the battle that began on September 19: "The people and soldiers who had been consistently anti-imperialist were finally forced to defend themselves as a result of President Sukarno's speech on the night of September 19, 1948. In his speech the President ordered a general armed attack, and the arrest and brutal slaughter of those branded troublemakers." This passage was an open challenge to Sukarno, who was apparently expected to recognize that, in this era when his prestige was still virtually unchallenged, the Communists felt powerful enough to criticize him. At the same time, they withdrew from an earlier propaganda line, which had called him a "collaborator" with the Japanese Fascists.

Despite the fact that the White Paper appeared not long after the PKI had attempted to establish a *modus vivendi* with Murba, it is Tan Malaka and his followers who are accused therein of having spread false information about the program and plans of the FDR, information which is supposed to have instigated Sukarno's speech. Finally, the "Madiun incident," it is flatly stated, "absolutely was not an attempted *coup d'état*, as was falsely alleged by domestic and foreign reactionaries." Then, contradicting the official Soviet line used in 1948, the document stated: "To have made Sukarno's action legal, it would have been necessary to have definite proof [that] at the specific time of these accusations, the night of 19 September 1948 a Soviet Government had been set up in Madiun."

In this rewriting of history, a eulogy of Musso contains indications that not only the Madiun incident but some earlier Communist errors needed rectification. Thus, it stated: "From the first, Musso and the Soviet people did not believe Dutch accusations that the Republic was Japanese inspired. This was due to the fact that the revolution was then clearly anti-imperialistic," and "Comrade Musso patriotically published the independence proclamation in the USSR capital."[159]

The document ended with a plea that the anniversary of Madiun be marked by continuing the spirit of the united national front and quoted a statement adopted by the PKI Central Committee on February 6, 1951:

> The success of the provocation plan of the Sukarno-Hatta government resulted in the division of the national anti-imperialist union, which was being built up by the PKI, based on a national program which had been approved by all parties and people's organizations. The destruction of the anti-imperialist national revolutionary strength was brought about, among other things, by the killing and arrest of 36,000 people who were the backbone of the revolution. These incidents aided the Dutch attacks during the second police action, and the Sukarno-Hatta government's policy of capitulation to the Dutch.

In spite of the fury that was aroused in many better-informed quarters by the final and other paragraphs quoted above, the Communists were fairly successful in the use of this document to repair their damaged name. Except for those who had fought in the Madiun area against the Communists, and those who were consistently well-informed about the internal situation, the exact details of the Madiun revolt had doubtless been blurred in the memories of most Indonesians, who had been remote from the scene and who were soon thereafter fully occupied with the Dutch onslaught of December 1948.

Having launched its campaign to clear its name and to refabricate the history of the Madiun revolt, the PKI kept forging ahead both in its efforts to gain mass support and in its parliamentary activities, garnering strength in the latter sphere from the general dissatisfaction with the Sukiman cabinet's handling of the Japanese Peace Treaty in the fall of 1951 and reaping a harvest of unearned profit from Subardjo's clumsy handling of the Mutual Security Act incident in February 1952. Soon after that event, which brought down the Sukiman cabinet, the PKI made its bid for a broad national front, which was in effect a bid to the dissatisfied elements in the PNI leadership who had lost out to the Wilopo wing of that party in the reshuffling of the government. The new plans were introduced in May 1952 on the grounds that "the national bourgeoisie who had fled the democratic camp in 1948 were now sufficiently disabused of their imperialist allies that the restoration of four-class cooperation was again possible."[160]

This was an opportune time for the PKI. Though the Masjumi and the PNI were both represented in the cabinet, the former found itself increasingly at odds with a wing of the PNI which felt deprived of cabinet position. The latter group, led by Sidik, was willing to work with the PKI parliamentary faction even to the disadvantage of its own party. Later in 1952, there occurred the already mentioned October 17 affair which adversely affected the fortunes of the PSI. The badly weakened PNI cabinet, led by the Wilopo-Mukarto wing which favored cooperation with both Masjumi and the PSI, managed to limp through until June 1953, when it was brought down by the Kertapati motion on the eviction of squatters from the oil lands in Sumatra—an issue manufactured by local leaders of the PNI and blown up to national dimensions by the PKI. It was at this point that the PKI's strategy of cooperating with willing leaders in the PNI moved into high gear. The first Ali Sastroamidjojo cabinet was formed in July 1953, with the blessing of the President and the support of the PKI. In some respects, the key to the cabinet was the new Minister of Defense Iwa Kusumasumantri,[161] then a member of the Progressive Party, one of the splinter groups under the wing of the PKI. His handling of the Defense Ministry in this cabinet suggests either that he did not recognize the true strength of the PKI and hoped to utilize the Communist-oriented officers he placed in key spots for his own purposes, or else that he had revised the views he held in 1946 and also presumably at the time of Madiun and later, and was now ready to work with the PKI.

The PKI announced that, while not participating in the government, it would support the Ali cabinet. Still somewhat vulnerable as a result of Madiun, the party needed a close tie with a nationalist organization led by respected public figures whose loyalty to the Republic had never been doubted. Furthermore, the PNI, with its carefully nurtured following in the villages, especially in outlying areas where the Communists had never gained a foothold, and with its first line of supporters, the civil servants, offered a new potential base to the organizing and propaganda skills of the PKI. At the same time, the PKI provided the PNI with a source of support through its well-organized unions (SOBSI) and through its purveying of a right line always closer to the nationalists than the reverse.

The members of the Ali cabinet had barely taken their seats when the PKI put its first card on the table. Sakirman, leader of the PKI in the parliament, cited the new cabinet as "the outgrowth of a violent struggle between the forces of democracy and the reactionaries"[162] and immediately called for an active program to eliminate Darul Islam (DI) and other terrorist gangs. In this speech, he made the first demand for supplying arms to volunteer battalions and village self-protection units to fight DI; he also suggested that the apparatus used to fight DI be cleaned of any possible pro-DI elements by transfers and dismissals from its ranks—a clear recommendation to the Minister of Defense to start reorganizing the armed forces along lines more amenable to the new government.[163]

There were two other ways in which PKI-PNI cooperation fitted into mutually agreeable patterns. One was the violent antipathy of the PNI wing represented in the Ali cabinet for the PSI; the other was the close tie between many of these PNI leaders and that essential figure in Indonesian politics, the President. On the first point, the PNI group then in power had until that time been the most aggressive in its attacks on the PSI. The PKI now joined in the fray in the parliament, expanding its attacks on the PSI as the "compradors of the capitalists," knowing that these attacks would be fully supported by the government's spokesmen. Apparently, there has never been any doubt in the minds of the PKI leadership about which group constituted their most serious ideological rival; not long after the transfer of sovereignty, Sjahrir remarked on several occasions that the only thing that had kept a number of the disillusioned younger students and army officers from joining the PKI was the existence of his party as an alternate rallying point for those opposed to the old-line nationalist leaders and parties. While the election results in 1955 demonstrated that the PSI had grossly overestimated its popular following and had shown little ability in the realm of political campaigning, the PKI, like other perceptive observers, realized that the PSI's central leadership still had an influence far beyond the boundaries of its own small membership or election-time supporters.

The other feature of this new and open PKI-PNI cooperation was the attempt to capture the President's ear and at the same time to utilize his overwhelming prestige. Many of the Ali cabinet members were associates and friends of the President from prewar days. Although there is little doubt that the PKI's leadership could have carried on its own public-relations job of wooing the President singlehanded, it was unquestionably faster and easier to use the numerous doors into the Presidential Palace opened with so little effort by the PNI ministers. Thus, the PKI used its new role of government-supporter to build a closer relationship with the President through a friendly approach, while at the same time brandishing its growing power rather ostentatiously in the background to remind the President that, back door or front door, the PKI intended to move into the Palace courtyard.

Throughout this period of PKI-PNI cooperation, there were several basic issues in behalf of which the Communists utilized their position to heighten the alignment with the PNI and to extend their influence in the country. Their treatment of foreign policy is an example of the first, and their handling of the "Chinese question" illustrates the second.

The PKI started with the advantage that Indonesian foreign policy, no matter the party in power, is committed to a neutralist formulation, closer in practice to that of India than to other expressions of neutralism. On most questions of the day, it agrees with the predominating temper of the African-Asian bloc within the United Nations. Present international Communist policy to the greatest extent possible is prepared to accommodate itself to this view. The PKI in Indonesia finds little or no fault with this policy as it has been carried out by the first and second Ali Sastroamidjojo PNI cabinets. The PKI also has been able to make political capital out of the travels of Khrushchev and Bulganin to India and Burma, widely reported throughout the Asian press, and President Sukarno's trip to the U.S.S.R. In Indonesia, the Communists were able to utilize the opportunities offered by the Bandung Conference for their own ends and make it in part a triumphal tour for the Peking delegates. Although there was hostility evident at Bandung between anti-Communist delegates and the Chinese Foreign Minister's entourage, the net effect of the conference on many Indonesian first- and second-rank figures was an impressive picture of Chinese strength and Chinese "friendship."

The complex of problems surrounding the Chinese in Indonesia and the rise of Red China has been dealt with by the PKI in a highly opportunistic fashion. On the one hand, the party has not hesitated, especially in areas where there have been particularly strong local grievances against the Chinese, to jump on the prevailing anti-Chinese band wagon. On the other hand, the PKI has rather deftly spread the word not only of Peking's might and relative proximity but of Peking's answers to the rapid industrialization of a primitive economy. Peking in turn has done its part with a continual parade of grand tours through its territory by visiting Indonesians—at first mostly Indonesians of Chinese descent, later any willing

Indonesian, and, more recently, top-ranking political leaders, including Sukarno and Hatta. Scholarships for study in China have been handed out in generous proportions, and the numerous visiting cultural, trade, technical, and other missions to China have been lavishly treated.

In the first phase of their upward climb, the PKI defied local antagonism toward the Chinese by having Indonesian Chinese play prominent roles in the party's central leadership. This was partially the result of the leadership's respect for the obvious vigor of the new Chinese People's Republic—a respect which was shared by a large part of the Indonesian political elite and which led the Indonesian government to recognize Red China quite early.[164] It was also in part the result of the pro-Mao leanings of Alimin and other figures in the PKI who were beginning their rise to the top. Once the Chinese embassy was established in Djakarta, it became a valuable source of support for the PKI. At a peak it maintained a staff of over three hundred in the embassy, as well as a string of well-staffed consular offices, ostensibly concerned with the interests of the overseas Chinese.[165]

Meanwhile, in the fall of 1953, the PKI had reversed its earlier position by removing from conspicuous posts the Chinese members of its leading cadre (cf. above, fn. 154). While playing down its partnership with the local Chinese Communists, the party has, however, relied on a variety of organizations of Indonesian Chinese[166] as well as on less open but equally effective liaison with "bourgeois" Chinese, who recently seem to have come to the conclusion that the wind is blowing in the direction of Peking. Thus the Communists rarely tend to forfeit popular Indonesian support because of too open reliance on local Chinese, while at the same time they reap the benefits of their "Peking" stance.

At this writing, July 1957, the PKI has demonstrated its ability to revive in strength from the defeat at Madiun. Its command of votes and parliamentary seats, its roots in important functional organizations, and its ability to present a persuasive, persistent propaganda line in a political context marked by high volatility assures it a considerable place in any analysis of contemporary Indonesian life. Its development as revealed in the 1955 elections surprised many in and out of Indonesia. The surprise has yielded in part to a decision to face the issue openly. The anti-Communist political forces centering around Masjumi and some of the smaller parties have, since the elections, re-examined their past performances and mistakes as a preliminary to organizing to do battle with the Communists. The PKI's current espousal of its "right" line makes it more difficult for the anti-Communists to oppose it without simultaneously appearing to yield their presumed common Socialist goals. What has begun to emerge in Indonesia is a more widespread recognition of the totalitarian, dictatorial essence of Marxist communism. This has not yet meant that the Western opposition to communism in the name of democracy is believed or, if believed, accepted. As anti-communism becomes clearer, more thoroughly understood by its newer adherents in Indonesia, it tends to balance more equitably the older, stronger views of anti-(Western)colonialism and anti-imperialism. This would appear to be the major consequence among those who have apparently resolved that there is need for them to add an anti-Communist dimension to their programs and organization.

But this view is not yet accepted throughout the non-Communist leadership. The reluctance in some quarters revolving about the PNI, and even the NU, to admit that the PKI is not just "another Indonesian party" no doubt contributed to the President's decision to launch his "conception" of an extraparliamentary body which would give representation to the Communists. Sukarno's idea, first presented in December 1956, came after more than a year of continued interparty strife, which followed in the wake of the election. His plan called for a National Council, representing all elements in Indonesian society—political, religious, racial, occupational—which would function in the manner of the traditional Indonesian village council, reaching agreement through discussion (*musjawarat*) and compromise (*mufakat*), so that all could work peaceably together in a spirit of *gotong rojong*. The National Council would seek, among other things, to resolve in this fashion the problem created by the rise and development of the PKI. In his attempt to solve this problem, President Sukarno proposed to "take them in"—to give the PKI a place figuratively among the elders so that their views could be "compromised" with the others. In principle he is trying to utilize an Indonesian cultural device to resolve a situation of conflict. This is the heart of his new conception, which encourages the illusion that communism and the PKI are like everything else in Indonesia—Indonesian. On the surface he has won the point. His conception with some modification has been accepted. It represents, at best, a truce before the next storm.

THE SITUATION TODAY

As the preceding pages have shown, some elements of Marxist doctrine have pervaded most, if not all, articulate Indonesian sociopolitical and economic organs of expression. Gradually, this Marxism has become differentiated into its historic contending wings, communism and socialism. But this distinction, as noted immediately above, is still not fully accepted, and the reluctance to accept it is not limited to those who have been lulled by the siren songs of the Communists or stand transfixed by the growing power of Red China. To accept the view that the PKI is by nature essentially different from other Indonesian political parties would mean to give up the long-cherished idea that Indonesia can remain aloof from the storms sweeping the globe today. It would mean recognition of the fact that, like it or not, Indonesia's future is inextricably and irrevocably bound up with the forces animating the international political scene. It would also mean abandoning the hope that Indonesia's problems can be resolved in an Indonesian fashion: by arriving at a mutually agreeable compromise to be carried out in a spirit of *gotong rojong*.

6

THE IMPACT OF MARXISM: HISTORICAL OVERVIEW AND JUDGMENT

FRANK N. TRAGER

The present chapter provides a review of the development of Marxism from a region-wide point of view. Since for a large part of its history the Marxist movement in this area was oriented toward revolution, it will be useful to examine the various historical shifts in revolutionary strategy, particularly on the part of the Communists, to evaluate the success or failure of each strategy, and to point out any general effects each had on the structures of the regional Marxist movements.

During most of the period under consideration, doctrinal and organizational distinctions between different Marxist and non-Marxist nationalist groups did not preclude joint action. With the attainment of independence, and particularly as a result of postwar Communist tactics, a sharper differentiation of these groups with respect to doctrine, organization, and action is observable.

The application of Communist doctrine in areas under Communist control after independence is outside the scope of this study. The present chapter, however, will evaluate the significance of Communist and non-Communist Marxism as a factor in the formulation of domestic (primarily economic) and foreign policies in the four countries under consideration; and it will trace the effect on non-Communist Marxism itself of the assumption of political responsibility in the postwar period. It concludes with a brief comparison of the different roles of Marxism in the four countries.

Whatever the consequences of the introduction of Marxism in Asia, it is abundantly clear that in Southeast Asia indigenous nationalism pre- ceded the penetration of Socialist and Communist ideas. When the modern idea of a national state emerged in these countries, it was not as a wholly novel concept. The peoples of Southeast Asia fell naturally into groups, each of which shared, within a more or less homogeneous territory, simi- larities of language, custom, religion, ethnic and racial origin, historical memory, and in some periods dynastic continuity.

There is no longer any doubt that the arrival of the Western powers in Southeast Asia and their struggle for colonies fractured well-developed existing societies, just as it suppressed many well-organized existing states. Van Leur's description of the Indonesian peoples supports this view.[1] He holds that among the societies which the Western powers found on their arrival each revealed its own historical and geographical milieu, its own continuing processes of long-lasting and independent development in a variety of governmental, legal, and socioeconomic forms. "In the course of history," he writes, "[these peoples] had been subjected to the greatest tests of strength and have proved to have the power of resistance." Caesar Fredericke, a Venetian who came to Burma in 1569, described the royal city of Pegu as consisting of two parts, the old and the new. "In the old Citie are the Merchant strangers and the Merchants of the Countre for there are the greatest doings and the greatest trade. This Citie is not very great but it has very great suburbs." His fulsome description of the new city, which contained the palace of the king, shows his respect for the power of the Burmese ruler. His careful descriptions of trade and com- merce reveal advanced enterprises involving traffic throughout the Indian Ocean and the South Seas.[2]

It must be admitted that neither indigenous nor Western historical writing has been especially illuminating on these precolonial societies and states. Although there is promise of improvement in the future,[3] the West hitherto has seen these Southeast Asian societies primarily through the eyes of Western writers, who often treated the history of these peoples from what has been called a "Europe-centric" standpoint.

If some students find the term "nationalism" inapplicable to precolonial Southeast Asia, none can deny that nationalist feeling had appeared by the closing decades of the nineteenth century. In the last years of the nineteenth century and the first of the twentieth, Burma, Indochina, and Indonesia gave evidence of budding nationalist movements directed against the respective imperial powers. Even Thailand, spared as a buffer state in the power struggle between England and France, experienced during this period the force of modern nationalist ideas introduced by the absolute monarchy of the Chakri dynasty.

The first forms of this modern Southeast Asian nationalism were built on the perduring features of its pre-Western culture. That these forms were associated with Buddhism in Burma, Buddhism together with Confucianism in Indochina, and Islam in Indonesia may be partially explained by the fact that the people of these three countries had been allowed by the colonial powers to organize semireligious institutions. Beginning in the 1890's the Burmese Buddhist societies served as the base from which a full-grown nationalist movement emerged. In Indonesia, Budi Utomo Day (The Day of the Glorious Endeavor), May 10, 1908, has been called "the earliest demonstration of Javanese nationalism as a living creed."[4] Sarekat Islam, organized in 1912 as a trade organization to protect Indonesians from Chinese competition, soon became a strongly Moslem organization, drawing its nationalist inspiration from the Modernist Islamic movement which animated Egypt at the turn of the century. Its Burmese nationalist counterpart was the Young Men's Buddhist Association, later reorganized as the General Council of Burmese Associations. In both countries religion was the matrix from which a nationalist movement took shape. In Indochina, Cochinchinese Buddhist secret societies and elements of the Confucian-based mandarinate served the same purpose until they were effectively bottled up by arms or absorbed, in a subordinate position, into the French civil administration.

This early nationalism, drawing upon indigenous sources for its institutional expression, found response in the peoples of the whole region. It had roots in a patriotic countryside, no matter how "urbanized" the leadership may have become. Its leaders may or may not have had some Western education in the schools established for them by the colonial powers. Certainly they experienced the impact of the West—if not through schools, then by contact with European individuals and associations. But on the whole there was very little opportunity for Western education in the colonies until World War I. Essentially, the early nationalist movements were vernacular, modest in outlook and demand, and, with the possible exception of Viet Nam, not yet committed to full self-government or independence. Ideas of the latter type were to emerge with force only after World War I, nurtured by such events as America's entry into the war, Japan's victory over Russia in 1905, the rise of Sun Yat-sen, and the Russian revolution of 1917.

PREWAR SOCIALISM

These events were among the positive influences on Southeast Asian nationalism. By contrast, the absence of Marxist influence during the same period is remarkable. No evidence has yet appeared of the export of Marxism from Europe to Southeast Asia before 1914. It seems that neither the First nor the Second International (of the Socialist and Labor parties), nor any European Marxist party, had reached out into the colonial empires.[5] This important omission requires some comment.

It would not be unfair to say that the European Marxist movement, from its inception down to World War I, was either indifferent to Asian developments or unable to fit them into its schema. Marx himself, following the classical economists and particularly the British Utilitarian writers on India, never went much beyond referring to Asian countries as "Asiatic" or "Oriental" societies. For him, these terms stood for stagnant despotisms to which he had not given any extended study or treatment. He was, on the whole, content to characterize them and place their development alongside of, if not in sequence to, the dialectical unfolding of primitive, feudal, and capitalist societies, having their own mode of production in which the government and its bureaucracy (not a class in the Marxist sense) acquired the surplus value of the system. Lenin and his followers, as we shall see, began with fewer and perhaps less prejudiced preconceptions concerning Asian countries and peoples. Marx's creation, the First International (embracing the rising trade-unions and the Socialist movements), was primarily "European-centered." Whether or not Marx had familiarized himself with Asian developments, the very nature of his theory required that the Socialist revolution take place in a technologically advanced country, and not in the typical agrarian societies of Asia. Hence his major concern was with the problems of these technologically advanced countries. Prior to World War I, European Marxists did not fail to criticize the excesses of colonial policies,[6] but their theoretical position as Marxists was postulated upon the existence of a bourgeoisie, an industrialized society, and an international market. These were the necessary capitalist preconditions of socialist development. Since the Asian colonies did not exhibit such property and class relations, Asian lands and peoples were "backward" in development. Hence their advancement would come either after the working-class revolution in Europe, which in due course would lead to the liberation of Asians, or after they had gone through their own capitalist stage of development.

The Second International and the parties affiliated with it had less reason to take such a position. By the time it was organized in 1889, conquests and colonial development had led to a greater knowledge in Europe about Asia and its peoples. Logically, the professed ideals of the Second International should have required the member parties to deal with the problems of the subject peoples. However, although resolutions endorsing the right to self-determination were passed at various congresses, they were primarily directed to the nationality groups within the larger European states, such as Russia and Austria-Hungary. In short, before World War I

the Labor and Socialist movement in Europe, to say nothing of that in the
United States, had little sympathy for, understanding of, or desire to participate in the nationalist struggles which already animated the Asian
scene.[7]

Whether Lenin's subsequent criticism, to the effect that the Second
International was "betraying" the interests of the colonial peoples, was
justified is no longer a question of practical significance; but the fact that
the Marxist parties of the metropolitan powers did not significantly concern themselves with the colonial peoples before World War I contributed
to the anti-Western, antiwhite attitudes that became so deeply rooted in
the nascent nationalist movements of colonial Southeast Asia.

Before World War I, it may be said, members of the Second International regarded internationalism, specifically workers' internationalism, as
an inspiring cause. Nationalism they regarded, if not as anathema, certainly as a danger to their primary cause.[8] If the Socialists at home succeeded in winning power, presumably they would then be able to extend
self-determination and perhaps freedom to the colonies.[9]

After World War I, the parties of the Second International sought to
overcome the suspicion and anti-Western feeling which their earlier policies had helped to foster. But by that time they faced the competition of
the Third, and later the Fourth, International, which did not suffer from
such a stigma. Though a very few European Socialists (mainly Dutch in
Indonesia) found their way to Southeast Asia just before World War I,
Marxism came to the area chiefly under the aegis of the Comintern. The
first indigenous Marxists, therefore, became Communists or "sympathizers"
rather than Socialists. The European Socialist parties and their International subsequently made valiant efforts to redress this imbalance in their
relations with the non-Communist Southeast Asian nationalists and Marxists. Nevertheless, when the Asian Socialists organized their regional group
in January 1953, they carefully refrained from becoming a constituent section of the (European) Socialist International.

THE EARLY COMINTERN LINE: 1920–27

Where Marx had concentrated his attention upon Europe, Lenin, before
the Russian revolution and without discarding the Marxist view of a backward Asia, had convinced himself that "Russia belongs not only to Europe
but also to Asia." He had been deeply impressed by the Persian revolution
of 1908 and the creation of the Chinese republic in 1911.[10] He was certain
that the anticolonial grievances of the Asian peoples could be exploited
against the metropolitan powers. It was in this context that he developed
the views on imperialism which led to his support for wars of national
liberation and for political parties and organizations made up of indigenous

"blocs" and classes. Before the revolution, Lenin wrote a "scant dozen articles on China,"[11] including *Imperialism, the Highest Stage of Capitalism*. These constitute the indispensable prelude to his policy formulated in the eighth of the "Twenty-one Conditions" for admission to the Third International and to the crucial discussion on national and colonial questions which took place at the Second Comintern Congress.

The eighth condition is:

On the question of the colonies and oppressed nationalities an especially distinct and clear line must be taken by the parties in those countries where the bourgeoisie possesses colonies or oppresses other nations. Every party desirous of belonging to the Third International must ruthlessly denounce the methods of "their own" imperialists in the colonies, supporting, not in words, but in deeds, every independence movement in the colonies. It should demand the expulsion of their own imperialists from such colonies, and cultivate among the workers of their own country a truly fraternal attitude towards the toiling population of the colonies and oppressed nationalities, and carry on systematic agitation in its own army against every kind of oppression of the colonial population.

The Second Comintern Congress met from July 17 to August 7, 1920, in Petrograd and Moscow. Lenin's report was delivered in a Moscow session July 26. It is interesting to compare it with the *Manifesto* of the Comintern prepared by Trotsky and unanimously adopted at the First Communist International Congress in Moscow, November 2–6, 1919. The language of the latter holds in fairly classic Marxist terms that "the emancipation of the colonies is possible *only* [italics added] in conjunction with the emancipation of the metropolitan working class"; whereas Lenin's theses show greater flexibility simply by changing the word "only" to "primarily."[12]

The strategic and tactical consequences of the congress of 1920 dominated Communist anti-imperialist policy in Asia until the Sixth Comintern Congress in 1928, and helped to shape the ideological baggage of the anticolonial Asian leadership as well. The modifications in this policy can always be tied in with some discussion which arose at the 1920 meeting. Many of the principal actors in the Communist movement in Asia appeared on the scene during the early Comintern sessions of the twenties. In addition to the Indians and Chinese, one finds there Ho Chi Minh, Tan Malaka, Darsono, Alimin, Musso, Semaun, and others.[13] Eudin and North, quoting from Russian sources, report the Communist summation of the importance of the Second Comintern Congress:

The Second Congress of the Communist International held its last session on August 6, and its decisions set the stage for intensive work in the colonial and semicolonial countries. A leading article in *Izvestiia* summarized the results of the Congress in the following manner: "A new world is awakening to life and to struggle—the world of the oppressed nationalities which has been compre-

hended by us, though not quite correctly under the name of the East. For here
are found not only the peoples of Asia, but also those of Africa and America."

The article spoke with scorn of the platonic protests of the Second International against imperialist colonial policies, and pointed out that the Communist
International acted quite differently. Not only did it stand in close solidarity
with the revolutionary uprisings of oppressed peoples against capitalist domination, but it also required that the communist parties of all countries, and particularly the countries that were doing the oppressing, give active support to
colonial revolutionary movements directed against imperialist bourgeoisie. The
article concluded:

"When the news of the decisions of the Second Congress of the Communist
International reaches the hundreds of millions of Indians, Chinese, Negroes,
Malays, and other oppressed peoples, it will be happy tidings for them, and also
the call for a new and greater struggle against the capital that exploits them.
. . . The fact that the Communist International was the first openly to raise
the banner of the struggle, and to call to this banner all the oppressed peoples
and the organized proletariat, will stand to its eternal credit."[14]

Strip the foregoing passage of its propaganda, and there remains a
solid core of fact: the colonial and semicolonial countries were fashioning
a struggle against imperialism. The Third International did recognize the
explosive value of this struggle for its own ends. Outstripping the Second
International, the Comintern appeared as the protagonist of the "oppressed
peoples" against the imperial powers. Much of Communism's influence
in Asia can be traced to this source.

The lack of contact between the Second International and colonial Asia
before World War I left the ground clear for the acceptance of a Marxism
emanating mainly from Bolshevik sources. In Southeast Asia as elsewhere
the Communist version of Marxism was aided by the extraordinary effect
of the October Revolution. It is perhaps difficult for us today to recapture
the sense of excitement and achievement which the events in Russia inspired in many parts of the world, and particularly among those in the
nationalist movements who looked upon the overthrow of tsarism as a
pregnant symbol for their future liberation. The *élan* of the Russian
revolution spread rapidly to India, China, Indonesia, Indochina, and
Malaya. Communist movements directed against the imperial powers were
launched even before the Second Comintern Congress had met. The Comintern by and large gave them encouragement, leadership, financial support, and training for their subsequent activities in Asian countries.

Though Burma was at this time a province of India, no Burmese seem
to have been involved in Indian Communist activities, nor were the Communists particularly interested in Burma. In fact, the Russians seemed
either ignorant of, or indifferent to, Burma. As for Thailand, the first Communist visit took place in 1925, when Indonesian party members banished
by the Dutch came to Bangkok.[15] Thailand is first mentioned as having

a Communist party in Wang Ming's report to the Seventh Comintern Congress in 1935.[16]

In the twenties the major ingredients in Southeast Asian Marxism were nationalism and anti-imperialism. The movement in Indonesia, for example, exhibited the full complement of Communist patterns for this area. It acquired a highly centralized party organization led by a cadre of individuals who had received Comintern training. It proceeded to organize a membership based on Lenin's conception of a proletarian-*cum*-peasant base. Its program was always revolutionary; that is, it sought to oust the imperial power and to replace it in one or two leaps with Communism, but it also seized upon any "immediate" programmatic issue which in its opinion would enhance its leadership over the masses. Using programs of "immediate demands," the Communists sought out existing indigenous organizations whose members could be won over, subverted, or otherwise influenced. Depending upon the "situation" and upon Comintern zigs and zags, the Communists used the tactic of the "united front from above" or "from below" to achieve their organizational purpose. The movement suffered from internal dissension as the struggle for party leadership led to emphasis on one or another of the strategic and tactical questions of the times. The factions seeking party power looked for the approval of the Comintern as they attempted to interpret and apply its directives. The party succumbed temporarily after its unsuccessful bid for power in the revolt of 1926–27. As always, the Comintern blamed the local leadership for its errors, not its own policies.[17]

Developments initiated at the Second Comintern Congress in 1920 were steadily carried forward by the Third, Fourth, and Fifth Comintern meetings (1921, 1922, and 1924, respectively), even though the debate between Lenin and M. N. Roy, which began at the 1920 meeting, had not yet been resolved. Lenin had called for an alliance between the Communists and the non-Communist nationalists, whether proletarian, peasant, or petty bourgeois—an alliance, in short, between the Communist and nationalist liberation movements without respect to the social or religious origins of the latter.[18] Roy had persistently argued against bloc alliances within the struggle for liberation. He urged instead the classic Marxist formula of a movement led and engineered by the Communist parties on their proletarian base. Lenin maneuvered Roy into accepting a verbal compromise, at the Second Comintern Congress, which did not substantively alter his own position. At the Fourth Comintern Congress, Roy came quite close to Lenin's position, but the issue of the role assigned to the nonproletarian, nonparty nationalist movements remained unresolved.[19] At the Fifth Comintern Congress, Manuilsky, pointing with pride to Communist success in Asia, referred to this historic debate between Lenin and

Roy but indicated that the Executive Committee of the Comintern "had wisely handled" the issue as it arose in various countries.[20] His optimism was misplaced, for the unresolved issue split the Indonesian Communist leadership and in major part contributed to the abortive 1926–27 revolt against the Dutch. A similar failure, and for the same reason, followed in China.

FROM "LEFT" STRATEGY TO "POPULAR FRONT"

The Third International's advance into Asia was arrested in 1927. The Dutch suppression of the Communist revolts in Java and Sumatra, the bloody collapse of the Kuomintang-Communist alliance with its repercussions in Indochina, and the British and French police actions against leading Communists in India, Indochina, and Singapore from early 1929 were the chief external factors which inhibited the Communist advance at this time. Under other circumstances the Communists might have won misplaced sympathy and support as martyrs in the cause of national liberation.[21] For a brief time, indeed, during the Meerut trials (1930–32), they did win some sympathy from the Indian National Congress (Nehru served as one of their unpaid lawyers). And despite French police action, Ho was successful in organizing the Indochina Communist Party. But the vital decision that blocked the spread of Communism among the nationalists of South and Southeast Asia was taken by the Comintern itself at its Sixth Congress, in 1928. It is the launching of the classic "left" strategy, which followed closely on the defeats in Indonesia and China, that must be held largely responsible for the decline in Communist strength in Asia after 1928. This Comintern line required proletariat-based Communist parties, utilizing "united-front-from-below" tactics. All non-Communist organizations, even of trade-union workers, were by definition composed of, or led by "social fascists" or worse. Since the Communist parties of Asia were severely affected by the defeats and the arrests, and since there were few industrial areas in Asia which offered a proletarian class for potential recruitment, the Comintern made little if any progress during the so-called third period, i.e., between the Sixth and the Seventh Comintern Congress.

Correlatively, during this period non-Communist Marxist and other Socialist ideas for the first time appeared in the arsenal of the anticolonial nationalist elites. While retaining the inevitable anti-imperialist and, to some extent, the anticapitalist line, the Indian National Congress led by Gandhi and Nehru, the Indonesian nationalist movement led by Sukarno, Hatta, and Sjahrir, and even the burgeoning nationalist movements in Burma and Indochina all fought for, or returned to, concepts and tactics designed to win and retain mass followings rather than risk losing them by the application of doctrinaire Communist class-struggle strategy and tactics. Masani rightly describes Communists in the period up to the

Seventh Comintern Congress as living in the "wilderness."[22] Though he was writing of the Indian Communist party, his observation applies to Communists in Southeast Asia, except for Indochina.

The Sixth Comintern Congress also abandoned Lenin's flexible approach to the anticolonial struggle in favor of the strict class approach originally espoused by Roy.[23] In its turn to the left, the Sixth Comintern Congress determined "to overthrow the rule of foreign imperialism, of the feudal rulers and of the landed bureaucracy; to establish the democratic dictatorship of the proletariat and the peasantry on a Soviet basis"; to nationalize industry and "the land"; and to organize "revolutionary workers' and peasants' armies." To accomplish this, the Communist parties, both in the imperialist countries (which sought the destruction of the U.S.S.R., "the only fatherland of the international proletariat") and in the colonies, were to secure "predominant influence in the broad mass proletarian organizations . . . over wide sections of the toiling masses . . . the lower strata of the intelligentsia . . . the petty bourgeois strata generally [and] the peasantry." The party as "the vanguard of the working class . . . bound by iron discipline and strict revolutionary rules of democratic centralism" would carry out these assigned tasks while combating the "reactionary force" of the "labor movement" and such tendencies as "Sun-Yat-senism," "Gandhism," and "the mediaeval influence of the clergy, of the missionaries and other similar elements." In order to acquire proletarian "hegemony," the prerequisite of "the dictatorship of the proletariat," it was to "capture" the trade-unions and otherwise "to change and 'remove from their posts' the reformist leaders."[24]

In sum, the consequences of this Sixth Comintern Congress *Program,* together with the repressive, anti-Communist measures instituted by the colonial governments and the home rule granted the colonies, effectively contributed to the decline and disintegration of the indigenous Communist parties and organizations. Increasingly the Communist movement became isolated from the main, ongoing nationalist struggle.[25]

The Comintern's policy during its "third period" can be said to have had uniformly negative effects on the various Asian Communist parties. In contrast to this, it appears that the "People's Front" line, adopted at the Seventh Comintern Congress, in August 1935, gained widespread acceptance among non-Communists and strengthened the various Communist parties and front organizations. By 1935, Western governments and peoples were somewhat alarmed by the threat of Fascism, which gave evidence of growing international strength. The Nazi-Fascist Axis did not hesitate to sponsor vigorous tactics for infiltrating and subverting non-Fascist countries. This gave rise to what came to be called a "fifth column" movement in the democracies.

In the period 1935–39, the slogan "Democracy versus Fascism and War"

had a widespread popular appeal. It was basically on this account that
Stalin scored his successes of those years. The U.S.S.R., admitted to the
League of Nations, and joining in alliances and pacts with countries it had
formerly castigated as "imperialist," posed as a "democratic," anti-Fascist,
antiwar champion. The various sections of the Comintern concerned with
"the defense of the Soviet Fatherland"—Stalin's phrase—now sought eagerly
and effectively to join with non-Communist parties and organizations
everywhere, including Asia.[26]

For a variety of reasons, however, the anti-Fascist, anti-Nazi line of
the Seventh Comintern Congress was less successful in Asia than in the
West. Its reception varied from country to country, according to local
situations and personalities.

In the first place, Germany did not appear to be so much an enemy
to Asia as to Europe. Nehru ascribed this attitude in part to the fact that
Berlin had served as a center for political refugees and radical elements
from abroad, in part to the fact that Germany—no longer a colonial power
—had watched with "benevolent neutrality" the growth of anti-imperialist
agitation in the colonies.[27] In addition, as Sjahrir has pointed out in his
autobiography, "many of the Dutch in Indonesia had openly expressed
pro-German sympathies [and] could not be otherwise because in a sense
the entire white community was fascistic and there was certainly no
inclination to fight a war against Hitler and Germany."[28] It was during
this period that Burmese nationalists began their short but important
flirtation with the Axis partner, Japan. In brief, however much Asian nationalists understood the threat posed by the Fascist powers to the democratic powers, they had little inclination to side with the latter since they
were not particularly happy with their lot under the colonial policies of
the democracies.

In the second place, Marxists and nationalists in the colonies, especially
those who had not already slavishly committed themselves to the Comintern, were distressed after 1935 by the "collaborationist" role of the metropolitan Communist parties and front groups. In order to carry out Comintern policy in their respective countries, the European parties subordinated their role as ardent anticolonialists to one which permitted them to
pose as ardent anti-Fascists. Thus, for example, the Netherlands Communist party dropped its demand for the immediate independence of Indonesia; and the "Perhimpoenan Indonesia," now under Communist control,
swung toward the party line by changing the name of its journal from
Free Indonesia to *Indonesia*.[29]

These negative factors, which diluted the appeal of the Seventh Comintern Congress policy in Asia, were balanced by some more favorable.

Masani calls attention to the Communist wooing of Nehru, Jayaprakash Narayan, and other leftist nationalist and Socialist leaders.[30] From 1936 on, relations between the Indian National Congress and the Thakin movement in Burma became closer. An exchange of visits and ideas took place before and after the 1938 anti-Indian riots in Burma.[31] Much of the Seventh Comintern Congress's anti-Fascist phraseology was echoed in the pronouncements of the Thakins. They apparently absorbed their Marxism initially in this period. And despite the split in Indochina over support of the French Communists in their attitude toward the Fascist danger, the Vietnamese Communists won support among the masses because some of their "immediate demands" were granted by the Popular Front government in France.[32] In Indonesia, where the Communist party was still illegal, Musso, since 1928 an elected member of the ECCI, returned to Indonesia from exile in April 1935 for at least one year, and in the spring of 1936 Sjarifuddin (his future comrade in the Madiun revolt of 1948) and others organized a new and highly successful nationalist party called Gerindo. Though this party was "militant," it regarded independence as a consequence of a successful struggle against international Fascism. Because Fascism was the main danger, according to the Communist party line between 1935 and 1939, Gerindo "called for short-run solidarity with the Dutch," participated in the Indonesian Volksraad, and "operated on a generally cooperative basis" while exhibiting "strong and constant pressure for the granting of self-government to Indonesia."[33]

In summing up the mixed effects of the Seventh Comintern Congress in South and Southeast Asia, two points need to be made. First, despite the particularized, local role of the Communist parties in the colonies and in the metropolitan countries, the Soviet Union itself won many admirers in the area during these years. The anti-Soviet critic S. K. Mohan Das has tied the Soviet Union's enhanced prestige in Asia to the gathering war clouds in Europe.[34] The U.S.S.R. was for "peace" and for "collective security." The shortcomings of the metropolitan Communist movements were not ascribed to the U.S.S.R., but to the normal vagaries of Englishmen, Netherlanders, and Frenchmen who were members of these parties. The U.S.S.R. presumably was basically anti-imperialist and anticapitalist. Its "turn to the right" was accepted as understandable self-protection.

The second point is equally significant. Non-Communist forces—European Marxists, Social Democrats, liberals—in increasing measure were displaying sympathy for, and establishing connections with, nationalists in the South and Southeast Asian countries. Metropolitan Socialist parties and movements affiliated with their International began increasingly to advocate self-government or independence for the Asian colonies. The

Indian National Congress and the Indian Socialists established strong bonds
with their sympathizers in England; the non-Communist but Marxist-influenced nationalists in Indonesia were once again in serious contact with
the Dutch Social Democratic Party—virtually for the first time since World
War I. The Socialist-led, Popular Front government of Leon Blum was
responsible for sending an Investigating Commission to Indochina. Though
Burma did not yet have a range of international contacts, its most ardent
nationalists began to exhibit connections with British Fabians, "Left Wing
Book Clubs," and other mixed Socialist sources. They were also preoccupied with their nationalist development following the 1935 Government of India Act, which gave to India and to Burma new and separate
constitutions with additional measures of home rule. In sum, there were
alternative sources of ideas, of political philosophy, to those so vigorously
propagandized by the Communists.

WORLD WAR II AND ITS AFTERMATH

World War II greatly accelerated the pace of developments in the area.
The Nazi-Soviet pact of August 1939 and the opening of the war a few
days later caused a revulsion of feeling in the democracies against the
Soviet Union and the Communist parties. In Europe the Communist parties
lost members; but this was not the case in Southeast Asia, where many
nationalists, some Socialists, and all Communists regarded the war in
Europe as none of their affair. As Asians, they objected to their involvement by fiat of the metropolitan capitals. They uniformly offered some
degree of cooperation, but at the price of increasing home rule or independence. Not only were their offers either ignored or rejected, but they
experienced in varying degrees the effects of stringent police action and
wartime security measures. Typical of the activities in the region at this
time were the 1939 program of Gapi (the union of the eight leading
nationalist organizations of Indonesia), which called for a democratically
elected Indonesian parliament dedicated to the right of self-determination
and based on the principles of political, economic, and social democracy;
the 1939 Freedom Bloc in Burma, a coalition of the Thakins with Ba Maw's
Poor Man's Party, which vigorously opposed British rule; and the Gandhi
"Quit India" campaign.

Japan's entrance into the war and the welcome extended to her by
Southeast Asian nationalists had a decisive effect on the situation. Japan
had long occupied in the minds of Asian nationalists a favorite position,
which her invasion of China had not destroyed. Not only did the Japanese
have the advantage of the popular Javanese myth, the Djodjobojo, which
predicted that after white rule a yellow people would come from the north
and rule for "100 days," but they also had the advantage of again repre-

senting an antiwhite force capable of beating the "arrogant imperialists."
On August 19, 1937, while Sjahrir and Hatta were exiled in Banda Neira,
the former wrote prophetically:

As far as I can make out, the whole Islamic population of our country is now
pro-Japanese! Japan is continually increasing in popularity as was formerly the
case with Germany. I still try to make the people here realize that the Japanese
are really not angels. That what they are now doing [in China] is nothing else
but murder and pillage. I do not, however, really doubt that Japan will still be
able to profit from the sympathy that our people now feel toward that country.[35]

In Burma the nationalists, the Socialists, and Communists associated
with Ba Maw's Freedom Bloc had concluded an agreement with the Japanese some time in 1939 which called for setting up an underground organization to be known as the National or People's Revolutionary Party.
This party in turn organized the Burma Independence Army, which was
supplied with Japanese arms and funds and trained by the Japanese. Thus,
when the war finally came to Southeast Asia, the Japanese were largely
accepted by non-Communist Marxists and nationalists, and even by some
Communists.[36] After all, the Soviet Union's policy toward Japan still followed the line of their neutrality agreement of April 1941, which was not
denounced by the U.S.S.R. until four years later, when the Soviet Union
was preparing to declare war on Japan.[37]

The Japanese contribution to Southeast Asian nationalism, despite all
its shortcomings, was highly significant. It accelerated the development
of indigenous administrative organizations. Japan treated various areas,
at least symbolically, as national units. She liberated an entire generation
of nationalist leaders, who were able to find their levels of status and power
within their own societies. It is not without significance that except in the
Philippines the Japanese have quietly rewon much lost ground since the
end of the war.

A number of the Southeast Asian Communists turned to the Allies after
the Nazi invasion of the U.S.S.R. in June 1941. Among the Burmese, Thein
Pe, Tin Shwe, Soe, and their followers offered their services to the British
and started a resistance movement. In Indonesia, Sjarifuddin, still closely
adhering to the twists in Soviet policy and supported by the illegal PKI,
took his section of the Gerindo into the first underground resistance movement in that country. After the Japanese joined the Nazis, Ho Chi Minh
was able to seek and receive aid from Chiang Kai-shek against the Vichy
French in Indochina. This resistance activity on the part of the Communists might have been matched quickly by the non-Communist nationalists,
once they decided that the struggle for independence could not be achieved
through Japanese overlordship, but for the powerful aid extended to the
Communists by the Allied powers. The Dutch government supported

Sjarifuddin financially and otherwise, and he, though probably not a Dutch agent, was willing like other Stalinists to accept such support. The British, who had major military responsibility for Southeast Asia, also did not hesitate very long before deciding to accept Communist offers of aid both in the archipelago and on the mainland. The British gave the Communists formal recognition, arms, and constant cooperation through Force 136, the British Special Operations Executive (SOE, equivalent to the United States OSS).[38]

It is usually argued that the support given to the Communists by the Allies "saved lives," and this is probably true. Usually ignored, however, is the offer made by non-Communist nationalists, such as U Nu and his group in Burma. They were prepared to assist the Allies at the beginning of the war in Asia in return for some definite promise concerning self-rule at the end of the war. They were not able to extract such promises. Not even the Atlantic Charter was deemed applicable to them. Prime Minister Churchill specifically excluded Burma from its provisions; Queen Wilhelmina vaguely broadcast on December 6, 1942, her "intention . . . to create the occasion for a joint consultation about the structure of the Kingdom and its parts"; President Roosevelt and Secretary Hull gradually yielded to De Gaulle their modest hope for an Indochina trusteeship.

Dedicated non-Communist nationalists, with the belated exception of General Aung San of Burma, seldom found favor in the councils of the Allies. There is no record, for example, that Sjahrir's underground in Indonesia was ever helped by the Dutch, and, though Aung San emerged as the outstanding Burmese leader, the Allied Command was willing, right up to the end of the war, to deal with the Communists in Burma.

There can be little doubt that Allied material aid and American recognition helped the Communists in the resistance movement to assume prominent positions in the postwar nationalist struggles. Nor can there be doubt that Allied unwillingness to face the end of the Asian colonial era contributed much to the old reservoir of anti-Western, antiwhite feeling which remained in Asia after the forced departure of the colonial masters. Soviet propaganda was to thrive on this issue.

The war made it clear that nationalism in Asia—in every sense of that term—had its mainspring in Asia. It was in part inspired to action by the impact of Western rule, specifically by Western education and by experience of Western methods acquired either in the colonies or in the metropolitan centers. Colonialism or imperialism[39]—that is, the imposition of external power on indigenous societies with all the consequences of that imposition—was never accepted no matter what benefits it conferred upon the conquered peoples. Periods of peace and stability were fewer and less extensive than the Western public commonly supposes. Periods of agitation and of vain rebellions against the imperial powers—the histories of which are yet to be written—were numerous and intense, as the colonial archives reveal.

Marxism, first in its Leninist anti-imperialist formulation, later in its democratic Socialist form, added to indigenous nationalism a social rationalization for its fight against the imperial powers. It gave to the nationalists a sense of participation in world history on a scale not provided by the formal bases of Western or vernacular education. It gave them a teleological view according to which the future necessarily belonged to them.

The combination of nationalism and Marxism gave some coherence to a struggle that was marked, at least until World War II, by a fourfold Asian revolt: against alien political domination, against alien economic domination, against the white man's racial domination, and against alien cultural and religious influence. So long as a leadership sponsored a platform which included one, some, or all of these elements, it could acquire a following in the plural agrarian and urban societies which commonly characterized the English, French, and Dutch colonial order in Southeast Asia.

These were the elements of Asian nationalism from which even Marxism and Marxist leaders could not depart if they wished to retain mass support, both agrarian and urban. To this fourfold revolt the Marxists contributed various more or less violent strategies and tactics for achieving the goals implied by the revolt. They instituted techniques of organization and propaganda, dramatized specific demands and grievances, called the world's attention to their struggle, and attracted funds and encouragement from abroad. Nationalists and Marxists, as individuals, cliques, groups, organizations, or parties, frequently agreed on the goals of the revolt but with almost equal frequency disagreed on the means. A history of the nationalist-Marxist internal struggle between the wars could conveniently be written on the single theme of cooperation versus noncooperation with the colonial powers (including Japan) as the means for achieving self-determination. At any given period the leadership, both Marxist and non-Marxist, can be found on both sides of this issue.

Neither the nationalist nor the Marxist leaders of the anticolonial struggle bothered with philosophizing about the meaning and responsibilities of nationhood. They assumed the prior existence of Asian nations which would almost automatically begin to function on the morrow of success. They were aware of internal religious, ethnic, and, particularly in Indonesia, class differences. They relied on the cementing effect of the common struggle against imperialism to hold together the ethnic and religious groups in some kind of assumed but unreal harmony.

It cannot be too strongly emphasized that this nationalist-Marxist leadership was composed of men and women who were bicultural. They had whatever strengths and weaknesses their own indigenous cultures had

given them, and they had acquired aspects of Western culture from which
they could draw some strength to use against the colonial masters. In each
of the four Southeast Asian countries there was—and is—an urgent need to
solve problems arising from such biculturalism and from the pluralist
character of the nation.[40] In eliminating alien political domination, the
Southeast Asian nationalists do not appear to have considered a return to
the dynastic past; without debate they decided to retain some aspects of
polity derived from Western sources, whether Marxist or non-Marxist.
They did not elect to restore the indigenous forms of kingship, though they
were willing to accept for a limited time the continued existence of local
rulers, such as the Shan Sawbwas in Burma and the Sultans in Java. The
Southeast Asian republics are in principle democratic, based largely on
Western models and infused with some moderate Socialist and social welfare concepts.

In getting rid of alien economic domination,[41] sometimes called economic colonialism, the nationalist leadership resolved, even before its
ultimate victory, to continue and extend the inherited colonial pattern of
nationalizing some sectors of the economy and regulating, rather than
excluding, foreign enterprise. What they wanted to eliminate was exploitation by the outsider of industry and agriculture. Under the colonial
regime, they saw the "native" society at the bottom of the economic heap,
and they identified the regime with capitalism—"sinful capitalism" as it
was called in Indonesia. Since under the colonial regimes these countries
had primarily agrarian and extractive economies and were mainly producers and exporters of raw materials, the nationalist leadership, whatever its degree of radicalism, determined to sponsor an industrial revolution. They held that countries which remained primary producers were
still stigmatized by colonialism. This feeling was well expressed by President Ngo Dinh Diem in a notable speech before a joint meeting of the
United States Congress on May 9, 1957:

> The Asian people—long humiliated in their national aspirations—their human
> dignity injured—are no longer, as in the past, resigned and passive. They are
> impatient. They are eager to reduce their immense technical backwardness.
> They clamor for a rapid and immediate economic development—the only sound
> base for democratic political independence.
> The leaders of Asia—whatever their ideologies—are all faced with the tragic
> urgency of the economic and social problems of their countries. Under the strong
> pressure of their peoples, they are compelled to adopt economic planning. Such
> planning is bound to cause serious political repercussions. It is for this reason
> that the main theme of domestic political debates in Asian countries centers
> around—the extent of planning needed—the indispensable method required to
> bring urgent practical results. Should everything be planned or—should plan-
> ning be restricted to essential sectors? Should democratic or should ruthless
> totalitarian methods be adopted?

These words from the non-Socialist, anti-Communist president of Viet Nam could be paralleled by considered pronouncements from most non-Communist nationalist leaders in Southeast Asia.

Little comment is necessary to point up the revolt of Southeast Asians against the white man's racial supremacy. Color prejudice and discrimination were the inevitable accompaniments of colonial power. The reaction of the indigenes was to be expected when one recalls that under the Dutch there was a descending racial ladder from the whites to the Eurasians to the Chinese to the majority Indonesians, and that similar patterns obtained in Burma and Indochina. The manifestations of racial discrimination were not only social, that is, of the home and the "club," but they permeated every aspect of colonial life. Neither the acquisition of wealth nor education nor both guaranteed equality of "social class" treatment.

The forceful introduction of Western institutions broke down pre-Western social and cultural structures. The necessity of acquiring Western education and language as the precondition for employment above the menial level in any Western enterprise, the disregard or the studious nonregard for the dominant religions of the area, the imposition of Western law in the main population centers as a substitute for customary law contributed to this breakdown. Lament over such facts relieved feelings of alienation in one's own country. It led to the adoption of nationalist songs and banners, to the revival or the re-creation of a national language, to the creation of "national" schools as opposed to "colonial" schools.

These reactions, however, did not mean that the leadership desired or advocated a complete return to the past. Some return has been necessary. Burma and Indonesia, respectively, have witnessed strong Buddhist and Islamic revivals. Viet Nam leadership is striving to rebuild Confucian morality. (Completely secular nationalism or Marxism would probably run afoul in those countries.) The varieties of Burmese national dress for both males and females are vigorously maintained and encouraged, though elsewhere in Southeast Asia this cultural phenomenon is more frequently left to females. The traditional arts and crafts are being revived where necessary and nurtured where they continue to exist, but adaptations of nonindigenous art and literary forms are also approved. Praise of customary law may be heard, but little effort is being made to use it in place of concepts of law derived from the Western colonial experience. Education is not being returned to the monastery school or to the Islamic academy, though these institutions continue their educational functions. The precolonial lunar calendar, which still conditions the life of the people, will not be substituted for the Western import. Folk medicine, which remained the practice in colonial societies having a ratio of one trained physician for from fifteen to twenty thousand people, may be "investigated scientifically, but otherwise Western medical science is being extended as fast as circumstances permit. When Indonesia adopted as its national motto "Bhinneka Tunggal Ika" (There Is Unity in Diversity), it was careful to point out that the phrase came from a Madjapahit poet, Empu Tantular. But this phrase is also a variation of E Pluribus Unum.

In brief, the attempt to be rid of alien domination in the political, economic, racial, and cultural aspects of life is giving rise to some as yet incomplete synthesis between indigenous traditions and external influences.

THE MARXIST APPEAL TO NATIONALISM

That Asians responded with alacrity to the ideas which Lenin popularized and subsequently crystallized in the theses of the Second Comintern Congress needs to be understood, however much it may be lamented in the West. Such ideas naturally belonged to a very small leadership group —one which could afford to acquire education and the tools for Western study. The number of Asians who, between the wars, introduced and spread Marxist-Leninist ideas and grafted such ideas onto indigenous nationalism was exceedingly small; yet, by any estimate the effect of their work was exceedingly large.

After Lenin and the Comintern faced the East, the Communists expected that first India would successfully revolt, then China, to be followed by the other colonial and semicolonial countries.[42] The Communist timetable on this matter and others had to be revised on numerous occasions. What is important is not the revision of the timetable or of the strategy, but rather the effectiveness with which Marxist ideas of anti-imperialism and anticapitalism permeated the non-Marxist movements for national liberation. There was a response to these ideas far beyond the limited circles of the Roys and Danges, the Mao Tse-tungs and Chou En-lais, the Tan Malakas, Alimins, Darsonos and Semauns, or the Ho Chi Minhs.

No single study illuminates more clearly this early Southeast Asian response to Marxist ideas below the level of the leadership cadre than that contributed by B. J. O. Schrieke in the "Causes and Effects of Communism on the West Coast of Sumatra."[43] The imperial power found itself governing a pre-capitalist or subsistence society. The basis of that society was self-sufficiency, primitive barter, and customary law. It was a society that cherished many communal features. The introduction of a money and export economy disturbed traditional land-tenure practices guarding against alienation of land, fostered the growth of wage labor, weakened the force of *adat* law, and in sum broke down the self-sufficing, self-sustaining, communal nature of the society while increasing the individualizing demands of external authority. This created a basis for social malaise, which can be handled in good times, when jobs are available and exports sell at good prices. When internal migration, modest welfare improvements, and opening of new lands are feasible, much of the potential danger can be drained off. But given any kind of crisis the latent social malaise will respond explosively to sympathy and the prospect of improved conditions. The Marxist postulation of "increasing misery" is thereupon considered proved. As Schrieke puts it, capitalism in general (and in particular its presumed last stage, imperialism) could be charged with having created the troubles which harassed the people's daily lives. The government could be identified with capitalism and the chances were that everything would continue to get much worse. Some of the now differentiated social and economic groups—"industrial" labor, plantation workers, small landed proprietors, and tradesmen, in short, any groups affected by a crisis—were in the mood to respond to agitation, nationalist or Communist. The Communist leaders derived from socially disillusioned and dislocated groups: elementary school teachers, impoverished nobility, people dismissed from government service, minor teachers of religion wishing to increase their importance, and so on.

Schrieke's analysis of Sumatra can be legitimately generalized. The colonial governments did in fact alter the system of production and exchange. The very nature of their enterprise transformed the societies of Southeast Asia so that they in turn became capable not only of sustaining the colonial administration but also of providing considerable profits.[44]

Local, national, and international Communist propaganda never abandoned its anticolonial, anti-imperialist tune, no matter how many variations it played. It was a constant theme that the capitalist oppressor, symbolized by the white colonial administration, should be thrown out, peacefully if possible but violently if necessary. Thus the Communists, and other Marxists, had no difficulty in accommodating their strategy and tactics to the fourfold antialien revolt which characterized the Asian nationalist movements prior to World War II and independence.

Non-Communist nationalists were handicapped by their mutual support for this essentially "negative" line and by the fluent dogmatism of the Communists. They had initiated and wished to maintain the struggle against the colonial administrations. To differ with the Communists, the nationalists would have had to conduct a "fight on two fronts."[45] Questions of strategy and tactics, such as cooperation versus noncooperation and separation versus nonseparation, frequently promoted differences; but such questions were divisive *within* the nationalist fold as well as between nationalists and Marxists. Between the Second and the Sixth as well as after the Seventh Comintern Congress the nationalists were hard pressed to maintain a basic doctrinal difference with the kind of Marxism operating in South and Southeast Asia. They were deprived for the most part even of the argument based on the Marxist atheology.

However much Marxism in the West was atheistic and anticlerical, and however personally secular the Marxists may have been, in Southeast Asia they carefully, except during the "third period," concealed or otherwise tempered classic doctrine on this point. The views put forth by Asian Communist leaders, such as Tan Malaka, at the Fourth Comintern Congress generally governed Communist tactics in Southeast Asia. More than most, Tan Malaka was keenly aware of the role of religion in a traditional society. Accordingly, Communist propaganda was designed to take into account this element. Schrieke quotes one of the propaganda leaflets used in Sumatra.[46] By any standard an extremely skillful job, the leaflet attempted to show that "religion, *adat* and prosperity" were one with Communism, and quoted directly from the Koran. The government and the capitalists were dubbed *Kafir*, or unbelievers. The word "capitalist" was translated into the local language as equivalent to the money-grubbing unbeliever, *Kapisetali*, "the skinflint *par excellence*, the tax-demanding government."

When, much later, anticlericalism crept into the writing of one leading Burmese Communist, a storm broke loose and he had to be publicly disciplined. Though some Burmese leaders attempted to reconcile "Marxist theory and Buddhist philosophy," more recently U Nu, in distinguishing Socialism from Marxism and in equating the latter with Communism, indicated that to identify Marxism with Buddhism was "ill-considered and unfounded."[47]

No trick in the arsenal of propaganda was overlooked when it conformed to the purpose of the Communists. Consequently, even when they lost favor as a result of changes in the Comintern line, as for example during the "third period," or when many nationalists became suspicious after the Seventh Comintern Congress that the Communists in Europe were yielding on the anticolonial struggle, there still remained a pervasive receptivity to the broad generic concepts of Marxism: anti-imperialism (or anticolonialism) and anticapitalism. These ideas were merged by almost all nationalist groups with the ongoing struggle for liberation from alien masters.

Schrieke concludes his study with some lines which may serve as a summation for this section. He was writing specifically of the significance of Communist propaganda on the west coast of Sumatra, but what he says can be generalized for the nationalist-Marxist amalgam ubiquitous in all Southeast Asia before World War II:

This discord between the traditional standard of justice and the present day order [the colonial administration], this sense of inequality before the law, this feeling of inferiority in connection with the administration of justice . . . education, public life and official relations . . . has also created . . . a feeling of negative solidarity in resisting the undue pressure of the present system of justice. The metaphor of the *sapu lidi*, the bundle of sticks, each stick of which was incapable of doing anything alone but which as a united whole was able to sweep, has taken hold of the popular imagination.[48]

When called upon, the popular imagination overwhelmingly supported the revolt against political, economic, racial, and cultural domination.

The existence of this nationalist-Marxist amalgam between the two world wars must not be allowed to obscure factors, already mentioned in passing, which in time affected significant sociopolitical variations in the area. We have already noted the pervasive influence of the dominant religiocultural systems. The early (Communist) Marxists in Indonesia felt the need to maintain a public posture of friendliness or neutrality toward Islam. Simultaneously, their nationalist opponents emphasized the historical atheism of Communism. While this continuing conflict does not exclude the possibility of a successful Communist coup in Islamic Indonesia, it has become an inhibiting element to the extent that non-Communist Marxists, Religious Socialists and other Socialists, and secular and religious nationalists have tempered their programs for a population still largely influenced by Islamic teachings. In analogous fashion, when Burmese Marxists (Communists) attempted to exploit a vein of typical atheism directed against the Buddhist "clergy," the popular and stimulated non-Communist outcry was immediately felt. The Communists in Burma have not publicly tried this again. The secular Socialists and other nationalists in Burma have publicly acknowledged the role of Buddhism while supporting the government's policy of friendship for all religions. In Viet Nam the residual elements of the traditional Confucian state system—the family system, the semiautonomous commune, and the central state authority—are still strong enough, even among the numerous Roman Catholic Vietnamese, to help explain the phenomenal migration since partition of almost one million northerners (8 per cent of the population) to the Republic of Viet Nam. Their deep loyalties obviously aroused in them a response to anti-Communist Vietnamese nationalism.

In Burma, perhaps more than elsewhere in Southeast Asia, Western education has been a factor making for distinctions within the amalgam. There the conception of Western law, of an independent judiciary, of due process, of commitment in principle to parliamentary, democratic government may be seen at work. Non-Communist Marxists and nationalists voted for a republic with a constitutional system of checks and balances and have adhered to a multiparty state in spite of rebellion and their own large parliamentary majorities. The 1958 split did not alter this commitment.

In general, within Southeast Asia, Marxist ideas and the vocabulary of class struggle gradually recede where they had been present among non-Communist Marxists and other nationalists once independence is achieved. If, as Sacks points out, the French conquest of Viet Nam "opened the door of the closed society . . . to such concepts as . . . nationalism and Marxism," it also brought "individualism" and "social humanism." Dutch education, as Sjahrir has indicated, at its best did the same for Indonesia.

The Japanese occupation and the immediate postwar confusion both accelerated developments and sharpened the inherent ideological and organizational conflict in Southeast Asia. What had been movements directed against imperial power were, suddenly as in Burma and Indonesia, belatedly as in Indochina, transformed into *de facto* national administrations. The war was the immediate cause for the coming to power of the erstwhile "extremists." However much their power was limited by the Japanese authorities, it progressively increased during the war. The Dutch and the British were forced from the scene. Some nationalists, for example U Nu in Burma, would have exerted influence to support the Allies in return for clear-cut commitments for future self-rule. But neither Downing Street nor the Dutch government-in-exile in London and Brisbane would offer any promises for the future.

After disillusionment had set in over the Japanese occupation, the wartime Southeast Asian collaboration between the Allies and the Communists, both pursuing their own purposes, was broadened to include non-Communist nationalists. Japan had given much to both the Marxist and nationalist movements, but it lost their support, literally and figuratively, by the "slap in the face." There was never any doubt but that at the war's end the nationalists would not, short of successful military counteraction, return to the *status quo ante*. They had acquired some power and were resolved to extend it at the expense of the former metropoles.

Throughout Southeast Asia the reputation of the Soviet Union during and after the war was climbing steadily. The Soviet stand against the German war machine, its equal membership among the leading Allies, its continuing propaganda in behalf of peoples' liberation, now received and published throughout the world, gave it a tremendous advantage. This development occurred at a time when the other Allied powers were either uncertain of their policy on colonial issues or determined to return to their prewar possessions. Alone among these powers the Soviet Union seemed prepared to encourage nationalist movements and the Communist element within such movements. Propaganda to this effect not only was heard and felt throughout Southeast Asia but became a world-wide topic of discussion through the Security Council and the General Assembly of the United Nations.[49]

An interesting example of such indigenous propaganda is a play written by Thein Pe of Burma—called by the publisher "one of the leaders of the young Communist Party in Burma." *Over the Ashes: A Play About Resurgent Burma* is a typical example of "agit-prop." The young Communist teaches his family and the villagers to unify all anti-Japanese forces "even . . . the loyalists of the British" in order to "disperse . . . the fascist invaders." However, Soviet Russia and the "good . . . progressive forces . . . dominating the United Nations" will help to bring about the retreat of "world imperialism." The "decaying, old forces" will give way "to the becoming" and the "new upheavals." A religious character in the play promptly recognizes this "exposition" of the dialectic as "our Abid-hamma." "Every son of Buddha," he says, can "follow the road you [the Communists] are going." Thein Pe was one of the first Burmese to get the cooperation of the British Force 136.

THE CALCUTTA CONFERENCE OF FEBRUARY 1948

On February 9, 1946, Stalin made an election speech rededicating the energies of the Soviet Union to the policy of world revolution.[50] This was not merely a restatement of the ultimate aims of the Communist movement; it signalized yet another turn in the shifting strategy. Until October 5, 1947, the line could be said to be in the making, for Stalin's "new" policy had not yet been made uniformly official. Communists in Indochina and Indonesia were still relying upon big-power and related negotiations to further their cause, whereas in Burma (as in India) they gave early evidence not only of rejecting such negotiations but also of intensifying the struggle for power within the nationalist-Marxist amalgam. In October 1947, however, the Cominform, a revised version of the Comintern, was organized—not to be dissolved until after the Twentieth CPSU Congress in April 1956. This turn to the left had crucial significance for Southeast Asia, as the February 1948 Calcutta Conference was to indicate. Because of the importance of this conference and the presumed difficulties of interpreting it, it may be worth while to examine it and related events in some detail.

The outbreak of Communist-led insurrections in Southeast Asia after the Calcutta Conference leads unavoidably to an examination of possible causal connections between the Conference, the Cominform, and the insurrections. A number of scholarly opinions have been advanced. Joseph Frankel states that some Western journalists have attributed the uprisings in Burma, Malaya, and Indonesia to instructions received at Calcutta, but that there is no tangible evidence for this contention.[51] McVey, reviewing Calcutta from the point of view of Indonesian developments, admits to some plausibility in a connection but tends to agree with Frankel that there is an absence of positive evidence to support the connection.[52] Kautsky cites Das and Masani, among those who had "implied that the insurrections . . . were ordered at this meeting."[53] Actually, Das and Masani did more than merely imply it; the former asserted that there was a direct connection between Moscow and the Calcutta Conference, and the latter argued the existence of such a connection.[54] Kautsky, however, apparently endorses Frankel's position.

Documentary evidence is hardly likely to be found. The assumption that a written directive from Moscow ever existed is, to begin with, gratuitous; even if it did exist, it is reasonable to assume that, in much the same way as the Soviet encyclopedia is periodically rewritten to conform to policy changes, Communist government files are subject to occasional cleaning out or doctoring. Hence, in common with most students of Communist affairs, the present author is inclined to be satisfied with conclusions of high probability based on inference from strong circumstantial evidence.[55]

Study of Communist behavior indicates that the making of decisions about party strategy and tactics takes place in a series of steps over a period of months prior to their announcement at a Comintern, Cominform, or party congress. Potential changes in the line are discussed and to some extent foreshadowed in public communications long before the meeting at which they are proclaimed. The announcement is frequently followed by a period of readjustment, including the shifting of personnel. For example, Stalin's political report of December 3, 1927, in which he announced that "the period of a certain equilibrium and peaceful coexistence between the USSR and the capitalist countries . . . is receding into the past[,] making way for the period of imperialist raids and preparation for intervention against the USSR,"[56] preceded by many months the Sixth Comintern Congress (July 15–September 1, 1928), which adopted as its program the positions Stalin had already clearly developed. In much the same way, Stalin's speech of February 9, 1946, initiated a series of steps culminating in the October 1947 announcement of the new left line. During this interval of almost two years, a number of relevant events occurred. The well-known Soviet economist E. Varga, whose views at that time did not support the existence of "objective conditions" for a "new revolutionary upswing," was publicly disciplined and repudiated.

At the June 1947 meeting of the U.S.S.R. Academy of Sciences, there appeared a series of reports on India by leading Soviet members, including E. M. Zhukov, the head of the Pacific Institute of the Academy. These reports held that India had become ripe for a revolutionary policy to be executed by the working class. The class emphasis of these "studies" was accompanied by a sharp attack on the Indian National Congress and Nehru, now regarded as reactionary nationalist forces to be placed in the same camp as the imperialists.[57] Obviously, it then became the task of the Indian Communists to attack both groups and to break off any wartime association or united-front relations with them.

The Academy reports may be regarded as straws in the wind, for the shift in the party line was clearly announced by Andrei Zhdanov at the opening of the first Cominform meeting in September 1947. His thesis, in effect a reiteration of the now well-worn view of the world as divided into two camps, the imperialists led by the United States and the "emancipationist anti-imperialist forces . . . based on the USSR and the new democracies," coincided approximately with the end of the postwar Russian advance in Central Europe. The speech had little to say about the colonies, but it did insist that "the ruling classes of the metropolitan countries can no longer govern the colonies on the old lines." They had to resort to military force, as in Indonesia and Viet Nam. Zhdanov's views were given prominent space in Communist journals throughout the world.

At various times in the past the Comintern had been able to anticipate the announcement of a new line through the actions and publications of a European Communist party outside the U.S.S.R. The French Communist Party, especially under the leadership of Duclos, and its organ L'Humanité had served this purpose in times past. The device could not be as effectively used in Asia for several reasons: the parties were at various times illegal; they were not organized on a truly national basis; and they had limited access to conventional channels of communication. Hence a different procedure was devised for Asia and was introduced after the Second Comintern Congress. Continued into the postwar period, this procedure was based on the practice of having a few trusted representatives serve openly as the channel and intermediate authority of the Comintern at conferences or congresses or other meetings of the party and front organizations.[58] There was no exception in 1947–48 to this practice. S. A. Dange, a leading member of the Indian Communist movement, who had spent a long time in the U.S.S.R. and other parts of Europe, reappeared in India immediately after the 1947 Cominform meeting. He was apparently present at a meeting of the CPI Central Committee held in Bombay, December 7–16, 1947, at which time it adopted a "left" policy and took steps to install a "left" leadership to replace the earlier "right" one.

The new line in India was an adaptation of the Zhdanov thesis on "imperialism," "feudalism," and the "national bourgeoisie," with which the Indian Congress was identified in Communist eyes. The Mountbatten agreement, which led to independence in India, was denounced as a "fake."[59] There was a call for "peoples' struggles," strikes, student and mass demonstrations, and peasant "unrest." The leadership was to seek a "democratic front of all left parties" and groups. It was to employ the classic left tactic of the "united front from below" in order to lead an intertwined bourgeois-Socialist revolution.[60]

All this became the subject matter first of the Youth Conference of Southeast Asia, convened by the two front organizations, the World Federation of Democratic Youth and the International Union of Students. It was followed almost immediately by the Second Congress of the Communist Party of India. Both meetings took place at Calcutta in February 1948. Present at these conferences were representatives from the three South Asian countries and from Burma, Malaya, Indonesia, Indochina, and the Philippines. Soviet, Yugoslav, and Australian delegates were also present, as were guests from elsewhere in the Communist world.[61]

If the period prior to the Cominform meeting be regarded as one of preparation, that immediately after, including the series of meetings in India attended by "international" delegations and ending on March 6, 1948, falls in the category of intense indoctrination.[62] The period of violent Communist struggle in South and Southeast Asia against imperialist- as well as against nationalist-achieved power follows on the Cominform and subsequent meetings. The Communists in India launched a series of violent campaigns in the rural districts of Telengana in Hyderabad, before that state acceded to Delhi, and they sponsored a country-wide strike movement. State governments in India variously declared the party illegal (West Bengal, March 26, 1948), arrested important leaders (Bombay, April 2), and sent troops to disturbed areas (Madras). Nehru characterized the campaign of violence as "bordering on revolt," which, happily, his government was able to suppress.[63] The insurrection in Burma began in March 1948, within weeks after Communist leader Than Tun, who had already had the advantage of Goshal's attendance at the December 1947 meeting in Bombay, returned from the Second Congress of the CPI. As for Malaya, the leading Australian Communist, Lawrence Sharkey, who also attended the Calcutta meetings, on his way home stopped off for two weeks in Singapore and conferred with the Malayan Communist party leadership. According to one authority, there is some evidence of a direct connection between this visit and the opening of the Malayan rebellion in June 1948.[64]

Doubts about an Indonesian connection with the Calcutta meetings stem in part from the fact that the Indonesian Communists present at Calcutta were of the second rank. Any demand for action they may have made upon returning home, however, was doubtless reinforced by delegates to a conference of the World Federation of Trade Unions and the International Youth Conference in Prague, who got back to Indonesia early in the summer of 1948. Refusal on the part of the Indonesian Communist leadership to adopt policies communicated to its subordinates at Calcutta would have led to a serious challenge to their position within the party.[65] There may well have been a factional struggle within the Indonesian Communist party as to the wisdom or the timing of the left turn. But hesitations were resolved by the action of the Cominform. Just as Moscow sent Dange back to India, so it secretly returned Musso to Indonesia in August 1948. An early member of the first Indonesian Communist party, founder of the "illegal PKI" in the thirties, Musso had been living in the U.S.S.R. for a decade. He now came back in the company of a PKI Politbureau member, Suripno, who had been at the Prague meeting. As subsequent events demonstrate, Musso was sent back to take leadership in the PKI, since in Moscow's eyes he had enough stature to handle whatever doubts and confusions may have remained among Indonesian Communists. The Communist revolt against the Indonesian nationalists started the next month.

Events in Indochina are not directly related to the meetings in India, but rather they are more regularly pegged to the fortunes of the French Communist Party, which was forced out of the postwar Paris coalition in May 1947, and to the tangled skein of big-power negotiations, e.g., British military support for, and diplomatic recognition of, the French civil administration south of the Seventeenth parallel on October 9, 1945; the French-Chinese agreement of February 28, 1946, whereby France ceded her position in China in return for Chinese withdrawal of support from "President" Ho Chi Minh's provisional government proclaimed on September 2, 1945; and negotiations between the Viet Minh and the French carried on from August 1945 through the fruitless mission of Paul Mus in May 1947. However, these negotiations took place in a setting of growing guerrilla warfare in which many genuine Vietnamese nationalists willingly participated because they did not trust the Communist-French negotiations. In this warfare Communist guerrilla leaders, such as Vo Nguyen Giap in the North and Tran Van Giau in the South, were not inhibited by the negotiations. Nor during this period did the Communists fail to assassinate non-Communist opposition leaders: Ta Thu Thau (Trotskyite); Huynh Pho So (Hoa Hao sect leader); Nguyen Van Sam (Front of National Union, or United National Front, in the South); Truong Dinh Tri (Chairman of the Northern Administrative Committee); and others.[66]

Additional research will add to the "Calcutta story," especially when some of the actors who participated in these scenes become willing either to talk or to make available their personal records. From what is already known, one may conclude that the Calcutta meetings were the signal for the postwar re-entry of the Soviet Union into South and Southeast Asian affairs. The strategy of this period called for world revolution in the interest of Communist domination, even in those countries where Marxist-influenced nationalist movements had succeeded in achieving independence. For Moscow there was to be no "third force" or "third camp." In the light of everything we have learned about Communist strategy and tactics, it is sufficiently clear that Moscow ordered the rebellions which broke out after the series of meetings in India between December 1947 and March 1948.

In this period the Maoist line in relation to colonial Asia followed Moscow's lead: that is, it is "right" up to the end of 1947, and turns "left" after 1948. Mao Tse-tung applied the line more successfully than any other Asian Communist leader. In the postwar period Red China displayed the same attitudes as Moscow toward the non-Communist, nationalist liberation movements and the independent governments set up by them. In 1945, Mao had expressed his sympathy for Burma's independence.[67] In December 1947, however, while uttering the conventional warnings against "ultra-left" sectarianism as practiced in the U.S.S.R. in 1931–34, he and his colleagues restated all the major propositions associated with the left strategy. The opponents to be attacked included the liberation movements and the independent governments of Southeast Asia.[68]

Mao's support for the 1947 left line of the Cominform can best be examined in his important *On People's Democratic Dictatorship,* dated June 30, 1949. Here he reiterated the doctrine of the two camps, "the side of imperialism" and "the side of Socialism" (i.e., the Communists). He decried fence-sitting: "a third road does not exist." The four classes, united "under the leadership of the working class and the Communist Party," would join with the Soviet Union, the new Peoples' Democracies, and "the proletariat and masses of the people in other countries to form an international united front." There was never any doubt that in Asia the new formula excluded the non-Communist nationalist leaders from what Mao called the "revolutionary forces" united with, and led by, the Soviet Union. The Nehru government was characterized as a "lackey of British and American imperialists." "Wars of national liberation" (Communist rebellions) were endorsed in Burma and Indonesia. Sukarno was neatly dismissed as among the "new nobility" who, together with the

"Nehrus, Jinnahs, Luang Pibul Songgrams, Quirinos, Rhees, and other feeble-minded bourgeoisie of the East," had to be eliminated. Only then could the revolutionary workers, in a "united national front," successfully wage the "struggle against imperialism and its agents."[69]

Preoccupation with the domestic organizational structure and tactics of Maoism should not obscure the object of its strategic external attack. Maoism at any given time may have wooed wider sections of the Chinese class structure in order to hold or to advance its base of operation. But before and after the accession to power in September 1949, Mao was prepared to put the influence of the Chinese Communist Party behind the armed Communist attacks on the newly independent governments of Southeast Asia and its arms behind the sister parties in Korea and Indochina. By December 1949, Chinese Communist power had reached the border of Viet Nam. On January 16, 1950, China recognized the "Democratic Republic" of Ho Chi Minh, and the U.S.S.R. followed suit on January 30. According to non-French sources, Chinese military equipment began to appear in quantity in Viet Nam in February.

Like many Chinese, both Communist and non-Communist, Mao has not yielded China's interest in the *Nanyang*. Chinese tradition regards the "South Seas" as feudatory. Its records frequently and inaccurately reflect a relationship of vassalage between the countries of Southeast Asia and various ruling Chinese dynasties. The more China succumbed to Western (including Russian) and Japanese imperialist encroachments in the nineteenth and early twentieth centuries, the more her intellectuals and nationalist leaders asserted claims and former glories arising from earlier alleged Chinese suzerainty in Southeast Asia.[70] China always regarded Chinese immigrants to these lands, the "overseas Chinese," as its citizens. In this respect, Chinese Communists are making prescriptive claims based on China's imperial past, though their strategy and tactics vary according to Communist winds of doctrine. Peripheral territories are no longer described as feudatory or tributary, but in effect these terms might well be applied to Tibet, the borderlands claimed from Burma and India, and in the relationship of North Viet Nam and North Korea to Peking. China needs the Southeast Asian mainland rice bowl both for food and for emigration.

Speculatively, one might ask why Moscow turned so energetically to South and Southeast Asia after the Zhdanov speech, when it appeared as if its major preoccupation was with Europe. It has already been indicated that, according to Stalin's "law of ebb and flow," a revolutionary upswing after World War II was to be expected. The alleged "crisis in capitalism" may account for a general disposition to change the line after the war, but it does not appear to be a satisfactory reason for ordering the struggles and rebellions signalized by the change in strategy at the Cominform's first meeting in 1947.

We have established the high probability that the new rebellions in India, Burma, Malaya, Indonesia, and the Philippines, as well as the on-going one in Indochina, were directly inspired and where possible aided by Moscow and, certainly during and after 1949, by Peking. However, though these rebellions are set down as a consequence of the new Cominform policy, it would seem that Moscow must have known that they were ill prepared and ill timed and that, short of massive aid, they were reasonably certain to fail. After all, in 1947, Moscow intelligence about Asian affairs had vastly improved since 1927, if only because it had acquired the services of at least one generation of Moscow-trained "students" from Asian countries. Why then did Moscow promote actions that seemed doomed from the start?

They may have been decided on in Moscow primarily to capitalize as far as possible on the unrest that had been accentuated by the war and postwar dislocations. If they proved successful, so much the better; if not, the defeats could be accepted as in the past. This explanation presupposes that Moscow expected at the most a limited success as far as the actual establishment of Communist-dominated regions was concerned. Such an assumption is surely not inconsistent with the fact that neither the Soviet Union nor Red China gave these rebellions (Viet Nam excepted) the quantity and quality of material and propaganda support which would have made a substantial difference in their outcomes. The rebellions were "expendable." Alternatively, Stalin and the Moscow leadership looked to South and Southeast Asia because they in effect revived the timetable of revolutions which was current after World War I and which might be applicable to the post-World War II period; India first, then China, etc. In this connection some authorities have suggested that Stalin lacked faith in the ability, or did not especially relish the idea, of a Chinese Communist victory. If such a timetable were resurrected, the Communist rebellious effort in India in the spring of 1948, though vigorous, as indicated above, was quickly snuffed by Nehru's government and by the overt refusal of the Cominform to support the Indian Communist leader, Ranadive, in his controversy with Mao and the Chinese Communists.

If it were not for the fact that Stalin first announced this left turn in early 1946, some weight could be assigned to a hypothesis based on psychopathology—that Stalin, merely because he had the power, caused to be acted out his own diseased conceptions of the revolutions he had predicted in the aftermath of the war. Conceivably, Stalin was as "senile," as "paranoid," or what you will, in 1946 as he seemed to show himself to be in January 1953, when he dictated the arrest of the "Jewish doctors." But in the absence of pertinent data, this case is difficult to make for the years following 1946 and at least through the nine-week conference with Mao Tse-tung in late 1949 and early 1950.

It is here suggested as a more tenable hypothesis regarding Stalin's motives that he was animated by the desire to be vindicated in China. This desire must rate as one of the powerful drives in his life. He could force Communist historians to distort the facts, but he could not conceal from himself that his policy in China had failed. Postwar Asian confusion and American policy in China gave him another chance. He announced the beginnings of the new left turn when the United States was again vainly trying to bridge the gulf between Mao Tse-tung and Chiang Kai-shek. When this policy gave evidence of its inherent futility, Stalin must surely have known that Chiang would get some Western support and that the U.S.S.R., despite its agreements with Chiang, would give its support to Mao. The Soviet leader turned over to Mao large quantities of Japanese arms. The common border between Soviet Asia and China, as well as the Russian occupation of the port of Dairen, provided supply lines which could be easily used to serve the interests of the Chinese Communists. The supplies thus provided were later augmented by American equipment obtained through Kuomintang defeats and defections.

Stalin had reason to regard Mao as the emergent power in China, with or without his aid. As one commentator put it, both the American President and his Secretary of State "hoped for a united, democratic China but gave up the active attempt to bring it about. Henceforward, the United States would watch the opposing factions fight it out."[71] The American "China policy" of "cautious non-involvement" in late 1946 and 1947 cannot have been unwelcome to Soviet leaders. Though Stalin ordered the withdrawal of Soviet troops from Manchuria, thus strengthening Chiang, this move was no more than an expedient adoption of the "correct" posture of fulfilling some of the terms of the Big Three meeting in Moscow in December 1945.

But Stalin had more to do than this. After his "hardening of the line" speech in February 1946, one can begin to discern a change of pace in China. The Soviet public position developed through several phases, from finding fault with Chinese Nationalist fulfillment of the 1945 Sino-Soviet agreement, through accusations that the Nationalist government was conducting a "campaign of lies directed against the Soviet Union," until by December 1946, the attack on the American "imperialist" role in China and the "reactionary" Kuomintang "had become a stock phrase of the Russians."[72]

What was at stake throughout the years 1945–49 was, first, the security of the U.S.S.R. and, second, the advancement of Communist power by "peaceful" means during the temporary alliance with the Western Allies and by revolutionary means when this alliance was no longer needed. Diversionary tactics would help Mao. If the United States, now partially disengaged from China, and the Asian colonial powers—Britain, France, and the Netherlands—could be kept busy elsewhere, Mao would benefit. Revolutions in the newly free or soon to be free countries, even if abortive, might help Mao by taking attention away from China and diminishing the assistance that might be given to Chiang. It is here suggested that Moscow ordered the expendable Calcutta revolutions not only to aid its policy in Europe but also to aid Mao in China. When it is remembered that Chiang's stock in the United States had dropped severely during 1947–48, after the failure of the Marshall mission and while President Truman was intensely preoccupied with Europe, it seems all the more likely that the unpromising revolts in South and Southeast Asia were Stalin's ultimate attempts to insure his vindication in China.[73]

There are, in addition, negative arguments for the view here suggested. In contrast with its continuous connection with Northern Asia and China, the Soviet Union's interest in South and Southeast Asia had been sporadic and episodic. Even a casual analysis of Soviet journals reveals the comparative infrequency of articles about this area.[74] (After the war, it is true, Soviet interest in Indonesia and Viet Nam was effectively demonstrated in the United Nations.) Despite Calcutta, the Soviet Union does not appear to have supplied direct "military" aid to the revolutions it inspired in 1947–48. Finally, on the eve of Mao's great victory in China, the Moscow-controlled World Federation of Trade Unions announced on August 11, 1949, that the annual conference of trade-unions would be held in Peking, beginning in mid-November. Stalin was later willing to assign to the Permanent Liaison Bureau, based in Peking, the task of dealing with the Asian Communist movements,[75] an indication that China was the main focus of his interest in the East.

It is not suggested that Stalin, by this act, was elevating Mao and China to equality with himself and the Soviet Union but only that his conduct further supports the view of the lesser importance to Moscow of the Southeast Asian area. Stalin exacted a considerable price for his aid to Mao, particularly in Outer Mongolia and Sinkiang, in "war-industrial-booty" from Manchuria, and in war debts imposed on China on behalf of the North Korean war machine.

The Permanent Liaison Bureau never became particularly important. The Southeast Asian Communist rebellions—with the exception of Ho Chi Minh's—were allowed to run their course, but were not called off even after the death of Stalin. Four years before his death, Stalin could boast that

Communism had triumphed in China, could find satisfaction in a Chinese Communist Party with 3,000,000 members, and could welcome alliance with a victorious Chinese army of 1,500,000. He need not fear Mao, who had supported him in every twist and turn of policy since the Sixth Comintern Congress.

THE NEW COMMUNIST LINE OF 1953

The rigor of Moscow's left strategy in Asia began to diminish after the consolidation of Chinese Communist power and, noticeably, just before and immediately after the death of Stalin in March 1953. The Korean Armistice, concluded on July 27, 1953, may be taken as a new dividing line for Communist strategy and tactics in Asia. It has been suggested that possibly a new policy, placing less emphasis on the two-camp conflict, was under consideration for some time before Stalin's death.[76] Burma felt the change in 1954, as Prime Minister U Nu pointed out in a speech to the Burma Chamber of Deputies in September 1957.[77] He said of China:

But our relations with the new Chinese regime (even after mutual recognition and exchange of ambassadors) remained uncertain for a number of years. The Communist rebellion was still going strong, and the new Chinese Government seemed inclined to give our Communists their moral support, apparently regarding us as stooges of the West. Broadcasts from Peking radio at that time did not attempt to disguise this attitude. . . . Premier Chou En-lai's visit to India and Burma in 1954 proved to be the turning point in Sino-Burmese relations. [The Soviet Union at first treated] us as "on probation." . . . But later, as the Communist rebellion gathered momentum, her attitude underwent a change, and indications were that she came to look upon us as reactionaries standing in the way of the people's liberation. . . . [A]s time passed . . . the Soviet Union's attitude changed. . . . We shall always remember that it was the Soviet Union which, in the difficult days of 1954 and 1955, came to our assistance by entering into barter arrangements involving substantial quantities of our surplus rice.

The Calcutta policy had served a major purpose. It gave to the Communist parties and groups in South and Southeast Asia a more vigorous role than they had ever played before. The history of the area since the Calcutta conference cannot be written without full recognition of this Communist thrust for power. Nevertheless, it failed everywhere in Southeast Asia except in North Viet Nam, where, as noted above, the Communists pursued a policy not directly related to the Calcutta decisions.

Since Stalin's death, Soviet policy has been marked by an extraordinary outward acceptance of non-Communist Asian nationalism in general and of the newly independent neutralist countries in particular. Geneva in 1954, Bandung in 1955, and the innumerable visits of missions between the Moscow-Peking bloc and India, Burma, and Indonesia represent diplomatic gains for the present Communist strategy. The "peace-loving, outstretched hand," first used when the "right" line was adopted at the Seventh Comintern Congress, may prove in many ways more dangerous to Asian nationalists because it is more flexible and opportunistic. The illegality of the Communist parties in Burma, Thailand, and the Republic of Viet Nam may provide more of a shield against Communist subversion and infiltration than Indonesian toleration of that party at the presidential and cabinet levels, but neither practice in itself insures the nationalists against their irreconcilable opponents. Since 1953 the Moscow-Peking bloc has been willing to accept both treatments of the local Communist parties. They have found ready channels for extending their influence in the interest of their long-range revolutionary aims: embassies, peace movements, barter-trade-aid agreements, border problems, and even the agitation for self-determination for minority peoples, particularly at the northern perimeter of Southeast Asia.

This Sino-Soviet policy, which still prevails, is designed to conceal from the newly independent peoples a long-range revolutionary strategy. Like the proverbial iceberg, much of it is below the surface; but enough of it appears above to be recognized by discerning eyes. The Asian neutrals can hardly be won by threats to their territorial integrity. Thus, if China's "rights" to Tibet are accepted in India as justified by history, India nevertheless does not want Chinese forces probing in Nepal and publicly protests China's ruthless suppression of Tibetan autonomy and incursion over her borders. Whether or not China is entitled to certain border rectifications with Burma, if the Burmese are obliged to make territorial concessions to keep the peace, they are not going to forget it, nor will they forget that they were kept dangling for years while China temporized about accepting a proposed agreement.

Moreover, rumors of Chinese Communist sponsorship of Free Kachin, Free Thai, and similar movements based in Yunnan are disturbing to some southern Asians, whose fears have more recently been intensified by external Communist support for the Pathet Lao rebels.[78] The Moscow-Peking embassies in the new Asian countries, particularly the Chinese embassies, are sometimes said by the indigenes to have attempted to influence elections. The five principles of peaceful coexistence, so ably sold by Chou En-lai since 1954, have been taken up prudently by many politically wise Asians in the hope that they have not paid too big a price for what may after all be shoddy stuff. In the meantime, the spirit of Bandung begins to arouse skepticism where Peking is involved.

CONFLICT AND DIFFERENTIATION WITHIN SOUTHEAST ASIAN MARXISM

We have already seen that the nationalist-Marxist amalgam was forged in the struggle for independence in Burma, Viet Nam, and Indonesia. It did not last beyond independence. Since then it has been exposed to two major tests. The Communist-led rebellions inspired or ordered by Moscow split the Marxists into non-Communist and Communist groups in Burma and Indonesia. The Communists who remain in South and Southeast Asia are followers of the Marxist-Leninist-Stalinist line, whatever it happens to be. They are true pro-Moscow die-hards. It appears that no well-known Communist in Asia has defected, even after the revelation of Stalin's crimes at the Twentieth CPSU Congress or on the Hungarian issue. The second test, the more dangerous one, which arose after the shift to the "right" strategy in 1953, still continues.

The Communist rebellions took a tragic toll of lives and resources. They also forced leadership groups in Burma and Indonesia to deepen the process of ideological re-examination which had started earlier; and though Viet Nam was not affected directly by the Calcutta decisions, the ruthless measures adopted by Ho against other Marxists (Trotskyists) and nationalists who disagreed with the Communist party of Indochina produced a related effect. This ideological re-examination can best be illustrated in the context of the Asian Socialist Conference.

However they differentiated themselves within the nationalist-Marxist amalgam, Asian Socialists and Communists had found little difficulty—except during the Comintern's "third period"—in living together before and during World War II. During the postwar independence drive some who still called themselves Marxists began to recognize the irreconcilability of the differences between themselves and the Communists. Burmese documents, made available in 1952, trace the rise of the split between those who formed a "Socialist party" and the Communist party. A similar story emerged from a few records and conversations with the Vietnamese and Indonesians. The Calcutta rebellions of 1948 in effect marked the end of any Socialist-Communist organizational unity. U Nu, in May and June 1948, made one last attempt to heal the breach in Burma, in order to end the rebellion. His efforts at "Marxist unity" were publicly scorned by the Communist party. No such attempt at Marxist unity has since been tried by non-Communist Marxists anywhere else in Southeast Asia.

The Burmese have indicated that they raised the question of an Asian Socialist identity at the 1947 Asian Relations Conference held in Delhi. In and after 1948, Asian Socialists moved toward defining the distinctions between their outlook and that of the Communists. In March 1952, a preparatory conference of Indian, Burmese, and Indonesian representatives was held in Rangoon to plan for the first Asian Socialist Conference, to be held January 6–15, 1953.

That it should have taken place at all was in itself a mark of the great change in Asia. In the twenties Asian nationalist movements— forerunners of today's Socialist parties— had got short shrift from their European counterparts. In 1925 the European parties "hailed the awakening of

the great masses of the Chinese, Indian, and Mohammedan world" but did
not pursue the kind of aggressive anti-imperialist policy propagandized by
Moscow.[79] Events of the late 1920's in China, India, and North Africa induced the Socialist International to discuss the issues of political and economic self-determination for Asian and African peoples. Before World
War II, however, the European parties found themselves either too preoccupied with European problems or too fearful of disturbing "the basic
relations of their home countries with their colonial dependencies" to do
more than concur in expressions of sympathy. Hence it is remarkable that
in 1953 there should have been an Asian Socialist conference and that it
should have invited delegates from the European parties and the present
Socialist International.

Some two hundred delegates, "fraternal delegates," and observers from
fifteen countries were present. None was invited from the U.S.S.R., Communist China, or the satellite countries. Clement Attlee, who, as Prime
Minister, had helped Burma achieve independence, was lionized at the
conference. He and Saul Rose of England, André Bidet of France, and Kaj
Bork of Sweden were the official representatives of European Socialism,
and they sought organizational ties between the Asian groups and the
European International. These ties were rejected by the Asians as being
unnecessary or undesirable at the time.[80]

In all, thirteen resolutions were unanimously adopted.[81] The chief ones
were:

1. A statement on the "Principles and Objectives of Socialism," which
overtly rejected Communism and determined upon a "struggle to supersede capitalism and feudalism by democratic socialism." The two approaches were contrasted as follows:

The essence of democratic socialism is the striving to attain greater happiness, justice and dignity, and the fullest possible chance of self-expression for
the human being. In seeking to abolish exploitation of class by class and of man
by man, socialism recognizes man both as an integral part of a class or group
and as a human individual. It therefore avoids totalitarian forms of government
and methods of mass coercion. Communism, on the other hand, as practiced
today in its totalitarian form in the Soviet Union and its satellites, has degenerated
into a regime of the complete subordination of the individual and the group to
the centralized power of the leadership of the ruling party. Under the Soviet
system, state power imposes absolute domination and exacts blind obedience;
man is expected to give up his freedom and individuality, obliterating himself
as an abstract part of an all-powerful state in which only one will prevails. Communism, therefore, stands for the negation of all concepts of freedom, individual
self-expression and genuine mass responsibility which are the very breath of
democratic socialism.

2. A resolution on "Asia and World Peace," which re-emphasized Asian
Socialist "determination to ensure that such a solution be arrived at by

democratic means and be conducive to the strengthening of democracy. . . . World Peace is threatened by . . . colonialism, economic disequilibrium and the politics of spheres of influence." Hence Asian Socialists pledged support for the principles of the United Nations Charter and their determination to combat "the causes of world tension and to oppose aggression in any form."

3. A section on "Common Asian Problems," which restated the need to overcome the "evil forces" which "corrode within": poverty, religious fanaticism, the politics of linguistic separatism, Communism, capitalism-feudalism, lack of integrated thinking, political apathy, methods of terror and assassination, handicaps of women, and fence-sitting. To counteract these, "we must devise a system whereby the entire mass of the people could be associated with economic and political activity. It should be our endeavor to decentralize the political and economic power, wherever this is possible, and whenever economic and political factors demand this. Asia must realize that Bread and Freedom are indivisible." Asian Socialism must be dynamic instead of gradual, and, if necessary, must develop its own methods (instead of merely copying those of Europe) of peaceful mass action.

In a joint statement appended as a separate document to the resolutions of the First Asian Socialist Conference, the Socialist parties of Burma, India, and Indonesia restated their definitions of, and opposition to, both capitalism and Cominform Communism. The former "gave birth to imperialism and colonialism, . . . the exploitation of man by man." The latter "denies in practice [the] dignity and equality of man. . . . Its views and convictions cannot be separated from the position of Soviet Russia which it regards as its bulwark. . . . In Cominform countries there exists a dictatorship of the Cominform parties, employing the methods of terror of the secret police, which is also felt in the sphere of production." The statement, "employing the methods of analysis used by Marx and Engels," then continues to restate the principles and objectives of Socialism in terms of a commitment to democratic political, economic, and social rights, fully attainable "only in a society based on Socialist Economy."[82]

4. Freedom of all peoples, irrespective of race, color, and creed is a fundamental article of faith with the Asian Socialists. "The struggle against colonial rule is, in essence, the human protest against the dejection, degradation and poverty, against the frustration and indignity, which this system necessarily entails for the people suffering under it." All vestiges of colonialism were roundly condemned.

Specific resolutions were passed on Malaya, Uganda, Kenya, and North and South Africa, but there was no mention of Indochina. This omission was most significant. Burmese leaders and many others in Asia had no use for French hegemony in Indochina. They originally believed that Ho Chi Minh and many of his Vietnamese supporters were fighting a battle for national liberation. They regarded the French-controlled struggle in Indochina and the restoration of Bao Dai as leading to failure in this long-drawn-out anti-Communist fight. However, they refrained from mentioning Indochina in the enumeration of Asian countries to be liberated from imperialist control because they condemned the "imposition by force from outside of totalitarian regimes upon countries in Europe and Asia" as much as they regretted the existing French control.[83]

It should be noted that the Burmese government was represented at the conference. No other Asian nation (except Israel) was so represented. Burma's neighbors, India, Pakistan, Indonesia, and Ceylon, with whom Burma was trying to concert its foreign policy, sent high dignitaries (e.g., Jayaprakash Narayan and Sutan Sjahrir) but no governmental representatives. It is safe to say that the First Asian Socialist Conference meant more to Burma and its leadership than to other Asian countries.[84]

The years from 1948 to 1953, then, mark the firm differentiation of the Southeast Asian Socialist parties from the Communist parties. The significance of the Asian Socialist Conference is that it ratified positions previously taken by Southeast Asian Socialists. Perhaps more than others among them, Sutan Sjahrir of Indonesia led the way to a written formulation of this outlook that was both anticapitalist and anti-Communist. Unlike Ba Swe or Kyaw Nyein and other Burmese leaders preoccupied with Communist rebellion, Sjahrir had time to reflect upon Marxist philosophy. He began to express an outlook which, while still retaining the "method of analysis used by Marx-Engels in their dissection of the development and organization of capitalist society,"[85] came to look upon Marx and Engels as historically important but of questionable contemporary use. Increasingly he wrote and talked of "democratic socialism and humanism" as basic principles in opposition to Communism, which he identified as "the Leninist-Stalinist school of thought."[86] Increasingly his colleagues in the Asian Socialist Conference found themselves in agreement with such views, especially after the Burmese Socialists took the initiative in branding Soviet imperialism as "more ruthless, more systematic and more blatantly unjustified" than the older forms of imperialism.[87]

The nationalist-Marxist amalgam was irreparably broken as the meaning of Communism became clarified. Sjahrir's remark concerning Indonesia, that "political thinking in general is socialist oriented," is largely true of the leaders who "made the revolution" in South and Southeast Asia, whether they call themselves nationalists, Socialists, independents, or patriots. But since the First Asian Socialist Conference there has been a better understanding of the differences between democrats of whatever persuasion and totalitarians. The lines of demarcation can be crossed. Non-Communist and Communist political parties can and do make common cause for domestic political reasons; for example, the Nationalist and Communist parties of Indonesia. But in the main such political conduct must take place in the open and must be rationalized in the face of the clarity which the Asian Socialist Conference signalized.

The Second Asian Socialist Conference, in 1956, accentuated without adding new substance to this fundamental clarification. Without the strong support of the Burmese government and the AFPFL party, it is doubtful whether the Conference, as a permanent regional body, would survive. Regional organizations have not yet taken firm root in South and Southeast Asia. Whether or not the ASC survives, it has already succeeded in giving to many Asians an identifiable Socialist philosophy as a guide to action.[88]

Thus, to sum up, the Communist parties of Southeast Asia, whether in power, as in North Viet Nam, or constituting an above ground or underground opposition, as elsewhere in the region, remain standard exemplars of the policies of the Moscow-Peking bloc. Theirs is a crude and opportunistic adherence to whatever is the current international Communist party line. The Socialist parties, in theory and in practice, are moving toward a new synthesis of imported and indigenous elements which reflects, more than anything else, European "utopian" and "revisionist" Socialism. Humanistic, cooperativist, nonclass-struggle values have become the theoretic essentials for a benevolent and active central state power exercised in principle through democratic institutions.

MARXISM AND SOUTHEAST ASIAN ECONOMICS

Thus far the analysis has centered on the political consequences of the introduction of Marxism as a factor in the nationalist movements of Southeast Asia. There is little doubt that in a general sense—but only in a general sense—it also supplied a framework for nationalist thinking on economic matters and the type of economy to be established once independence had been achieved.

Though there are national variations, the countries of Southeast Asia, and especially those treated in this study, share a generally similar economic development, which in major part has determined their present economic policies. Modern capitalism, developed by Western nations, was grafted onto an indigenous, precapitalist economic and social system. The latter, then, as now, was devoted to pursuits of agriculture (including forestry and fishing) and mining for domestic use, and to such regional trade as resulted from this type of production. Western capital, which followed colonial conquest, developed the area; and a significant but lesser role was played by Indian and Chinese capital. Sparked by the Indian banking caste, the

Chettyars, Indian investment had been important in Burma;[89] Chinese capital had been important everywhere in Southeast Asia.[90] After the invasion of Western capital, Asian investment continued in subordinate sectors of the colonial economies. By the beginning of World War II, at a conservative estimate, the equivalent of some $4,000,000,000 had been invested in the Netherlands Indies, British Malaya, Thailand, the Philippines, French Indochina, and Burma.[91] This investment, both private and governmental, was amply protected from nationalist aspirations. It gave rise to the "dual economy" in which profits largely went overseas and subsistence modified by the amount of welfare necessary and useful to the ongoing entrepreneurial system remained behind.[92]

International public and private investment protected by colonial governments developed these countries and created a trade which depended on increased production of the area's natural resources and raw materials. Prewar Burma, Thailand, and Indochina were capable of feeding themselves and exporting annually approximately 6,000,000 tons of milled rice. Malaya and Indonesia accounted for 800,000 tons of exported rubber; Indonesia and Burma produced 8,500,000 metric tons of crude petroleum; Malaya, Indonesia, and Thailand mined 90,000 metric tons of tin in concentrates, and Malaya alone produced 65,000 metric tons of tin metal. Indonesia, the Philippines, and Malaya produced 1,600,000 tons of copra. Raw materials and primary products came forth in abundance; but industrial power, manufacturers, and the production of capital goods were conspicuously weak.[93]

As Boeke tartly remarks: "Three centuries ago, Europeans did not sail to the Indies to collect butterflies." The European market "was insatiable" and the demand for profits steadily imposed on the "native" society ever-increasing forms of economic (and other) power. The pre-European subsistence economy remained side by side with the newer one. This and its cultural, traditional setting gave rise to the description of the combination as a dual or plural society.[94]

As the pace of Western capitalist enterprise in the colonies accelerated and as it responded to the vagaries of the market, the total economy gave every evidence of polarization. The entrepreneur who came from, or followed the practice of, the West was able to reap the benefits of colonial investment, while the native producer declined in relative importance and the self-sufficiency of the rural population progressively deteriorated.[95]

Thet Tun, a Burmese economist, defines an economy as "colonial" when it is based primarily on agriculture and extractive industries, when the role of foreign capital control is either substantial or complete, and when the jobs requiring managerial techniques and administrative skills are mainly in the hands of foreigners. In such a society, output and consumption per capita are extremely low. Social services are limited both in scope and quality, and substantial amounts of dividends, interest, and profits are withdrawn by the foreign investors.[96] Long before the advent of any kind of Marxism in Southeast Asia, capitalism, the name for the hated system of economic exploitation, was regarded as the concomitant of the political power structure imposed on the Asian societies by the metropole. In the early days after independence, nationalists acutely feared the power of remaining foreign investments—hence the rapid moves toward nationalization—and acquired new suspicions of needed foreign capital.

Also useful in explaining present attitudes is the fact that the metropolitan powers, in varying degrees but always extensively, introduced state-owned and -operated industry and, in some instances, monopoly.[97] Probably the Dutch were more directly involved in the development and ownership of industry and agriculture in Indonesia than the British in Burma or the French in Indochina, but these are differences in degree which in no way impair the conclusion that the colonial plural economy witnessed widespread state ownership, control, and monopoly, while at the same time it assigned an inferior role to the indigenes. Though state-dominated economic development was more extensive in colonial times than before, it should be noted that the indigenous societies had been accustomed to state monopolies under their own rulers. This is well illustrated in Thailand under both the absolute and constitutional monarchies.[98] Since 1932 the constitutional government (or the ruling clique of the day) has increased government ownership and operation of industry. The variety of state-owned, -controlled, and equity shares in industry in Thailand is probably proportionately higher and more varied today than in the other countries of this study.[99]

As state enterprise had been normal in Southeast Asia both before and since the colonial period, it is not surprising that the Marxist emphasis upon state or public ownership, upon nationalization of economic enterprise, found a ready audience in Southeast Asia even among those who might not have been attracted to other aspects of Marxist ideology. It conflicted neither with traditional culture patterns nor with recent experience.

Despite the present willingness of Southeast Asian economists to accept a Marxian economic alternative for the colonial economy, it would be difficult to point to any non-Communist among them, in or out of government, who bases his views exclusively on Marxian economic theory. The typical Marxian economic problems—commodity exchange production, value and its determination as socially necessary labor time, the nature of labor power and its relation to wages and surplus value, etc.—are absent from Southeast Asian economic literature.

On the other hand, the Marxian sociology, which deprecates the social

effects of a capitalist economy, its "misery," "poverty," "inequality," etc.—
will be found as part of the doctrinal and propaganda equipment of almost
any literate Southeast Asian. He sees in the disparities of a free market,
particularly the world market, baneful effects upon the prices of the primary products produced in his country and of the manufactured goods
which he must still import. He is critical of the accumulation and concentration of capital in the hands of resident and nonresident aliens. He is
fearful of a possible crisis of capitalism, particularly if he is old enough to
have lived through the great depression of the thirties. He recoils from the
contrast between the levels of profits and wages, and from the under-
employment of indigenous labor. He is acutely aware, because he usually
has rural roots, of the consequences of large-scale land alienation, sharecropping, and preindependence forms of indentured or contract labor systems. From historic knowledge and personal experience, Southeast Asians
have little love for what they call capitalism, and what we in the United
States frequently call the free enterprise system.[100] Nationalists and Marxists found no difficulty in joining forces to oppose it.

Postwar independence for Southeast Asia has meant among other things
the decision to end this colonial economic system. In its place the various
governments, naturally and necessarily, have stepped in to diversify their
monocultures and to build new national economies. These governments,
as the primary investors, with or without planning have adopted the spirit
of Western technology and a residue of European economic ideology. The
policy may be called "Socialistic," as in contemporary India; "Socialist," as
in Burma; by no name, as in Thailand and Viet Nam; or by various names in
Indonesia, such as President Sukarno's coinage *marhaenism* ("proletarian
nationalism"). Whatever the name, the policies have uniformly sought
to improve agriculture, which still embraces from 80 to 85 per cent of the
population, and to create an industrial base which will utilize in part indigenous primary products. This double effort, it is hoped, will make their
national economies less dependent upon the fluctuations of the international commodity trade.

Despite their initial hostility to foreign investments and entrepreneurial
skills, the Southeast Asian nations have rapidly come to understand that
there can be no release from the wheel of poverty until there is economic
development, which is consequently a prime requirement not only among
the newly independent nations but also in Thailand and what is left of the
former colonial empires. Economic development demands a rate of net
investment which exceeds internal capital accumulation. The underdeveloped countries of Southeast Asia, lacking an entrepreneurial class, private savings, banks, insurance companies, and other aids to domestic in-

vestment, have had to rely upon their governments as the primary internal sources for capital.[101]

The problem for nationalists and Marxists alike, once power was achieved, was to avoid a return to economic colonialism and to the non-monetary subsistence economy which had so largely characterized their homelands under various precolonial dynasties. Economic planning was their ready solution to this problem. The crucial question became: What kind of economic planning? Any model which the Southeast Asian leaders would adopt or develop was bound to contain a large element of state control. Both their own cultural inheritance and the Western impact had prepared them for this. They were prepared to give the Soviet model a large degree of approbation because it had been visibly successful in transforming a backward economy into one capable of competing with the technologically advanced capitalist countries of the West, and because this had been done within the lifetime of the present generation of Southeast Asian leaders. They too wished to raise themselves quickly by their own bootstraps. Having "made the revolution," they now wished to carry it forward on its economic front. Initially they were prepared to overlook or to excuse the human costs and the loss of freedom which the Soviet system had imposed upon its people.

How widespread this attitude may have been, how consciously it was articulated during the early postwar years, is difficult to say. One might speculate that, if the First Cominform Congress and hence the Calcutta Conference had adopted a "right" instead of a "left" strategy, Soviet Marxism might have been more effectively advanced in Southeast Asia. But freedom was given another chance and the free world a respite by the superlative Communist blunder (as far as Southeast Asia was concerned) of the Sino-Soviet bloc policy. The Communist rebellions of 1948 and the fear engendered by Communist China in 1949, and since then, raised a further question respecting economic planning: Could it be achieved without totalitarian methods and within a democratic political structure? The non-Communist answer in Southeast Asia has been almost everywhere in the affirmative. In this context the Southeast Asians have begun, casually or deliberately, to develop plans for a "mixed economy," or what has been called, in Scandinavia, "the middle way." The search is on for a road between totalitarian Communism and unfettered capitalism.[102]

Given the similarities among the countries involved, the over-all uniformity of their plans and policy statements is not surprising. They called for higher standards of living; a new industrial base for an essentially rural population; improved health, sanitation, education, housing, transport, and communications; and increased per capita production and consumption.

In the original Burmese Pyidawtha plan, these goals received moderate expression in concrete plans for raising the gross domestic product about 30 per cent above the prewar level, so as to achieve an increase of almost 9 per cent in per capita consumption by 1960.[103] The projects adopted to realize these goals also show a uniformity such as one might expect: new industries—some of doubtful value in regional terms but "justified" by nationalist considerations—using indigenous raw materials; public utilities; transport and communications; land reform, reclamation, and irrigation; crop diversification and yield improvement; and a great variety of social capital projects.

No matter how much these governments "tighten their belts," that is, tax, impose import restrictions on nonessentials, control export trade, float domestic loans, and otherwise "save" for investment, they inevitably come to the point where their capital accumulation and net investment fall behind the scheduled requirements of their expansion programs. The westernized elites who run these governments are, in a sense, "people in a hurry." Since they have explicitly rejected the Russian (and Chinese) economic model and its dictatorial method, they have discarded any doctrinaire approach to the solution of their economic problems. They have not hesitated to revise or discard plans where necessary. After initial suspicion, they have all made increasing efforts to attract private foreign capital, while making as much use as possible of the resources of the United Nations, the Colombo Plan, United States aid agencies, and, more recently, Sino-Soviet instruments of aid.[104]

In the West, these developments in Southeast Asia have been overshadowed by concern about the developmental "race" between democratic India and Communist China. The results in India, down to the start of her Second Five-Year Plan, have supported the conclusion that a democratic, planned economy, however "mixed" it may be between the public and private sectors, can increase production and consumption in a heavily populated country. Though Southeast Asia as a whole is less advanced economically than India and is still plagued by problems of security and regional conflict and by a dearth of top-level skills of every kind, it has nonetheless been able to recapture economic ground lost in the war and in subsequent rebellions.[105] The trend has been upward even where prewar levels of economic activity have not yet been reached. To sum up, necessity, design, and tradition, in varying combinations, have placed the governments of Southeast Asia in the role formerly occupied by Western private and public sectors of the colonial dual economy.

The similarity of goals is reflected also in the policies adopted by these nations, be they "Socialist" as in Burma, "capitalist" as in Thailand and Viet Nam, or "people's frontist" as in Indonesia. In the first place, though land reform and land redistribution have occurred, there has been a complete avoidance of action even remotely resembling Stalinist or Maoist collectivization. On the contrary, there has been a firm resolve to retain a free basic agarian structure while simultaneously extending to the working farmer and agricultural laborer the benefits of legislative and social reform. In Southeast Asia the domestic agricultural producer and his market are free. Government price-fixing and government marketing affect only production for export. An important Burmese minister inspected the agricultural systems of the U.S.S.R. and Israel, after which he strongly recommended the democratic Israeli cooperative in preference to either the Soviet *kolkhoz* or *sovkhoz*.

Cooperatives of every variety, nonusurious credit facilities, new agricultural technology, rural health, education, and welfare programs, bonus incentives for improving the quality and quantity of yields—these and many other devices typify land-reform and land-redistribution policies in Southeast Asia. In the entire area only Java need worry about population growth. Despite poor agricultural methods, low yields, and the prevalence of one-crop farming, there is little pressure of population. The present comfortable ratio of population to arable land represents a considerable margin of political and economic safety for nontotalitarian Southeast Asian governments.

Second, Southeast Asian governments uniformly expect industrialization to relieve them eventually of the real and fancied liabilities of an economy based mainly on primary products. The urge to industrialize was characterized at first by what has been called the "steel-mill complex." This emphasis on the production of capital goods has gradually been modified, partly by the force of circumstances and partly by the recognition that an underdeveloped country can perhaps more effectively build its industrial base by starting with manufacturing processes that make use of indigenous raw materials, thus conserving or gaining foreign exchange.

Southeast Asian governments have increasingly clarified their positions with respect to those economic ventures which should remain exclusively within the public or nationalized sector, those which should be handled in a combined or joint venture between government and private capital, both internal and external, and those which should be in the field of growing indigenous private capital. The joint venture has been used to attract needed foreign capital and as a means of avoiding the dangers of, and unfavorable external reaction to, expropriation of private capital.

The joint agreements have usually assigned management to the providers of private capital, with the stipulation that facilities be set up for training nationals. On June 9, 1957, Prime Minister U Nu announced that his government, besides providing foreign exchange credits and technical advice for domestic capital investors, would further narrow its own sector and thereby encourage "profit motives" among those capable of handling industrial and mining enterprises. Throughout Southeast Asia any citizen with capital is free to start a business, subject to licenses for imports and a ban on manufacturing certain military items. Whatever the degree of professed Socialism or "statism" in economic affairs, the Southeast Asian governments have increasingly taken steps to encourage and support domestic capital when it is willing to venture beyond its typical export-import commercial pattern.

In Southeast Asia non-Communist Marxists and non-Marxist national-ists alike have made their goal economic development in the interests of public welfare, not conformity to previously held concepts of Marxist planning. Behind this there appears to be a general desire—even among anti-Marxist leaders of Thailand and Viet Nam—to achieve a balanced, industrial-agrarian economy which will be characterized by three factors: state ownership or control of a limited number of industries; state partner-ship with private capital, external or domestic, in various enterprises; and a growing field for domestic private investment and initiative, encouraged by the state, especially if it adds to development. The resulting combina-tion may well be called a "mixed economy" or one that has found a "middle way" between Communism and capitalism as both these terms are com-monly understood.

The "mixed economy" or "middle way" are terms which do not lend themselves to easy definition. At best they stand for a determination to favor the coexistence and continued development of public and private sectors of an economy. What is put into each sector depends in part on ideas of Socialist planning, the absence of significant amounts of private capital, available skills, and traditional concepts of the proper role of central authority. Doctrine and necessity reinforce and refine each other. They have been supported also by the "Marxist ethical critique of capi-talism." If at the beginning of independence these countries were suspi-cious of nonindigenous investment because they accepted the critique of capitalism, they have more recently sloughed off some of their suspicion. If planning and investing in the public sector (chiefly capital but also some consumer goods) of industry; if public ownership of utilities, transport, telecommunications, defense industry; if agricultural and other coopera-tives and credit institutions are regarded as Socialism or Socialist, then in varying degrees each of the four countries in the study is "Socialist" in economic practice, if not in outlook.

On the other hand, individual enterprise in agriculture and local com-merce now constitutes the largest sector of domestic economic life. There appears to be every disposition on the part of the state to leave these in private, indigenous hands and to better the prospects of these private hands as well as to encourage indigenous investment in, and operation of, productive enterprise. It is this combination of public and private sectors which has been here called the middle way.

MARXISM AND SOUTHEAST ASIAN FOREIGN POLICY[106]

A general discussion of the foreign policy of Southeast Asia falls outside the scope of this study, but comment on the relationship between Marxism and foreign policy is pertinent.

The Communist parties, legal and illegal, their front organizations, and their press follow the current Sino-Soviet foreign policy line. Their propaganda task has been vastly simplified since 1953. In Burma and Indonesia, they offer support to neutralism while vigorously attacking the "camp of Western imperialism"; in Thailand, whatever underground movement exists probably finds ways to support, if not to inspire, the outburst of neutralist, anti-SEATO sentiment which has been prominent in a considerable section of the Thai press since the end of 1956. In Viet Nam, underground Communists cannot risk expression on foreign affairs, but radio propaganda activity from the Communist North is fairly successful in reaching the South. More recently there is some evidence that infiltrated personnel from the North have rebuilt some Communist cadres and have renewed guerrilla-type actions in provincial areas.[107] The Twentieth CPSU Congress and the Eighth Congress of the Communist Party of China reinforced the line which calls for friendly relations between the Moscow-Peking bloc and Southeast Asia. In the effort at peaceful conversion of neutrals into allies, Peking appears to retain the primary role awarded to it at the 1949 WFTU Peking conference.

The revelations of the Twentieth CPSU Congress do not appear to have had any appreciable effect upon the Communists in Southeast Asia, nor did the subsequent events in Poland and Hungary. This may be accounted for by the fact that since 1949 they have looked to Peking for guidance.[108] On two issues local Communist parties and propaganda must tread warily: first is the endemic problem of the citizenship of "overseas Chinese." Communist China has, if anything, been more willing than Kuomintang China to negotiate the problem. The agreement with Indonesia, concluded at Bandung by Chou En-lai, was intended to serve as a model for other countries. It appears to have been ratified in late 1957, but hardly any information is available about its implementation. In August and September 1956, President Ngo Dinh Diem authorized decrees which imposed Vietnamese nationality on all Chinese born in Viet Nam and restricted certain trades and professions to persons of Vietnamese nationality. Severe penalties could be, but have not as yet been, applied for disobedience. In this instance Nationalist China through its embassy

in Saigon has taken up the cause of the overseas Chinese. Since 1955 the
Thai government has relaxed suppressive policies against overseas Chinese. This has made for an entente between the Chinese business community and political and military leaders. It has been estimated that the
number of overseas Chinese in Burma has doubled in recent years, from
350,000 to 700,000. Concern has been expressed in various Burmese circles
over illegal Chinese immigration via the northern border.[109]

The second problem which tends to embarrass local Communists is
China's border with Southeast Asia, particularly the current Sino-Burmese
border dispute. The frontier has been poorly demarcated at least since
the days of the last Burmese king, Thibaw (1878–85). Sino-British agreements in 1886, 1894, 1897, and 1941 have not been accepted by the Chinese
Communists. They, as their predecessors, have laid claim to a considerable
area in the north of Burma, above 25° 35', and two other slices east of
Lashio and Bhamo. At one point Communist Chinese troops occupied
parts of these areas but presumably withdrew under Burmese protest.[110]
Since 1954, inconclusive high-level negotiations have been carried on between the two governments. Each time Burmese officials renew "peaceful
negotiations" with Communist China, Burmese Communists and their front
organizations provide a claque for the Chinese; but as the negotiations
proceed with the probability that Burma will have to yield some land on
which Burmese citizens have lived for generations, the Communists per-
force quiet down under attacks from their opponents. Local Communist
foreign policy in Southeast Asia is opportunistic, designed primarily to
exhibit local Communist leaders as loyal defenders of the Moscow-Peking
line, insofar, presumably, as this does not weaken their position with their
own peoples. The dominant consideration is what will strengthen Communist power as a whole in the long run.

In Burma and Indonesia the Socialist parties have frequently stated
their views on foreign policy. Spokesmen such as former Prime Minister
Ba Swe and Deputy Prime Minister Kyaw Nyein of Burma and former
Prime Minister Sjahrir of Indonesia, highly trained political interpreters
of policy, have been the chief Asian Socialists to recognize and condemn
as imperialistic the various forms of Soviet aggression. Kyaw Nyein has
found them more degrading and even more dangerous than "that typical
19th and 20th century colonialism or imperialism, which is the consequence
of the growth of capitalism."[111] The Socialist parties see "world peace
. . . threatened by three main factors, namely colonialism, economic disequilibrium and the politics of spheres of influence," and they feel that
the role of the Asian countries in the maintenance of peace lies in "opposing
aggression in every form." This they propose to do by upholding

the principles of the Charter of the United Nations; by coordinating their policies with states "internationally independent" [of the power blocs] . . . [I]n this way it will be possible for the Asian countries to ensure sufficient room for political freedom of movement necessary for them to play their part in the maintenance of peace in Asia and throughout the world. The contribution to the maintenance of world peace which Asian countries could make, therefore, lies not in their identification with the so-called world peace movements, which have become tools of the cold war, nor necessarily in joining any military security system, but essentially in their efforts to strengthen themselves.[12]

This is the policy of "neutralism," which Socialists in South and Southeast Asia share in some degree with nationalists outside the SEATO countries. The distinctive contribution of the Socialists to this policy emerges from their analysis of imperialism. Their public recognition that a self-styled "Socialist" country has been guilty of this major political crime was a significant development too frequently overlooked in the West.[113] The announcement of this recognition was made by Kyaw Nyein at the May 1954 bureau meeting of the Asian Socialist Conference held in Kalaw, Burma. He was supported vigorously by Ba Swe, then Burmese Minister of Defense and chairman of the conference, by the Indonesians, and by the majority group of the Indian Praja Socialists. Though the Indians and Indonesians gave currency to these views, on return to their respective countries, they were not "of the government." Because of the major role of the Socialist party of Burma in the ruling government coalition, the Anti-Fascist People's Freedom League, it appeared that the Burmese government had rationalized its foreign policy in terms of the Socialist principles for which Kyaw Nyein adopted the European Social Democracy term "Third Force,"[114] though the policy generally continues to be called "positive neutralism."

The Socialists of South and Southeast Asia have been consistent in supporting the "Third Force" even where, as in India and Indonesia, they have had to be critical of their respective governments. However, the role of Marxist ideas in the area of foreign policy does not go beyond this: condemnation of all forms of colonialism and imperialism and resistance to an alliance which would endanger "political freedom of movement." For the rest, foreign policy is an expression of the indigenous analysis of the structure of power and its relationship to national security.

The great foreign policy questions in Southeast Asia today, as in the past, relate to the power, international position, and economic requirements of China. Southeast Asians, for the most part, think of the present regime on the mainland as a permanent phenomenon. Their attitudes toward Communist China are compounded of respect and fear in varying combinations, depending on the distance between themselves and China, the degree of their confidence in their own economic future, and so on. The desire to preserve their independence vis-à-vis China under future conditions of either war or peace is universal. Other foreign policy questions are subsidiary. Southeast Asian positions on, for example, the reunification of Viet Nam and Korea are more comprehensible as extensions of the positions taken by each country toward China than as derivations from one or another ideological position.

The relationship between Marxism and foreign policy needs, however, to be stated with such precision as can be achieved. On the surface it would appear that Burma and Indonesia, where some aspects of Marxism have been congenial to the significant sections of power elites, have developed a neutralist or Third Forcist foreign policy; whereas the corresponding elites in Thailand and Viet Nam, who for different reasons find any form of Marxism, overtly so labeled, uncongenial, have welcomed a foreign policy which looks to Western alliances such as SEATO. (Technically, Viet Nam is not a member of SEATO, but by protocol it is included, along with Laos, Cambodia, and Malaya before its independence, in the protective area of the treaty.) But any attempt at generalizing a connection between Marxism or Socialism and neutralism withers before the variety of foreign policies adopted or approved by Socialist governments or Socialist parties throughout the world. There has been a strain in Marxism which persistently identified wars with capitalism and imperialism and regarded Socialism either as pacifist or supportive of "wars of liberation." This element in Marxism led to notable antiwar resolutions at various Socialist and later Communist International congresses. It split the Socialist International at the beginning of World War I, and it helped to bring to the fore Leninist ideology during and after that war.

The present Asian Socialists for the most part (and all Communists) had accepted this reading of history. It fitted into their interpretation of their colonial experience, and it conditioned their anti-Western response. To that extent there is a limited ideological connection between Asian Socialism and neutralism. But foreign policy is only in part compounded of ideology. The need for security, the promotion of interests, the conception or image a nation has of itself or wishes to project, its "pooled self-esteem," its actual historical and cultural experience subject always to time and fortune—these, too, embodied in the vagaries of personality enter into the making of foreign policy and control decision-making.

The effective leadership in Burma and Indonesia, nationalist and Socialist (not orthodox Communist), did not start out as neutralist at independence. Burma in 1948 and early 1949 and Indonesia after 1945 and at least up through the period of the Renville agreement in January 1948 (perhaps even up to early 1952, when an Indonesian government fell because it accepted the military provisions of the U.S. Mutual Security Act) actively and successfully sought Western aid. Only after both the Communist and the Karen rebellions had started in Burma, in 1949, and after the combination of the Communist rebellion and the continuing imperialist intervention in Indonesia, does one begin to find the expression of a neutralist note, as in a 1948 Partai Sosialis Indonesia manifesto calling for Asian unity, keeping away from alliances with the United States and with the Soviet bloc and thus becoming a factor in determining the future of the world.[115] Asian disillusionment with Western response over the traditional colonial or imperialist issue reasserted itself. This, coupled with the always prominent component of Asian nationalism and the growing fear of Communist China after 1949, led to the formulation of neutralism and to its adoption by all avowedly Asian Socialist parties and by other Asian nationalists. Since 1949, Burmese and Indonesian Socialist and nationalist leaders, frequently in concert with their friends in India, have held to their neutralist policy, with or without reference to its Marxist derivation. They are aware that it separates them from their comrades in many of the European Socialist parties, but they continue to feel that as a policy it fits their situation.

Neutralist expression in Thailand arises not from the Socialist thinking of the real or fancied Thai Socialists, but from another set of circumstances. It is related to the fear of China, to the fear that SEATO does not have the firm commitment to be found in NATO, and to interest in potential trade with China. The Thai, historically conscious of big-power rivalries, have no desire to be caught in a political and economic squeeze. Neutralism as a Thai policy is a bargaining weapon or a future insurance policy. The Republic of Viet Nam exists today because finally in 1954 the United States decided to back a regime which had then acquired a momentum of its own. It has no use for neutralism since its continued external security and, for some time to come, its ability to thwart domestic subversion and infiltration require U.S. Support. Thailand with or without any ideology continues to do what the present dynasty began to do at the beginning of the nineteenth century. Viet Nam whether anti-Marxist or otherwise can do no other than what she is doing.

What meaning has this in terms of freedom and democracy? Most observers would agree that the Burmese and Indonesian Socialists are in the vanguard of those who advocate and support "democracy" as the term is understood in the West. Viet Nam has not yet felt it could afford this. Thailand, under both the absolute and the constitutional monarchy, and Viet Nam enjoy a curious combination of domestic social freedoms and political constraints.

The ideological elements which make up foreign policy are not the critical factors when a decision has to be made concerning the actual conduct of foreign relations. Every nation seeks its own security and interest in its own way. The critical test of any foreign relationship is the compatibility of the concepts of security *and* of the value systems held by the parties to the relation. If these two tests of compatibility are of equal weight, there is no reason for the United States to cherish the members of SEATO more or less than the non-SEATO countries. Non-Communist Marxism has been a relevant but not decisive factor in the making and execution of Asian foreign policy. Neutralism has been one particular form of the Asian response to changing experience.

MARXISM AND SOUTHEAST ASIA: IN CONCLUSION

This study has attempted to set forth the development and meaning of Marxism in Southeast Asia. The four historical chapters have established that the development began primarily with the Communist version of Marxism. In this sense the arrival and establishment of Marxism in Southeast Asia reverses the pattern which has been familiar in the West, where more than half a century had to go by before the totalitarian potential in Marxism began to be organized by the Bolsheviks. During this second half of the nineteenth century a democratic Marxist or Socialist movement had grown up and taken fairly firm root in Western Europe. It was, however, mainly as a result of the Bolshevik seizure of power in Russia that Marxism came to Southeast Asia.

Since 1920, despite setbacks, there has been a persistent Communist movement in Southeast Asia, which, like its counterparts throughout the world, has slavishly followed the Soviet and Chinese model. The party line, now furnished by the Moscow-Peking bloc, is periodically revised, but it retains certain perduring tenets: (1) An ideology which, according to the "faith," is destined to triumph in the world—an ideology of social revolution. Capitalism, like Carthage, must be destroyed—even while it is destroying itself. The revolution is bound to occur, but its advent will be hastened by the midwifery of the well-disciplined vanguard party, which from time to time seeks a variety of allies and keeps them as allies so long as they are subservient to the party. (2) Dictatorship is necessary before, during, and after the seizure of power. Some day, when there are no more "class enemies," it, too, will pass. (3) The presumed will of the revolution is the only law, and he who interprets and controls the revolution is the only lawyer and judge.

Inevitably there will be some who see in the often interesting speeches and articles of Mao a hope that he is changing, that he will become a Tito, or that China in some mysterious way must necessarily reject what is not Chinese, i.e., Marxism, or transform it to the point of obliteration. Such interpretations seem to be a species of wish-fulfillment, springing from a romantic view of Chinese history. The extraordinary thing about Mao has not been reliance on the bloc of four classes, the parity role assigned to the peasantry, or the creation of a military force in China; it has been the consistency and essential changelessness of his views for the past thirty years. Mao is, if anything, a rock-ribbed Leninist in his adherence to Bolshevik ideology, including its conceptions of revolution, the nature of the party, the road to power, and the conduct of the party's dictatorship after it comes to power. Because Mao is not a Stalin, we should not be blinded to what he is. The view here expounded is that Mao and Maoism are simulacra, insofar as is humanly possible, of Lenin and Leninism.

Thus the Communist version of Marxism, whether it comes from Moscow or Peking or both, has become even more committed to the essential aims set out by Lenin. Communism in Southeast Asia has to be understood in global as well as in local terms. Its strategy in Southeast Asia, as elsewhere, is designed for the ultimate achievement of monopolistic power, whether it pursues the varieties of its classical left or right tactics. An implicit argument of this study—one which required frequent reference to Communism in China—concerns the strategic importance of Southeast Asia to Peking. Communist China covets the rice bowl both as a source of food and as an area for emigration. All of Southeast Asia represents a source of raw materials and, eventually, a market for an industrialized China. It would be folly to underestimate the area's pre-eminent importance to Communist China, and hence to the Moscow-Peking bloc.

In Thailand, Communism has not yet anchored itself strongly enough to make a bid for power. Since the late 1920's it has been forced to operate underground. Aboveground front organizations and internal propaganda have been singularly ineffective, but this is hardly a basis for complacency. The strength of Communism among the numerous overseas Chinese in Thailand cannot yet be accurately gauged.

Communism has been successful in splitting Viet Nam at the seventeenth parallel. North Viet Nam and North Korea are Soviet bloc satellites, in different degrees under the control of both Moscow and Peking, but otherwise entirely comparable to the Eastern European satellites. That the Republic of Viet Nam has outlawed Communism has not prevented the Communist movement from carrying on a persistent campaign of subversion and even a type of guerrilla warfare, though the latter has not yet been mounted, perhaps cannot be mounted, in strength.

In Burma and Indonesia the Communist bid for power initially failed. A crypto-Communist party has operated openly in Burma since December 1950. It has some parliamentary strength, which grew between the elections of 1951 and 1956. Though the Burmese government has largely succeeded in mopping up the remaining insurrectionary pockets, it faces two new dangers: the legalization of the Burma Communist Party, and elec-

tions which, in view of the split in the Anti-Fascist People's Freedom
League and the accelerated rate of Communist surrenders, may strengthen
the Communist minority. The phenomenal growth of the Indonesian Communist Party, both in the local Javanese and the national elections, has
obviously worried many anti-Communists inside and outside Indonesia.
Internal and regional conflicts between the center and the outlying islands
have weakened Indonesian stability, while President Sukarno's concept
of "guided" or "balanced" democracy has not yet evidenced its hoped-for
therapeutic qualities. In the late spring of 1958, Sukarno indicated his
concern about all this by downgrading Communist representation in his
advisory council. But Communist electoral strength and Communist labor
organization do not appear to have lost their momentum. It is important
to note, however, that the leadership of the Armed Forces in Burma, no
matter how committed to democracy they may be, will not permit any
"legal" Communist electoral victory. A "Kerala" is not probable in Burma,
nor under the present Army leadership in Indonesia. This is one of the
basic meanings of the politico-military involvement in those two countries.

Why the Communists have been so successful in Java since their defeat
at Madiun in 1948 ought to be the subject of a special study, though some
of the reasons have been suggested in the chapter on Indonesia, above.
That they have been successful cannot be denied. As has been noted
above, Communist "right" strategy may be more dangerous than the "left"
variety, particularly in Asian countries.

But Marxism has also had a democratic component, and it is this aspect
which, after an aborted start in Indonesia in World War I days, came later
to Southeast Asia. In this process it has, as in Western Europe, sloughed
off many of the doctrinal niceties which used to be debated at various
congresses of the Second International.

In the final analysis, if Marxism is to be democratic, it logically must
respond to new experience; for that is what the democratic element in it
stands for. This kind of Marxism in Southeast Asia, as in Western Europe,
has come to be called "democratic Socialism." In broad outline it has given
some positive definition and content to postindependence nationalist philosophies.

Some authorities on, and practitioners of, Socialism would refuse to
use the word "Marxism" with a "democratic component." U Nu in Burma
has taken this stand. But Marxism has produced a considerable European
movement which is both truly democratic and avowedly Socialist. Its
supporters equate democratic Socialism with something called Marxism.
"Democratic Socialism," or Socialism with a firm commitment to the rights
and freedoms of the individual, is a phrase increasingly used in Southeast
Asia, instead of the generic term "Marxism."

The split in the Anti-Fascist People's Freedom League of Burma has left both sides, that of U Nu and Thakin Tin and that of U Ba Swe and U Kyaw Nyein, with a generous number of committed Socialists. The issues that gave rise to the split were domestic policies and personalities, not doctrinal differences. Whichever side wins in the 1960 elections will not substantially alter the ideology of democratic Socialism as defined at length by U Nu at the Third All-Burma AFPFL Congress, in January 1958. A new party system may emerge, at least for a time. If the split is not eventually healed, the "single-party" Socialist parliamentary democracy in Burma, comparable to that of the Congress party in India, will probably develop into a three-party or three-part political system not dissimilar from Western prototypes: Liberal-*cum*-Socialist, Socialist, and Communist.

Indonesia is already on the way toward such a three-party system: a secular nationalist-socialist group, a religious-state nationalist group, and a Communist party. Democratic Socialist ideas and programs, whether so designated or not, pervade the first two. It is questionable whether the present Indonesian Socialist party, PSI, despite its ideological influence and especially its clear understanding of totalitarian Marxism and Communism, will regain in the immediate future the political power it once wielded. Its future may resemble the history of the British Independent Labor Party in the framework of the absorptive capacity of the Labor Party.

In Thailand, Socialism as an ideology is at best vague and meagerly understood. Its stage of development is pre-Marxian, highly eclectic, and not particularly sophisticated; and it constitutes little more than a borrowing of not very appropriate symbols for the purpose of expressing partially analyzed discontents with the prevailing military governments. Unlike Burmese, Indonesian, and Vietnamese Marxism, Socialism in Thailand cannot appeal to a previous colonial history to rationalize its development. Moreover, it cannot be fully expressed unless its leaders are prepared to suffer political and perhaps economic reprisals. The short-lived, Phibul-inspired Hyde Park and related movements do not seem to have much of a future, primarily because there is still some expectancy regarding the paternalistic endeavors of General Sarit's government.

Viet Nam presents a different level of development. Its official hostility to Marxism, regarded as Communism, does not prevent various members of the ruling elite and assorted intellectuals from espousing Socialist ideas and programs, provided that the ideas and programs are not so identified. The country's leaders include a number of ex-Marxists in addition to well-educated, politically sophisticated individuals. The orientation in Saigon is still predominantly nationalist and centralized—an environment which can move in any political direction. The Socialist party, as indicated earlier, is a pious gesture in the direction of traditional Marxian Socialism.

The continuing ideological relationship between democratic Socialism and nationalism has affected both. Socialism has largely retained the Marxian analysis of capitalism and imperialism, with its emphasis on economic causation in history, but it has yielded to nationalism by de-emphasizing or abandoning the Marxian concepts of the division of (indigenous) society into contending classes and of class struggle based on the aspirations of the proletariat. Thus Socialism and nationalism, particularly in Burma and Indonesia, are jointly directed toward overthrowing colonialism, developing national strength, and gaining a rightful place for the Southeast Asian countries among the democracies of the world.

"Socialism," "democratic Socialism," or "People's Socialism" (terms used interchangeably by Asian non-Communists) gained acceptance in Burma and Indonesia and avoided dogmatic rejection in Thailand and Viet Nam because they were able to convert into a positive social philosophy the fourfold negative revolt which characterized the preindependence struggles. Resentment of alien political domination now became a positive commitment to political democracy based on universal suffrage, respect for law, an independent judiciary, and a constitution in which individual and social rights were protected. Opposition to alien economic domination was transformed into planning and building a mixed economy in which public, private, and joint enterprise were employed to advance the public's welfare. The struggle against alien cultural domination turned into a movement for free public education at every level, state encouragement of indigenous arts, and a new concern for museums, libraries, and historical monuments. Hostility to racial domination gave rise to theories of cultural pluralism which recognized and respected religious, ethnic, and racial differences without sacrificing national unity.[116]

The merger of nationalism and Socialism is not easily dissolved again, because both standpoints rest on the same experiences. It might be expected, for example, that the current religious revivals in Burma and Indonesia would separate the nationalists from the Socialists—the former as potential or actual supporters of the revival, and the latter as neutral or negative toward it. The Socialists, however, are on record as "respecting religious conviction and sentiment," although they oppose religious "fanaticism," especially where it is "employed as a weapon for political ends." In addition, many Socialists in Burma and Indonesia are completely convinced religionists. They see their respective religions in complete harmony with their Socialist principles. There are secular, neutral, and religious elements among both Socialists and nationalists. The issue of a secular versus a theocratic state would range all Socialists and most nationalists on the same side. Many Asian Socialists, however, and most nationalists would accept a state in which religion occupied a special place, as it does in several European countries.

Socialists and nationalists in Southeast Asia are committed at least in principle to democracy both as means and ends and to large degrees of state responsibility for public welfare. Since the Socialists have never been particularly doctrinaire, nationalists can join them when they describe their outlook in such terms as "fighting for the independence and maturity of mankind . . . free from oppression and exploitation and humiliation," and having "the humanitarian spirit" which "rejects" and "abhors Communist methods that lead to spiritual degradation."[117] Neither in Southeast Asia nor elsewhere, however, does practice conform to philosophy. Two examples may be cited. Asian societies, both on the mainland and in the islands, place high value on communal responsibility whether of the family, village, clan, tribe, or region. Hence a philosophy which puts primary emphasis on individual rights does not receive prompt acceptance in these societies. When the Burma government had to meet this problem after independence, it asked the question: What kind of system should be used for administering the areas outside the capital city and provincial urban communities? Gradually it formulated a concept to which it gave the name "Devolution of Power." This concept did not aim to restore to the village its precolonial, communal character, but offered a compromise between that and the respect for "individual rights" bequeathed by the colonial experience. The Burmese were aware that the national government would be to a considerable extent imposing a new kind of democracy upon that which had been historically associated with village life. The latter proceeds by consensus and compromise, the former by the assertion and upholding of an individual claimant if his claim is validated. Indonesia, too, must face the same question which the Burmese have begun to answer: Will the two kinds of democracy mix? "Time," as Ulysses said to Achilles, "has a wallet at his back."

The second example concerns race relations. Under the colonial system, Asians were treated as beings inferior to the white masters. Upon gaining independence, they were resolved to put an end to racial and ethnic discrimination. The major Socialist-nationalist leaders now display, in their interethnic relationships, the human values which they extol, but beyond this display not much is done to face the ethnic problem in legislative or educative ways. Burma, having at the outset created a Federal Republic which constitutionally recognizes the major geographic-ethnic divisions, has gone further than any other Southeast Asian country in attempting to solve the problems of a multiethnic or multicultural society. In conversation, even educated Burmans would probably deny the existence of ethnocentric attitudes as between the majority Burman and the various minority peoples. But these attitudes do exist, as the outsider soon discovers.[118] In Indonesia the persistence of the concept of a unitary state has in no small measure been responsible for recent conflicts between the Javanese majority and the Sumatran, Sulawesian, and other minorities. Even within Java, differences are found between the Javanese and the Sundanese minority. In Viet Nam, besides the long-standing attitudes of the dominant Vietnamese toward the "Moi" and other hill peoples, recent migrants from the North are not yet fully at home with their southern neighbors. In Thailand, with a more homogeneous population, such differences are much less significant than elsewhere in Southeast Asia.

During the summer of 1956 and again in 1958, the author revisited Southeast Asia, with stopovers in London, Paris, and The Hague, and recorded some five hundred interviews. While hardly comprising a scientific sample, the interviewees in the former metropolitan capitals comprised officers in the colonial and foreign offices, archivists, research professors, and representatives from all Southeast Asian countries who were then resident in these capitals. In Southeast Asia the interviewees were cabinet members, scholars, journalists, civil servants, politicians, trade-unionists, businessmen, and personnel from various embassies in the Southeast Asian capitals. Among the indigenes were ex-Communists who had an intimate knowledge of some of the events treated in these pages, since they had participated in them. The questions put to these individuals varied, but in most instances an attempt was made to elicit some kind of descriptive and normative answer about the role of Socialism and Communism in the area or country with which the interviewee was most familiar. The Westerners, whether interviewed "at home" or abroad, generally replied that non-Communist Marxism in Southeast Asia was nondoctrinaire and little concerned with "the books." It was based on ideas and slogans derived from anticolonial and anticapitalist attitudes and nearly always included nationalist ideas of culture and welfare.

One of the most able British Labourites expressed regrets at his party's lack of interest in Burmese (not Indian) preindependence affairs. An able civil servant at the Quai d'Orsay felt that the French in Indochina had been like the British in Burma and unlike the Dutch in Indonesia, in that even so-called left or Socialist coalition governments at home did not attempt in their colonial policy to carry out Marxist ideas. He described their policies in a well-worn French political mot: "They were like a radish, red on the outside and white on the inside."

In Southeast Asia, leading ex-Communists and well-trained Socialists usually complained that, despite the numerous varieties of left-wing thought represented in the area, there were few well-read or well-trained Marxists to be found at any time. This may have been a plaint "over the snows of yesteryear," but they usually cited "in proof" the difficulty of setting up Marxist study groups, which had been an earlier fashion. One student indicated that the Communists in his country still conducted Marxist study groups for college students, texts for which could be bought cheaply or freely acquired at the Soviet embassy. However, he said, if one seriously raised questions at such group meetings, one would be branded as a "deviationist" or "opportunist" and either made to conform or be ostracized. There was general agreement that the idea of class struggle was foreign to the societies of Southeast Asia and that any kind of non-Communist Marxism had to take account of this fact. One of the leading Socialist theoreticians in the area pointed out that if Marxism should ever revert to its antireligious bias, it would irreparably suffer; but if its appeal was couched in terms of a welfare society guarding against extremes of poverty and wealth, it would prove highly acceptable to indigenous religious leadership.

No Asian among the interviewees failed to stress one or more of the four negative elements in the Marxist-nationalist revolt against colonialism. On the positive side, both nationalists and Socialists placed increasing emphasis on the values of human personality, human dignity, and human rights. The need to retain contact with the indigenous culture without being, or appearing to be, so Westernized as to cause rejection by the members of that culture was one of the reasons offered to explain why Socialism in Southeast Asia had to merge in a general way with nationalism. One, but only one, of the reasons offered for the poor showing of the Indonesian Socialists in the 1956 elections was their failure to observe this factor. On the other hand, because the Burmese Socialists gave attention to this, they were aided in repeating in 1956 their earlier 1951 victory. The Southeast Asian Socialists recognized that the time for advertising grandiose plans had long since passed. In the words of a leading Burmese cabinet minister, a Socialist, either they would be able to "deliver" on their plans for development and economic growth in the next few years or "they deserve[d] to be thrown out at the next elections."

Events of the past decade have slowly but surely extruded the Communists from the nationalist-Marxist amalgam. Political leadership today can, if it will, clearly identify and separate itself from the apparatus of international Communism. If it chooses not to do so, the choice is conscious, whatever the reason. What appears to be developing in Southeast Asia is a tropical variant of the Scandinavian pattern. Planned economic growth and social welfare, with heavy emphasis on education and cultural regeneration, accompany—or in fact help to compose—a philosophy based on Western democracy and Socialism and indigenous nationalism and culture.

NOTES

See Bibliography for full titles and publication data

CHAPTER 1: THE STUDY DEFINED

1. Karl A. Wittfogel, *Oriental Despotism*, p. 425.

2. John H. Kautsky, *Moscow and the Communist Party of India*.

3. *Ibid.*, especially Chapters 1 and 7, *passim*. See also the same author's "Neo-Maoism, Marxism and Leninism," *New Leader*, XL (December 16, 1957), 12–16.

4. I have here used the 71-page pamphlet edition published by Workers Library Publishers, New York, 1935. Wang Ming, in his speech of August 7, 1935, *The Revolutionary Movement in the Colonial Countries,* at the Seventh Comintern Congress, strongly supported Dimitrov. His argument runs that the anti-imperialist united front demanded the continuing effort of the Communist party to win this hegemony throughout China and over all allies, etc. (pp. 36–39).

5. Kautsky believes that the distinctive Neo-Maoist strategy was developed during World War II. He does not believe that "chief reliance on the peasantry" is "absolutely essential to the Neo-Maoist strategy," for he recognizes that "some reliance on the peasantry is not a new Communist policy." Thus he breaks with the views advanced in Benjamin I. Schwartz, *Chinese Communism and the Rise of Mao,* pp. 191 ff. The latter is concerned, among other things, with establishing the deviations of Maoism from "basic Marxist-Leninist tenets" precisely on the issue of the Maoist "heresy," i.e., a peasant- instead of a proletarian-based party. See also Lucian W. Pye, *Guerrilla Communism in Malaya*, pp. 27–40, for an interpretation differing from both Kautsky and Schwartz. Though Schwartz may have the better of the argument with Kautsky, both views are debatable because they posit in effect a *single* Marxist-Leninist orthodoxy. The futility of searching for it leads some writers into extravagances.

6. Benjamin Schwartz, in Howard L. Boorman *et al.*, *Moscow-Peking Axis*, Chapter 3, pp. 112–41, states, "at the risk of some oversimplification," that "in the prolonged and complex discussion of ['Ideology and the Sino-Soviet Alliance'] . . . over the past decade, the outlines of three overriding points of view can be discerned[:] . . . the monistic ideological approach, the sociological approach, and the power approach." Schwartz recognizes that there may well be overlap as well as subgroupings in these approaches. I would regard the use of the word "monistic" as question-begging. Marxists claim to be "scien-

tific" and "monistic," but in fact Marxism is shot through with varieties of meta-physical and epistemological dualism. Otherwise, the conception of the role of Marxism herein expounded is a combination of these three approaches in which the factor of shared ideology, however much it varies at different periods, is the necessary cement.

W. W. Rostow, in *The Dynamics of Soviet Society, passim,* defends an analysis of that society based upon "the concept of the priority of power." How-ever, he regards "the history of society [including Soviet society] as a fully in-teracting process . . . [in which] ideology contributed to the emergence of the priority of power. . . . [Ideology] furnishes a common vocabulary and agreed set of concepts. . . . [It is a] prism through which the regime looks at the world. . . . [It serves] as a rationale for the pursuit of power by a political dictatorship. . . . [It is even] an indispensable overt medium for conducting conflicts over power and policy substance." In short, though Rostow argues for the "priority" of power, neither he nor any other analyst of Marxism can avoid what I here call the crucial character of ideology. For historically the ideology created the movement and not the reverse, though admittedly the movement has changed the ideology. This assertion applies to the Russian as well as other Marxists, as L. H. Haimson amply demonstrates in his *The Russian Marxists and the Origins of Bolshevism.*

7. The system, like so much in Marxism, arose as a polemic. Its exposi-tion therefore is frequently fragmentary. Marx and Engels set forth their views in the early 1845–46 writings (*The German Ideology,* Parts I and III, pp. 6 f. and *passim;* this edition includes the *Theses on Feuerbach*). The views of 1845 remained substantially unaltered in Engels' *Ludwig Feuerbach and the Out-come of Classical German Philosophy* (1888); see Chapter 4. For the "seven meanings" and "a naturalistic" interpretation of the dialectic, see Sidney Hook, "Dialectic and Nature," *Marxist Quarterly,* I (April–June 1937), 253–84. Cf. Max Eastman, *Marxism: Is It Science?,* pp. 299–350. For the polemic aspect, see Hook, *From Hegel to Marx.*

8. Engels in *Anti-Dühring* (1877), Plekhanov in *In Defence of Materialism* (1895) and more particularly in *Fundamental Problems of Marxism* (1908), Lenin in *Materialism and Empirio-Criticism* (1909), and Stalin in *Dialectical and Historical Materialism* (1938) and *History of the Communist Party of the Soviet Union,* pp. 102–35, present classic examples of Marxist polemics and ex-positions of dialectical materialism. J. B. S. Haldane's *The Marxist Philosophy and the Sciences* is one of a number of attempts by a non-Russian scientist to demonstrate the pertinency of dialectical materialism to the natural sciences. For a contemporary treatment of Marxism as philosophy, see H. B. Acton's *The Il-lusion of the Epoch* and a discussion of this interesting volume by J. and M. Miller, "A New Stage in the English Study of Marxism," *Soviet Studies,* VII (January 1956), 275–95, with a reply by Acton in *ibid.,* pp. 409–11.

9. Pp. 10–15. See also *The German Ideology,* pp. 16–43; and Engels, *Socialism Utopian and Scientific* (this version, with a special introduction by the author, in 1892, was first prepared for a French edition in 1880). Engels quotes the Goethean "Im Anfang war die That." This idea and a class interpre-tation of the Hobbesian *bellum omnium contra omnes* are apposite summations of dialectical and historical materialism.

10. Marx, as Trevor-Roper clearly points out, never claimed originality for discovering "the existence of classes" or "the class struggle." He claimed, as he wrote to Joseph Weydemeyer in March 1852: "[W]hat I did was to prove:

(1) that the existence of classes is only bound up with particular, historic phases in the development of production; (2) that the class struggle necessarily leads to the dictatorship of the proletariat; (3) that this dictatorship itself constitutes the transition to the abolition of all classes and to a classless society." (Hugh Trevor-Roper, "Marxism and the Study of History," *Problems of Communism*, V, [September–October 1956], 38.)

11. In this sense, Lenin's *What Is To Be Done?* (1902) and *Two Tactics of Social-Democracy in the Democratic Revolution* (1905), his stand on the antiwar resolution of the 1912 Basle congress of the Second International, his analysis of World War I and hence his call for "revolutionary defeatism" at the first and second Zimmerwald meetings of 1915–16 (the latter was held at Kienthal), and his preparation in 1916, publication in 1917, of *Imperialism, The Highest Stage of Capitalism* represent because of subsequent events the most significant undergirding and expansion of the Marxist philosophy of history.

12. Especially Lenin's formulation on "National and Colonial Questions." (See *The Second Congress of the Communist International*, "as reported and interpreted by the newspapers of Soviet Russia," pp. 38–45. The theses of this meeting and others of the Comintern are reprinted in *The Communist Conspiracy*, Part I, Sec. C, "The World Congresses of the Communist International.") Lenin here addresses himself particularly to the relation of Communists to the peasants and nationalist movements in colonies and semicolonies. He had the support of Maring (H. J. F. M. Sneevliet), who had recently come from "Dutch India," but was opposed by M. N. Roy, who unsuccessfully defended the thesis opposing collaboration with nationalist liberation movements. There is little difference between Leninist strategy in 1920 and Maoism. For an interesting "Third Period" formulation which clearly combines the "block of four classes" with "united front from below" tactics, see Orgwald, *Tactical and Organizational Questions of the Communist Parties of Indo-China and India: In Questions and Answers*, printed in the U.S.A. at the press of *The Pan-Pacific Worker* [n.d., ca. July 1933].

13. Lenin, *Marx-Engels Marxism*, particularly "Imperialism and the Split in Socialism" (1916), pp. 389–409. I do not mean to ignore the work of the Austrian and other Socialists (O. Bauer, Hilferding, Rosa Luxemburg, etc.) on imperialism; in the final analysis, however, it is Lenin whose work, and more particularly whose name, has been identified with the politically consequential "theory" of imperialism. It was this development which turned his attention to the colonies and semicolonies, particularly in Asia; and further it led directly to the assignment of the national and colonial question to Stalin, for whom it became a major preoccupation in the 1920's.

14. The import of the Marxist historical synthesis has been commented upon frequently; Joseph A. Schumpeter's Chapters 1–4 in his *Capitalism, Socialism and Democracy* are extremely perceptive.

15. It may be said that Marxism in the West had a theoretical need to "welcome" the historical tendencies of capitalism: the more capitalism the better. For as enterprise increased in scale and concentration, as the individual employer and his small labor force succumbed, the "system" was increasingly readied for revolutionary change and socialization.

16. E.g., *The Eighteenth Brumaire of Louis Bonaparte*. "Man makes his own history. . . . The tradition of all past generations weighs like an alp upon the brain of the living. At the very time when men appear engaged in revolutionizing things and themselves, in bringing about what never was before, at

such very epochs of revolutionizing crises do they anxiously conjure up into their service the spirits of the past, assume their names, their battle cries, their costumes, to enact a new historic scene." There is more of this, amply describing, exhorting, and analyzing the differences between bourgeois and proletarian revolutions and above all predicting the end of proletarian fear, the awareness of "that situation . . . which renders all retreat impossible and [in which] conditions themselves cry out: 'Hic Rhodus, hic salta.' "

17. *What Is To Be Done?*, p. 175.

18. *Communist Manifesto*, p. 30.

19. Among others, R. N. Carew Hunt, in his *Theory and Practice of Communism*, p. 161, points out that Lenin's central thesis, imperialism as a "direct continuation of the fundamental properties of capitalism in general," is "not a work of any theoretical originality, and is simply an excellent popularization of J. A. Hobson's *Imperialism* (1902) and Rudolph Hilferding's *Finanz-Kapital* (1910) to which Lenin added certain practical political conclusions of his own." For the purposes of the present study, the presumed lack of originality in Lenin's work is of far less significance than its effectiveness. Stalin's evaluation is the more pertinent one, especially for an understanding of Marxism in Asia. Lenin, according to Stalin, yoked the national and colonial questions together. He broadened the issue so as to include "the countless millions of Asiatic and African peoples that were suffering under the yoke of national oppression." (*Problems of Leninism*, pp. 73–80.) By contrast with Lenin and Stalin, the Marxist leaders of the Second International had certainly minimized their attention to the colonial peoples of Asia and Africa.

20. "What the 'Friends of the People' Are" (1894), in Lenin, *Marx-Engels Marxism*, pp. 112 f.

21. E. H. Carr, *The Bolshevik Revolution, 1917–1923*, p. 7.

22. Stalin, *The Foundations of Leninism*, pp. 96–110. That the manipulation of the party—and the purges—remained as an essential element in Stalin's dictatorship does not require further comment. But it is important to note that Stalinism retained until the dictator's death this organizational conception. He was thus able to identify himself, the party, and the U.S.S.R. with one of the "two camps" in the world, the other being the class-imperialist enemy. At the Fourteenth CPSU Congress, December 18–31, 1925, Stalin developed, at some length, his views on the "international question," and particularly on the "two camps, two centers of attraction." (*Works*, VII, 289.) From this view he never deviated. It underscored his hostility to any European or Asian "third force" conceptions. See R. C. Tucker, "The Psychology of Soviet Foreign Policy," *Problems of Communism*, XI (May–June 1957), 3 f. Tucker dates Stalin's "two-camp" polarization "as early as 1927," but it can be found at least as far back as an article in *Izvestiia*, February 22, 1919.

23. U Ba Swe, *The Burmese Revolution*.

24. "The Indonesian Communist Party," *Eastern World*, XI (December 1957), 22. Darsono outlined these views to me in an interview in August 1956.

CHAPTER 2: MARXISM IN BURMA

1. Geoffrey Fairbairn, "Aspects of the Burmese Political Scene," *Pacific Affairs*, XXIX (September 1956), 211.

2. *The Nation*, Rangoon, January 30, 1958.

3. Kyaw Nyein, "A Burmese View of New Colonialism: The Elements of Soviet Imperialism," *Socialist Call*, XXII (October 1954), 13.

4. Rupert Emerson, "The Progress of Nationalism," in P. W. Thayer (ed.), *Nationalism and Progress in Free Asia*, p. 73.

5. Htin Aung, "The Progress of Nationalism, Commentary," in Thayer, p. 83.

6. Kyaw Thet, "Burma: The Political Integration of Linguistic and Religious Minorities," in Thayer, p. 167.

7. Htin Aung, in Thayer.

8. G. E. Harvey, *British Rule in Burma, 1824–1942*, London, 1946, pp. 25–29. Theravada Buddhist tradition frowns on such worldly activity as politics, but it nonetheless demands and receives a recognized place in the state.

9. "K," "Burma in My Life-Time," *The Guardian*, III (March 1956), 22.

10. *Ibid.*, III (February 1956), 25.

11. *Ibid.*, III (March 1956), 23.

12. F. Tennyson Tesse, *The Story of Burma*, London, 1946, p. 70.

13. Frank N. Trager, review of Dr. Maung Maung, *Burma in the Family of Nations*, in *Far Eastern Survey*, XXIV (February 1957).

14. Virginia M. Thompson and Richard Adloff, *The Left Wing in Southeast Asia*, p. 77.

15. See his introduction to Thakin Nu, *Burma Under the Japanese*, London, 1954. J. S. Furnivall writes on Burmese affairs from more than fifty years experience there.

16. Thakin Nu, *Burma Under the Japanese*, p. 3. Whether these Communists were responding to the threat of Fascism, in the fashion of the Seventh Comintern, or to the invasion of the U.S.S.R. by Nazi Germany and the formation of the wartime "Western" Alliance is not clear.

17. *Ibid.*, p. 7.

18. Tun Pe, *Sun Over Burma*, Rangoon, 1949, p. 94.

19. See Trager, "Political Dynamics," Chapter 18 in Trager (ed.), *Burma*, III, 959–1005. See also Maung Maung Pye, *Burma in the Crucible*, Rangoon, 1951, pp. 1–50; and John L. Christian, *Modern Burma*, Berkeley, Calif., 1942, or *Burma and the Japanese Invader*, Bombay, 1945, Chapters 5 and 13.

20. The writings of U Ba Choe (Deedok) have not yet been collected. He may have early been attracted to Marxism and was certainly a socialist in the thirties. Teacher, journalist, and writer, Ba Choe in 1936 founded both the Burmese Journalists' Association and the Fabian League, neither one of which appears to have established any foreign ties. Elected to the legislature as a Fabian Socialist, Ba Choe formed an opposition bloc with three radical candidates of the Dohbama Asiayone (We Burmans Association), who had campaigned under the title Komin Kochin (One's Own King, One's Own Kind) Party.

21. Maung Maung Pye, p. 28.

22. Tun Pe, p. 34. Others say the purchases included "complete sets" of Marxist writings.

23. Notes from an unpublished lecture by Kyaw Thet, Professor of Far Eastern History, University of Rangoon, delivered at the University of Rangoon, November 24, 1954.

24. *Ibid.*

25. Maung Maung, "Mr. Justice Chan Htoon," *The Guardian*, II (December 1954), 35. It should be pointed out that such study groups exist at the present time, a number of them the particular target of Marxist groups. It was

through such groups that the Burmese Workers and Peasants Party, for example, built up its student following. One young Burmese Foreign Service Officer, recently graduated from the University of Rangoon, reports that he was a member of a Marxist study group which obtained its literature from the Soviet embassy. The FSO so reporting was expelled from the study group for "deviationism"—he had expected a critical study and questioned both the content and interpretation of the literature.

26. Christian, *Burma and the Japanese Invader*, p. 243.

27. Government of Burma, *Burma Handbook*, Simla, 1944, p. 106.

28. John S. Furnivall, introduction to Thakin Nu, p. xxiv.

29. Kyaw Thet, unpublished lecture notes.

30. Maung Maung Pye, p. 40. In later years the slightness of the provocation so embarrassed U Nu that he wrote to Mr. Sloss in 1955, apologizing for his irresponsibility and asking forgiveness. As quoted in the *New Times of Burma* of December 29, 1955, Mr. Sloss replied: ". . . [I]n taking, I am able honestly to say, the chief place in the provision of a students' Union, I knew it would involve us in political differences arising out of the impetuosity of the younger and the caution of the older people. But our conviction was that the University and . . . the Union must train the men who would replace us in the administration and government of all the affairs of the Burmese people."

31. In retrospect, the student strikes of the thirties appear to have been on the whole quite orderly. Newsreel films of them have recently been incorporated into a documentary film on the Burmese nationalist movement put out by the A.1. Studios in Rangoon. In the films one can see and hear Burma's contemporary leaders U Nu, Aung San, and U Raschid as students leading demonstrations before the Secretariat Building in Rangoon.

32. Christian, *Burma and the Japanese Invader*, p. 187.

33. Harvey, p. 48.

34. Maung Maung, "U Ba Swe," *The Guardian*, III (March 1956), 28. *The Guardian* since late 1954 has carried a remarkable series of profiles of Burmese leaders prepared by Dr. Maung Maung. Among others, he has written of U Nu, U Ba Swe, U Kyaw Nyein, Bogyoke Ne Win, U Tun Win, U Thant, U Vum Ko Hau, U Hla Maung, M. A. Raschid, and Thakin Than Tun.

35. According to the official biographical sketch put out by the Ministry of Information, "he left the University for national politics . . ." *Burma Weekly Bulletin*, New Series, V (June 21, 1956), 74.

36. Trager (ed.), *Burma*, III, 1010. Chapter 19 of the same work, "The Labor Movement," pp. 1006–62, summarizes the development of the labor movement and its political interconnections.

37. Maung Maung, "U Ba Swe," p. 28.

38. Quoted in *ibid*.

39. Trager (ed.), *Burma*, III, 1021.

40. See, e.g., P. P. Pillai, *Labour in Southeast Asia, a Symposium*, New Delhi, 1947, p. 118. There is in this study no mention of ABTUC, while the Burmese labor movement is described in terms of "inertia and apathy."

41. Kyaw Thet, unpublished lecture notes. Malcolm Kennedy, in his *A History of Communism in East Asia*, pp. 221 f., 304, refers to Thakin Thein Pe and Goshal as having formed a Burma Communist Party in August 1939. This date must be that of the founding of the People's Revolutionary Party, which

under the leadership of Thakin Mya, Aung San, U Ba Swe, and U Kyaw Nyein evolved into the Socialist party.

42. *Burma Handbook*, pp. 114–23; at p. 114.

43. The ten were Thakins Nu and Shu Maung (Ne Win), to become Prime Minister and Commander-in-Chief, respectively; Aung San, Mya, and Deedok Ba Choe, who have since died; and Thakins Than Tun, Ba Sein, Tun Oke, Kadaw Hmaing, and Thammami Tun Shein, who came to stand in the opposition or have dropped out of politics. Membership in the RUSU, participation in the student strike of 1936, membership and official capacity in the Dohbama Asiayone or the Thakin party and in the 1939 Thakin-sponsored good-will mission to Chungking, and visits to India and the National Congress conferences were items considered worth mentioning.

44. Cf. M. Collis, *Last and First in Burma*, London, 1956, *passim*.

45. Thakin Nu, pp. 2 f.

46. Collis, p. 205.

47. Cf. Maung Maung, "Thakin Than Tun," *The Guardian*, III (October 1956), 33–36, among others.

48. *Who Is Right, the AFPFL or the Communist Party?* This is a compila tion of Communist party documents and AFPFL commentary originally published in mimeograph form in Burma sometime in 1952. The Burmese document was made available to Frank N. Trager, who had a literal translation prepared in New York and has circulated it privately.

49. Maung Maung, "U Kyaw Nyein," *The Guardian*, II (March 1955), 16.

50. Collis, pp. 232–36.

51. Maung Maung Pye, pp. 177–83; at p. 183.

52. Maung Maung, "Thakin Than Tun," p. 36.

53. Cf. *Who Is Right?* throughout.

54. Maung Maung, "Thakin Than Tun," p. 35.

55. *Who Is Right?*

56. *Ibid.*

57. Maung Maung, "U Kyaw Nyein," p. 17. The reference is to the then governor of Burma.

58. *Ibid.*

59. *Who Is Right?*

60. Thakin Soe was described by the Burmese government in 1949 as "one of the most picturesque personalities Burma has produced in recent years . . . [He] reads voraciously and writes profusely . . . [He is] ruthless in his methods and combines in himself the qualities of a terrorist, a voluminous pamphleteer and a dauntless campaigner." (See Government of Burma, *Burma and the Insurrections*, Rangoon, 1949, pp. 2 f.)

61. This remains the policy of the CP(B) today.

62. *Who Is Right?*

63. Thakin Nu, *Towards Peace and Democracy*, Ministry of Information, Rangoon, 1949, p. 26.

64. For a detailed discussion, see Albert Somit and Janet Welsh, "The Constitution and Government," Chapter 17 in Trager (ed.), *Burma*.

65. *The Constitution of the Union of Burma*, Rangoon, 1947.

66. Somit and Welsh, in Trager (ed.), *Burma*, p. 910.

67. *The Constitution of the Union of Burma*, p. 5.

68. *Ibid.*

69. *Ibid.*, p. 6.

70. *Ibid.*, Sec. 41.

71. *Ibid.*, pp. 53 f. Actually, though the constitution has not been amended, these strictures have had to be modified, and currently the government is doing its utmost to attract foreign investment into the country to carry out much-needed development programs.

72. U Mya, *Two-Year Plan of Economic Development in Burma*, Rangoon, 1948, p. 40.

73. *Ibid.*, p. 21.

74. Directorate of Information, Union of Burma, "Chronology of Events," in *Burma's Freedom, The First Anniversary*, Rangoon, 1949, pp. 56–61.

75. J. Russell Andrus, *Burmese Economic Life*, Stanford, 1948, p. 356.

76. Document (typewritten) in possession of F. N. Trager. It includes in addition fourteen pages of "Notes on the Program" for the "decisive period of revolutionary possibilities."

77. Interview, dated Calcutta, December 20, 1947 (mimeographed).

78. Thakin Nu, *Towards Peace and Democracy*, p. 51.

79. "Than Tun's Greetings to the Second Congress of the Communist Party of India," dated February 28 [1948] (mimeographed).

80. Government of Burma, *Burma and the Insurrections*, p. 41.

81. *Ibid.*, p. 16.

82. *Ibid.*, p. 18.

83. *Ibid.*, Appendices.

84. *Ibid.*, p. 32.

85. For a detailed discussion of the struggle between the government and the insurgents and of the reasons for the government's survival, see "Insurgent Movements," and "Why the Insurgents Failed," Chapters 20 and 21 in Trager (ed)., *Burma*, III.

86. Even today, June 1957, after more than nine years of strife, though the general amnesty offer ended on March 31, 1956, the government is still allowing private citizens to act as go-betweens and is willing to guarantee to surrendering insurgents clemency for their crimes.

87. Thakin Nu, *Towards Peace and Democracy*, pp. 55–64.

88. *Ibid.*, pp. 92–94.

89. "Will the United Nations be a repetition of the League of Nations? Will the member nations only think of their own safety and leave the smaller nations to their fate . . . ? Korea has dispelled these doubts . . . Henceforth, if aggression occurs elsewhere, there too the United Nations must step in . . . This is the great hope, the only hope for small member nations like us . . . It is only fitting that Burma whole-heartedly supports the United Nations in the step they have taken in Korea." (Thakin Nu, *From Peace to Stability*, Rangoon, 1951, p. 100.)

90. Milton Sacks, "The Strategy of Communism in Southeast Asia," *Pacific Affairs*, XXIII (September 1950), 232, 234. Certainly the victory of the Chinese Communists over Chiang Kai-shek heavily reinforced the left-wing parties of Southeast Asia—and whetted their appetites for power.

91. *New Times of Burma*, December 9, 1950.

92. *The Nation*, December 12, 1950.

93. The competing labor organization founded by the BWPP after its

ouster, the Burma Trade Union Congress (BTUC), attracted only a small following and remains weak.

94. *The Nation*, December 24, 1950.

95. *The Nation*, June 9, 1957.

96. Founded at Rangoon with the sponsorship of the government in January 1953, the Conference claims a membership of over 600,000 in nine countries, 16,000 of these members being Burmese. Burma also provides the Conference with three of its major officers: Ba Swe as chairman, Kyaw Nyein as treasurer and chairman of the Anti-Colonial Bureau, and Hla Aung as one of its joint secretaries.

97. *Three Years of the Asian Socialist Conference*. Though it is not affiliated with European Socialist parties, the Conference looks on them with approval and cooperates where possible.

98. U Ba Swe, *The Burmese Revolution*, 1952.

99. *Ibid.*, p. 3.

100. *Ibid.*, p. 5.

101. *Ibid.*, p. 6.

102. *Ibid.*, pp. 6 f.

103. *Ibid.*, p. 7.

104. Cf. "N. N." (U Mya Sein), "Buddhism and Marxism," *The Guardian*, III, No. 8, 18–20. Cf. also Francis Story, *Buddhism Answers the Marxist Challenge*, Rangoon, 1952.

105. U Ba Swe, p. 7.

106. *Ibid.*, p. 11.

107. *Ibid.*, p. 17.

108. *Ibid.*, p. 18. This is one of the very few "class" references applied to Burma by government leaders in the postindependence period.

109. *Ibid.* See also U Ba Swe, "The Burmese Revolution," *Burma*, II (July 1952), 10.

110. *Ibid.*, p. 24.

111. U Ba Swe, "May Day Address," *Burma*, III (July 1953), 1–10.

112. *Ibid.*, p. 4.

113. *Ibid.*, p. 10.

114. *Burma Weekly Bulletin*, New Series, III (May 5, 1954), 25, 28–31.

115. *Ibid.*, p. 28.

116. U Ba Swe, "Burma Builds for Socialism," *Socialist Asia*, II (March 1954), 4.

117. *Ibid.*, p. 6; italics added.

118. Directorate of Information, *The Pyidawtha Conference*, August 4–17, 1952.

119. See U Kyaw Nyein, "Burma's Eight Year Plan," *The Guardian*, III (November 1955), 41 f. For an over-all presentation, see Donald Wilhelm, Jr., and Louis Gordon, "Planning for Economic Development," Chapter 23 in Trager (ed.), *Burma*, III. See also Trager, "Toward a Welfare State in Burma," New York, 1954 (mimeographed). Note further modifications currently under way, as reported in *The Nation*, June 9, 1957.

120. *The Nation*, June 9, 1957.

121. *Ibid.*, May 31, 1955.

122. The chamber of commerce in Rangoon is by far the most influential economic group to be found in the country. Its membership represents the major sources of private capital available for investment purposes in Burma.

123. *Burma Weekly Bulletin,* New Series, IV (March 1, 1956), 380.
124. *Ibid.,* V (March 14, 1957), 394.
125. In 1951 the AFPFL and its associated parties won 53.4 per cent of the total vote; and the combined opposition, 46.6 per cent. In 1956 it was 55.2 to 44.8 per cent.
126. *New Times of Burma,* May 2, 1956.
127. U Ba Swe, "The Socialism of Asia—When Democracy Looks Ahead," *Socialist Call,* XXIV (June 1956), 15.
128. Foreign Affairs Committee of the Burma Socialist Party, *Socialism,* Rangoon, 1954, p. i.
129. U Ba Swe, "The Socialism of Asia—When Democracy Looks Ahead," p. 14.
130. *Ibid.,* p. 15.
131. See the *Reporter,* November 15, 1956, p. 8.
132. *Asian Socialist,* June 1954, p. 9.
133. U Ba Swe, "Asian Socialists Look Ahead—excerpts from the Chairman's Report," *Socialist Call,* XXV (January–February 1957), 20.
134. Maung Maung, "U Kyaw Nyein," p. 8.

CHAPTER 3:   THAILAND AND MARXISM

1. John F. Embree, "Thailand — A Loosely Structured Social System," *American Anthropologist,* LII (1950), 181–93.
2. *Ibid.,* p. 182.
3. Dr. Luang Suriyabongse, *Buddhism in Thailand,* p. 20.
4. James C. Ingram, *Economic Change in Thailand Since 1850,* pp. 43 f.
5. Happily, more information is becoming available all the time. The extensive researches of the Cornell Thailand Project in Bang Chan (see Lauriston Sharp *et al., Siamese Rice Village*) and individual scholars are building up the stock of information.
6. Embree, p. 188; Sharp *et al.,* pp. 153–55. Note also Sharp's definition (pp. 16–18) of the Bang Chan community as the clients of the school and temple, with its implication, supported by evidence, that there are few, if any, other community institutions. Charles Madge, in his *Village Communities in Northeast Thailand,* finds somewhat greater elements of cooperation in his area but also notes the free and open nature of the Thai village.
7. The population of Phra Nakhon (Bangkok) province increased at a rate of 37.62 per cent in the period 1919–29 and 29.86 in the period 1937–47, against the national rate of 24.97 and 20.59 for the same periods, respectively. It should be noted that the 1937–47 period includes the war years, which temporarily arrested the urban flow. (*Statistical Year Book of Thailand* [1952], p. 8.) A population survey of Bangkok Municipality in 1954 showed that about 38 per cent of the population had migrated to the city within the previous seven years. Of these about 96 per cent were from other areas of Thailand. (*Economic and Demographic Survey, 1954,* 1st Series, Municipality of Bangkok. Thailand, Central Statistical Office, 1954, mimeographed, Tables 15 and 16.)
8. The village of Bang Chan, which has been under study by the Cornell Thailand Project, is known to have been founded, so to speak, about eighty years ago. Migration into the village, however, has been going on continually.

How widespread this situation is, of course, remains an open question. (Sharp et al., pp. 23 f.)

9. H. G. Quaritch Wales, *Ancient Siamese Government and Administration*, p. 59; W. A. Graham, *Siam*, I, 237–38.

10. Mary Rosamond Haas, "The Declining Descent Rule for Rank in Thailand: A Correction," *American Anthropologist*, XXIII (1951), 585–87.

11. Quaritch Wales, pp. 35, 49 f.; M. R. Kukrit Pramoj, "The Social Order of Ancient Thailand (II)," *Thought and Word*, I (March 15, 1955), 17 f.; Graham, I, pp. 234–37.

12. The *sakdi na* as a part of the civil service organization has been replaced by a civil service law along competitive lines. As a mode of structuring society, it disappeared with the reorganization of interior administration and the abolition of slavery and *corvée* obligations in the reign of Čhulalongkọn (1868–1910). (See Walter F. Vella, *The Impact of the West on Government in Thailand*, pp. 332–50; and Graham, pp. 223–29.)

13. Sharp (ed.), *Handbook on Thailand*, pp. 158–91.

14. *Ibid.*, p. 165.

15. *Ibid.*, pp. 162–64.

16. Discussion of the Chinese minority as such has been excluded from this chapter. This social group will be considered only insofar as it affects the attitude of the Thai people toward Marxism. There are several good studies of the Chinese in Thailand, for which see Sharp et al., *Bibliography of Thailand*, Data Paper No. 20, Ithaca, N.Y., 1956, pp. 59–64. Virginia M. Thompson and Richard Adloff's *The Left Wing in Southeast Asia* has considerable discussion of the role played by Marxism among the Chinese in Thailand.

17. *Statistical Year Book of Thailand* [1952] pp. 336–42.

18. The remaining 5 per cent are unclassified.

19. Ingram, pp. 56 f.

20. Sharp (ed.), *Handbook on Thailand*, pp. 431–35.

21. Manich Jumsai, *Compulsory Education in Thailand*, "UNESCO Studies on Compulsory Education," VIII, Paris, 1951, 56–61.

22. Kasem Udyanin and Rufus D. Smith, *The Public Service in Thailand*, p. 41.

23. The following discussion is impressionistic, based upon several years of teaching in Thai schools and universities and associating with educated Thai men and women.

24. See "USIS Press Section Summary of Editorials and Special Articles from the Thai Language Daily Newspapers," Bangkok (mimeograph ed.), e.g., November 21 and December 21, 1956, and *passim*.

25. Ingram, p. 209.

26. *Economic Farm Survey, 1953*, p. 38.

27. Ingram, p. 208.

28. *Farm Survey*, p. 38.

29. *Ibid.*, p. 32.

30. *Ibid.*, pp. 62–63.

31. *Ibid.*, pp. 70–73.

32. Ingram, pp. 210–11.

33. *Ibid.*, pp. 144 f.

34. Thailand, Central Statistical Office, *Economic and Demographic Survey, 1954*, 1st Series, Municipality of Bangkok (mimeograph ed.), Table 20.

35. *Ibid.*, pp. 26–29.

36. *Ibid.*, pp. 87–92. Government trading in rice was abandoned in 1955. *Economic Survey of Asia and the Far East, 1956,* Bangkok, UNECAFE, 1957, p. 162.

37. Ingram, pp. 139–44.

38. *Economic Survey of Asia and the Far East, 1956,* pp. 163, 166.

39. *Statistical Year Book of Thailand* [1952], p. 340.

40. Ingram, p. 142.

41. Richard Coughlin, "The Status of the Chinese Minority in Thailand," *Pacific Affairs,* XXV (December 1952), 378–89.

42. M. Sivaram's *Mekong Clash and Far Eastern Crisis* gives an account of the Franco-Thai dispute heavily biased toward the Thai point of view.

43. This was written before the *coup d'état* of October 1958, which ended the "democratization" policy, and dampened—not to say soaked—press criticism of, among other things, Americans.

44. Vella, pp. 334–49; Graham, pp. 305–7. The king brought foreign advisers from a number of European countries, as well as from Japan, in a studied policy aimed to avoid the domination of any single country.

45. *Bangkok Times,* August 13, 1932, as quoted in Kenneth P. Landon, *Siam in Transition,* p. 23.

46. Landon, pp. 15–17.

47. *Ibid.*, p. 259.

48. John Coast, *Some Aspects of Siamese Politics,* p. 17.

49. *Ibid.*, pp. 27–32. Two recently published autobiographical volumes by Netr Kemayothin, who, as an officer attached to the army general staff, was involved in anti-Japanese activities with the approval of Phibun Songkhram, throw considerable light on the Thai attitude of the time: *Chiwit Nai Phon* (*Life of a General*), Bangkok, 1954; and *Ngan Dai Din Khọng Phanek Yothi* (*The Underground Activities of Colonel Yothi*), Bangkok, 1957.

50. Vella, pp. 317–31. The term "bureaucracy" as used here includes both civil and military officials. This usage is particularly justified by history in Thailand. In the traditional administrative system before the end of the nineteenth century, although there was a formal distinction between civil and military affairs, in fact there was little distinction in the administrative activities of these two divisions of government. After the reorganization of government under Čhulalongkọn, this distinction became something of a reality, but since the ascendancy of the military group in politics after the *coup d'état* it has become a formal distinction again. Almost all high officials and political leaders are now generals and vice versa, whether they be professional soldiers or not.

51. "Thai Noi," *Phraya Phahon,* Bangkok, n.d., pp. 15–17; Vella, pp. 356 f.

52. Coast, p. 31.

53. Vella, pp. 388 f.

54. *Royal Thai Government Gazette from the Thai version,* Bangkok, LXXII (1955), 725–27.

55. Ernest L. Fogg, "Labor Organization in Thailand," *Industrial and Labor Relations Review,* VI (1953), 368.

56. Medhi Dulyachinda, "The Development of Labour Legislation in Thailand," *International Labour Review,* LX (November 1949), 473.

57. Fogg, p. 369.

58. Richard Deverall, "Thailand: Free Unions' Difficult Path," *International Free Trade Union*, VIII, No. 5 (1953), 5.

59. Fogg, p. 370.

60. *Bangkok Post*, July 7, 1954.

61. *Ibid.*, January 4, 1957.

62. Ingram, p. 68.

63. *Ibid.*, p. 69.

64. *Ibid.*, p. 74.

65. Vella, pp. 327–31.

66. Thompson and Adloff, pp. 51–75.

67. *Ibid.*, pp. 56 f.

68. *Ibid.*, p. 60. Some observers think, on the other hand, that the Communist Party of Thailand is a creature of the Chinese Communist Party in Thailand.

69. Vella, p. 364.

70. *Ibid.*, p. 389.

71. Nai Pridi Phanomyong, *Khaw khrong kansetakit khǫng Luang Pradit Manutham Lae Phrabaromarachawinitchai* (*The Economic Plan of Luang Pradit Manutham and the Royal Judgment on It*), Bangkok, 1956. A translation of this pamphlet plus various other documents related to it are available in Landon, Appendix III.

72. Landon, p. 260, italics added.

73. *Ibid.*, p. 261.

74. *Ibid.*, p. 265.

75. *Ibid.*, p. 267.

76. *Ibid.*, pp. 281–83.

77. *Ibid.*, pp. 285–88.

78. *Ibid.*, pp. 283 f.

79. *Ibid.*, pp. 278–80.

80. *Ibid.*, p. 306.

81. *Ibid.*, p. 307.

82. *Ibid.*, p. 314.

83. *Ibid.*, p. 304.

84. *Ibid.*, p. 306.

85. *Ibid.*, pp. 251–52. The act was amended in 1935, after Pridi's plan was out of the way, making the use of force a restricting qualification upon the definition.

86. *Ibid.*, p. 34.

87. Thompson and Adloff, pp. 70–72.

88. *Ibid.*, p. 71.

89. *Ibid.*, pp. 74 f. This does not mean that international communism lacks contacts in Thailand. Reports are, however, that contacts are made from China through Hong Kong.

90. *Royal Thai Government Gazette*, LXIX (1952), p. 489.

91. *Bangkok Post Supplement*, January 1, 1953.

92. Thompson and Adloff, p. 54.

93. *Khǫmmunit Thai čha Tham Arai nai Prachuban* (*What the Thai Communists Will Do Now*). 1945.

94. *Ibid.*, p. 4.

95. *Ibid.*, p. 5.

96. *Ibid.*, pp. 29–35.

97. *Ibid.*, pp. a–d.

98. Thompson and Adloff, p. 61. The two papers were *Chon Kammachip* (*Working People*) and *Lok Mai* (*New World*).

99. Alexander MacDonald, *Bangkok Editor,* New York, 1949, pp. 205–6.

100. The daily *Khao Phap* is an old paper which has been through many lives. The two weeklies—*Muan Chon* (*Masses*) and *Phithuphum* (*La Patrie*)—appeared to be financed more fully than advertising and circulation revenues would permit.

101. Vella, p. 388.

102. Coast, p. 47.

103. Thompson and Adloff, p. 63. There is an apocryphal version of this story still current in Bangkok. After meeting with a representative of the British Labour Party, who carefully explained the party and British Socialism to him, Phibun is reported to have turned to a cohort and declared, "This Labour Party business sounds like a good thing. See what you can do about getting one organized."

104. *Bangkok Post,* November 10, 1952, *et seq.*

105. Suphot Tantrakun, *Khabuan kan ku chat* (*National Liberation Movement*). Bangkok, 1957.

106. See pp. 181–82 and note 54. The act was repealed and parties outlawed again by the *coup d'état* in October 1958.

107. *Bangkok Post,* January 16, 1957.

108. *Royal Thai Government Gazette,* LXXII (1955), 780.

109. Darrell Berrigan, "Thailand: Pibul Tries Prachathipatai," *Reporter,* XIV (June 14, 1956), 30–33.

110. *Royal Thai Government Gazette,* LXXIII (1956), p. 252.

111. Born in Bangkok, the son of a carpenter, Prakǫb passed through secondary school in the capital. He was an employee of the Bangkok Water Works and worked in the State Railway workshop. In 1950 he became head of the Railway Workers Union in the workshop. In 1952 he became an employee of the Thai National Trade Union Congress. In 1955 he became head of the Labour Party of Thailand. Some observers believe him to be a front man for other more militant union organizers in the Labour Party.

112. *Royal Thai Government Gazette,* LXXII (1955), p. 785. This reference to "just fruits of their labour" is as near to Marxism as the party policy comes.

113. *Bangkok Post,* January 8, 1957. In the February 1957 election the Socialist Front won ten seats: eight Economist seats in three northeast provinces, one Hyde Park in the northeast, and one Hyde Park in a central province where two slates of government party candidates ran against each other. In December the Economists lost two of their eight and the Hyde Park one of their two. The Free Democrats went from eleven in February to five in December. Many of the more vocal leaders of the Socialist Front were arrested following the *coup d'état* in October 1958.

114. By "Ong Aphiradi" (pseudo.), *Daily Mail,* July 28, 1952 (weekly edition), pp. 12 f., 46–49.

115. By "Navaboon" (pseudo.), *Phithuphum* (*La Patrie*), November 12, 1951, pp. 28 f., 36–38.

116. Thep Chotinuchit was born the son of a lawyer and government official in Nakhǫn Phatom, just west of Bangkok. He was educated there through

secondary school and then took a law degree from the old Law Institute in Bangkok in 1924. He also has an M.A. in economics from Thammasat University. His first job was as manager of a government opium den. He then began his legal and political career. He was appointed a judge in 1937. He was elected for the short parliament of that year, serving as M.P. from Srisaket province in northeast Thailand. Defeated in 1938, he was reappointed to his judgeship, which he held until 1946. In 1947 he was elected again from Srisaket. From 1949 to 1951 he was Assistant Minister of Commerce in Field Marshal Phibun Songkhram's fourth government. In 1955 he organized the Economist Party with two other M.P.'s from the northeast. In 1956 he took a trip to China at the invitation of the Canton Institute of Foreign Affairs. Upon his return he was arrested for this presumption. He is now the acknowledged leader of the Socialist Front, and as such was arrested in October 1958.

117. Born in Pattani province in south Thailand, the son of a rubber planter, Suthep was educated in Singapore. He studied at Thammasat University in Bangkok but received no degree. Before the 1957 election he had no political experience. He says that in 1956 a group of friends urged him to organize a political party on the left. As head of the Social Democrat Party, he was one of the party's two candidates, both in Bangkok. He joined in the Socialist Front with the three other so-called Socialist parties. He has been a white-collar employee of an import-export firm for ten years.

118. Born in a village southwest of Bangkok in 1912, Wisit lived and received his elementary education there. At the age of seventeen he went to the Khlong Rangsit area in the central plain to find work. At the age of twenty he joined the army and was stationed in Bangkok. From 1936 to 1951 he was a worker in the shops of the State Railway organization. For four years he appears to have had no regular job. In 1956 he became known as the head of the tiny Socialist Party and was its only candidate in the 1957 election.

CHAPTER 4:   MARXISM IN VIET NAM

1. The text of the Declaration of Independence may be found in Harold R. Isaacs, *New Cycle in Asia*, pp. 163–65. A slightly different text taken from an English translation by an agency of the Viet Nam government may be found in Allan B. Cole (ed.), *Conflict in Indochina and International Repercussions*, pp. 19–21.

2. French Indochina was the geographic area in mainland Southeast Asia bounded by China to the north, the South China Sea to the east and south, and Thailand and Burma to the west. It consisted of the French-conquered kingdoms of Laos and Cambodia and the former Viet Nam Empire. Legally, Laos and Cambodia were protectorates. The Viet Nam Empire was divided into three parts, corresponding to its three major territorial divisions: North, Central, and South Viet Nam, and designated respectively as Tonkin, Annam, and Cochinchina by the French. Tonkin and Annam were legally one protectorate, while Cochinchina was a French colony.

3. The name Vietnamese is applicable to the principal linguistic and ethnic population stock of the former Viet Nam Empire. The Chinese also referred to this state as Annam (Pacified South), whence the alternate name "Annamese" to designate the people. The French adopted this term and then narrowed its use for the inhabitants of Central Viet Nam (Annam), as distinct from the "Tonkin-

ese" in the north and "Cochinchinese" in the south, to foster separatism. Since 1945 ,the older usage has been restored and is officially used in both North and South Viet Nam today.

4. Official material on the negotiations and settlement may be found in *Documents relating to the Discussion of Korea and Indo-China at the Geneva Conference, April 27–June 15, 1954, and in Further Documents relating to the Discussion of Indo-China at the Geneva Conference, June 16–July 21, 1954.*

5. This period is treated extensively in Pierre Pasquier, *L'Annam d'autrefois: Essai sur la Constitution de l'Annam avant l'intervention française.*

6. The religious conceptions of the Vietnamese are treated in Raymond Grivaz, *Aspects Sociaux et Economiques du Sentiment Religieux en Pays Annamite.*

7. Cora Du Bois, *Social Forces in Southeast Asia,* p. 31.

8. A fuller description of the Viet Nam monarchy may be found in Robert Petit, *La Monarchie Annamite.*

9. The most extensive treatment of Vietnamese secret societies is contained in Georges Coulet, *Les Sociétés Secrètes en Terre d'Annam.*

10. This economic transformation is treated extensively in Charles Robequain, *The Economic Development of French Indo-China.*

11. Le Thanh Khoi, *Le Viet-Nam Histoire et Civilisation,* pp. 381–85.

12. Marius B. Jansen, *The Japanese and Sun Yat-sen,* pp. 112–26.

13. Virginia M. Thompson, *French Indo-China,* p. 480.

14. Leon Trotsky, "Manifesto of the Communist International to the Workers of the World," adopted at the First World Congress of the Communist International (March 2–6, 1919), reprinted in Leon Trotsky, *The First Five Years of the Communist International,* I, 23–25.

15. No authoritative biography of Ho Chi Minh exists. Most accounts repeat the French Indochinese police data given in Gouvernement Général de l'Indochine, Direction des Affaires Politiques et de la Sûreté Générale, *Documents,* Vol. IV: *Le "Dong Duong Cong San Dang."* Curiously enough, even the propaganda agencies of the Viet Nam government have issued contradictory versions based on this data. Cf. Viet Nam News Service, *Fifty-eighth Birth Anniversary of Ho Chi Minh;* or Viet Nam Information Service, *Viet-Nam's President Ho Chi Minh* (the English version appeared in November 1947). Paul Rivet, "Le Drame Franco-Vietnamien," *Cahiers Internationaux,* June 1949, p. 46, claims that Ho was a member of the Socialist party as early as 1914. The present author has tried to reconcile the conflicting versions emerging from his research in France. The biographical data which follow are a reconstruction from personal interviews and documentation as indicated.

16. Leo Figueres, *Je reviens du Viet-Nam Libre: Notes de Voyage,* p. 130.

17. Le Thanh Khoi, p. 440, gives as his original name Nguyen Van Cung. This is incorrect. His original name is Nguyen Tat Thanh (Nguyen Who Will Certainly Succeed). Other of his aliases include Ly Thuy and Song Man Cho. Cf. Viet Nam News Service, pp. 11 f.

18. Robert S. Elegant, *China's Red Masters,* p. 205.

19. Gerard Walter, *Histoire du Parti-Communiste Français,* p. 73.

20. *Ibid.,* p. 104.

21. S. R. Mohan Das, *Ho Chi Minh: Nationalist or Soviet Agent?,* pp. 2 f.

22. Vème Congrès de l'Internationale Communiste (17 June–8 July, 1924), *Compte-Rendu Analytique*, p. 231.

23. *Ibid.*

24. Nguyen Ai Quoc, *Le Procès de la Colonisation Française.* The succeeding material paraphrases and quotes from this pamphlet.

25. Roy Jumper, "Mandarin Bureaucracy and Politics in South Viet Nam," *Pacific Affairs*, XXX (March 1957), 47–58.

26. A government official and agricultural engineer who founded the newspaper *La Tribune Indigène* in 1917 to support the liberal program of the then Governor-General Albert Sarraut.

27. A former customs official and current journalist who published the newspaper *L'Echo Annamite* to support the demands of civil servants.

28. A prominent Saigon lawyer.

29. *La Lutte*, Saigon, November 1, 1934.

30. George Garros, *Forceries Humaines*, pp. 89 f. The appendix contains documents outlining the program of the Constitutionalist Party.

31. *La Cloche Fêlée*, Saigon, December 12, 1923.

32. A prominent nationalist who later turned toward Communism.

33. See Gouvernement Général de l'Indochine, Direction des Affaires Politiques et de la Sûreté Générale, *Documents*, Vol. I: *Le Tan Viet Cach Menh Dang.* The bulk of this study of the New Viet Nam Revolutionary Party was prepared by a leader of the organization. Restoration of Viet Nam was the first name of this organization. See below, pp. 119 ff.

34. Le Thanh Khoi, pp. 403 f.

35. See below, pp. 120 ff.

36. Thompson, p. 314.

37. Jean Chesneaux, *Contribution à l'Histoire de la Nation Vietnamienne*, p. 203.

38. *La Lutte*, November 22, 1934, contains information to this effect in a letter written by Nguyen An Ninh.

39. Gabriel Gobron's *Histoire et Philosophie du Cao Daisme* contains an official statement of the views of this religious movement.

40. William Henry Chamberlin, *Blue Print for World Conquest*, Washington, D.C., 1946, contains the full text of the "Theses and Statutes" of the Communist International's Second World Congress, July 17–August 7, 1920. These include the "Theses on the National and Colonial Questions" pp. 118–31.

41. Allen S. Whiting's *Soviet Policies in China, 1917–1924* contains an excellent treatment of part of this problem.

42. See Benjamin I. Schwartz, *Chinese Communism and The Rise of Mao*, pp. 46–78.

43. The history of this group is covered in Gouvernement Général de l'Indochine, *Documents,* Vol. IV, dealing with the Indochina Communist Party. All quotations and information, unless otherwise indicated, are taken from this document.

44. A. F., "The Revolutionary Movement in French Indochina," *International Press Correspondence (Inprecor)*, Vol. VI (September 2, 1926).

45. Xenia J. Eudin and Robert C. North, *Soviet Russia and the East, 1920–1927*, pp. 269 f.

46. *Inprecor*, Vol. VIII (November 21, 1928), indicates that Piatnitsky

ber 15, 1932, cited in Anh Van and Jacqueline Roussel, *Mouvements Nationaux et Lutte de Classes au Viet-Nam*, p. 53.

83. Orgwald, *Tactical and Organizational Questions of the Communist Parties of Indo-China and India*. pp. 69–93.

84. The Indochinese Communists were advised to join all the "national reformist, trade union, peasant and other organizations with a mass following and form Communist fractions inside them." It was necessary to conduct illegal work but at the same time the Communists were to "avoid being buried," etc.

85. "Under the direction of the Communist Party, through armed insurrection, the Indochinese workers will drive the imperialists out of their country, will create a workers' and peasants' power, will return the land to the laboring peasants. Through the anti-imperialist and agrarian revolution, the Communist Party will lead the revolutionary masses forward towards the struggle for the final transition to socialism." (Quoted in Anh Van and Roussel, p. 53.)

86. "Indochina—The Construction of the Revolutionary Party," *Quatrième Internationale*, November–December 1938.

87. *Labor Action*, October 27, 1947.

88. *La Lutte*, April 24, 1933.

89. *Ibid.*, April 29, 1933.

90. *Ibid.*

91. *Inprecor*, XIII (June 16, 1933), 575.

92. Chesneaux, p. 215.

93. Gouvernement Général de l'Indochine, *Documents*, V, 293–307, contains the text of Indochina Governor-General Pasquier's reply to the Committee's memorandum.

94. G. Péri, "The Workers' Delegation in Indochina," *Inprecor*, XIV (June 8, 1934), 884 f. Most commentators usually refer to the Chinese Communist Party as having achieved this leading position in the period following its conquest of the Chinese mainland in November 1949. This quotation and later admonition by the Chinese Communists of the Indochina party (see below, p. 136) would indicate that the Chinese Communist Party had achieved pre-eminence in some Asian Communist circles at a much earlier date.

95. Personal interview with individuals who have direct knowledge of this period.

96. *Cahiers du Bolshevisme*, 11th Year (July 1, 1934), pp. 796–800. Subsequent quotations are from this source.

97. *Ibid.*, August 14, 1934, pp. 957–68.

98. Franz Borkenau, *European Communism*, pp. 115–62, contains an extended discussion of this policy of the French Communists and of the Communist International.

99. This action was in line with Trotsky's call for a new Fourth International, since the Communist International was, after its debacle in Germany, now deemed irrevocably bankrupt as a revolutionary force.

100. *La Lutte*, October 4, 11, 25, and November 1, 1934, issues *et seq.*

101. *Ibid.*, January 17, 1935.

102. It is said that the Communist party was able again to hold a congress in Macao under the aegis of an "exterior directing committee" in 1935. This congress reaffirmed the support by the Indochina Communist Party of the Communist International, adopted a form of party organization equivalent to that of

the other national sections of the Comintern, and tightened the party organizationally and politically. The Central Committee was transferred to Saigon-Cholon. Le Thanh Khoi, p. 447, places the date of this congress in February 1935. Other sources, such as Philippe Devillers, *Histoire du Viet-Nam de 1940 à 1952*, p. 68, fn. 16, indicate that the Macao congress took place after the Seventh World Congress of the Communist International, July 25–August 25, 1935.

103. Nguyen Van Dinh, *Ta Thu Thau: Tu Quoc-Gia Toi Quoc-Te (Ta Thu Thau: From Nationalism to Internationalism)*, p. 66.

104. *La Lutte*, May 18, 1935.

105. *Ibid.*, June 8, 1935.

106. G. Péri, "The Anti-Imperialist Front in the Elections of the Colonial Council in Indo-China," *Inprecor*, XV (March 23, 1935), 353.

107. *Ibid.*, October 7, 1935, p. 1294.

108. *VII Congress of the Communist International—Abridged Stenographic Report of Proceedings*, Moscow, 1939, p. 604. This probably formalized the action of the April 1931 Comintern Executive Committee.

109. J. Lun, "The Popular Movement in Indochina after the Victory of the People's Front in France," *Communist International*, March–April 1937, p. 193.

110. Anh Van and Roussel, p. 56.

111. Personal interview with Louis Caput, January 15, 1954. He indicated that there had been a previous Socialist organization founded in Hanoi in 1928 consisting of French citizens. During the troubled period of 1930–32, it had called for action against the insurrectionary Vietnamese nationalists and Communists. This led to a split and its disintegration.

112. *La Lutte*, August 22, 1937.

113. Walter, p. 377.

114. The Trotskyist leader Ta Thu Thau engaged in a series of public debates in *La Lutte* with Nguyen An Ninh, the veteran revolutionary, who favored the People's Front. (Cf. *La Lutte*, March 18, 23, and April 1, 1937.) In the same issue that contained an article by Nguyen Ai Quoc under the new pseudonym of Hong Qui Vit (Hong Who Is Alive: to signify that he had not died in Singapore as was believed by many) in support of the People's Front, Ta Thu Thau wrote an article entitled "Against the People's Front of Betrayal," in which he directly attacked the French Communist Party. (Cf. *La Lutte*, May 13, 1937.) This internal struggle did not interfere with the joint presentation of candidates by La Lutte in the Saigon Municipal Council elections of May 1937. Ta Thu Thau, Nguyen Van Tao, and Duong Bach Mai were elected again.

115. Referred to in *La Lutte*, May 30, 1937.

116. This difficult situation produced rifts in the ranks of the Communist Party of Indochina. Duong Bach Mai, a leading Stalinist, was loath to accept the split policy. He indicated that there was an abyss between Stalinists and Trotskyists, "but in the particular situation in Indochina, unique in the world, where through the fault of Moutet and Brévié [French Colonial Minister and Governor-General of Indochina, respectively] the anti-imperialist struggle remains unchanged, the breaking of our fighting front, the only one which can be built with the Trotskyists and ourselves, will engender inextricable confusion among the masses, and kill all the combative ardor of our people. We do not overestimate in the slightest the strength of the Trotskyists. However, at the same time that we see their errors which arise from a sterile revolutionarianism,

we also acknowledge, until some new pattern emerges, that they are still trustworthy anti-imperialist elements, who deserve all our aid." (*La Lutte*, June 6, 1937.)

117. *Quatrième Internationale, op. cit.*

118. *La Lutte*, August 29, 1937.

119. Jean Hovan, "60 ans de lutte pour l'independence nationale," *La Verité sur le Viet Nam*, cites the Cochinchina Sûreté report which quotes the Communist newspaper *Le Peuple* at end of July 1939 to this effect.

120. *Labor Action*, October 27, 1947.

121. Devillers, p. 79.

122. *Ibid.*

123. The material in this section is similar to that in *Political Alignments of Vietnamese Nationalists*, prepared by this author. The account was based on the same Cochinchina Sûreté report cited above in Hovan. Quotations used by Devillers, pp. 78–80, are probably drawn from the same source.

124. An account of his role in Indochina during this period may be found in Jean Decoux, *A La Barre de l'Indochine*.

125. Devillers, p. 97, suggests that this decision was made because of "fear that an important part of the nationalist bourgeoisie would rally to the Japanese, and its example would influence profoundly the masses in the same direction." By "muting its 'class struggle' program and concentrating all its efforts on the nationalist plane, [the Viet Minh] thus would disarm (or at least attenuate) the fears of the anti-Marxist elites of China and Indochina."

126. Nguyen Van Dam, *Le Viet Nam en Marche*, pp. 27 f.

127. The attitude of the Viet Minh toward the European war is not known at this time. Germany did not attack the Soviet Union until June 22, 1941. Le Thanh Khoi, p. 457, is obviously quoting a later Viet Minh document which indicated that the Viet Minh was formed to "struggle in accord with the Allies against French colonialism and Japanese imperialism." Nor does Devillers, pp. 98–100, specify the date of the "fifteen page" Viet Minh program whose second major point, in contrast to Nguyen Van Dam's version above, reads: "alliance with the Democracies who are fighting fascism and aggression." The history of the Viet Minh at this early period is still obscure. Devillers, p. 97, indicates that Nguyen Ai Quoc first announced on September 8, 1941, the formation of the Viet Minh, constituted "to struggle against French and Japanese fascism until Viet Nam is totally liberated." Devillers further reports that the "first manifesto" of the Viet Minh was issued on October 25, 1941, and called for "union of all the classes, of all the revolutionary organizations, of all the ethnic minorities; alliance with all the other oppressed people of Indochina; collaboration with all the anti-fascist French elements; one aim: the destruction of colonialism and fascist imperialism."

128. Le Thanh Khoi, p. 458, suggests that the Kuomintang reacted to the Communist character of Viet Minh propaganda when its own alliance with the Chinese Communists was broken following the new Fourth Army incident. Nguyen Ai Quoc later said ironically that he had been arrested as a "French spy." (Isaacs, *No Peace for Asia*, p. 164.)

129. The best published account of this period is contained in Devillers, pp. 103–5.

130. The very day that the Viet Nam Revolutionary League was founded, the Viet Minh issued an independent appeal to "French nationals" and "French

soldiers" to "form an anti-fascist, anti-Japanese Viet-Nam–French front on Indo-chinese territory!" (Cited in *A Chronicle of Principal Events Relating to the Indo-China Question, 1940–1954*, p. 4.)

131. *Le Viet Nam en Lutte contre le Fascisme*, pp. 52–54, has excerpts of some Viet Minh documents.

132. "For the Complete Independence of Indochina," June 4, 1944, statement of the Indochina Communist Party. Text in *Témoignages et Documents Français Relatif à la Colonisation Française au Viet Nam*, pp. V5 f.

133. *Ibid.*, pp. V3 f., contains the complete text of the September 5, 1944, leaflet of the Viet Minh League: "To the French Soldiers and Legionnaires, To the Patriots and Anti-Fascist French in Indochina."

The dual policy of the Stalinists is borne out by Devillers, pp. 110 f., who detects "disappointment" on the part of the Viet Minh with respect to support from the Allies at this time and cites a Viet Minh document of August 6, 1944, which affirmed: "Our principle is to eliminate our enemies by playing one off against the other. It is necessary to exploit the others without letting ourselves be exploited. In the interior, we must compromise with the Gaullists and the Chinese. The Gaullists will struggle as a matter of fact against the French fas-cists, the Chinese will rise against the Japanese and the French from the moment that the Chinese army enters Indochina . . ." That this document is authentic is verified by excerpts used in an official publication of the Democratic Republic of Viet Nam–Nguyen Van Dam, pp. 32 f.

134. Devillers, pp. 106, 108, indicates that the Decoux administration col-laborated with the De Gaulle mission in Kunming and informed it that "Nguyen Ai Quoc and Ho Chi Minh were one and the same person, and that the Viet Minh to its own advantage was undoubtedly in the process of fooling the Chinese." The De Gaullists then tipped off the Chinese government to information they were clearly aware of!

135. The propaganda effect of this American aid was far more important than the limited military value of the trickle of arms provided. It contributed to the Viet Minh claim that it would have American support in the postwar period.

136. Official Communist sources now all specify December 22, 1944, as the "birth" of the Viet Nam Liberation Army, and it is so celebrated in the Democratic Republic of Viet Nam. Cf. *Ten Years of Fighting and Building of the Vietnamese People's Army*, Hanoi, 1955, pp. 11 f., which reads: "The first platoon of the Vietnamese People's Army initially called the Vietnamese People's Propaganda Unit for National Liberation and afterwards the Tran-Hung Dao platoon, was created on December 22, 1944, in the jungles of Cao Bang province. It consisted of 34 men and cadres and was equipped with 2 revolvers, 17 rifles, 14 flint lock rifles and one light machine gun. In the night after its formation, this platoon inaugurated its activities by completely annihilating two enemy posts, thus scru-pulously observing the order of President Ho Chi Minh that the first attack ought to be a victorious one."

The extent of guerrilla warfare actually conducted by the Viet Minh is a much-disputed question. Devillers, pp. 107–8, attributes the Viet Minh with having organized guerrilla forces in October 1943 in Bac Kan and Thai Nguyen provinces "of which, however, the major part had been furnished by Chu Van Tan [a leader of the Tho, an ethnic group inhabiting this mountainous region]." Devillers indicates that the Decoux administration cleared the region thereafter. This may account for the Communists' unwillingness to include the events as part of the history of their army. Chesneaux, p. 231, writes: "But up to 1943, directives counseled them [the guerrillas] to engage themselves rather in a 'labor of preparation and organization.' . . . In 1944, a true 'liberated region' was organized around Thai-Nguyen, while the partisan network consolidated itself in Nghe An (North Annam), in Quang Ngai (South Annam), and in Cochinchina. The Viet Minh Congress of July 1944, under these conditions, envisaged the eventuality of an immediate general insurrection; a project which Nguyen Ai Quoc, now called Ho Chi Minh, dismissed as premature." A Viet Minh source published very early makes no reference to the above and indicates that guerrilla operations began following the Japanese coup of March 9, 1945 (*Factual Records of the Vietnam August Revolution*, pp. 12 f.). Given the limited arms it possessed, most Viet Minh claims of extended guerrilla activity during World War II must be discounted as propaganda to substantiate their claims to leadership as a pro-Ally fighting force.

137. March 15, 1945, "Appeal to the population to fight the Japanese," *Factual Records of the Vietnam August Revolution*, pp. 19 f.

138. *Ibid.*, p. 13. The formal date for the merger of these zones is now officially June 4, 1945. (*A Chronicle of Principal Events Relating to the Indo-China Question, 1940–1954*, p. 7.)

139. Lucien, "Quelques Etapes de la Révolution au Nam-Bo du Viet-Nam," *Quatrième Internationale*, September–October 1947, p. 43. (Nam Bo is South Viet Nam, corresponding to Trung Bo, Central Viet Nam, and Bac Bo, North Viet Nam. This is the new nomenclature adopted in place of Cochinchina, Annam, and Tonkin by Vietnamese nationalists and Communists.)

140. See below, pp. 154–56.

141. *Factual Records of the Vietnam August Revolution*, pp. 21–23, contains the text of this appeal of July 1, 1945.

142. Devillers, p. 134, reproduces the text of this memorandum: "We of the Viet Minh League ask that the following points be announced by the French and observed in their future policy in Indo-China:

1) A parliament shall be elected by universal suffrage. It shall legislate for the country. A French governor will exercise the functions of president until our independence is assured. This president shall choose a cabinet or a group of advisers accepted by the parliament. The precise powers of all these organs will be delineated in the future.

2) Independence shall be given to this country in a minimum of five years and a maximum of ten.

3) The natural resources of this country shall be returned to the inhabitants after a just compensation of the present holders. France will benefit from economic privileges.

4) All the liberties proclaimed by the United Nations shall be guaranteed to the Indo-Chinese.

5) The sale of opium shall be prohibited.

"We hope that these conditions will be judged acceptable by the French government."

143. *Factual Records of the Vietnam August Revolution*, p. 13.

144. *Ibid.*, pp. 23 f., contains the text of this order.

145. *Ibid.*, p. 14.

146. Quoted from Devillers, p. 137.

147. Author's translation from *La République,* Hanoi, October 1, 1945. See also Isaacs, *New Cycle in Asia,* pp. 161 f., or Cole, pp. 18 f.

148. Tran Huy Lieu, "The Emperor's Golden Sword." Translated excerpts from this account by the Minister of Propaganda in the new Viet Minh government appear in *Factual Records of the Vietnam August Revolution,* pp. 25–32, and clearly show how skillfully the Communists utilized this historic occasion to legitimate their regime in the popular mind. The fuller implications on the popular level of this coming to power of the Viet Minh are explored in Paul Mus, *Viet-Nam: Sociologie d'une guerre.* Professor Mus also advances his interpretation of the impact of Communism in Viet Nam.

149. *President*: Ho Chi Minh. *Ministers* (all on the former Viet Minh People's Liberation Committee except as otherwise indicated): Foreign Affairs, Ho Chi Minh; Interior, Vo Nguyen Giap; Propaganda, Tran Huy Lieu; National Defense, Chu Van Tan; Youth, Duong Duc Hien; National Economy, Nguyen Manh Ha (a nonparty Catholic); Social Welfare, Nguyen Van To (nonparty technician); Health, Pham Ngoc Thach; Public Works and Communications, Dao Trong Kim (nonparty technician); Labor, Le Van Hien; Finance, Pham Van Dong; Without Portfolio, Cu Huy Can and Nguyen Van Xuan; Justice, Vu Trong Khanh; and National Education, Vu Dinh Hoe. (The latter two, together with Duong Duc Hien and Cu Huy Can, constituted the Democratic Party contingent in this government. The Democratic Party, founded in June 1944, was always an affiliate of the Viet Minh. Its role can best be compared to that of the officially approved minority parties in Communist China.)

150. The readers of *Cuu Quoc (National Salvation),* an official government newspaper, would have been surprised to know that the Nguyen Ai Quoc who signed an "Old Comrade's Heartfelt Letter" and Ho Chi Minh, President of the Democratic Republic of Viet Nam, were one and the same. (*Cuu Quoc,* Hanoi, August 29, 1945.)

151. The Declaration of Independence of September 2, 1945, was couched in terms taken from the American Declaration of Independence and from the French Declaration of the Rights of Man and of Citizens. Vo Nguyen Giap, in his speech on that day, said: "However, as far as China and the United States of America are concerned, we have had particularly intimate relations which it is for me a pleasant duty to dwell on. . . . The United States of America is a Republic which has no territorial interests in this country. They have paid the greatest contributions to the Vietnamese fight against fascist Japan, our enemy, and so the Great American Republic is a good friend of ours." (Quoted in Cole, p. 26.)

152. The United National Front was set up by a nationalist congress in Can Tho province in the period following the Japanese coup of March 9, 1945. Can Tho province during much of this period, March–August, was virtually an independent state under control of the Hoa Hao. Similarly, Tay Ninh province was controlled by, and the seat of, the Cao Dai.

153. Leaflet published by the Indochina Communist Party, August 17, 1945 (copy in possession of author). A portion of this leaflet is quoted in *La Verité sur le Viet Nam,* p. 42.

154. The members were Tran Van Giau, Nguyen Van Tao, Pham Ngoc Thach, Duong Bach Mai, Nguyen Van Tay, Hoang Don Van, Huynh Van Tieng, Pham Van Bach, and Nguyen Phi Oanh. With the exception of Pham Van Bach

and Nguyen Phi Oanh, these were all members of the Indochina Communist Party, although Huynh Van Tieng was now formally a member of the Democratic Party.

155. Even this committee had a majority of six Viet Minh members out of ten. Huynh Phu So, the Hoa Hao leader, was made a member. Phan Van Hum, of the Trotskyist Struggle Group, was made one of three alternate members. (*Bulletin d'Information*, Saigon, September 10, 1945.)

156. *Ibid.*

157. Now formally known as the Viet Nam Lao Dong Xa Hoi Dang (Viet Nam Socialist Workers Party). It published *Tranh Dau* (*The Struggle*) as a daily newspaper of 30,000 circulation in September 1945.

158. Lucien, p. 45. This agitation was opposed by the Viet Minh, whose representative, Nguyen Van Tao, is quoted as saying: "All those who have instigated the peasants to seize the landowners' property will be severely and pitilessly punished. . . . We have not yet made the Communist revolution which will solve the agrarian problem. This government is only a democratic government. That is why such a task does not devolve upon it. Our government, I repeat, is a bourgeois democratic government, even though the Communists are now in power." See below, p. 156.

159. In the provinces, there were clashes between the Viet Minh and Cao Dai or Hoa Hao troops. (*Bulletin d'Information.*)

160. Leaflet, September 7, 1945.

161. *Bulletin d'Information.*

162. Lucien, p. 48.

163. Among the more prominent opponents of varying political beliefs who were killed by the Viet Minh in this period were Pham Quynh (prominent mandarin), Ngo Dinh Khoi (mandarin brother of Ngo Dinh Diem), Bui Quang Chieu (Constitutionalist), Ho Van Nga (leader of the National Independence Party), and the Trotskyists Ta Thu Thau, Tran Van Thach, and Phan Van Hum. Devillers, p. 181, says: "The Communists gave the appearance of coldly applying a systematic program of elimination of their eventual adversaries."

164. "September 11, 1945, an Indochina Communist Party Congress posed, among others, the following fundamental principle: 'The Party takes for itself alone the leadership of the Viet Minh Front.'" (*Ibid.*, p. 143.)

165. Devillers, p. 181, reports that Duong Bach Mai told him: ". . . he was employed in calming the tempestuous ardor of the militants at the base, in showing them that the task of the moment was not to make a proletarian revolution but to smash 'colonialism' by calling on *all* the people to struggle against it." This verifies the remarks attributed to Nguyen Van Tao. (See above, fn. 158.)

166. Devillers, p. 184, cites government circular text in *Quyet Chien*, Hué, November 21, 1945.

167. See above, p. 142. This same policy was later summed up in an article by French Communist Raymond Barbé: "At the present time, faced with imperialists' designs, the common interest of the Overseas people and the French people is to remain united and to put everything to work so that the brotherhood of diverse races be really ensured. In a world where, the war barely ended, and apart from the fifth of the globe where socialism is being built, the great world powers are looking for new pretexts, every attempt to leave the French Union can only lead to an illusory and momentary pseudo-independence, and the

strengthening of imperialism." ("Les Problèmes de l'Union Française," *Cahiers du Communisme*, New Series, October 10, 1946.)

168. Isaacs, *No Peace for Asia*, p. 173.

169. An extended discussion of the events associated with the Chinese occupation and an interpretation thereof from a French point of view may be found in Pierre Célerier (pseud.), *Menaces sur le Viet Nam*, pp. 1–80.

170. See above, p. 149.

171. *La République*, October 25, 1945, contains the text of declaration of unity and statements.

172. *Ibid.*, November 18, 1945. This move was opposed by Tran Van Giau and others, mostly from South Viet Nam, where the Indochina Communist Party had been functioning independently and Viet Minh organization was weak.

173. The elections originally had been provided for in a decree dated September 8, 1945. An official description is contained in *Les Elections Générales et L'Assemblée Nationale Constituante Vietnamienne*.

174. Devillers, p. 216, reports that Ho Chi Minh offered to step down as president in favor of Bao Dai in February because "the Viet Minh could not obtain Viet Nam's independence since all the powers mistrusted it." Apparently, the Viet Minh leadership, or at least part of it, was prepared to relinquish power at that time. The Chinese forced the opposition groups to enter into the coalition, thereby permitting Ho Chi Minh to retain his office.

175. For the text of this agreement, see Cole, pp. 40–42. The fate of South Viet Nam was to be decided by a popular referendum whose results the French would accept. The best discussion of these negotiations and subsequent Franco-Vietnamese relations is contained in Devillers, pp. 241–356.

176. Devillers, p. 230, cites the translation of the speech made from *Quyet Chien*, Hué, March 8, 1946.

177. *Ibid.*, p. 231.

178. The Chinese and French signed an agreement on February 28, 1946, prior to the March 6 agreement (text in Cole, pp. 7–9). French troops actually entered Hanoi on March 18, 1946, after arranging for the withdrawal of Chinese troops to begin on March 15, with complete withdrawal by March 31, 1946.

179. *Political Alignments of Vietnamese Nationalists*, pp. 97–99. I have reproduced essential data on the Socialist Party from my earlier study here.

180. See above, p. 141. The new party did invite its former Vietnamese members to join. Vu Dinh Hoe, a prewar member of the Socialist Federation and then listed as a Democrat (see above, fn. 149), has since been referred to, by Communist sources, as a Socialist member of the Ho Chi Minh government.

181. Subsequently, the Socialist Party comprised a bloc of twenty-four delegates in the National Assembly. Party representatives have occupied leading positions through all the shifts and changes of the Viet Minh governmental coalition. Its newspaper *Tien Len* (*Forward*) was given prominence during the 1946–49 period in official broadcasts even when it mildly criticized government policy. On balance, however, despite the genuine social-democratic convictions of some of its founding leaders, it has been used by Ho Chi Minh and his Communist collaborators in the same way that the legal minor parties of Communist China have been manipulated by Mao Tse-tung.

182. The main features of the operations and structure of the army and government during the period up to Dien Bien Phu have been dealt with in Bernard Fall, *The Viet-Minh Regime*.

183. To show deference to the Chinese and to deny the charge made against his government as "Communist," President Ho Chi Minh said: "We are realizing the people's three principles of Asia's Great Revolution as stated by Dr. Sun Yat Sen. The French reactionary colonialists mistook them for 'the class principle' of Karl Marx." (Viet Nam American Friendship Association News Release, New York, July 7, 1947.) This implied no deviation from the practice of the Chinese Communists who had appropriated long since Sun Yat-sen's principles. (Cf. Mao Tse-tung, "The Chinese Revolution and the Chinese Communist Party," in *Selected Works of Mao Tse-Tung*, III, 57.)

184. Viet Nam News Agency, March 1, 1949.

185. Virginia M. Thompson and Richard Adloff, *The Left Wing in Southeast Asia*, p. 37.

186. This strategy, and its application to Viet Nam referred to below, is discussed in this author's "The Strategy of Communism in Southeast Asia," *Pacific Affairs*, XXIII (September 1950), 227–47.

187. Belated French efforts to counter the Viet Minh's political strength among nationalists had led finally to the creation of a government and a political movement around former Emperor Bao Dai.

188. Documents setting forth the platform and position of the Viet Nam Workers' Party may be found in Cole, pp. 96–110. Some of the more important documents relating to the war in Indochina have been excerpted and may be consulted in this volume.

189. At least, I would like to say, with respect to the attitude of the Chinese Communists toward Viet Nam, that they are likely to demonstrate a continuing interest in what was historically a Chinese tributary state and that even the Vietnamese Communists share some of the age-old fears of their "elder brother." Mao Tse-tung, p. 78, has remarked vis-à-vis the "imperialist powers" that, "having defeated China in war, they not only occupied many states bordering on China that were under her protection . . . [*sic*]."

190. I refer here to the perceptive comments of Benjamin Schwartz, pp. 191–204, who explains convincingly the way in which the Chinese Communists attempt to conceal the divorce of their party as a vanguard organization from its proletarian class base. His remarks are germane to the Viet Nam Workers' Party.

191. Hoa Mai, *The "Nhan-Van" Affair*, n.p. [Saigon?], n.d. [1957?], contains a significant amount of translated material from this heretical Communist publication issued in Hanoi.

192. Mao Tse-tung, "On the Correct Handling of Contradictions Among the People" in "Let a Hundred Flowers Bloom," *New Leader*, Sec. 2, September 9, 1957.

193. In this connection, see Fall, "Crisis in Viet Nam," *Far Eastern Survey*, XXVI (January 1957), 12–15.

194. See J. A. C. Grant, "The Viet Nam Constitution of 1956," *American Political Science Review*, LII (June 1958), 437–62, for an analysis of the constitutional structure of the Republic of Viet Nam.

195. William Henderson, "South Viet Nam Finds Itself," *Foreign Affairs*, XXXV (January 1957), 283–94.

196. Jumper, "The Communist Challenge to South Viet Nam," *Far Eastern Survey*, XXV (November 1956), 161–68.

197. Grant, pp. 457–62.

198. David Wurfel, "Agrarian Reform in the Republic of Viet Nam," *Far Eastern Survey*, XXVI (June 1957), 81–92.

199. For two of the most recent views on this matter, see John T. Dorsey, Jr., "South Viet Nam in Perspective," *Far Eastern Survey*, XXVII (December 1958), 177–82, and Francis J. Corley, "Viet Nam Since Geneva," *Thought, Fordham University Quarterly*, XXXIII (Winter 1958–59), 515–68.

CHAPTER 5:   MARXISM IN INDONESIA

1. Sjahrir, p. 31.
2. Ruslan Abdulgani, "Ideological Background of the Asian-African Conference," *United Asia*, VII (March 1955), 43–45.
3. The Socialist literature that reached Indonesia in the early days of the nationalist movement was a heterogeneous mixture, including, for example, the works of Domela Nieuwenhuis, of Henriette Roland Holst, the writings of Bakunin, and a good deal written about him. (See Sutan Sjahrir, *Indonesian Socialism*, p. 27.) In many ways this situation resembles that in former British colonies, where, according to several Indian Socialists, the vehicle of Marxism was often the writings of Laski.
4. Karl Marx, *Capital*, p. 824; see also pp. 823, 826.
5. Among the chief historical sources are John Theodoor Petrus Blumberger, *De Nationalistische Beweging in Nederlandsch-Indie*, and articles in *Encyclopaedie van Nederlandsch-Indie*; and L. M. Sitorus, *Sedjarah Pergerakan Kebangsaan Indonesia*.

A somewhat less analytical account than that of Sitorus is found in A. K. Pringgodigdo, *Sedjarah Pergerakan Rakjat Indonesia*. A study of the nationalist movement in the decade before the Japanese occupation is given in J. M. Pluvier, *Overzicht van de Ontwikkeling der Nationalistische Beweging in Indonesie*. The book of D. M. G. Koch, *Om de Vrijheid*, offers some interesting observations by a Dutch journalist who was close to the nationalist movement almost from its inception.

Among the standard works in English which contain valuable sections on the nationalist movement are Rupert Emerson, *Malaysia*; John S. Furnivall, *Netherlands India*; and Bernard H. M. Vlekke, *Nusantara*.

The social environment out of which Indonesian nationalism arose may be examined in such works as A. D. A. de Kat Angelino, *Staatkundig beleid en bestuurszorg in Nederlandsch-Indie* (an abridged edition of this work in English was published in The Hague in 1931 under the title *Colonial Policy*); B. J. O. Schrieke, several of whose studies have now been collected and published as *Indonesian Sociological Studies*; and W. F. Wertheim, *Indonesian Society in Transition*.

The most complete, and indeed the indispensable, study of Indonesia's nationalist movement and its culmination in the Republic of Indonesia is found in George McT. Kahin, *Nationalism and Revolution in Indonesia*. This writer, as the reader of these pages will soon discover, is deeply indebted to Professor Kahin's book and to his numerous articles and papers on Indonesia.

6. Raymond Kennedy, *The Ageless Indies*, pp. 90 f. For a useful summary, see Raden Supomo, "The Future of Adat Law in the Reconstruction of Indonesia," in P. W. Thayer (ed.), *Southeast Asia in the Coming World*.
7. Some Indonesians prefer the term "unanimity" to describe this process and its end result. Whether one calls it compromise or unanimity, essentially the process consists of discussion in which varying points of view are aired, differ-

ences reconciled, and a unified view—which does not necessarily represent any single viewpoint—emerges.

8. Some 90 per cent of Indonesia's population are nominally Moslem.

9. For details on the impact of Modernist Islamic ideas on Indonesia, see Kahin, pp. 44–49. The analogy between Modernist Islam and the contemporary "Social Gospel" movement in American Protestantism merits further study. These movements and their European Roman Catholic counterpart were part of the response to the "evils" of capitalism.

10. The program to unify the Dutch and "Native Civil Service," first cautiously offered for Java in 1867 and for the whole archipelago in 1905, was repeatedly shelved. In 1921 limited concessions were made to meritorious ruling Indonesian regents under the term "emancipation" (*ontvoogding*), but this experiment "was found unsatisfactory and there were few regrets when it came to an end . . . in 1931." See Furnivall, pp. 266–69.

11. *Ibid.*, p. 238. For a discussion of the Ethical Policy (referred to below), see *ibid.*, pp. 229 ff. "The public," says Furnivall, "might have been less sensitive to the appeal of these reformers to its conscience if circumstances had not at the same time touched its pocket."

12. Blumberger, *Le Communisme aux Indes Neerlandaises,* p. 1.

13. Kahin, pp. 43 f. Although Furnivall does not discuss this movement, he supplies data which shed light upon it: displaced villagers were recruited by the "coolie agents" (pp. 355 f.); the peasantry suffered during the depression of 1884 (p. 220), after which "plantation agriculture made rapid progress . . . at the expense of the natives"; progress in welfare at the end of the Culture System "was followed by stagnation and relapse" (pp. 222 f.); "to sum up the general opinion (after the introduction of the Ethical System), the natives grow in numbers and the other sectors of the community, the Europeans and the Chinese, in wealth" (p. 404).

14. S. J. Rutgers, *Indonesie,* II, 146. (This was issued by a firm which publishes much Communist material.)

15. Furnivall, pp. 239–42, 408–14. See also Victor Purcell, *The Chinese in Southeast Asia,* Part VII and particularly pp. 511 ff. For an account of the Chinese in the early part of the twentieth century, see P. H. Fromberg, "De Chineesche Beweging op Java," *Verspreide Geschriften,* Leiden, 1926. For a study of the legal position of the Chinese in Indonesia from the middle of the nineteenth century to the treaty on dual nationality between the Republic of Indonesia and the People's Republic of China in 1955, see Donald E. Wilmott, *The National Status of the Chinese in Indonesia,* Ithaca, N.Y., 1956.

16. H. H. van Kol, "De Strijd der SDAP op Koloniaal Gebied," *Gedenkboek SDAP ter gelegenheid van het vijf en twintig-jaarig bestaan van de sociaal-democratische arbeiderspartij in Nederland,* p. 89.

17. Founded in 1912, with a membership of Eurasians and Indonesians, the NIP developed a program of racial equality, social and economic justice, and freedom.

18. Ki Hadjar Dewantoro was the founder of the Taman Siswa school system, which played a vitally important role in building a generation of conscious nationalists emancipated from the bonds of much of the traditional education expounded in the villages and in the official government schools.

19. H. J. F. M. Sneevliet, the man generally credited with playing the key role in establishing Indonesia's Communist movement, had been a member of

the radical wing of the SDAP, the Tribunist group which split off in 1909 to form the Sociaal-Democratische Partij (SDP), the forerunner of the Communist Party of Holland (CPH). In the thirties the CPH altered its name to Communist Party of the Netherlands (CPN). For the sake of simplicity, we will refer to the party throughout as the CPN. (See Blumberger, *Le Communisme aux Indes Neerlandaises*, p. 2; and Vlekke, pp. 338 ff.) Among the founders of the ISDV, along with Sneevliet, were H. W. Dekker, J. T. Brandsteder, A. Baars, and P. Bergsma.

20. See Blumberger, *Le Communisme aux Indes Neerlandaises* and *De Communistische Beweging in Nederlandsch-Indie*; Sitorus; and Ruth T. McVey, *The Development of the Indonesian Communist Party and Its Relation with the Soviet Union and the Chinese People's Republic.*

21. P. Bergsma, "A Letter from the Dutch East Indies," *International Press Correspondence (Inprecor)*, III (September 27, 1923), 699.

22. By the end of 1919, SI's central leadership had united twenty-two Indonesian trade-unions, with a total membership of 77,000, under the direction of one of its own men. The Communists immediately sought to take control of this organization. Although Semaun, the key figure among the Communists, managed to have himself elected chairman of this trade-union federation, he found his attempts to control it blocked by the resistance of SI men who had retained the other top posts. Semaun then left to set up a rival trade-union federation, taking with him fourteen unions, including the highly important VSTP, the Association of Railway Workers, one of the oldest and most revolutionary trade-unions. (See *Vakbeweging [The Labor Movement]*; and Kahin, p. 75.)

23. An example of this is the often-quoted distinction which the SI's leaders made between "sinful," presumably Western, capitalism as opposed to other forms, presumably indigenous capitalism. (See Vlekke, p. 340; E. S. De Klerck, *History of the Netherlands East Indies*, II, 534; and B. Alkema, *De Sarikat Islam*, p. 49.) Alkema lists the resolutions adopted at the SI's National Congress on October 21, 1917, including as point 3: "The SI will always fight against the domination of sinful capitalism."

24. At the SI congress at Madiun in February 1923. (See Blumberger, *Le Communisme aux Indes Neerlandaises*, p. 38.)

25. *Semangat Moeda*, Tokyo, 1920. Tan Malaka recommended the use of religion especially in such markedly orthodox Moslem areas as Solo, Jogjakarta, Atjeh, and Bandjermasin. (See Blumberger, *De Communistische Beweging in Nederlandsch-Indie*, pp. 65 f.)

26. Schrieke, "The Causes and Effects of Communism on the West Coast of Sumatra," *Indonesian Sociological Studies.*

27. Tan Malaka, speech to the Fourth Comintern Congress, *Inprecor*, II (December 5, 1922), 875.

28. *Ibid.*, pp. 875 f.

29. Blumberger, *De Communistische Beweging in Nederlandsch-Indie*, p. 48, and Semaun, "International Imperialism and the Communist Party of Indonesia," *Communist International*, No. 17, 1926, pp. 75–82. In Semaun's article, the rival organization is called *Sarekat Hindyu*, and its members are charged with killing several PKI members.

30. Semaun, p. 7.

31. "X," "The Revolutionary Movement in the East," *Communist International*, No. 18–19, 1926, pp. 97–115.

32. In March 1925, the ECCI had directed the PKI to form a united anti-

imperialist front with the non-Communist nationalists and to continue to work through the SR's. (See article by "X.") This Moscow criticism becomes a more important issue in connection with the interpretation of the rebellion and its relation to Moscow.

33. Tan Malaka, *Thesis*; and Alimin, *Analysis*. Summarized in Kahin, pp. 81–87.

34. Rutgers, pp. 162 f.

35. The original edition of this pamphlet is virtually unavailable except for one edition, printed in Djakarta in 1947, which Kahin indicates is a reprint of the 1926 edition published in Singapore.

36. See *Toward the Indonesian Republic*, Canton and Tokyo, 1925, as quoted in Blumberger, *De Communistische Beweging in Nederlandsch-Indie*, pp. 62–67. In this pamphlet Tan Malaka stressed the need for strengthening the party and its cells in the armed forces as a preliminary to any violent action.

37. Sjahrir, *Out of Exile*, pp. 73 f.

38. See, e.g., Schrieke, esp. pp. 111 f., 149, and 160 f. It is obvious that Schrieke's comments on the lasting result of Communist propaganda in the area to which he confined his examination were undoubtedly applicable to other parts of Indonesia which had been similarly propagandized.

39. See Blumberger, *Le Communisme aux Indes Neerlandaises*, pp. 46, 49 ff.

40. Blumberger, *Le Communisme aux Indes Neerlandaises*, pp. 42 f. Apropos of the increased use of Comintern symbols, it is interesting to note that the pictures used to decorate the hall at the PKI congress in Batavia in June 1924 included, in addition to portraits of Marx, Lenin, and Trotsky, pictures of Sun Yat-sen, Sneevliet, and the exiled PKI leaders Tan Malaka and Semaun.

41. This was apparently one of the first attempts by a Communist party to infiltrate another party and form cells within it as a means for developing its own propaganda and contacts among the masses. Sneevliet, in 1922, proposed this technique to the Chinese Communist Party. (See Harold R. Isaacs, *The Tragedy of the Chinese Revolution*, pp. 58 f.)

42. Semaun, "The Situation in Indonesia," Coreport to the Sixth Comintern Congress, *Inprecor*, VIII (October 4, 1928), 1243. Kahin, p. 84, offers figures which would reduce Semaun's claim of party membership to "some 3000 party members."

43. Sneevliet represented the Indonesian Communists at the Second Comintern Congress.

44. Semaun, p. 1245.

45. Semaoen (Semaun), *Hoe het Hollandsche Imperialisme het Bruine Millioenenvolk Aanzet tot een Massamoord op Europeanen in Indonesia*.

46. For a review, see Xenia J. Eudin and Robert C. North, *Soviet Russia and the East, 1920–1927*, pp. 75–90.

47. Although few Indonesians had more than a hazy idea of where Moscow is, or what the Russian peoples' racial origins are, the ideas and revolutionary slogans attributed to Moscow tended to make Russia seem like a fellow Asian country. Furthermore, to a handful of Indonesians, Russia had offered recognition on a footing of equality with the representatives of Western countries, through participation in the Comintern. Finally—a point which is still significant today—few Indonesians had ever seen a Russian, but most of them had seen a

number of Dutch, English, and French; and this familiarity with the representatives of colonial powers had all too often not been conducive to mutual respect or liking.

48. See *Inprecor*, VI (November 25, 1926), 1390 and (December 2, 1926) 1438. Musso returns to this theme in "How the Social Democrats Betray the Workers in Indonesia," *ibid.*, VIII (January 5, 1928), 13.

49. De Visser, statement at the Sixteenth Session of the enlarged ECCI, December 6, 1926, *ibid.*, VI (December 30, 1926), 1635 f.

50. In 1933 the CPN for the first time elected an Indonesian Communist, Roestam Effendi, as a member of the Dutch parliament. The propaganda value of this move should not be underestimated. There are Indonesians who were not yet born at the time when Effendi took his seat in the Dutch parliament, who today point to that event as evidence that the sole group in Holland which genuinely fought for Indonesian rights was the Dutch Communist party.

51. Kahin, p. 83.

52. Speech, May 1925, before the Communist University of the Toilers of the East, in *Marxism and the National and Colonial Question*, p. 192. "X" (see above, fn. 31), reports similar criticism from the ECCI meeting of March 1925. See also McVey, p. 11.

53. *Inprecor*, VI (November 1926), 1429.

54. See, e.g., "Leninist Teachings on the Colonial and National Revolutionary Movement and the Current Problems of the Revolutionary Movement in the East," *ibid.*, VII (January 13, 1927), 93–95, and, more important (December 8, 1927), p. 1562.

55. *Ibid.* (December 8, 1927), pp. 1562–63.

56. Mauawar, "(Report to the) Thirty-fourth Session, Moscow, August 17, 1928," *Inprecor*, VIII (October 17, 1928), 1325.

57. "The Situation in Indonesia," Coreport of Comrade Semaun, *ibid.*, VIII (October 4, 1928), 1243–47. Semaun apparently used the analysis of the ECCI as it appeared in *ibid.*, VII (December 8, 1927) (cf. above, fn. 54). But he also appealed to revolutionary sentiment. "We believe," he said, "that it would be better to die fighting than to die without fighting, . . . and many of our members were . . . killed." (*Ibid.*, VIII [October 4, 1928], 1246.)

58. *Program of the Communist International*, p. 20. Musso was elected to the ECCI while Tan Malaka became candidate member. The latter, identified by McVey as "Comrade Alphonso" at this congress, had engaged in vigorous and effective debate against Bukharin at a time when Stalin was preparing to be rid of the latter. In this debate Tan Malaka was called a Trotskyist, a label which stuck to him and his followers after his eventual purge. (For the debate, see *Inprecor*, VIII [September 4, September 25, and October 4, 1928].)

59. Cramer had been one of the founders of the ISDV when it was established in May 1914; the ISDV had contained both orthodox and revisionist Marxists. However, in 1917, when the extremist members of the ISDV, encouraged by the news of the Russian revolution, became increasingly emboldened, the less radical members of the party broke away to form the ISDP, which affiliated itself with the SDAP in Holland.

60. *Handelingen*, November 16, 1918, p. 211, quoted in Blumberger, article on the Radical Concentration, *Encyclopaedie van Nederlandsch-Indie*, Supplement No. 5, 1927, p. 201.

61. Insulinde: a predominantly Eurasian party. Budi Utomo: the earliest and one of the smaller Indonesian nationalist groups, founded by a group of medical students, mostly from aristocratic Javanese families, in 1908.

62. Blumberger, article on the Radical Concentration.

63. *Ibid.*, p. 203.

64. G. H. Bousquet, *A French View of the Netherlands Indies*, p. 5; see also Schrieke, p. 154.

65. PI was established in 1922 as the successor to a previous student organization that had been less political in character.

66. Earlier plans to form such a party had been deferred because of the strength of the PKI. By the time the accord was signed, however, shortly after the unsuccessful uprising of 1926 in Java, it was apparently clear to PI's non-Communist leaders that the PKI would now cease to exist in the open as a political force.

67. Blumberger, *Le Communisme aux Indes Neerlandaises*, p. 161. Semaun's repudiation of the accord appeared in the Dutch Communist paper *Tribune* on December 12, 1927.

68. In that speech, Hatta referred to the 1926 revolt in Java as a national insurrection of the Indonesian people against the tyrannical oppression under which they suffered; the PKI's role was not stressed. (See "Special Report on the International Congress against Colonial Oppression in Brussels," *Inprecor*, VII [February 25, 1927], 328.)

69. Blumberger, *Le Communisme aux Indes Neerlandaises*, p. 157.

70. See, e.g., the pamphlet written by a Dutch Socialist attacking the government's trial of these leaders: J. E. W. Duijs, *De Vervolging Tegen de Indonesische Studenten*.

71. Details on the history of PI and the League can be found in Blumberger, *Le Communisme aux Indes Neerlandaises*. For an analysis of these relations by a leading participant, see Mohammad Hatta, "Het Anti-Koloniale Congres te Brussel in het licht der Wereldgeschiedenis," "Het Brusselse Congres Tegen Imperialisme en Koloniale Onderdrukking en onze Buitenlandse Propaganda"; and especially "Een Nabetrachting van het Tweede Congres der Liga Tegen Imperialisme en voor Nationale Onafhankelijkheid te Frankfurt," in *Verspreide Geschriften*, pp. 160–86.

72. Persindo and the CPN rival press bureaus were in competition for space in the Indonesian nationalist press. The CPN, though harshly critical of the "bourgeois nationalists" of Indonesia in Holland, avoided such criticism in the selection of Communist material sent to Indonesia. Thereupon Persindo, indicating the source of such material, forwarded to Indonesia the critical CPN articles. As a result, the Communist press bureau soon fell into disrepute.

73. Daan van der Zee, *De Wereld Vrij*, pp. 156–61. For a detailed history of the SDAP's stand on the Indonesian question, especially in the Dutch parliament, see the same author's *De SDAP en Indonesie*. For an analysis, see M. Hatta, "De Tweede Internationale en de Onderdrukte Volken"; and "De Koloniale resolutie der Tweede Internationale," reprinted in *Verspreide Geschriften*, pp. 445–61.

74. The *Zeven Provincien* incident, the mutiny of the crew of a Royal Dutch Navy cruiser off the coast of Sumatra, was popularly supposed to have been an isolated event remote from the mainstream of Indonesian nationalist activities. However, information given the author by an Indonesian imprisoned for com-

plicity in the affair indicates that the mutiny was not the reaction of disgruntled Indonesian seamen but the outgrowth of plans laid by the Socialist trade-union to which the Indonesian crew members belonged. Like all Indonesian labor organizations of that era, the sailors' trade-union was primarily a political organization; despite its public protestations to the contrary, the Dutch Indies government was apparently aware of this connection between the mutineers and the nationalist movement and promptly arrested a number of Indonesians known to be active in the sailors' union or in the trade-union federation with which it was affiliated. In Holland, the entire affair caused considerable furor, especially since the mutiny had been ended by a Dutch naval aircraft dropping a bomb on the ship. In the public meetings on the incident and in the ensuing parliamentary debates, the SDAP's activities drowned out the minor public protests of the Communists. In Indonesia, the *Zeven Provincie* affair was quickly played down by the authorities, but a visitor to the islands some years later remarked on the uneasiness still visible in Dutch circles—an uneasiness which was attributed to overtones of the incident. (See Geoffrey Gorer, *Bali and Angkor*, Boston, 1936, p. 6.) As for the Third International, the mutiny was seen as a "part of the current tide of colonial revolution." (See Wang Ming, "The Revolutionary Movement in the Colonial Countries.") The fact that the sailors' trade-union involved was linked to the Socialist (NVV) rather than to the Communist trade-union federation was not mentioned.

75. The Dutch Socialist Trade Union Federation (Nederlandsch Vakbeweging Vereeniging) sent a delegation to Indonesia to establish contact with the Indonesian labor movement in the mid-thirties; in 1938 the SDAP sent Palar to report on the Indonesian labor unions and work out a more satisfactory basis for cooperation. There is some evidence that this mission was favorably received by Indonesian nationalists. The latter expected the Dutch unionists' aid in support of a demand for an Indonesian parliament. The SDAP later (February 10, 1940) waged an unsuccessful battle in the Dutch parliament for this. (See Pringgodigdo, p. 145; and Pluvier, pp. 145 f.)

76. In conversation with the editor, in August 1956, Sjahrir indicated among other things that Socialist failure in the elections earlier that year convinced him that it was time to change his conception from a cadre to a mass party, but one with "education."

77. Sjahrir, *Indonesian Socialism*, pp. 29 f.

78. Sukarno, one of the few top nationalist leaders of the era to have been educated solely in Indonesia, had been arrested in December 1929 and later tried and sentenced, together with three of his colleagues, on the charge of fomenting public disorder and recommending the overthrow of the Netherlands Indies authority. The PNI, taking a militant stand for complete political and economic independence and advocating the strategy of noncooperation, had become the most powerful nationalist organization in the country, with a membership of more than ten thousand within two years of its establishment.

79. Soekarno (Sukarno), *Indonesie Klaagt Aan!* These excerpts are taken from a photostatic copy of an edition published in Dutch for Het "Fonds Nasional" der Federatie van Indonesische Politieke Vereenigingen (PPPKI). (Author's translation.)

80. *Ibid.*, pp. 41 f.

81. On this point he had the support, whether he knew it or not, of several of his fellow Indonesians in Moscow. (See the characterization of the PNI as a

petty bourgeois party in the reports to the Sixth Comintern Congress by Semaun
and Mauawar, *Inprecor*, VIII [October 4, 1928], 1247 and [October 17, 1928]
1326.) On the other hand, PI, the Indonesian Students Association in Holland,
although by then largely under Communist domination, regarded the PNI with
somewhat more approval. Hatta noted in an unsigned article in the PI journal
that "on the ruins of the PKI and SRs there has been formed a new mass movement. . . . In these difficult times, only a few people believed in the possibility
of a new mass movement. Among these pioneers were the founders of PNI: Ir.
Soekarno, Mr. Sartono, Dr. Tjipto Mangoenkoesoemo, Soedjadi, Mr. Iskaq, Ir.
Anwari, Dr. Samsi, Mr. Soejoedi and Mr. Soenario . . . [This new party differs
from the PKI only in that] the ultimate aim of the PNI is national independence."
("De Groei van de P. N. I. en de Regeeringsteereur in Indonesia," *Indonesia
Merdeka*, January–February 1930, pp. 1 f.)

82. Both *kromo* and *marhaen* originally meant peasant, although *marhaen*
has come to mean proletarian or worker as well. *Kromo* is a kind of stock term
for a Javanese farmer. *Marhaen*, according to the *Ensiklopedia Indonesia*, is
derived from the name of a peasant in the Sunda region of Java.

83. Soekarno, p. 76.

84. For such detail, see Kahin, pp. 90–100; Pluvier, *passim*; and Pringgodigdo, pp. 121 ff. For a useful political profile of PNI's founder, see Leslie H.
Palmier, "Sukarno, the Nationalist," *Pacific Affairs*, XXX (June 1957), 101–19.

85. Ali Sastroamidjojo, "Survey of the Indonesian National Movement,"
Indonesian Life, I (March–April 1947), 6. The article claims that this was
the first time these principles were introduced by a political party in Indonesia.
More likely this was the first time these principles were explained and outlined
in detail rather than merely presented in slogans.

The eclectic nature of Hatta's approach to socialism can be seen, for example,
in his article "Marxisme of epigonenwijsheid?" ("Marxism or the Wisdom of the
Epigones?"), *Nationale Comentaren*, Nos. 10, 11, 12, 13, 14, 1940, and reprinted
in Hatta, *Verspreide Geschriften*, pp. 117–41.

86. Kahin, pp. 85–87; see pp. 313–19 for details on Partai Murba, the postwar party founded by Tan Malaka in 1948, much of whose leadership was drawn
from Pari. Tan Malaka gave to the word *murba*, normally translated as proletariat, a special definition: "people who have nothing except brain and body
. . . different from the Western proletariat. The Indonesian Murba is not yet
completely separated from the family, as in the West . . . [T]he struggle and
the enemy of the Indonesian Murba are different from [those] of the Western
proletariat." (*Ibid.*, p. 314.) *Murba* is not unlike the phrase, "workers of hand
and brain," used in the West during the 1930's.

87. Musso had returned from Moscow to Indonesia and remained in Java,
under an assumed name, for about a year.

88. Musso, "The National Parties and the Worker's Organizations of Indonesia," *Inprecor*, IX (June 7, 1929), 588. See also Blumberger, *De Communistische Beweging in Nederlandsch-Indie*, pp. 151–53.

89. Kahin, p. 86.

90. Reesema, "The Terror in Indonesia," *Inprecor*, IX, (August 16, 1929),
883. See also "Manifest uitgegeven op 2 Januari 1930, n.a.v. de Razzia tegen
de P.N.I.," *Indonesia Merdeka*, VIII (January–February 1930), 13 f.

91. According to McVey, in 1928, propagandists J. Waworoentoe, C. Wen-
toek, and K. Kamoe, students at the Communist University of the Peoples of the

East, were sent to Indonesia apparently to help reorganize the movement there, but were interned by the authorities in March 1929. (See McVey, pp. 19 f.)

92. Kahin, p. 91.

93. Mohammad Hatta, (*Statement on*) *The Conception of the President*, p. 2.

94. For example Parindra, which was formed in 1935 out of a fusion of several small moderate parties and was generally characterized as both "moderate" and "cooperative" (see Sastroamidjojo, p. 7) was on July 11, 1941, the sole party in the Volksraad to vote against the establishment of an Indonesian militia on the grounds that this long-sought nationalist goal would be acceptable only if preceded by political reform. (See Vlekke, p. 390.)

95. Kahin, pp. 94 f.

96. Hatta, *The Conception of the President*, p. 3.

97. See McVey, p. 21.

98. So called for its first signer, Soetardjo, who was chairman of the PPBB (Persatuan Pegawei Binnenlandsche-Bestuur, or Civil Servants' Association) and a leading figure among the moderate nationalists.

99. S. II. Tajibnapis, "De Laatste Tien Juren voor de Japanese Bezetting," *De Brug-Djambatan*, I (April 1946), 12 f.

100. See, e.g., Alexandre von Arx, *L'Evolution Politique en Indonesie de 1900 à 1942*; and Furnivall, p. 255.

101. J. A. Verdoorn, *The National Movement in Indonesia*, pp. 54–65.

102. Kahin, p. 115; and McVey, p. 21. McVey calls Gerindo "the powerful left wing of Indonesian nationalism."

103. Verdoorn, p. 62.

104. Pringgodigdo, p. 128.

105. "Right" and "center" are here defined in terms of socioeconomic, not political, programs. Parindra, for example, shortly before the invasion of Holland decided "spontaneously to cease all political actions" since "to fish in front of a net (i.e., to be opportunistic) is not a characteristic of Indonesians." (Quoted in Pluvier, p. 168, from *Suara Umum*, a Parindra paper in Surabaya.) On May 15, after the invasion of Holland, PSII and Parindra as well as other parties decided to offer their support to the government in every possible way, including financial support; Parindra actually did contribute to the War Fund. (*Ibid.*)

106. The Visman Commission, headed by Dr. F. H. Visman, a member of the Volksraad, was established by the Netherlands Indies government in September 1940 to investigate the views of the various racial and social groups in Indonesia with respect to the country's future political development. The commission's report was completed a few days after Pearl Harbor and was printed shortly before the Japanese invasion, thus negating any possible effect the report might have had on later developments.

107. Mohammad Natsir, "Gapi-Komisi Visman," *Capita Selecta*, pp. 343–46. The excerpts (author's translation) are on pp. 345 f.

108. "Naar een Nationale Samenwerking," *Indonesia*, January 1937, pp. 1 f. The name of PI's periodical had now been changed from *Indonesia Merdeka* to *Indonesia*.

109. "Het Ontwerp-Program, Samengesteld door Dr. Soetomo en de Perhimpunan Indonesia," *ibid.*, pp. 8 f.

110. Gerindo at its congress on August 1, 1939 (see Pringgodigdo, p. 128); and Gapi in 1941 (see Pluvier, p. 189).

111. See Pringgodigdo, p. 145; and Pluvier, p. 145.

112. See Kahin, Chapter 4, "The Japanese Occupation," pp. 101–33; Willard H. Elsbree, *Japan's Role in Southeast Asian Nationalist Movements, 1940 to 1945*, especially Chapter 3, "The Development of Political Participation in Indonesia"; and Muhammad Abdul Aziz, *Japan's Colonialism and Indonesia*.

113. For Sjahrir's doubts concerning such cooperation, see his *Out of Exile*, pp. 242 ff.; and also H. van den Brink, *Ein Eisch van Recht*, pp. 49 f., fn. 1.

114. Kahin, pp. 116–21.

115. Aziz, p. 228.

116. The best single source for the history of this period is Kahin, Chapters 5–13; see also Charles Wolf, Jr., *The Indonesian Story*. For the role of the United Nations in the Indonesian dispute, see *Peaceful Settlement in Indonesia*, UN Publications No. 1951/I/6, New York, 1951; James Foster Collins, "The UN and Indonesia," *International Conciliation*, CDLIX (March 1950), 115–200; and William Henderson, "The Indonesian Question, 1946–1949," *Pacific Settlement of Disputes*, New York, 1954. For a documentary chronology of the period from August 1945 to the end of 1946, see Osman Raliby, *Documenta Historica*, Vol. I.

117. The quotations given below are taken from an English translation of a stenographic record of the speech issued under the title *The Birth of Pantja Sila*.

118. *Ibid.*, pp. 7–9.

119. *Ibid.*, p. 10. Sukarno notes that, despite having been influenced originally by the Dutch Socialist Baars, who condemned nationalism, there was "another man who showed me the right way and that was Dr. Sun Yat Sen," whose works "exposed cosmopolitanism as taught by A. Baars." Another Indonesian nationalist whose socialism was rooted in vastly different origins from Sukarno's, Hadji Agus Salim, had condemned the Marxist concept of internationalism almost twenty years earlier and advocated in its stead the internationalism of Islam that "wants to unite all of mankind in a united community but, contrary to Marxism, it makes only positive demands rather than negative. Therefore it does not demand the abolition of individualism and nationalism. The rights of the independent free individual to exist, of the family, of village and other communities, of independent nations or nationalities are recognized and guaranteed by Islam." "Onwelwillend, onbillijk, onwaar, maar niet onpartijdig," *Het Licht*, No. 1, Th. 2, reprinted in *Djedjak Langkah Hadji A. Salim. Pilihan Karangan Utjapan dan Pendapat Beliau dari Dulu sampai Sekarang*, pp. 96–103.

120. The order in which the Five Principles are customarily listed today varies somewhat from that used in the original speech. They are normally given as belief in God, humanitarianism, nationalism, democracy, and social justice.

Sukarno, in the Pantja Sila speech, indicated that the five principles could be reduced to three: God, socio-nationalism, and socio-democracy; these three could be further reduced to the single guiding Indonesian concept, *gotong rojong*, or mutual cooperation.

121. Mohammad Hatta, *Indonesian Aims and Ideals*. This statement, with very minor alterations, can be found in Hatta, *Verspreide Geschriften*, pp. 311–13, where the date is given as August 23, 1945.

122. The Political Manifesto has been reprinted in numerous editions. The introduction to the Manifesto is signed by Hatta, in his capacity as Vice-President, and the body of the document is unsigned, which has led many observers to credit its authorship to Hatta.

123. *Het Inzicht* (*Insight*) was the Republican government periodical

aimed at an audience of intellectuals. It was followed closely by official observers abroad for what it revealed about the views of the men in authority. Its editorial staff was headed by Sudjatmoko and Sudarpo Sastrosatomo, two former leaders of the students' wartime underground resistance movement that had been closely linked with Sjahrir's underground, and the magazine generally reflected the stand of the groups close to Sjahrir and Hatta.

This particular series of articles was signed only with the initial "S"; often attributed to Sjahrir, they are actually the product, in part if not in full, of the leading economist of the Republic in that era, Sumitro Djojohadikusumo.

The excerpts given here are taken from an English translation of the articles which appeared under the title "Our Nationalism and Its Substance: Freedom, Social Justice and Human Dignity" in *The Voice of Free Indonesia*, Vol. I, April 27, May 4, and May 18, 1946.

124. The quotations given here are from the Dutch edition of the pamphlet, published under the auspices of PI: *Onze Strijd*, Amsterdam, 1946, pp. 20, 22.

125. The excerpts from this work (Jogjakarta, 1948) given below are taken from the paragraphs found in Kahin, pp. 309 f. See also Palmier, "Modern Islam in Indonesia: The Muhammadiyah After Independence," *Pacific Affairs*, XXVII (September 1954), 255–63.

126. *Kepartaian dan Parlementaria di Indonesia*, Djakarta, 1954, pp. 441 ff. This wing of the party is careful to avoid any confusion between its stand and the concept of a theocratic state. As explained by Mohammad Natsir, "Islam cannot conceive of a separation of religion and community, or society, or nation, or state, or for that matter of mankind. But this is a far cry from what is understood as theocracy." (Natsir, *Some Observations Concerning the Role of Islam in National and International Affairs*, p. 4.)

127. The postwar PNI was not a reconstruction of the prewar PNI founded by Sukarno. The similarity in name did help it to win popular support, especially since many of its leaders had been active in the 1927 PNI, its successor Partindo, and the PI of the twenties.

128. In evaluating the Dutch premises concerning this famous flight, it should be remembered that a number of Indonesian Communists had become national Dutch heroes during the war as a result of their activities in branches of the Dutch underground.

129. At the time that Suripno was dispatched to Eastern Europe, it was not generally known that he was a Communist, and it was definitely not known by the non-Communist government officials who selected him for that job. Suripno's increasingly open pro-Soviet stand caused considerable confusion at the time in the offices of other Republican diplomatic missions abroad.

130. For details of the Madiun rebellion, see Kahin, pp. 290 f. SOBSI is discussed below.

131. This issue is discussed in detail in Chapter 6 of this book.

132. See, e.g., Kahin, pp. 284, 287; and McVey, pp. 63 f. Kahin, however, clearly indicates that the PKI leaders had made plans for a coup and did not hesitate to put themselves at the head of the Madiun uprising. Kahin writes that the PKI bid for power could not have been readied until November.

133. Ambassador Merle Cochran was the American representative on the United Nations Commission for Indonesia.

134. The Indonesian view of the Cochran proposals as favoring the Dutch was shared in other circles. (See, e.g., Collins.)

135. It is difficult to identify Subardjo's political affiliations in this era. He had been a leader of PI in Holland in the early twenties. Thereafter he spent at least a year in Moscow (see Kahin, p. 115, fn. 2) and was apparently active in the League Against Imperialism in Berlin in the late twenties (see Blumberger, *De Communistische Beweging in Nederlandsch-Indie*, p. 140). Despite numerous conversations with Mr. Subardjo in 1950, the author has not been able to form a clear-cut picture of his basic political views. This blurred impression was not dispelled when, in 1951, Subardjo as Foreign Minister signed the Japanese Peace Treaty and in 1952 reached an agreement with the American Ambassador to Indonesia, Merle Cochran, for U.S. aid with the military security provisions (Sec. 511A) of the Mutual Security Act. This forced Subardjo's resignation and ultimately helped to bring down the cabinet in which he sat.

136. It is of some interest that later official summaries of the attempted coup by the PP list as the prime movers only Tan Malaka, Major General Sudarsono, and Mohammad Yamin. See, for example, *Lembaran Sedjarah* (*Pages of History*), p. 9.

137. Murba has been claimed by the Trotskyist Fourth International, though the claim is open to some question. See *Kepartaian dan Parlementaria di Indonesia*, pp. 547, 551. It is pertinent that the trade-union confederation of this group, known as SOBRI (Sentral Organisasi Buruh Republik Indonesia), joined the Communist World Federation of Trade Unions after the death of Stalin and the execution of Beria, and announced in late 1953 that it would cooperate with the Communist-controlled SOBSI.

138. The observations in this section are based in part on the author's assignment in Indonesia in 1950, where she worked on the United Nations Desk of the Indonesian Foreign Ministry and otherwise assisted the then Prime Minister and Foreign Minister, Dr. Hatta. Unless otherwise indicated, she alone is responsible for what is here stated.

139. At the height of the revolution, when newsprint was painfully scarce and shortages of personnel crippling, both the newspapers and the Ministry of Information's publications devoted a significant amount of space to international affairs and especially to the war in Indochina. See, for example, "Outburst in Vietnam," *Voice of Free Indonesia*, II (December 28, 1946), 125–26, which gives a rather cynical but highly perceptive analysis of the attitudes of the big powers on the fighting that had just broken out in Viet Nam. While this publication was meant for foreign consumption, it is typical of articles then appearing in the Indonesian-language press. See also *Rakjat* (otherwise unidentified), quoted in *Sari Pers*, January 11, 1947.

140. The author was surprised to find the extent to which villagers in fairly remote parts of Java were aware of the war in Viet Nam in 1950. The name of Ho Chi Minh was recognized in a number of places far from Djakarta or any other major city. This might have been the result of a rather successful propaganda tour conducted in the area some months before by an emissary of the Ho government. Among his campaign materials was a film which included a number of battle scenes; the first time this movie was shown, in a small theater in Glodok, in Djakarta, the audience, many of whom apparently mistook these battle scenes for pictures of their own revolution, became so overwrought that they charged down the aisles and ripped the screen apart.

141. The Ambassador arrived without his family but with some sixty-seven trunks of personal luggage. Twenty-four hours later, a tour of the bookshops in

the Chinese section of Djakarta revealed a newly acquired supply of books and pamphlets, in Indonesian or Chinese, which included works of Mao Tse-tung, Lenin, and some simplified summaries of Marx. Rather well printed, these books sold for the equivalent in purchasing power of a nickel, in contrast with the very few and prohibitively expensive books then available elsewhere in the Indonesian language.

142. The shortage of reading matter for the younger generation was a serious problem, since English-language books were extremely expensive even for those whose knowledge of English was sufficient to read them; furthermore, unlike their older brothers and sisters, the postwar crop of students did not know enough Dutch to read the many books available in that language.

143. Those political leaders who originally took the view that there was no point in focusing public resentment on Irian when so much of a positive nature remained to be done soon learned that this was one question which would not permit any deviation: Irian must be restored to Indonesia as rapidly as possible. Too much political capital has been made of the question by various individuals and parties to let any political group seeking popular support sidestep the issue. Thus, each and every Indonesian party includes the return of Irian to Indonesia as part of its political program.

144. In the developments that have taken place since this chapter was written in the spring of 1957, it is noteworthy that with few exceptions even the severest critics of the president's policies have hesitated to cut their ties with the president completely. There was more to this than an unwillingness to reject the still popular president and risk losing the support that his name lends; it was very much in keeping with the traditional Indonesian social preference for seeking to accommodate divergent points of view, as well as a reluctance to create an open and seemingly final break.

145. The first "pure and simple" Indonesian trade union, the Staatspoorweging Bond, an organization of employees of the government railway system, founded in 1905, predated the first nationalist organization. However, it was not only the first but the last of its kind, disbanding in 1912 after having lost much of its membership to the Vereeniging van Spoor-en Tramweg Personeel, VSTP, established in 1908 under the aegis of Dutch Socialists. The VSTP rapidly developed a political character, especially under the leadership of Sneevliet and Semaun. See *Vakbeweging*, p. 1.

146. On November 30, 1946, the Ministry of Information announced the "fusion" of the "labor movement . . . embracing around 750,000 members." SOBSI, it went on to say, "counts 85,000 railway workers, 2,000 oil-laborers, 6,000 marine and waterfront workers, 5,000 postal employees, 10,000 electrical mechanics, 100,000 sugar mill workers, 5,000 nurses, 5,000 pawnbroking service workers, 3,000 banking clerks . . . [T]he oil workers alone in Sumatra count 23,000." If the figure did not then reach 750,000, there was never any doubt then or now concerning the substantial character of the organization.

147. SOBSI techniques and their appeal to the masses are worth a little study. Utilizing whatever the local employees' grievances may be, willing to counsel tactics of violence without regard to the effects on the economy or stability of the country, running a kind of claims bureau in each locality where the personal problems and needs of its members are met, SOBSI probably reaches more individual Indonesians than any other organization in the country. SOBSI makes full use of the value of recognizing individual merit and achievement; awards

and decorations are handed out in impressive public ceremonies to which are invited not only union members but the whole population of the vicinity; speeches by well-known leaders are followed by dramatically staged presentations in which the recipients of the awards are called forward individually over the microphone from the platform and treated to enthusiastic ovations. The look on the face of an Indonesian oil field worker as he marches back to his seat from the platform where he has been decorated—a formerly obscure man now raised to the heights of fame and prestige among his fellow villagers—is sufficient explanation of the kind of devotion and loyalty that SOBSI can depend upon from so many of its followers.

148. The years of contact with the Netherlands, with its multiparty system, no doubt have had some effect as far as the multitude of parties goes.

149. For a review article citing some of the factors in the current scene, see Justus M. van der Kroef, "Instability in Indonesia," *Far Eastern Survey*, XXVI (April 1958), 49–62.

150. For a discussion of the election proceedings and results, see Irene Tinker and Mil Walker, "The First General Elections in India and Indonesia," *Far Eastern Survey*, XXV (July 1956), 97–110. For a more detailed analysis, see Herbert Feith, *The Indonesian Elections of 1955*.

151. This insistence that the struggle between Communism and anti-Communism is irrelevant to Indonesia was the burden of numerous conversations that the author has had in the course of the past ten years with Indonesian leaders in Indonesia, Western Europe, and the United States.

152. *Kepartaian dan Parlementaria di Indonesia*, p. 27. (Author's translation.)

153. See *ibid.*, p. 78, for a brief characterization of the Masjumi's basic principles and program.

154. Alimin, who had been the scapegoat for the Communist rebellion in 1926–27, had the responsibility for rebuilding the PKI after Madiun. He worked with a group of Indonesian Chinese party members including Tan Ling Djie; Siauw Giok Tjhan, founder of the PKI newspaper *Harian Rakjat*; and Tjoa Sik Ien, Indonesian delegate to, and presidium member of, the Warsaw World Peace Conference. By 1951 they had been replaced in the top posts by the present leadership of the PKI: Aidit, Lukman, etc. (McVey, pp. 70, 74, 87.) Both Alimin and Aidit had had their "time" in China, the latter particularly in 1949. In 1953, Aidit was responsible for eliminating the Indonesian Chinese from leading positions in the PKI.

155. Pesindo, led by Wikana and with many graduates of the Japanese-sponsored Asrama schools in key positions, was closely affiliated with the PKI by the time of Madiun.

156. The document appeared as an article by Miradsi in *Bintang Merah* (*Red Star*), Vol. VII, No. 12–13 (1951). (All quotations are from a translation in the possession of the author.)

157. The use of the old Comintern term "white terror" has a rather special anti-Dutch meaning of which, no doubt, the authors of this document were fully aware.

158. Although this was not the only target at which the charge about foreign participation in government politics was leveled, the Republican leadership was open to attack on this issue to the extent that it related to the handful of foreigners working in its offices in Jogjakarta and abroad during the revolution. Any

foreign assistants in the PKI were, naturally, not publicly visible. By the time the White Paper on Madiun appeared, there were a number of foreigners working for the government in Indonesia, most of them technical experts assigned under the terms of Indonesia's Technical Assistance agreement with the United Nations. Although in government circles attitudes toward these foreign experts vary, depending upon the individual expert's competence and personality, it has never been too difficult to create mass resentment against their presence, in the current atmosphere of dissatisfaction and injured national pride.

159. Musso is reported to have carried out negotiations for the Soviet Union's recognition of the Republic since: "Musso's conviction was that recognition by the USSR would be beneficial because, as a land of workers, the USSR was necessarily anti-imperialistic."

160. McVey, p. 78.

161. Iwa Kusumasumantri appears to be one of those Indonesian Marxists whose views are sufficiently eclectic to permit them to vacillate between the Stalinist and non-Stalinist camps.

162. *Kementerian Luar Negeri, Bagian Penerangan,* daily news cable for August 31, 1953.

163. *Ibid.*

164. The ease with which recognition of Red China was achieved was no doubt to some extent the result of the ambivalent attitude the Nationalist Chinese government had displayed toward the Indonesian revolution. It might be noted that this official attitude was softened somewhat at the United Nations by the fashion in which the Chinese delegate interpreted his government's instructions. As for attitudes toward the local Chinese, the fact that a sizable proportion of Indonesia's Chinese population had sided with the Dutch, passively if not actively, coupled with the traditional resentment of this minority, left anti-Chinese feeling running strong at the time of the transfer of sovereignty.

165. AP dispatch by William L. Ryan, Washington *Post,* August 13, 1954. Reference has already been made to the large supply of low-priced reading matter made available by Peking and, after the opening of the USSR embassy in Djakarta in the summer of 1954, by Moscow. Several Indonesians have commented on the very high proportion of these books which deal with military tactics and place special emphasis on guerrilla strategy.

166. Baperki, largest of these organizations, is headed by Siauw Giok Tjhan, former editor of the Communist daily *Harian Rakjat.* The PKI election showing outside of Java where it won thirty-five of its thirty-nine seats—the remaining four in Sumatra—was not impressive. However, Chinese communities in the outer islands are presumably being reached through Chinese teachers "drawn mostly from Peking." (Article by Arnold Brackman reporting about West Borneo, *Christian Science Monitor,* Boston, December 17, 1954.)

CHAPTER 6: THE IMPACT OF MARXISM

1. J. C. van Leur, *Indonesian Trade and Society,* Chapters 3 and 4; see especially pp. 95, 165 ff.

2. D. G. E. Hall, *Europe and Burma,* pp. 15–20.

3. In June 1956 at the London School of Oriental and African Studies, there was held what is probably the first, certainly a most important and valuable, series of seminars dealing with "Historical Writing on the Peoples of South and

Southeast Asia and the Far East." (For a brief review of the conference, see Holden Furber, "New Approaches to Asian History," *Journal of Asian Studies*, XVII [November 1957], 188–92.)

4. John S. Furnivall, *Netherlands India*, p. 243.

5. Various efforts were made to organize Socialist parties in Japan from 1882, and Vietnamese students in Japan in 1906–1909 were able to pick up Socialist ideas. In 1904 the *Communist Manifesto* was translated into Japanese and published in the *Heimin Shimbun*. This Marxist development in Japan does not appear to have reached into Southeast Asia, although just before World War I began, some members of the Netherlands Socialist Democratic Party arrived in Indonesia.

6. James Joll, *The Second International, 1889–1914*, pp. 123 f. Socialists desired to raise the living standards of backward people and to improve the way they were governed, but not to work for their political independence.

7. Cf. Lewis L. Lorwin, *Labor and Internationalism*, p. 89; and Franz Borkenau, *World Communism*, p. 18.

8. Borkenau, p. 94, where he says: "It became almost a mark of an orthodox Marxist to despise every nationalist feeling. . . .

"Lenin's practical genius here as always subordinated theory to the requirements of practice. He made no serious attempt to reconcile the existence and growth of nationalism with Marxism, but he gave it due attention in practice. He clearly saw that the world was full of national grievances, that these grievances were inflammable material to be used by the revolutionary, and that if he disregarded them they would become the greatest imaginable obstacle to the revolutionizing of the proletariat of all the oppressed nations. Much of the later policy of the Comintern is based on this insight."

Borkenau's language is too sweeping and his generalizations about Marx and Lenin too uncritical, but the passage as a whole genuinely reflects the spirit of the Marxist movement.

9. Philip E. Mosely, "Soviet Policy and the Revolutions in Asia," *Annals of the American Academy of Political and Social Science*, CCLXXVI (July 1951), 94.

10. Borkenau, p. 284.

11. Allen S. Whiting, *Soviet Policies in China, 1917–1924*, Chapter 1, usefully summarizes these.

12. Jane Degras (ed.), *The Communist International, 1919–1922*, pp. 38–47, especially p. 43; and pp. 138–44, especially p. 141.

13. It is interesting to note that Semaun has returned from his long exile and toured Java with President Sukarno in 1957. (New York *Times*, April 28, 1957.)

14. Xenia J. Eudin and Robert C. North, *Soviet Russia and the East, 1920–1927*, p. 44. This study is superbly documented and conveniently organized. During the period covered by the book, neither Burmese nor Thai personnel appear on the Communist scene, though conceivably some Burmese and Thai may have attended the "universities" for cadre training and/or the various "Asian" conferences. Full lists of "students" and delegates or observers at the conferences have not yet turned up either in Communist or other sources. Conversations with former Asian Communist leaders of this period, e.g., Darsono of Indonesia, now a valued civil servant in Djakarta, have tended to support the presumed fact of their absence.

15. Malcolm Kennedy, *A History of Communism in East Asia,* pp. 200, 204, 207, 218, asserts that Tan Malaka, an official Comintern agent, visited Bangkok in 1925 and 1927 and Rangoon for a second time in 1931. Ho Chi Minh visited Thailand in the interest of Vietnamese exiles in 1928. Tan Malaka and Alimin are supposed to have visited Rangoon in 1929. In 1928, some Chinese in Burma are supposed to have formed a Communist Committee to keep in touch with the Singapore South Seas Communist Center.

16. Wang Ming, *The Revolutionary Movement in the Colonial Countries,* p. 4. If anything, the paucity of these Communist contacts with Burma and Thailand supports the views expressed in the text.

17. Borkenau, pp. 287–89, vastly underrates the Comintern's relationship with the Asian movements. Admittedly, the Comintern increasingly turned attention from India to China between the Second and the Sixth Comintern Congress. However, it continued to direct its attention to Southeast Asia from Singapore and from China. Several hundred Southeast Asians received their Communist training in bureaus, conferences, and universities set up for this purpose between 1920 and 1928.

18. Lenin arrived at this position because he regarded "the peasant movements against the landowners . . . and all feudal survivals" as an essential element in the revolution against colonialism, especially so in those countries where the smallness of a proletarian base dictated the need for other allies. In this he had the support of Bukharin, who, just prior to the Second Comintern Congress, had called for "an agrarian revolution" as a means of winning support in Asia for the Comintern. Lenin, as far back as 1905, had begun to break with Marx's "anti-peasant prejudice," modifying Marx's unilinear conception of historical materialism (feudalism, capitalism, Socialism) by positing the possibility that a proletariat- and peasant-based revolution could leap over the bourgeois or capitalist stage directly into a Socialist one.

19. It is interesting to note that at the Fourth Comintern Congress Tan Malaka strongly supported the Leninist position, arguing specifically the need to win over Islamic elements in Indonesia. According to the published report, he was "loudly applauded." (See *Report* published for the Fourth Congress of the Communist International by the Communist Party of Great Britain, pp. 85 f. The *Report* carries the Credentials Committee proceedings, which credit the Communist party of Java with 1,300 members. China is credited with 300 members, of whom 180 are "full-paying members.") As late as August 1, 1927, Stalin in a speech on "The International Situation and the Defence of the USSR"— mainly because of his China policy—was still arguing for the Leninist line of 1920. See *Marxism and the National and Colonial Question,* pp. 204 ff. Pages 107 f. point out that Stalin evidenced little concern with China as such prior to 1924; I find, however, that during the early years Stalin clearly supported Lenin's policy for the colonial and semicolonial areas in Asia and elsewhere. (See Robert C. North, *Moscow and the Chinese Communists,* p. 26.)

20. Eudin and North, p. 271. The above interpretation of the Second through the Fifth Comintern Congress is amply supported and documented in the Eudin and North work. See also Ruth Fischer, "The Indian Communist Party." Fischer was a delegate to the Comintern from Germany during this period.

21. It is interesting to observe that the Indonesian Communist Party (PKI) is currently attempting to glorify the Communist revolt of 1926–27 as their early

anti-imperialist struggle for "national liberation." This propaganda is not without effect among non-Communists in Indonesia who were contemporaries of the event, as well as among other younger elements. (See *Harian Rakjat,* editorial, November 12, 1957.)

22. M. R. Masani, *The Communist Party of India,* Chapter 3; and Virginia M. Thompson and Richard Adloff, *The Left Wing in Southeast Asia.* Note the "Socialistic" influences in the Indonesian nationalist movement attendant upon its revival under the three leaders mentioned in the text. (See also George McT. Kahin, *Nationalism and Revolution in Indonesia,* p. 89.) The 1931–32 Saya San "peasant" rebellion and the slightly later organization of Ba Maw's Sinyetha (Poor Man's) Party in Burma can be cited as examples. Similarly, Vietnamese Nationalist Party activity (in contrast to that of the Communist Viet Nam Revolutionary Youth League) increased in tempo and importance after 1928.

23. This debate of the Second Comintern Congress had never been fully resolved. By the time the Comintern came to support Roy's original thesis, he was destined for expulsion from the Comintern as a "right-winger," most probably for his prominent association with Stalin's final, failing efforts in Kuomintang China.

24. All quotations in this passage are from the *Program of the Communist International.* It is interesting to note—especially in connection with the 1948 Calcutta meetings (discussed below)—that a new edition of this *Program* was published in Bombay in 1948.

25. Madhu Limaye, *Communist Party,* quotes various sections of the "Platform of Action of the Communist Party of India" (1930), pp. 18–19: "The greatest threat to the victory of the Indian revolution is the fact that great masses of our people still harbour illusions about the National Congress and have not realized that it represents a class organization of the capitalists working against the fundamental interests of the toiling masses of our country. . . . The National Congress and particularly its 'left' wing have done and are doing all in their power to restrain the struggle of the masses within the framework of the British imperialist constitution and legislation. . . . *Ruthless* war on the 'left' national reformists is an essential condition if we are to isolate the latter from the workers and mass of the peasantry and mobilize the latter under the banner of the Communist Party and the anti-imperialist agrarian revolution in India." (See also Masani, pp. 42 f.)

26. The program of the Seventh Comintern Congress has been briefly discussed in the first chapter of this study. The conditions here mentioned tended, at least temporarily, to shield Stalin and the Communist Party of the Soviet Union from criticism of the Soviet purges (1935–37) and the tragic subversion of the legitimate Spanish Republican government.

27. Jawaharlal Nehru, *Toward Freedom,* pp. 123–27.

28. Sutan Sjahrir, *Out of Exile,* pp. 217–19. Pro-German sympathies were also evident in China.

29. Ruth T. McVey, *The Development of the Indonesian Communist Party,* p. 18. See also Kahin, pp. 88 f. Kahin points out (p. 51) that the Communist Party of the Netherlands dropped its plank calling for Indonesian independence in 1938 and did not resume it until 1947. The Indochinese Communist Party not only cooperated with a French People's Front Parliamentary Commission which visited Saigon in 1936, but also acquiesced in the French Communist Party's "abandonment of the struggle for separation." This split the nationalist

movement in Indochina. The influence of Trotskyites and noncooperating nationalists grew at the expense of the official Communists because of the more conciliatory line of the latter toward the colonial administration.

30. Masani, pp. 65–75.

31. Frank N. Trager (ed.), *Burma*, III, Chapter 19, "The Labor Movement," 1006–62.

32. Thompson and Adloff, p. 28; see also Ellen J. Hammer, *The Struggle for Indochina*, pp. 91 f.

33. Kahin, pp. 96 f. Kahin typically states the facts; the inference is my own.

34. Das, *Mainsprings of Communist Activity: India, 1925–1950*, p. 7.

35. Sjahrir, pp. 186 f.

36. A valuable study of the Japanese success and failure in Asia is Willard H. Elsbree, *Japan's Role in Southeast Asian Nationalist Movements, 1940–1945*; see especially pp. 75, 164–69.

37. Max Beloff, *Soviet Policy in the Far East, 1944–1951*, Chapter 6.

38. F. S. V. Donnison, *British Military Administration in the Far East, 1943–1946*, pp. 344–69, 378, 403. It should be noted that all the Allies, including the U.S., concurred.

39. These two terms are used interchangeably in the present study, as is commonly done by Southeast Asians. No new theory of imperialism was ever developed in the region by either nationalists or Marxists. The definitions most commonly cited in response to demands are variants of Lenin's or occasionally of Hobson's. For the purposes of this study, Schumpeter's formulation (in Joseph A. Schumpeter, *Imperialism and Social Classes*, p. 6) is accepted: "Imperialism is the objectless disposition on the part of a state to unlimited forcible expansion" —except that for "objectless" I substitute "purposive," without, however, excluding from the imperialist drive nonrational elements of the type Schumpeter wishes to designate by the term "objectless."

40. The contemporary relevance of this issue can be seen in the Sumatran-Javanese conflict in Indonesia, 1956–57. (See the author's "Roots of Indonesian Conflict," *Foreign Policy Bulletin*, XXXVI [February 1957], 77–79.)

41. Throughout this study noncitizen Indian and Chinese elements are included in the phrase "alien economic domination."

42. As late as 1924, Stalin, in *The Foundations of Leninism*, was still putting India first: "The front of capital will not necessarily be pierced where industry is most developed . . . [I]t will be broken where the chain of imperialism is weakest." He went on to cite the revolution in Russia as having first exemplified this view. He suggested that the chain would next be broken "once more precisely where it will be the weakest[;] it is not impossible that this may be in India."

43. Schrieke, *Indonesian Sociological Studies*, pp. 83–166 (this was prepared as a report of the Investigating Committee appointed under a government decree of February 13, 1927). See also Paul Mus, *Viet-Nam: Sociologie d'une guerre*, Chapters 7 and 18, for a perceptive account of the acculturation of Marxist ideas in a Vietnamese setting.

44. For another example, see Furnivall, *An Introduction to the Political Economy of Burma*. This book, long out of print, was first published in 1931; the new impression is unchanged except for the addition of a new preface.

45. Trotskyists in Indochina after 1928 and Socialists in India after 1934

had no difficulty in finding differences with the Stalinists, but this implied a sophisticated level of Marxist knowledge and factional skill which one does not find either in Burma or in Indonesia, and certainly not in Thailand, in the thirties.

46. Schrieke, pp. 155–57.

47. See the author's "Insurgent Movements," Chapter XX in his *Burma*, Vol. III, esp. pp. 1080 ff.; U Ba Swe, *The Burmese Revolution*, p. 7; and speech by U Nu at the Third All-Burma AFPFL Congress, January 29, 1958, in *Burma Weekly Bulletin*, February 6, 1958.

48. Schrieke, p. 166.

49. Beloff, p. 15.

50. From 1925 onward, Stalin, in accordance with his law of the ebb and flow of revolutionary tides, had talked in reporting to the party congress of the inevitability of war and its aftermath of revolutions. The expected imperialist war "will," he reported to the Seventeenth CPSU Congress, "surely turn loose revolution and place in jeopardy the very existence of capitalism, as happened in the course of the first imperialist war." In 1946 he said that "the war in fact arose as the inevitable result of the development of world economic and political forces on the basis of contemporary monopolistic capitalism." It was no longer a war of "Democracy versus Fascism." The crises of capitalism would deepen. The imperialist camp would deteriorate because of internal contradictions. Hence, it was necessary for the U.S.S.R. to aid and abet the "revolutionary upswing." (Historicus, "Stalin on Revolution," *Foreign Affairs*, XXVII [January 1949], 19.)

51. Joseph Frankel, "Soviet Policy in Southeast Asia," Chapter 8, in Beloff, p. 209.

52. McVey, p. 53; see also pp. 52–65. She concludes that it is "difficult to determine what, if any, major direct influence the Soviet Union exercised on the course of events." McVey, in her more recent study, *The Calcutta Conference and the Southeast Asian Uprisings*, retains the same doubts with, perhaps, less reason.

53. John H. Kautsky, *Moscow and the Communist Party of India*, pp. 33 f. Kautsky appears to argue that because the Communist party of India had embarked upon a "decisive shift" two months before the Calcutta Conference, the latter was not the "literal" instrument for conveying "instructions to adopt a new line."

54. Masani, pp. 89 f. Das, *op. cit.*, p. 9.

55. Harold R. Isaacs, *The Tragedy of the Chinese Revolution*, pp. 58 f., writing of the early period (1922), refers to both written and oral communication between the Comintern and its affiliates. However, he also indicates that after 1926 the system of publication of documents was "scrapped." Semiconspiratorial techniques were henceforth employed (pp. 239 f.).

56. *Political Report of the Central Committee to the 15th Congress of the CPSU, (B)*, December 3, 1927. (This is also available in *The Communist Conspiracy*, Part I, May 29, 1956, pp. 132 ff.) In this report Stalin heralds "a new revolutionary upswing." He then defines the tasks of the party to include the "fight to develop the Communist parties all over the world," to strengthen revolutionary [i.e., nonreformist] trade-unions, and to build "a workers' united front." Here he foreshadowed the break with nonproletarian nationalist forces.

57. Kautsky, pp. 25 f.

58. It is not to be inferred that this practice of using representatives and

advisers was exclusively an Asian tactic. The Comintern assigned the well-known "C.I.Rep." to Western parties as well. However, in Europe the C.I.Rep. was seldom known, except by rumor, to the rank and file of the party. In Asia those selected by the Comintern for this purpose were openly known and were frequently leaders within the various Asian national parties.

59. The Burmese Communists, who were represented at the Bombay meeting by Goshal, took the same line on the Nu-Attlee agreement. Goshal's thesis, brought back from India, was based on the resolutions adopted at the Indian party's Central Committee meeting.

60. Between the Bombay and Calcutta meetings, Zhukov's "The Sharpening of the Crisis of the Colonial System" appeared. If anything, Zhukov's amplification of the new line as it affected the "liberation struggle" gave additional support to this left interpretation of Zhdanov's thesis. Though Zhukov's article appeared in print after the Bombay meeting, it is probable that Dange knew of it before his arrival at that meeting.

61. Frankel, in Beloff, p. 209, reports that nine hundred and eight hundred delegates, respectively, attended the Youth and Party meetings. He also indicates that a Soviet delegate by the name of Kharlamov reported the conference in the *Moscow News* of April 3.

62. It is not without irony that the First Asian Relations Conference, held in New Delhi, March–April 1947, had invited delegates from all the Asian countries including the Soviet Asian "Republics"; also observers from "Australia, New Zealand, Britain, the U.S.A. and the Soviet Union." The observer for the U.S.S.R. was none other than E. M. Zhukov, who, in June and later in December 1947, did so much to organize the left line against his Indian hosts, Gandhi and Nehru. (See Asian Relations, pp. 5, 278.)

63. See Masani, pp. 89–96.

64. Lucian W. Pye, *Guerrilla Communism in Malaya,* p. 84.

65. Kahin, p. 258.

66. See Philippe Devillers, "Vietnamese Nationalism and French Politics," in William Holland (ed.), *Asian Nationalism and the West*, pp. 199–265.

67. Shen-Yu Dai, *Peking, Moscow and the Communist Parties of Colonial Asia,* p. 28.

68. Milton Sacks, "The Strategy of Communism in Southeast Asia," *Pacific Affairs*, XXIII (September 1950), 227–47.

69. See H. Arthur Steiner, *The International Position of Communist China,* pp. 8–13, for a valuable, documented, and brief exposition of this Maoist line.

70. For example, C. C. Tan, in his otherwise fine study, *The Boxer Catastrophe,* remarks (p. 8): "One after another, China's dependencies were hacked away. Russia took part of Turkestan in 1881, France seized Tonkin in 1885, and in 1886 Britain annexed [Upper] Burma." He seems oblivious of the fact that Burma had ceased being a Chinese dependency, certainly since it defeated China four times between 1766 and 1769, and that Tonkin had achieved independence from China—except for a short interlude in the fifteenth century—as far back as the end of the Tang dynasty. Tan's is a typical reading of Chinese history from Chinese sources.

71. John C. Campbell, *The United States in World Affairs, 1945–47,* p. 467. Among the climactic events accenting the U.S. decision to disengage were President Truman's statement of December 18, 1946, in defense of the Marshall mission; Secretary of State Marshall's announcement on January 29, 1947, of

the dissolution of the mediation machinery in Peking and the withdrawal of remaining U.S. forces; the failure of General Wedemeyer's mission of July–August 1947 to effect any basic improvements in Chiang's regime; and the partisan political dispute which subsequently broke out in the U.S. concerning the Wedemeyer report. (See also Campbell, *The United States in World Affairs, 1947–1948,* pp. 184–202.)

72. Beloff, pp. 48–53. Beloff gives April (1949) as the month when the Soviet government underwent a radical public alteration in favor of the Chinese Communists (p. 65). Official references were then made to the "liberation" of China by the Communists and to the "new China." There can be little doubt that the Communists in the Soviet Union and in China had had close political relations throughout the war and the postwar period. Special note also should be taken of Liu Shao-chi's *Internationalism and Nationalism,* published in November 1948, which supported Stalin against Tito. One difficulty of interpreting the period 1945–49 is that the Chinese edition of Mao's writings for these years has not as yet been published. (For a review of this issue, see Steiner, " 'On the Record' with Mao and His Regime," *Journal of Asian Studies,* XVII [February 1958], 215–23.)

73. After the decline of the Communist parties in France and Italy, the fall of Czechoslovakia in February 1948, and the Berlin Airlift, Stalin had moved as far west in Europe as he could at that time without inviting a new war. It might be argued that to have captured Germany for Communism would have been more significant than to capture China, especially since Germany has meant so much to Soviet policy since World War I. Moves toward Germany, however, most probably would have entailed a greater risk of war, which Stalin then did not want and could not afford.

74. For the degree of interest in the post-Stalin period, see A. Z. Rubinstein, "Selected Bibliography of Soviet Works on Southern Asia, 1954–1956," *Journal of Asian Studies,* XVII (November 1957), 43–54. See also Ruth McVey, *Bibliography of Soviet Publications on Southeast Asia: As Listed in the Library of Congress Monthly Index of Acquisitions* (Cornell University Data Paper No. 34, March 1959).

75. Beloff, pp. 84–87. The conference was attended by 117 delegates representing thirteen countries, including India, Ceylon, Burma, Thailand, Viet Nam, Indonesia, Malaya, and the Philippines.

76. Barrington Moore, Jr., "The Outlook: Russia Since Stalin: Old Trends and New Problems," *Annals,* CCCIII (January 1956), 4. This view is based on the publication in October 1952 of Stalin's *Economic Problems of Socialism.*

77. U Nu, speech of September 27, 1957, printed as *Premier Reports to the People,* pp. 35 f., 41 f.

78. E. F. Stanton, "Spotlight on Thailand," *Foreign Affairs,* XXXIII (October 1954), 72–85.

79. Lewis L. Lorwin, *Labor and Internationalism,* p. 682; see also pp. 319, 321, 434, 440 f.

80. *Socialist Asia,* Vol. III (1955), Nos. 9–10, discusses editorially the differences between the Socialist International and the (nine parties of the) Asian Socialist Conference. The differences arise primarily from "their approach to the problem of colonialism and freedom of the dependent peoples." This in turn affects their views on world peace and world reconstruction. However, they resolved to cooperate and in July 1953 set up liaison machinery for this purpose.

Delegate Moshe Sharett, then Foreign Minister of Israel, also worked for European organizational ties. An influential delegation of observers came from Yugoslavia: Milovan Djilas and Ales Bebler.

81. The most convenient source is the *Report of the First Asian Socialist Conference*, IX, 114. (The Appendix, pp. 91–110, reprints the resolutions in full. See also *Three Years of Asian Socialist Conference*; and Saul Rose, "The Asian Socialist Conference of 1953," *Far Eastern Affairs*, (1957), pp. 75–93.

82. Rose, who attended the conference as a representative of the Socialist International, professes (p. 79) to find a "special ideological factor; a strong Leninist influence, in the Burmese and Indonesian parties which together with self-conscious Asianism, an element of anti-Europeanism and anti-colonialism and neutralism made them unwilling to join the Socialist International." As an unofficial observer at this conference, the author of the present chapter would argue that the ideological factor of Leninism, especially in the Indonesian Socialist party and to a major extent in the Burmese Socialist party, had become so diluted by the time of the conference as to be ideologically meaningless. Even Lenin's name, which by contrast to Stalin's was still used respectfully, was hardly heard at the conference. Sjahrir had already coupled "Leninism" and "Stalinism" as incompatible with Socialism. By 1954 the Burmese leadership stood out as non-Leninist or as anti-Leninist in their opposition to Soviet imperialism. It is worth noting that Rose in his subsequent work, *Socialism in Southern Asia*, pp. 4–13, drops this inaccurate charge of "Leninist tendencies" which he had earlier ascribed to the Burmese and Indonesian parties.

83. *Socialist Asia* (August 1954), pp. 1 f., editorially welcomed "the ceasefire in Indochina." It regarded the "liberation of Laos and Cambodia from the threat of communist occupation and from the shackles of French imperialism as the most impressive consequence of the [July] Geneva agreements . . . Vietnam, however, continues to remain a tragedy. Dr. Ho Chi Minh for instance has promised the Communists a complete liberation of the country south of the 17th parallel from the 'continued' stranglehold of the 'imperialist warmongers.' What that exactly means is not difficult to predict . . . [T]he fate of the Vietnamese, Cambodians and Laotians depends more on the countries of Asia pursuing an independent foreign policy than on the sincerity and desire for peace and co-existence of the Sino-Russian and Anglo-American blocs."

84. Subsequent meetings of one kind or another have been held roughly on a semiannual basis. *Socialist Asia*, originally a monthly, now a quarterly, has been published as the organ of the Conference. All these organizational arrangements are so far conducted from the Secretariat, located in Rangoon. The Second Asian Socialist Conference met in Bombay, November 1–10, 1956; the resolutions of the second conference were published in *Information Bulletin*, Asian Socialist Conference, Vol. I, No. 4 (November 1956), mimeographed.

85. Sjahrir, *Indonesian Socialism*, p. 10. The quotation is from a 1952 PSI document reprinted in this collection.

86. *Ibid.*, pp. 48 f., 65.

87. *Socialist Asia*, III (June 1954), 9–11.

88. Undoubtedly, some Asian Socialists will reject U Nu's identification of Marxism and Communism. They will retain what Sidney Hook has called "the Marxist ethical critique of capitalism"; i.e., that the latter supports property as a form of power capable of excluding others from its usufructs, because this critique squares with their experience. But they are increasingly skeptical of

Defence in Southeast Asia. There are also a few monographs on special topics, such as William Henderson, *Pacific Settlement of Disputes*; Frank N. Trager, Patricia Wohlgemuth, and Lu-yu Kiang, *Burma's Role in the United Nations, 1948–1955*; and Ralph Braibanti, "The Southeast Asia Collective Defense Treaty," *Pacific Affairs*, XXX (December 1957), 321–41.

107. See Tillman Durdin, "Red Activities Up in South Vietnam," New York *Times*, April 13, 1959.

108. See "Southeast Asia and Communism: The Psychological Effort of the Communists in Southeast Asia in 1956," *Far Eastern Economic Review*, January 17 and 24, 1957, pp. 75–79, 103–10.

109. G. William Skinner, "Chinese Assimilation and Thai Politics," *Journal of Asian Studies*, XVI (February 1957), 237–50; and New York *Times*, June 30 and July 20, 1957. For a brief discussion of Communist China and the overseas Chinese of Southeast Asia, see *Collective Defence in Southeast Asia*, pp. 83–90.

110. See Hugh Tinker, "Burma's Northeast Borderland Problems," *Pacific Affairs*, XXIX (December 1956), 324–46; "Eloquent Maps," *China News Analysis*, April 27, 1956; U Nu, "On the Sino-Burmese Boundary Question," *Burma Weekly Bulletin*, November 15, 1956; and Chou En-lai, "Report on the Question of the Boundary Line Between China and Burma," *People's China*, August 1957, Supplement. Burma has little choice except to negotiate peacefully. No matter how the frontier may finally be drawn, Burma will lose territory which it regards as Burmese.

111. Kyaw Nyein, "To prefer is not to choose," in *Socialist Asia*, III (June 1954), 9–11. See also *Partai Sosialis Indonesia*, Djakarta, 1956, pp. 24 f.

112. *Three Years of Asian Socialist Conference*, pp. 25–27.

113. The former secretary of the Socialist International visited South and Southeast Asia in connection with the Bombay meeting (November 1956) of the Asian Socialist Conference. Although Asian Socialists and many Asian nationalists had by this time criticized an exclusive equation between capitalism and colonialism, this observer still believed it to be pervasive. He remarks, somewhat ingenuously, that the Asian Socialists "are rather severe in their criticism of the international policy [on colonial questions] of some of the International's member parties," overlooking the fact that this has been the main issue in Asia since World War I and that it had been largely neglected or compromised by the member parties of the International. (See *Socialist International Information*, Vol. VII [June 1, 1957] 391–98; see also above, fn. 82.)

114. Frank N. Trager, "Burma's Foreign Policy, 1948–1956: Neutralism, Third Force, and Rice," *Journal of Asian Studies*, XVI (November 1956), 89–102; and John Seabury Thomson, "Burmese Neutralism," *Political Science Quarterly*, LXXII (June 1957), 261–83.

115. Sjahrir, *Indonesian Socialism*, p. 43.

116. There is no single exposition of the above summary, but a sampling of the following references may convince skeptics: almost any issue of *Socialist Asia*, the quarterly of the Asian Socialist Conference; *Three Years of Asian Socialist Conference*; Sjahrir, *Indonesian Socialism*; *Cultural Freedom in Asia*; and M. W. Fisher and J. V. Bondurant, *Indian Approaches to a Socialist Society*. Of President Sukarno's speech, *The Birth of Pantja Sila*, Kahin says (p. 123): "Probably in no other exposition of principle can one find a better example of the synthesis of Western democratic, Modern Islamic, Marxist and indigenous-

village democratic and communalistic ideas which forms the general basis of the social thought of so large a part of the postwar Indonesian elite."

117. The quotations are from the Indonesian *Socialist Bulletin*, Vol. I, No. 2 (1956), p. 5, and Vol. I (*sic*), No. 1 (1957), p. 5. See also L. M. Sitorus, *Socialist International Information Bulletin*, Vol. VII (May 4, 1957) 321–24: "People's Socialism, having emerged from the national struggle, today forms a separate broad current in Asia in particular, and in the world in general. In foreign policy it stands for non-participation in the cold war between the Russian and Western blocs, and for the development of a third force working for world peace and friendship. In home policy, it is based on the interests of the people, of the nation. Its method is the parliamentary struggle combined with efforts to organize the people for the defence of their interests and the improvement of their conditions by constructive efforts in all fields."

118. See the speeches by former Prime Minister U Nu on the subject of cultural pluralism. This theme is one of his favorites, and he is recognized by minority groups in Burma as a true and just friend. See also Kyaw Thet, "Cultural Minorities in Burma," in Herbert Passin (ed.), *Cultural Freedom in Asia*, pp. 228–40, and his chapter in P. W. Thayer (ed.), *Nationalism and Progress in Free Asia*.

BIBLIOGRAPHY

BOOKS AND GOVERNMENT DOCUMENTS

Acton, H. B. *The Illusion of the Epoch: Marxism-Leninism as a Philosophical Creed.* London, 1955.

Alimin. *Analysis.* Jogjakarta, 1947.

Allen, C. C., and A. G. Donnithorne. *Western Enterprise in Far Eastern Development: China and Japan.* London, 1954.

——. *Western Enterprise in Indonesia and Malaya.* London, 1957.

Anh Van and Jacqueline Roussel. *Mouvements Nationaux et Lutte de Classes au Viet-Nam.* Paris, 1947.

Ardenne de Tizac, Andrée Françoise C. (Andrée Viollis). *Indochine S.O.S.* Paris, 1935.

Asian Relations: Being a Report of the Proceedings and Documentation of the First Asian Relations Conference. New Delhi, 1948.

Aziz, Muhammad Abdul. *Japan's Colonialism and Indonesia.* The Hague, 1955.

Ba Swe, U. *The Burmese Revolution.* Rangoon, 1952.

Beloff, Max. *Soviet Policy in the Far East, 1944–1951.* London, 1953.

Blumberger, John Theodoor Petrus. *Le Communisme aux Indes Néerlandaises.* Paris, 1929.

——. *De Communistische Beweging in Nederlandsch-Indie (The Communist Movement in Netherlands India).* Haarlem, 1935.

——. *De Nationalistische Beweging in Nederlandsch-Indie (The Nationalist Movement in Netherlands India).* Haarlem, 1931.

Boeke, J. H. *Economics and Economic Policy of Dual Societies as Exemplified by Indonesia.* New York, 1953.

Boorman, Howard L., Alexander Eckstein, Philip E. Mosely, and Benjamin Schwartz. *Moscow-Peking Axis: Strengths and Strains.* New York, 1957.

Borkenau, Franz. *European Communism.* London, 1953.

——. *World Communism: A History of the Communist International.* New York, 1939.

Bousquet, G. H. *A French View of the Netherlands Indies.* London, 1940.

Brandt, Conrad, Benjamin Schwartz, and John K. Fairbank. *A Documentary History of Chinese Communism.* Cambridge, Mass., 1952.

(Burma) Economic and Social Board. *Pyidawtha: The New Burma.* London, 1954.

Callis, Helmut G. *Foreign Capital in Southeast Asia.* New York, 1942. Mimeo.

Campbell, John C. *The United States in World Affairs, 1945–1947.* New York, 1947.

————. *The United States in World Affairs, 1947–1948.* New York, 1948.
Carr, E. H. *The Bolshevik Revolution, 1917–1923.* London, 1950.
Célerier, Pierre (pseud.). *Menaces sur le Viet Nam.* Saigon, 1950.
Chamberlin, William Henry. *Blue Print for World Conquest.* Washington, D.C., 1946.
Chesneaux, Jean. *Contribution à l'Histoire de la Nation Vietnamienne.* Paris, 1955.
Chronicle of Principal Events Relating to the Indo-China Question, 1940–1950, Peking, 1954.
Chuong trinh hanh dong cua Dang Cong San Dong Duong: Chi bo doc lap cua quoc te Cong san (The Program of Action of the Indochina Communist Party: Independence Section of the Communist International). Berlin, 1932.
Coast, John. *Some Aspects of Siamese Politics.* New York, 1953.
Cole, Allan B., ed. *Conflict in Indochina and International Repercussions: A Documentary History, 1945–1955.* Ithaca, N.Y., 1956.
Cole, G. D. H. *A History of Socialist Thought.* London, 1953 and 1956. Vols. II and III.
Collective Defence in Southeast Asia: The Manila Treaty and Its Implications. London, 1956.
Comintern. Vᵉᵐᵉ *Congrès de l'Internationale Communiste (17 June–8 July, 1924). Compte-Rendu Analytique.* Paris, 1924.
Communist Party of Great Britain. *Report.* Published for the Fourth Congress of the Communist Party of Great Britain. London, n.d.
Coulet, Georges. *Les Sociétés Secrètes en Terre d'Annam.* Saigon, 1926.
Cultural Freedom in Asia. Rutland, Vt., 1956.
Das, S. R. Mohan. *Ho chi Minh: Nationalist or Soviet Agent?* Bombay, 1950.
————. *Mainsprings of Communist Activity: India 1925–1950.* Bombay, n.d. [1950].
Decoux, Jean. *A La Barre de l'Indochine: Histoire de mon Gouvernement Général (1940–1945).* Paris, 1949.
Degras, Jane, ed. *The Communist International, 1919–1922.* London, 1956.
De Kat Angelino, A. D. A. *Staatkundig beleid en bestuurszorg in Nederlandsch-Indie (Political Leadership and Administrative Policy in Netherlands India).* The Hague, 1929–30. 2 vols. in 3.
De Klerck, E. S. *History of the Netherlands East Indies.* Rotterdam, 1938. 2 vols.
Devillers, Philippe. *Histoire du Viet-Nam de 1940 à 1952.* Paris, 1952.
Donnison, F. S. V. *British Military Administration in the Far East, 1943–1946.* London, 1956.
Dorsenne, Jean. *Faudra-t-il Evacuer l'Indochine?* Paris, 1932.
Du Bois, Cora. *Social Forces in Southeast Asia.* St. Paul, Minn., 1949.
Duijs, J. E. W. *De Vervolging Tegen de Indonesische Studenten Mohammad Hatta, Mr. Ali Sastroamidjojo, Raden Mas Abdul Madjid Djodjoadhiningrat en Muhammad Nazir Pamontjak. Verdedigings-Rede, Gehouden in de Zitting der Arr. Rechtbankte s'Gravenhage op 8 Maart 1928 (The Prosecution of the Indonesian Students Mohammad Hatta, Mr. Ali Sastroamidjojo, Raden Mas Abdul Madjid Djojoadhiningrat and Mohammad Nazir Pamontjak).* Amsterdam, 1928.
Eastman, Max. *Marxism: Is It Science?* New York, 1940.

Elegant, Robert S. *China's Red Masters*. New York, 1951.
Elsbree, Willard H. *Japan's Role in Southeast Asian Nationalist Movements, 1940–1945*. Cambridge, Mass., 1953.
Emerson, Rupert. *Malaysia: A Study in Direct and Indirect Rule*. New York, 1937.
Encyclopaedie van Nederlandsch-Indie. The Hague, 1917–39. 8 vols.
Engels, Friedrich. *Anti-Dühring*. London, n.d.
———. *Ludwig Feuerbach and the Outcome of Classical German Philosophy*. London, n.d.
———. *Socialism, Utopian and Scientific*. Chicago, n.d.
Ensiklopedia Indonesia. Bandung, 1954–56. 3 vols.
Eudin, Xenia J., and Robert C. North. *Soviet Russia and the East, 1920–1927: A Documentary Survey*. Stanford, 1957.
Factual Records of the Vietnam August Revolution. Hanoi, 1946.
Fall, Bernard. *The Viet-Minh Regime*. 2d ed. New York, 1956.
Farley, Miriam S. *United States Relations with Southeast Asia, 1950–1955*. New York, 1955. Mimeo.
Feith, Herbert. *The Indonesian Elections of 1955*, Interim Reports Series, Modern Indonesia Project, Southeast Asia Program, Cornell University, Ithaca, New York, 1957, 91 pp.
Fifield, Russell H. *The Diplomacy of Southeast Asia: 1945–1958*. New York, 1958.
Figueres, Leo. *Je reviens du Viet-Nam Libre: Notes de Voyage*. Paris, 1950.
Finkelstein, Lawrence S. *American Policy in Southeast Asia*. Rev. ed. New York, 1951. Mimeo.
Fischer, Ruth. "The Indian Communist Party." Unpublished paper presented at the Russian Research Center, Harvard University, July 11, 1952.
Fisher, M. W., and J. V. Bondurant. *Indian Approaches to a Socialist Society*. Berkeley, Calif., 1956.
(France) Gouvernement Général de l'Indochine. Direction des Affaires Politiques et de la Sûreté Générale. *Documents*. Vol. I, *Le Tan Viet Cach Menh Dang—Parti Revolutionnaire du Jeune Annam, 1925–1930* (Hanoi, 1933); Vol. II, *Le Viet-Nam Quoc Dan Dang ou "Parti National Annamite" au Tonkin, 1927–1932* (Hanoi, 1933); Vol. III, *Le Viet-Nam Quoc Dan Dang ou "Parti National Annamite" des Emigres en Chine, 1930–1933* (Hanoi, 1933); Vol. IV, *Le "Dong Duong Cong San Dang" ou "Parti Communiste Indochinois," 1925–1933* (Hanoi, 1933); Vol. V, *La Terreur Rouge en Annam, 1930–1931* (Hanoi, 1934).
Furnivall, John S. *An Introduction to the Political Economy of Burma*. Rangoon, 1957.
———. *Netherlands India: A Study of Plural Economy*. New York, 1944.
Garros, George. *Forceries Humaines*. Paris, 1926.
Gobron, Gabriel. *Histoire et Philosophie du Cao Daisme*. Paris, 1949.
Goeldhieux, Claude. *Quinze Mois Prisonnier chez les Viets*. Paris, 1953.
Goodrich, Carter. *Report of the Economic Survey Mission of the United Nations and Specialized Agencies to the Republic of Viet Nam*. New York, 1956.
Graham, W. A. *Siam*. 2d ed. London, 1924. 2 vols.
(Great Britain) Foreign Office. *Further Documents relating to the Discussion of Indo-China at the Geneva Conference, June 16–July 21, 1954*. Miscellaneous No. 20, Cmd. 9239. London, 1954.

——. *Documents relating to the Discussion of Korea and Indo-China at the Geneva Conference, April 27–June 15, 1954.* Miscellaneous No. 16, Cmd. 9186. London, 1954.

——. *First and Second Interim Reports of the International Commission for Supervision and Control in Vietnam.* Vietnam No. 1, Cmd. 9461. London, 1955.

——. *Third Interim Report of the International Commission for Supervision and Control in Vietnam.* Vietnam No. 2, Cmd. 9499. London, 1955.

——. *Fourth Interim Report of the International Commission for Supervision and Control in Vietnam.* Vietnam No. 3, Cmd. 9654. London, 1955.

Grivaz, Raymond. *Aspects Sociaux et Economiques du Sentiment Religieux en Pays Annamite.* Paris, 1942.

Haimson, L. H. *The Russian Marxists and the Origins of Bolshevism.* Cambridge, Mass., 1955.

Haldane, J. B. S. *The Marxist Philosophy and the Sciences.* New York, 1939.

Hall, D. G. E. *Europe and Burma: A Study of European Relations with Burma.* London, 1945.

Hammer, Ellen J. *The Struggle for Indochina.* Stanford, 1954.

Hatta, Mohammad. *Indonesian Aims and Ideals.* n.p., n.d. Mimeo.

——. *(Statement on) The Conception of the President.* n.p., 1957. Mimeo.

——. *Verspreide Geschriften.* Amsterdam, 1952.

Heine-Geldern, Robert G. *Conception of State and Kingship in Southeast Asia.* Ithaca, N.Y., 1956. Mimeo.

Henderson, William. *Pacific Settlement of Disputes: The Indonesian Question, 1946–1949.* New York, 1954.

Higgins, Benjamin. *Indonesia's Economic Stabilization and Development.* New York, 1957.

Hilferding, Rudolph. *Finanz-Kapital.* Berlin, 1955.

Holland, William, ed. *Asian Nationalism and the West.* New York, 1953.

Hoa Mai, *The "Nhan-Van" Affair.* Saigon(?), 1957(?).

Hook, Sidney. *From Hegel to Marx.* New York, n.d. [1936].

Ho van Tao. *Le Mystérieux Ho chi Minh.* Paris, 1953.

Hunt, R. N. Carew. *Theory and Practice of Communism.* London, 1950.

(Indonesia) Ministry of Foreign Affairs. Division of Information. *Daily Press Cable.* Djakarta.

——. *Indonesia.* Djakarta, n.d.

——. *Indonesian Affairs.* Djakarta, monthly.

——. *Information Bulletins.* Issued by Indonesian diplomatic missions: Cairo, Colombo, Manila, New Delhi, and New York.

——. *Kepartaian di Indonesia (Parties in Indonesia).* n.p., n.d.

——. *Lembaran Sedjarah (Pages of History).* Jogjakarta, 1950.

——. *Press Releases.* Djakarta and Jogjakarta.

——. *Sari Pers (Press Review).* Djakarta.

——. *Vakbeweging (The Labor Movement).* Djakarta, 1947.

——. *Voice of Free Indonesia.* Djakarta, 1946–49.

Ingram, James C. *Economic Change in Thailand Since 1850.* Stanford, 1955.

Isaacs, Harold R. *New Cycle in Asia.* New York, 1947.

——. *No Peace for Asia.* New York, 1947.

——. *The Tragedy of the Chinese Revolution.* London, 1938. Rev. ed. Stanford, 1951.

Jansen, Marius B. *The Japanese and Sun Yat-sen.* Cambridge, Mass., 1954.
Joll, James. *The Second International, 1889–1914.* New York, 1956.
Kahin, George McT. *Nationalism and Revolution in Indonesia.* Ithaca, N.Y., 1952.
Kasem Udyanin and Rufus D. Smith. *The Public Service in Thailand.* Brussels, 1954.
Kaummunit Thai ca Tham Araj naj Prachuban (*What the Thai Communists Will Do Now*). Bangkok, 1945.
Kautsky, John H. *Moscow and the Communist Party of India: A Study in the Post War Evolution of International Communist Strategy.* New York, 1956.
Kennedy, Malcolm. *A History of Communism in East Asia.* New York, 1957.
Kennedy, Raymond. *The Ageless Indies.* New York, 1942.
King, John K. *Southeast Asia in Perspective.* New York, 1956.
Koch, D. M. Georg. *Om de Vrijheid* (*Toward Freedom*). Djakarta, 1950.
Kulski, W. W. *The Soviet Regime: Communism in Practice.* Syracuse, N.Y., 1956.
Landon, Kenneth P. *Siam in Transition.* Chicago, 1939.
Leites, Nathan. *A Study of Bolshevism.* Glencoe, Ill., 1953.
Lenin, V. I. *Imperialism, The Highest Stage of Capitalism.* Rev. trans. New York, 1933.
———. *Marx-Engels Marxism.* 5th English ed. Moscow, 1953.
———. *Materialism and Empirio-Criticism.* New York, 1927.
———. *The State and Revolution.* New York, 1932.
———. *Two Tactics of Social-Democracy in the Democratic Revolution.* New York, 1935.
———. *What Is To Be Done? Burning Questions of Our Movement.* New York, 1935.
Le thanh Khoi. *Le Viet-Nam Histoire et Civilisation.* Paris, 1955.
Limaye, Madhu. *Communist Party: Facts and Fiction.* Hyderabad, 1951.
Liu Shao-chi. *Internationalism and Nationalism.* Peking, 1948.
Lorwin, Lewis L. *Labor and Internationalism.* New York, 1929.
McVey, Ruth. *Bibliography of Soviet Publications on Southeast Asia: As Listed in the Library of Congress Monthly Index of Acquisitions.* Cornell University Data Paper No. 37, March, 1959.
———. *The Calcutta Conference and the Southeast Asian Uprisings.* Ithaca, N.Y., 1958.
———. *The Development of the Indonesian Communist Party and Its Relations with the Soviet Union and the Chinese People's Republic.* Cambridge, Mass., 1954.
Madge, Charles. *Village Communities in Northeast Thailand.* New York, 1954.
Mao Tse-tung. *On People's Democratic Dictatorship.* n.p., 1949.
———. *Selected Works,* Vol. III. London, 1954.
Marx, Karl. *Capital: A Critique of Political Economy.* Chicago, 1906–1909. 3 vols.
———. *A Contribution to the Critique of Political Economy.* Chicago, 1913.
———. *Critique of the Gotha Programme.* New York, 1938.
———. *The Eighteenth Brumaire of Louis Bonaparte.* Trans. by Daniel DeLeon. 3d ed. Chicago, 1913.
———, and Friedrich Engels. *Communist Manifesto.* Trans. by Samuel Moore. Chicago, 1955.

————. *The German Ideology.* London, 1940.

Marxism and the National and Colonial Question: A Collection of Articles and Speeches. Moscow, 1940.

Masani, M. R. *The Communist Party of India: A Short History.* New York, 1954.

Maung Maung (U). *Burma in the Family of Nations.* Amsterdam, 1956.

Mus, Paul. *Viet-Nam: Sociologie d'une guerre.* Paris, 1952.

Natsir, Mohammad. *Some Observations Concerning the Role of Islam in Nationl and International Affairs.* Ithaca, N.Y., 1954.

Nehru, Jawaharlal. *Toward Freedom: The Autobiography of . . . .* New York, 1941.

Nguyen ai Quoc. *Le Procès de la Colonisation Française.* Hanoi, 1946.

Nguyen van Dam. *Le Viet Nam en Marche.* Hanoi, 1955.

Nguyen van Dinh. *Ta thu Thau: Tu Quoc-Gia Toi Quoc-Te (Ta thu Thau: From Nationalism to Internationalism).* Cholon, 1939.

North, Robert C. *Moscow and the Chinese Communists.* Stanford, 1953.

Nu, U. *Premier Reports to the People.* Rangoon, 1958.

Orgwald. *Tactical and Organizational Questions of the Communist Parties of Indo-China and India: Questions and Answers.* n.p. [U.S.], 1933.

Pagniez, Yvonne. *Le Viet Minh et la Guerre Psychologique.* Paris, 1955.

Partai Sosialis Indonesia. Djakarta, 1956.

Pasquier, Pierre. *L'Annam d'autrefois: Essai sur la Constitution de l'Annam avant l'intervention française.* Paris, 1929.

Petit, Robert. *La Monarchie Annamite.* Paris, 1931. Vol. V.

Plekhanov, Georgii. *Fundamental Problems of Marxism.* New York, 1930.

————. *In Defence of Materialism.* London, 1947.

Pluvier, J. M. *Overzicht van de Ontwikkeling der Nationalistische Beweging in Indonesie (Survey of the Development of the Nationalist Movement in Indonesia).* The Hague, 1953.

Prasœt Sapsunthọn. *Chi wa that (View of Life).* Bangkok, 1949.

Pringgodigdo, A. K. *Sedjarah Pergerakan Rakjat Indonesia (History of the Indonesian People's Movement).* Djakarta, 1949.

Program of the Communist International. Adopted at the Sixth World Congress, September 1, 1928. New York, 1929.

Purcell, Victor. *The Chinese in Southeast Asia.* London, 1951.

Pye, Lucian W. *Guerrilla Communism in Malaya.* Princeton, N.J., 1956.

Quaritch-Wales, H. G. *Ancient Siamese Government and Administration.* London, 1934.

Raliby, Osman. *Documenta Historica: Sedjarah Dokcumenter dari Pertumbuhan dan Perdjuangan Negara Republik Indonesia (Historical Documents: Documentary History of the Growth and Struggle of the Republic of Indonesia).* Djakarta, 1953. Vol. I.

Report of the First Asian Socialist Conference. Rangoon, 1953.

Robequain, Charles. *The Economic Development of French Indo-China.* Trans. by Isabel A. Ward. London and New York, 1944. Supplement by John R. Andrus and Katrine R. C. Greene, *Recent Developments in Indo-China: 1939–1943.*

Rose, Saul. *Socialism in Southern Asia.* London, 1959.

Rostow, W. W. *The Dynamics of Soviet Society.* New York, 1953.

Rutgers, S. J. *Indonesie: het Koloniale systeem in de periode tussen de eerste en de tweede wereldoorlog (Indonesia: The Colonial System in the Period between the First and Second World Wars).* Amsterdam, 1947.

Schrieke, B. J. O. *Indonesian Sociological Studies: Selected Writings of B. Schrieke*. The Hague, 1955.
Schumpeter, Joseph A. *Capitalism, Socialism and Democracy*. 4th ed. New York and London, 1954.
———. *Imperialism and Social Classes*. New York, 1955.
Schwartz, Benjamin I. *Chinese Communism and the Rise of Mao*. Cambridge, Mass., 1951.
Semaoen (Semaun). *Hoe het Hollandsche Imperialisme het bruine millionen-volk aanzet tot een massamoord op Europeanen in Indonesia* (*How Dutch Imperialism Urges the Millions of Brown People to a Mass Murder of Europeans in Indonesia*). Amsterdam, n.d.
Sharp, Lauriston, ed. *Handbook on Thailand*. New Haven, Conn., 1956.
———, Hazel Hauck, Kamol Janlekha, and Robert Textor. *Siamese Rice Village: A Preliminary Study of Bang Chan, 1948–1949*. Bangkok, 1953.
Shen-Yu Dai. *Peking, Moscow and the Communist Parties of Colonial Asia*. Cambridge, Mass., 1954.
Sitorus, L. M. *Sedjarah Pergerakan Kebangsaan Indonesia* (*History of the Indonesian Nationalist Movement*). Djakarta, 1947.
Sivaram, M. *Mekong Clash and Far Eastern Crisis*. Bangkok, 1941.
Sjahrir, Sutan. *Indonesian Socialism*. Rangoon, 1956.
———. *Onze Strijd* (*Our Fight*). Amsterdam, 1946.
———. *Out of Exile*. Trans. by Charles Wolf, Jr. New York, 1949.
Skinner, G. William. *Chinese Society in Thailand: An Analytical History*. Ithaca, N.Y., 1957.
Sri Burapha (Kulab Saipradit). *Songkhram Chi wit* (*Struggle of Life*). Bangkok, 1932.
Stalin, Josef. *Dialectical and Historical Materialism*. New York, 1940.
———. *Economic Problems of Socialism*. New York, 1952.
———. *The Foundations of Leninism*. Rev. trans. New York, 1932.
———. *History of the Communist Party of the Soviet Union*. New York, 1939.
———. *Political Report of the Central Committee to the 15th Congress of the CPSU, (B)*. December 3, 1927. Moscow, 1950.
———. *Problems of Leninism*. Moscow, 1953.
———. *Works*. Moscow, 1952–55. 13 vols.
Stammhammer, Joseph. *Bibliographie des Socialismus und Communismus*. Jena, 1893–1909. 3 vols.
Starobin, Joseph R. *Eyewitness in Indochina*. New York, 1954.
———. *Viet Nam Fights for Freedom: The Record of a Visit to the Liberated Areas of Viet Nam in March 1953*. London, 1953.
Steiner, H. Arthur. *The International Position of Communist China*. New York, 1958. Mimeo.
Sukarno. *Indonesie Klaagt Aan! Pleitrede voor den Landraad te Bandoeng op 2 December 1930 Gehouden door Ir. Soekarno* (*Indonesia Accuses! Defense speech given before the District Court in Bandung, December 2, 1930, by Engineer Soekarno*). n.p., 1931.
———. *The Birth of Pantja Sila*. Djakarta, 1945.
Supha Sirimanond. *Khaphithalit* (*Capitalism*). Bangkok, 1951.
Suphot Tantrakun. *Khabuan kan ku chat* (*National Liberation Movement*). Bangkok, 1957.
Suriyabongse, Dr. Luang. *Buddhism in Thailand*. Bangkok, n.d.
Tan, C. C. *The Boxer Catastrophe*. New York, 1955.

Tan Malaka. *Massa Actie (Mass Action)*. Djakarta, 1947.
———. *Thesis*. Djakarta, 1947.
Témoignages et Documents Français Relatif à la Colonisation Française au Viet Nam. Hanoi, 1945.
(Thailand) Ministry of Agriculture. Department of Agricultural Economics. *Economic Farm Survey, 1953*. Bangkok, 1955.
———. National Economic Council. Central Statistical Office. *Statistical Year Book of Thailand*. Bangkok, 1953.
Thayer, P. W., ed. *Nationalism and Progress in Free Asia*. Baltimore, Md., 1956.
Thein Pe. *Over the Ashes: A Play about Resurgent Burma*. Bombay, 1945.
Thompson, Virginia M. *French Indo-China*. New York, 1937.
———, and Richard Adloff. *The Left Wing in Southeast Asia*. New York, 1950.
Three Years of Asian Socialist Conference. Bombay, 1956.
Tinker, Hugh. *The Union of Burma, A Study of the First Years of Independence*. London and New York, 1957.
Trager, Frank N. *Building a Welfare State in Burma, 1948–56*. New York, 1958.
———, ed. *Burma*. New Haven, Conn., 1956. 3 vols.
———, John N. Musgrave, Jr., and Janet Welsh. *Annotated Bibliography of Burma*. New Haven, Conn., 1956.
———, Patricia Wohlgemuth, and Lu-yu Kiang. *Burma's Role in the United Nations, 1948–1955*. New York, 1956.
Tran duc Thao. *Phénomènologie et Matérialisme Dialectique*. Paris, 1951.
Trotsky, Leon. *The First Five Years of the Communist International*, Vol. I. New York, 1945.
———. *The Permanent Revolution*. New York, 1931.
———. *Problems of the Chinese Revolution*. New York, 1932.
Tun Wai. *Burma's Currency and Credit*. Bombay, 1953.
U Ba Swe. *See under* Ba Swe.
(United Nations) *Economic Bulletin for Asia and the Far East*. Vol. VIII. United Nations, 1957.
———. *Economic Survey of Asia and the Far East, 1953: Statistical Yearbook*. United Nations, 1953.
(United States) Department of State. *The Sino-Soviet Economic Offensive in the Less Developed Countries*. Washington, D.C., 1958.
———. Department of State. Division of Russian Affairs. *The Second Congress of the Communist International*. Washington, D.C., 1920.
———. Department of State. Office of Intelligence and Research. *Political Alignments of Vietnamese Nationalists*. Report No. 3708. Washington, D.C., 1949.
———. House of Representatives. *The Communist Conspiracy: Strategy and Tactics of World Communism*. House of Representatives Reports 2241 and 2242. Washington, D.C., 1956.
———. House of Representatives. *The Strategy and Tactics of World Communism*. House Document 154. Washington, D.C., 1949.
———. Information Service. *Summary of Editorials and Special Articles from the Thai Language Daily Newspapers*. Bangkok, 1956. Mimeographed.
U Nu. *See under* Nu.
Vandenbosch, Amry, and R. A. Butwell. *Southeast Asia Among the World Powers*. Louisville, Ky., 1957.
Van den Brink, H. *Een Eisch van Recht: De Koloniale Verhouding als Vraagstuk*

Getoetst (*A Demand for Justice: The Colonial Relationship as a Test Case*). Amsterdam, 1946.

Van der Zee, Daan. *De SDAP en Indonesie* (*The SDAP and Indonesia*). Amsterdam, 1929.

———. *De Wereld Vrij: Socialistische Beschowingen over het Koloniale probleem* (*The World Free: Socialist Opinion on the Colonial Problem*). Amsterdam, 1931.

van Leur, J. C. *Indonesian Trade and Society*. The Hague, 1955.

Vella, Walter F. *The Impact of the West on Government in Thailand*. Berkeley, Calif., 1955.

Verdoorn, J. A. *The National Movement in Indonesia*. Jogjakarta, n.d.

Verité sur le Viet Nam, La: Une Etude Objective du Problème: Des Reportages Inédits sur la Guerre du Maquis: 60 Documents Photographiques. Paris, n.d. [late 1947 or early 1948].

(Viet Nam) Le Service d'Information Bureau de Paris. *Le President Ho chi Minh*. Paris, 1947.

———. *Le Viet Nam en Lutte contre le Fascisme, 1940–1945*. Paris, 1947.

———. Editions de l'Office d'Information. *Les Elections Générales et l'Assemblée Nationale Constituante Vietnamienne*. Paris, 1946.

———. News Service. *Fifty-eighth Birth Anniversary of Ho chi Minh: President, Viet Nam Democratic Republic, 19 May 1948*. Rangoon, 1948.

———. *Ho-chi-Minh: The Father of the Viet Nam People*. Calcutta, 1948.

———. *Viet Nam Information Bulletin*. Rangoon, n.d. Mimeo.

Vlekke, Bernard H. M. *Nusantara: A History of the East Indies Archipelago*. Cambridge, Mass., 1945.

Von Arx, Alexandre. *L'Evolution Politique en Indonesie de 1900 à 1942*. Fribourg, 1949.

Walter, Gerard. *Histoire du Parti-Communiste Français*. Paris, 1949.

Wang Ming. *The Revolutionary Movement in the Colonial Countries*. London, n.d. [1935].

Wertheim, W. F. *Indonesian Society in Transition*. The Hague, 1956.

Whiting, Allen S. *Soviet Policies in China, 1917–1924*. New York, 1954.

Wittfogel, Karl A. *Oriental Despotism: A Comparative Study of Total Power*. New Haven, Conn., 1957.

Wolf, Charles, Jr. *The Indonesian Story: The Birth, Growth and Structure of the Indonesian Republic*. New York, 1948.

ARTICLES IN BOOKS, NEWSPAPERS, AND MAGAZINES

Abdulgani, Ruslan. "Ideological Background of the Asian-African Conference," *United Asia*, VII (March 1955), 43–55.

Benda, Harry J. "Communism in Southeast Asia," *Yale Review*, XLV (Spring 1956), 417–29.

Berrigan, Darrell. "Thailand: Pibul Tries Prachathipatai," *Reporter*, XIV (June 14, 1956), 30–33.

Black, E. C. "Marxism, Leninism and Soviet Communism," *World Politics*, IX (April 1957), 401–12.

Braibanti, Ralph. "The Southeast Asia Collective Defense Treaty," *Pacific Affairs*, XXX (December 1957), 321–41.

Chou En-lai. "Report on the Question of the Boundary Line Between China and Burma," *People's China*, No. 15, August 1957, Supplement.

Cohn, David L. "The Communist Approach to Burma," *Atlantic*, CXCV (September 1956), 41–43.

Collins, James Foster. "The UN and Indonesia," *International Conciliation*, CDLIX (March 1950), 115–200.

Coughlin, Richard. "The Status of the Chinese Minority in Thailand," *Pacific Affairs*, XXV, No. 4 (1952), 378–89.

Darsono. "The Indonesian Communist Party," *Eastern World*, XI (December 1957), 21–23.

Deverall, Richard. "Thailand: Free Unions' Difficult Path," *International Free Trade Union*, VIII, No. 5 (1953), 8.

Devillers, Philippe. "Vietnamese Nationalism and French Politics," in William Holland, ed., *Asian Nationalism and the West*, New York, 1953.

Dhani Nivat, Prince. "The Old Siamese Conception of the Monarchy," *Journal of the Siam Society*, XXXVI (1947), 91–106.

Durdin, Tillman. "Red Activities Up in South Vietnam," New York *Times*, April 13, 1959.

"Eloquent Maps," *China News Analysis*, April 13, 1959.

Embree, John F. "Thailand—A Loosely Structured Social System," *American Anthropologist*, LII (April 1950), 181–93.

Fairbairn, Geoffrey. "Aspects of the Burmese Political Scene," *Pacific Affairs*, XXIX (September 1956), 211–22.

Fall, Bernard. "Crisis in Viet Nam," *Far Eastern Survey*, XXVI (January 1957), 12–15.

Fogg, Ernest L. "Labor Organization in Thailand," *Industrial and Labor Relations Review*, VI (April 1953), 368–77.

Frankel, Joseph. "Soviet Policy in Southeast Asia," Chap. 8 in Max Beloff, *Soviet Policy in the Far East, 1944–1951*, London, 1953.

Fryer, D. W. "Economic Aspects of Indonesian Disunity," *Pacific Affairs*, XXX (September 1957), 195–208.

Furber, Holden. "New Approaches to Asian History: A Report on the London Conference, July 2–6, 1956," *Journal of Asian Studies*, XVII (November 1957), 188–92.

Haas, Mary Rosamond. "The Declining Descent Rule for Rank in Thailand: A Correction," *American Anthropologist*, LIII (October 1951), 585–87.

Hatta, Mohammad, "Marxisme of epigonenwijsheid?" *Nationale Comentaren*, Nos. 10, 11, 12, 13, 14, 1940, reprinted in Hatta, *Verspreide Geschriften*, Amsterdam, 1952, pp. 117–41.

Henderson, William. "South Viet Nam Finds Itself," *Foreign Affairs*, XXXV (January 1957), 283–94.

Historicus. "Stalin on Revolution," *Foreign Affairs*, XXVII (January 1949), 175–214.

Hobbs, Cecil. "The Political Importance of the Buddhist Priesthood in Burma," *Far Eastern Economic Review*, XXI (November 8, 1956), 586–90.

Hook, Sidney. "Dialectic and Nature," *Marxist Quarterly*, I (April–June 1937), 253–84.

Jumper, Roy. "Mandarin Bureaucracy and Politics in South Viet Nam," *Pacific Affairs*, XXX (March 1957), 47–58.

Kautsky, John H. "Neo-Maoism, Marxism and Leninism," *New Leader*, XL (December 16, 1957), 12–16.

Kukrit Pramoj, M. R. "The Social Order of Ancient Thailand," *Thought and Word*, I [n.d.], 10–18.

Kyaw Thet. "Cultural Minorities in Burma," in Herbert Passin, ed., *Cultural Freedom in Asia*, Tokyo, 1956.
King, John K. "Thailand's Bureaucracy and the Threat of Communist Subversion," *Far Eastern Survey*, XXIII, No. 11 (1954), 169–73.
Kozicki, Richard J. "The Sino-Burmese Frontier Problem," *Far Eastern Survey*, XXVI (March 1957), 32–38.
Le Fort, Claude. "Les Pays Coloniaux," *Les Temps Modernes*, March 1947, pp. 1068–94.
Lucien. "Quelques Etapes de la Révolution au Nam-Bo du Viet-Nam," *Quatrième Internationale*, September–October 1947, pp. 41–48.
Marx, Karl. "Persia-China," New York *Daily Tribune*, June 5, 1857, in *Marx on China, 1853–1860: Articles from the New York Daily Tribune*, with an Introduction and Notes by Dona Torr. London, 1951.
Medhi Dulyachinda. "The Development of Labour Legislation in Thailand," *International Labour Review*, LX (November 1949), 467–86.
Miller, J. and M. "A New Stage in the English Study of Marxism," *Soviet Studies*, VII (January 1956), 275–96.
Mollegan, Albert T. "The Religious Basis of Western Socialism," in D. D. Egbert and Stow Persons, eds., *Socialism and American Life*, Princeton, N.J., 1952, 2 vols.
Moore, Barrington, Jr. "The Outlook: Russia Since Stalin: Old Trends and New Problems," *Annals*, CCCIII (January 1956), 1–10.
Mosely, Philip E. "Soviet Policy and the Revolutions in Asia," *Annals of the American Academy of Political and Social Science*, CCLXXVI (July 1951), 91–98.
Natsir, Mohammad. "GAPI-Komisi Visman" ("GAPI and the Visman Commission"), in Natsir, ed., *Capita Selecta*, Bandung, 1954.
Palmier, Leslie H. "Modern Islam in Indonesia: The Muhammadijah After Independence," *Pacific Affairs*, XXVII (September 1954), 255–63.
———. "Sukarno, the Nationalist," *Pacific Affairs*, XXX (June 1957), 101–19.
Rivet, Paul. "Le Drame Franco-Vietnamien," *Cahiers Internationaux*, June 1949, pp. 45–66.
Rose, Saul. "The Asian Socialist Conference of 1953," *Far Eastern Affairs*, 1957, pp. 75–93.
Rubinstein, A. Z. "Selected Bibliography of Soviet Works on Southern Asia, 1954–1956," *Journal of Asian Studies*, XVII (November 1957), 43–54.
Sacks, Milton. "The Strategy of Communism in Southeast Asia," *Pacific Affairs*, XXIII (September 1950), 227–47.
Salim, Hadji Agus. "Onwelwillend, onbillijk onwaar, maar niet onpertijdig" ("Unkind, unfair, untrue but not untimely"), *Het Licht*, II (March 1926).
Sastroamidjojo, Ali. "Survey of the Indonesian National Movement," *Indonesian Life*, I (March–April 1947), 1–9.
Silverstein, Josef. "Politics, Parties and National Elections in Burma," *Far Eastern Survey*, XXV (December 1956), 177–84.
Skinner, G. William. "Chinese Assimilation and Thai Politics," *Journal of Asian Studies*, XVI (February 1957), 237–50.
"Southeast Asia and Communism: The Psychological Effort of the Communists in Southeast Asia in 1956," *Far Eastern Economic Review*, January 17 and 24, 1957, pp. 75–79, 103–10.
Stanton, E. F. "Spotlight on Thailand," *Foreign Affairs*, XXXIII (October 1954), 72–85.

Steiner, H. Arthur. " 'On the Record' with Mao and His Regime," *Journal of Asian Studies*, XVII (February 1958), 215–23.

Supomo, Raden. "The Future of Adat Law in the Reconstruction of Indonesia," in P. W. Thayer, ed., *Southeast Asia in the Coming World*, Baltimore, Md., 1953.

Tajibnapis, S. H. "De Laatste Tien Jaren voor de Japanse Bezetting" ("The Last Ten Years Before the Japanese Occupation"), *De Brug-Djambatan*, I (April 1946), 10–14.

Thet Tun, U. "Outline of a Socialist Economy for Burma," *Journal of the Burma Research Society*, XXXVII (June 1954), 59–76.

Thomson, John Seabury. "Burma, A Neutral in China's Shadow," *Review of Politics*, XIX (July 1957), 330–50.

———. "Burma and China: A One-Sided Love Affair," *Progressive*, XX (November 1956), 26–29.

———. "Burmese Neutralism," *Political Science Quarterly*, LXXII (June 1957), 261–83.

T[inker]., H[ugh]. "Burma Today: Awaiting the Welfare State," *World Today*, XI (July 1955), 309–18.

Tinker, Hugh. "Burma's Northeast Borderland Problems," *Pacific Affairs*, XXIX (December 1956), 324–46.

———. "Nu, The Serene Statesman," *Pacific Affairs*, XXX (June 1957), 120–37.

Tinker, Irene, and Mil Walker. "The First General Elections in India and Indonesia," *Far Eastern Survey*, XXV (July 1956), 97–110.

Trager, Frank N. "Burma's Foreign Policy, 1948–1956: Neutralism, Third Force, and Rice," *Journal of Asian Studies*, XVI (November 1956), 89–102.

———. "Problems of Economic Development in Southeast Asia," *Journal of International Affairs*, X, No. 1 (1956), 59–68.

———. "Roots of Indonesian Conflict," *Foreign Policy Bulletin*, XXXVI (February 1957), 77–79.

———, and U Hla Maung. "Burma," *Journal of International Affairs*, X, No. 1 (1956), 11–18.

Trevor-Roper, Hugh. "Marxism and the Study of History," *Problems of Communism*, V (September–October 1956), 36–42.

Tucker, R. C. "The Psychology of Soviet Foreign Policy," *Problems of Communism*, XI (May–June 1957), 3 f.

U Nu. *See under* Nu.

U Thet Tun. *See under* Thet Tun.

Van der Kroef, Justus M. "Instability in Indonesia," *Far Eastern Survey*, XXVI (April 1957), 49–62.

———. "Marxism in Southeast Asia," *Current History*, XXVII (November 1954), 289–97.

Van Kol, H. H. "De Strijd der SDAP op Koloniaal Gebied" ("The Struggle of the SDAP in the Colonial Sphere"), *Gedenkboek SDAP, ter gelegenheid van het vijf en twintig-jaarig bestaan van de sociaal-democratische arbeiderspartij in Nederland* (*Anniversary Book of the SDAP on the occasion of the twenty-fifth year of the Social-Democratic Workers Party in the Netherlands*). Amsterdam, 1919.

Watnick, Morris. "The Appeal of Communism to the Peoples of Underdeveloped Areas," in Seymour Martin Lipset, ed., *Class Status and Power: A Reader in Social Stratification*, Glencoe, Ill., 1953.

———. "Continuity and Innovation in Chinese Communism," *World Politics,* VI (October 1953), 84–105.

Welsh, Janet. "Burma's Development Problems," *Far Eastern Survey,* XXV (August 1956), 113–22.

Wilbur, C. Martin. "Southeast Asia Between India and China: Burma's Peaceful Co-existence Policy," *Journal of International Affairs,* X, No. 1 (1956), 87–99.

Wurfel, David. "Agrarian Reform in the Republic of Viet Nam," *Far Eastern Survey,* XXVI (June 1957), 81–92.

Zhukov, Georgi. "The Sharpening of the Crisis of the Colonial System," *Bolshevik,* December 15, 1957, pp. 51–64.

NEWSPAPERS AND PERIODICALS

Aksonsan (The Newsletter). Bangkok, monthly.
Antara. Daily News Bulletin. Djakarta and New York, daily.
Bintang Merah (Red Star). Djakarta, weekly.
Burma Weekly Bulletin. Rangoon, weekly.
Cahiers du Communisme. Paris, monthly.
Communist International. London, monthly.
Cuu Quoc (National Salvation). Hanoi, daily.
De Brug—Djambatan Maandblad van de Vereeniging Nederland Indonesia (The Bridge—Monthly of the Netherlands-Indonesian Association). Amsterdam, monthly.
Harian Rakjat (People's Daily). Djakarta, daily.
Het Inzicht (Insight). Djakarta, weekly.
Indonesia Merdeka (Free Indonesia). Leiden, monthly.
Indonesian Socialist Bulletin.
International Press Correspondence. Moscow.
Isvestiia. Moscow, daily.
Khao Phap. Bangkok, daily.
Labor Action. New York, weekly.
La Lutte. Saigon, weekly.
La Lutte de Classes. Paris, monthly.
La République. Hanoi, weekly.
Les Temps Modernes. Paris, monthly.
L'Humanité. Paris, daily.
Lok Mai (New World). Bangkok, weekly.
Maha Chon (The Great People). Bangkok, fortnightly.
Muan chon (Masses). Bangkok, weekly.
Phithuphum (La Patrie). Bangkok, fortnightly.
Moscow News. Moscow, fortnightly.
Quatrième Internationale. Paris, bimonthly.
Royal Thai Government Gazette from the Thai Version. Bangkok, weekly.
Socialist Asia. Rangoon, quarterly.
Socialist International Information Bulletin.
The Bangkok Post. Bangkok, daily.
The Bangkok World. Bangkok, daily.
World News and Views. International Press Correspondence. London, weekly.

INDEX

Other Volumes of
RAND RESEARCH

Arrow, Kenneth J., and Marvin Hoffenberg. *A Time Series Analysis of Interindustry Demands.* Amsterdam: North-Holland Publishing Company, 1959.

Baker, C. L., and F. J. Gruenberger. *The First Six Million Prime Numbers.* Madison, Wisconsin: The Microcard Foundation, 1959.

Baum, Warren C. *The French Economy and the State.* Princeton: Princeton University Press, 1958.

Bellman, Richard. *Dynamic Programming.* Princeton: Princeton University Press, 1957.

Bergson, Abram, and Hans Heymann, Jr. *Soviet National Income and Product, 1940–48.* New York: Columbia University Press, 1954.

Brodie, Bernard. *Strategy in the Missile Age.* Princeton: Princeton University Press, 1959.

Buchheim, Robert W., and the Staff of The RAND Corporation. *Space Handbook: Astronautics and Its Applications.* New York: Random House, 1959.

Davison, W. Phillips. *The Berlin Blockade: A Study in Cold War Politics.* Princeton: Princeton University Press, 1958.

Dinerstein, Herbert S. *War and the Soviet Union: Nuclear Weapons and the Revolution in Soviet Military and Political Thinking.* New York: Frederick R. Praeger, 1959.

Dinerstein, Herbert S., and Leon Gouré. *Two Studies in Soviet Controls: Communism and the Russian Peasant, and Moscow in Crisis.* Glencoe, Ill.: The Free Press, 1955.

Dorfman, Robert, Paul A. Samuelson, and Robert M. Solow. *Linear Programming and Economic Analysis.* New York: McGraw-Hill, 1958.

Fainsod, Merle. *Smolensk under Soviet Rule.* Cambridge, Mass.: Harvard University Press, 1958.

Galenson, Walter. *Labor Productivity in Soviet and American Industry.* New York: Columbia University Press, 1955.

Garthoff, Raymond L. *Soviet Military Doctrine.* Glencoe, Ill.: The Free Press, 1953.

George, Alexander L. *Propaganda Analysis: A Study of Inferences Made from Nazi Propaganda in World War II.* Evanston, Ill.: Row, Peterson, 1959.

Goldhamer, Herbert, and Andrew W. Marshall. *Psychosis and Civilization.* Glencoe, Ill.: The Free Press, 1949.

Hastings, Cecil, Jr. *Approximations for Digital Computers.* Princeton: Princeton University Press, 1955.

Hoeffding, Oleg. *Soviet National Income and Product in 1928.* New York: Columbia University Press, 1954.

Janis, Irving L. *Air War and Emotional Stress: Psychological Studies of Bombing and Civilian Defense.* New York: McGraw-Hill, 1951.

Kecskemeti, Paul. *Strategic Surrender: The Politics of Victory and Defeat.* Stanford, Calif.: Stanford University Press, 1958.

Kramish, Arnold. *Atomic Energy in the Soviet Union.* Stanford, Calif.: Stanford University Press, 1959.

Krieger, F. J. *Behind the Sputniks: A Survey of Soviet Space Science.* Washington, D.C.: Public Affairs Press, 1958.

Leites, Nathan. *On the Game of Politics in France.* Stanford, Calif.: Stanford University Press, 1959.

—— *The Operational Code of the Politburo.* New York: McGraw-Hill, 1951.

—— *A Study of Bolshevism.* Glencoe, Ill.: The Free Press, 1953.

Leites, Nathan, and Elsa Bernaut. *Ritual of Liquidation: The Case of the Moscow Trials.* Glencoe, Ill.: The Free Press, 1954.

McKean, Roland N. *Efficiency in Government through Systems Analysis: with Emphasis on Water Resource Development.* New York: John Wiley and Sons, 1958.

McKinsey, J. C. C. *Introduction to the Theory of Games.* New York: McGraw-Hill, 1952.

Mead, Margaret. *Soviet Attitudes toward Authority: An Interdisciplinary Approach to Problems of Soviet Character.* New York: McGraw-Hill, 1951.

Melnik, Constantin, and Nathan Leites. *The House without Windows: France Selects a President.* Evanston, Ill.: Row, Peterson, 1958.

RAND Corporation, The. *A Million Random Digits with 100,000 Normal Deviates.* Glencoe, Ill.: The Free Press, 1955.

Rush, Myron. *The Rise of Khrushchev.* Washington, D.C.: Public Affairs Press, 1958.

Scitovsky, Tibor, Edward Shaw, and Lorie Tarshis. *Mobilizing Resources for War: The Economic Alternatives.* New York: McGraw-Hill, 1951.

Selznick, Philip. *The Organizational Weapon: A Study of Bolshevik Strategy and Tactics.* New York: McGraw-Hill, 1952.

Shanley, F. R. *Weight-Strength Analysis of Aircraft Structures.* New York: McGraw-Hill, 1952 (out of print).

Smith, Bruce Lannes, and Chitra M. Smith. *International Communication and Political Opinion: A Guide to the Literature.* Princeton: Princeton University Press, 1956.

Speier, Hans. *German Rearmament and Atomic War: The Views of German Military and Political Leaders.* Evanston, Ill.: Row, Peterson, 1957.

Speier, Hans, and W. Phillips Davison, eds. *West German Leadership and Foreign Policy.* Evanston, Ill.: Row, Peterson, 1957.

Williams, J. D. *The Compleat Strategyst: Being a Primer on the Theory of Games of Strategy.* New York: McGraw-Hill, 1954.

M